The World's Greatest Literature

THE Masterpieces of the World's Greatest Authors in *History, Biography, Philosophy, Economics, Politics; Epic and Dramatic Literature, History of English Literature, Oriental Literature (Sacred and Profane), Orations, Essays.* Sixty-one Crown Octavo Volumes :: :: ::

ILLUSTRATED WITH FRONTISPIECES, EACH A MASTER WORK OF ART IN PORTRAITURE OR HISTORIC PAINTING

Editors

LIBRARY COMMITTEE

JUSTIN McCARTHY, M.P.
Historian and Journalist

TIMOTHY DWIGHT, D.D., LL.D.
Ex-President Yale University

RICHARD HENRY STODDARD
Author and Critic

PAUL VAN DYKE, D.D.
Princeton University

ALBERT ELLERY BERGH
Managing Editor

ADVISORY COMMITTEE

JOHN T. MORGAN
United States Senate

FREDERIC R. COUDERT, LL.D.
New York Bar

EDWARD EVERETT HALE
Author and Editor

MAURICE FRANCIS EGAN, LL.D.
Catholic University of America

JULIAN HAWTHORNE
Literary Editor

TURKISH LITERATURE

COMPRISING
FABLES, BELLES-LETTRES, AND SACRED TRADITIONS

TRANSLATED INTO ENGLISH FOR THE FIRST TIME

WITH A SPECIAL INTRODUCTION BY
EPIPHANIUS WILSON, A.M.

REVISED EDITION

NEW YORK
P. F. COLLIER & SON

SPECIAL INTRODUCTION

THE national literature of Turkey is something with which the European and American mind is by no means familiar, and, indeed, it has only recently become a distinctive feature in the world's intellectual activity. Turkey is really an oriental country transplanted into a European environment, and the truest affinities of Turkey are with the far East, with Arabia and Persia. There are at least twenty-five written languages used in the Ottoman Empire, and Turkish is sometimes written in Arabian, sometimes in Persian characters, yet in spite of the babel of tongues which is found at Constantinople, the strong individuality of the Turk has manifested itself in literature as it has in politics and government, and there exists a considerable amount of epic and lyric poetry, drama, romance and apologue which is neither Arabian nor Persian, but is racy of the soil, the soil being principally that of Constantinople, where the Sultans, up to the present time, have been eminent patrons of the literary craft; some of them, Sultan Mustapha, for instance, in the sixteenth century, being writers of no mean accomplishments.

It is usual to divide the history of Turkish literature into three periods. The primitive literature of Turkey flourished between the years 1301 and 1520, during which time the Persian influence was paramount in the romantic and mystic productions of the Ottoman poets. The Shah-Nameh furnished many of the heroes to these Ottoman romances, and the forms of versification are all borrowed from Iran. "The Divan" and "History of the Forty Vezirs" belong to this period.

The middle period of Ottoman literature extends from 1520 to 1730. This is sometimes called the classic period, because in it the capabilities of the genuine Turkish language were tested, developed, and fixed. It opened with the reign of Suleyman I, whose splendid achievements, as a warrior by land and sea, won him the name of the Brilliant. The general history of literature teaches us that national triumph in war always gives a stimulus to national literature, and accordingly this era is adorned by the works of Fasli, and of a host of other poets, whose productions will be found represented in the translations contained in the present volume.

The third period of Ottoman literature shows the Turkish writers under the influence of European models, but ending at last in Drama, essentially the comedy of manners, and not of European, but of Turkish manners. The plays of Mirza Feth-Ali Akhoud-Zaidé, of one of which we publish a translation in this volume, reflect domestic, forensic, and official life at Constantinople during the last century as truly as those of Molière reflect the speech and manners of Parisian society as they existed in the reign of *le grand monarque*. The last development of literary activity at Constantinople is shown not only by the developments of the drama, but by the vigor displayed in the domain of journalism.

The Ottoman poems, of which we give the only English translation extant, that by E. J. W. Gibb, reveal the high rank taken by Turkish verse in the poesy of the East. The Turkish metres were many and varied, and the flexibility of the language lent itself to intricate forms of composition. In imagination and passion these Ottoman poems will hold their own in any company.

" The Rose and the Nightingale " of Fasli, which has been for the first time translated into English in the present volume, is the elaboration of an ancient Persian myth with regard to the loves of Gul and Bulbul. There are numberless allusions to this beautiful fable in such works as " The Divan " of Hafiz, as for instance where he says:

In blossom is the crimson rose, and the rapt Bulbul trills his song,
A summons that to revel calls you, Sufis, wine-adoring throng.

The author of this Turkish poem, Mohammed Fasli, " Black Fasli," as he was called from his swarthy complexion, was the son of a saddler of Constantinople, and early became a pupil of the poet Sati. He soon attracted the attention of the Court, and was made secretary to the Divan by Prince Mustapha, who, as we have seen, was himself a poet. Fasli wrote several poems of the same character as the present one, which is, however, his best and ripest production. He died in 1563.

" The Rose and the Nightingale " is a brilliant and gorgeous example of oriental poetry, whose charm is rather increased than diminished by the repetition and prolixity which characterize it. The poet gives it in his closing passages a profoundly mystical meaning, which has been so far developed by other writers that an Armenian Christian author says that the Springtime of Fasli means the Creation, the Rose is Christ, the Rosegarden the Church, the Brook is Baptism, the South Wind is the Inspiration of the Gospel, the Nightingale, the Soul full of ardent faith, and so on. This reminds one of Pico Mirandola reconciling Moses and Homer.

The drama, " The Magistrates," which is here for the first time translated into English, is the work of Mirza Feth-Ali Akhoud-Zaidé. He is the most original native dramatist whose works have appeared in Constantinople. Up to a comparatively recent period the theatres of Turkey were dependent for their comedies on translations from French, sometimes even from German or English comedies and farces. The Turk is fond of witnessing the exertions, the excitements and perturbations of others, while he himself remains indolent and imperturbable; hence his passion for story-telling and for the representations of the stage. In the dramas of Feth-Ali he sees the life of Turkey vividly reproduced. Love rules the scene, Eastern cruelty comes in with the bastinado, Eastern duplicity and fraud are vividly portrayed in the law-court scene. The arrangement and development of the play are good, and the. *dénouement* is natural and satisfactory.

This will appear from the following analysis of " The Magistrates." In the first place, the modern playwright will be astonished by the long list of personages in the play. There are twenty-seven in a short drama, consisting of a series of scenes, brief, even to jerkiness.

At the opening of the play we learn that Hadji-Ghafour, a rich merchant, has lately died and left no will; his property is therefore claimed by Sekine-Khanoum, his only daughter, a girl of eighteen, who is engaged to marry Aziz-Bey. The sum of money in which the legacy consists has been placed in the hands of the President of the Council, but before he can pay it over to the legatee, claims have been set up in favor of an alleged child of the late Hadji-Ghafour, borne him by his mistress Zeneib. A conspiracy is formed, with the aid of certain soldiers who are suborned to say that they saw the child in Hadji-Ghafour's arms, and that he acknowledged the paternity. The complications are increased by the fact that Zobeide, paternal aunt of Sekine-Khanoun, has promised the hand of her niece to a richer man than Aziz-Bey, namely, Aga-Hassan, a merchant. The young lady so enrages Hassan by the terms in which she repudiates him, that he joins the ranks of the conspirators, among whom the chief is Aga-Selman, who nevertheless has undertaken to be the advocate of Sekine-Khanoun in the coming lawsuit. The suit at last is opened, the witnesses come ready primed to the bar, but, instead of telling their perjured tale, relate how they were induced to promise their support to a fabrication. The tortuous diplomacy of Aga-Selman, the corruption of the judges, the despair of Sekine and Aziz are depicted in the liveliest manner, and the revelations of the soldiers, who are called by the false advocate as witnesses for Sekine-Khanoun, but bribed to testify against her, form a double climax which is a skilful stroke of dramatic art. The play will be interesting to the Teutonic reader, and seems even capable of adaptation to the American or English stage.

" The History of the Forty Vezirs " is evidently a collection of very old stories. Its compilation is attributed to Sheik-Zada, who lived in the reign of Murad II, 1421-1451. To this Sultan the tales are dedicated. They are like all oriental tales, barely tinged with any ethical significance; they aim principally at amusing and distracting the mind by a series of quickly changing incidents; there is no attempt at character-drawing, and an amazing element of the improbable spices the whole series. They form, however, the most notable work in prose produced in that period which saw the dawn of a Turkish literature, and are only inferior to the tales of Pilpay and the Hitopadesa in their frivolity, exaggeration and evident lack of all those features which would indicate an earnest and conscientious study of real life. They are none the less entertaining, and their genuine Turkish characteristics render them valuable to the student of Ottoman literature as well as to the general reader who may take them up merely *pour passer le temps*.

The fables by unknown authors, which we include in this volume, and which have never before been translated into English, are much later productions of Turkish genius. In Europe the fable has always been, in its original form, one of the most effective and pungent vehicles of appeal to public opinion. Witness " The Belly and the Members " of Menenius Agrippa, so nobly rendered in Shakespeare's " Coriolanus." It well illustrates La Fontaine's excuse for his own fables, namely, that under some circumstances a man must be silent or " strike from afar." From the vantage ground of the fable Menenius could rebuke a raging mob, and Le Fontaine score the ingratitude of kings, as in more recent times Krilof has satirized the despotic abuses of the Russian government.

The Turkish fables also " hit from afar." The tyranny of Turkish rulers is pointed out in "The Farmer and His Hounds." The corruption that surrounds access to the great is vividly suggested in " The Sailors in Distress." But the weaknesses of the Turkish character are also reflected in fables which contain but little wisdom; the apathy which puts up with everything is expressed in the moral of " The Candle "; the want of enterprise and energy which is characteristic of the Turk, in " The Shark " and " The Clown Turned First Soldier, then Merchant."

In the teachings of all these apologues there may be seen the same features of languid and unresisting acquiescence in things as they are, with a skit here and there on the oppression and ingratitude of those in power. Yet they bear a reality about them which is lacking in the artificial productions of Gay and Lessing. They come from the heart and go to the heart of the people, and some of them are neat and pointed, if not beautiful, in structure and expression. A collection of examples from Turkish literature would be quite incomplete without these specimens of the Turkish apologues, which reflect so plainly the ethical standard and general opinions of those to whom they were addressed.

Epiphanius Wilson. —

CONTENTS

CONTENTS

CONTENTS

TURKISH FABLES

—

[*Translated by Epiphanius Wilson, A.M.*]

TURKISH FABLES

The Gardener and His Wife

A CERTAIN Gardener had a young and pretty woman for his Wife. One day, when, according to her habit, she had gone to wash her linen in the river, the Gardener, entering his house, said to himself:

"I do not know, really, whether my Wife loves me. I must put it to the test."

On saying this, he stretched himself full length upon the ground, in the middle of the room, as if dead. Soon, his Wife returned, carrying her linen, and perceived her husband's condition.

"Tired and hungry as I am," she said to herself, "is it necessary that I should begin at once to mourn and lament? Would it not be better to begin by eating a morsel of something?"

She accordingly cut off a piece of *pasterma* (dried smoked meat), and set it to roast on the coals; then she hurriedly went upstairs to the garret, took a pot of milk, drank some of it, and put the rest on the fire. At this moment, an old woman, her neighbor, entered, with an earthen vessel in her hand, and asked for some burning coals.

"Keep your eye on this pot," she said to the old woman, rising to her feet. Then she burst into sobs and lamentations.

"Alas!" she cried, "my poor husband is dead!"

The neighbors, who heard her voice, rushed in, and the deceitful hussy kept on repeating:

"Alas! What a wretched fate has my husband met with!" and tears flowed afresh.

At that instant the dead man opened his eyes.

"What are you doing?" he said to her. "Finish first the

3

roasting of the *pasterma*, quenching your throat in milk, and boiling the remainder of it; afterward you will find time to weep for me."

First myself, and then those I love, says a proverb.

THE FLY

A Fly who had carelessly fallen into a pot full of food was at the point of death.

"What does it matter?" she said, "so long as hereafter I shall feel no more hunger, and for the present have eaten and drunk my fill, and have received a good bath."

Patiently to accept the misfortunes which can neither be hindered nor avoided is a proof of wisdom.

THE WIDOW AND HER FRIEND

A Widow, tired of single blessedness, was desirous of marrying again, but feared to draw down upon herself the remarks of the public.

A Friend of hers, to show her how the tongues of neighbors discussed everything, took in hand to paint the Widow's ass green; then leading the beast, she traversed all the streets of the town.

At first not only the children, but also their elders, who had never seen anything like it before, came to see the sight, and followed behind the ass.

At the end of a few days, when the Widow's ass went forth people simply remarked: "What a very singular animal!"

Soon, however, the people ceased to pay any more attention to the spectacle.

The Friend of the Widow who wished to marry again returned to her and said:

"You have seen what has just happened. It will be the same in your case. For some days you will be on the tongues of the people and have to endure the gossip and remarks; but at last they will leave off talking about you."

There is nothing so extraordinary in the world as not to become familiar in time.

The Two Young Men and the Cook

Two Young Men entered a cook-shop for the purpose of buying some meat.

While the Cook was engaged in serving one of them the other seized a huge piece of meat and popped it into his companion's pocket.

The Cook began looking about for his meat, but in vain. Then he addressed the two friends.

" I have not seen it," said one.

" As for me," added the other, " I am sure I have not taken it."

Then each one confirmed his statement with an oath.

" Really, gentlemen," said the owner of the shop, who well understood their rascality, " although I do not know who has robbed me, the God by whom you have sworn does."

Although a man may conceal things from men like himself, God is not deceived.

The Buffaloes and the Log

A pair of Buffaloes were harnessed to a heavy piece of elm wood, and were dragging it along.

" You are stupid," said the Log, reproachfully, " for when you are hitched to a light burden like me, why do you not gallop?"

" Poor wretch!" they replied, " we should doubtlessly move more quickly if we were not fastened to you. But if we moved quickly now, another log would be placed on top of you, to make up the load, and we do not wish to see you broken down by exhaustion."

This answer plunged the Log into profound thought.

The proverbial expression—" the Buffaloes' answer "—a pretext for laziness—is founded on this fable.

The Old Man and His Son

A feeble Old Man had given his home to his Son; soon the hapless father found himself driven from his home and forced to take refuge in a hospital.

Some time afterward, he saw his Son one day passing by, and called out to him.

" For the love of God, my Son," he said in a supplicating tone, " send me out of all that I have gained with the sweat of my brow a simple pair of sheets."

The Son promised his unfortunate father to do so.

" I will send them at once," he answered him.

When he arrived at home he said to his own son: " Take this pair of sheets, and carry them to your grandfather at the hospital."

The young man left one of the sheets at home and carried the other to his grandfather. Some time afterward his father happened to count his sheets.

" Why didn't you do as I told you, and carry the two sheets to your grandfather? " he asked of his son.

" When my father becomes old and goes to the hospital, I said to myself, I shall need this sheet to send to him."

Your child will behave toward you as you behaved toward your parents.

THE BIRD-CATCHER AND THE BLACKBIRD

A Bird-catcher was setting his snares; a Blackbird, as he flew by, caught sight of him.

" For the love of God," he said to him, " do tell me what you are building there? "

" I am founding a complete city."

The Blackbird believed this deceitful answer, and alighted on the net. Scarcely had he touched it, before he found himself caught.

When the Bird-catcher came up the Blackbird said to him: " If this is the way you build your city, you won't attract many inhabitants."

All men shun tyrannical magistrates and oppressors, who, by their violence, scatter ruin around them.

THE HENS AND THE EAGLES

The Hens were at war with the Eagles.

When the day of battle came near, the Hens went and asked the foxes to help them.

"We would willingly help you," replied the foxes, "if we could forget what you are, and what Eagles are."

He who enters upon a quarrel with one more powerful than himself runs a great risk, and is certain to meet with disaster.

THE PIGEON AND THE PAINTING

A Pigeon in its simplicity took for real water the stream represented in a Painting.

He flew down toward it with a sudden swoop, fell to the ground, and was quickly caught.

How many stupid and ignorant people ignore the real condition of things, follow entirely their own silly notions, and at last find themselves in serious trouble!

THE LION AND THE MAN

A Lion and a Man were journeying together as friends; they took turns in boasting each of his own merits. As they advanced on their way, they saw a mausoleum on which was carved in marble a man trampling a lion under his feet.

The Man called the attention of the Lion to this sculpture. "I need say no more," he remarked, "this is sufficient to show that man surpasses the Lion in strength and vigor."

"The chisel is in the hands of men," replied the beast, "so they represent in sculpture whatever they like. If we could handle it as you do, you would see what would be the subjects of our works."

Artists do not base their creations upon the realities of life, but follow the ideas which pass through their heads.

THE COMPLIMENT TO THE VEZIR

A Vezir had just received his appointment; those who had supported him came to compliment him on his promotion to a post of honor.

He was so inflated by the homage he received, that he came at last to pass by his former friends without noticing them.

"Who are you?" he asked one of them.

"My God," exclaimed the other, who was a wit: "I feel sorry for you indeed, for your Excellency, like most of those who have reached an eminent position, has suddenly lost sight, hearing, and memory, so that you no longer know your former friends."

It generally happens that those who attain to high station feel contempt for their friends.

THE ASS AND THE FROGS

An Ass was walking along loaded with wood; as he journeyed he fell into a pond, and lamented because he could not get out.

The Frogs, dwellers in the pond, heard his cries and came up to him.

"Pray tell us," they said to him, "how is it that you, who have been but a moment in this pond, cry out so vehemently. What would you do, if like us, you had been here for an infinite time?"

Such were the sarcastic consolations they addressed to him.

Young people full of vigor, and capable of enduring all sorts of hardship, too often deride the feebleness of the old.

THE TORTOISE AND THE KING OF ANIMALS

The quadrupeds and birds assembled one day at an entertainment given by the King of Beasts. Both those who go on foot and those who fly were there.

The Tortoise arrived late because of his slow motion, and asked pardon for his want of punctuality.

"I have such a pleasant home," said he, "that I never leave it without regret."

"At some future time," cried the Lion in a rage, "you will have a house of stone which you can never leave."

This fable is addressed to those who, instead of keeping to their own vocation, are anxious to attend the entertainments of the great.

THE FOX AND THE LION

A Fox who had never seen a lion in his life met one of the greatest size. In his terror and surprise, he thought that his last hour had come. At the second meeting, he was still somewhat alarmed, but less so than at first. At the third sight of the Lion, he felt no fear at all, but walked up to the Lion and began to converse with him.

By force of habit we become enabled to confront, unmoved, things the most terrible and dangerous.

THE FARMER AND HIS HOUNDS

A Farmer who lived remote from the city, was kept at home by the severity of the winter. Soon, his provisions were exhausted, and finally, he was compelled to kill his great black oxen.

On seeing this, his Hounds gathered together.

" If this man," said they, " butchers such strong oxen as these, the mainstay of his house, do you think he will spare us? Let us make our escape! "

Keep away from the man who without hesitation does injury to everyone else. To avoid him is a matter of haste and necessity.

THE BEAR AND HIS MATE

A Bear, in struggling with his Mate, used his claws with such violence that he tore her eyes out. He was immediately seized with such sorrow that he bit off his own claws.

A short time afterward, he conversed with her in a friendly manner in his cave.

" My dear," he remarked to her, " for your sake, I have sacrificed my weapons of war."

" What good," said she, " is that to me, now that I am blind, and deprived by you of my precious eyes? "

Repentance cannot repair an injury once inflicted.

THE EEL AND THE SERPENT

The Eel and the Serpent were talking together.

" Why is it," said the Eel, " that I, although I undoubtedly resemble you, in every point, am hunted by men, while they leave you in peace? "

" Because, if they caught me, they would do it to their cost."

No one attacks the person who always repays an injury.

a beating, and hit him so hard that it will kill him, and after that we will give him to the cat."

"Lord deliver us from the people of this house!" cried the Wolf, on hearing these words. "Nothing is less to be relied upon than their words; one moment they speak in one way, and the next in another!"

Saying this, he took himself off, and hurriedly retired.

Do not trust the promises of people whose word·is as changeable as the color of the chameleon.

The Candle

A Candle, made of soft and pliant wax, lamented over the fact that the slightest touch injured it. It did nothing but sigh, and burst out into bitter complaints against its dismal lot, especially dwelling upon the fact that bricks, although at first tender and pasty, grow hard from heat and thus acquire an age-long durability. In order to acquire the same hardness, and to reap the same advantages, it leaped into the fire, melted, and was consumed.

It is useless to rise up in irritation and revolt against the disadvantages which are inherent in our nature, our constitution, or our position.

The Clown Turned First Soldier, Then Merchant

A certain Clown, occupied in cultivating his field, guided the plough now this way, now that, and in the midst of his task felt sorry that he had not been more favored by fortune.

A number of volunteers, who formed part of a brigade, which had just come back victorious from war, happened at this moment to pass by, loaded with rich and abundant booty, and plentifully supplied with provisions. Moved by the sight of them, the laborer set to work to sell his sheep, goats, and oxen; with the price received for these he collected horses, weapons, and ammunition, with a view of joining the army on campaign. Just on his arrival, this army was beaten by the enemy, and utterly routed; the baggage of the new-comer was seized, and he himself returned home, crippled with wounds.

"I am disgusted with the military profession," he said, "and

I am going to be a business man. In spite of my slender income I shall be able to realize great profits in trade."

He accordingly sold his remaining arms and ammunition, and employed the proceeds in the purchase of goods which he put on board a ship and embarked himself as passenger. As soon as they had put to sea, a tempest fell upon the ship, which went down with the Merchant on board.

He who seeks for a better position in life, finds a worse one and falls at last into misery. Do not try to learn by experience the disadvantages of each several condition.

THE TWO KINGS AT WAR

A King, the hero of his age, had declared war upon one of his neighbors. The enemy for want of resources, had not been able to make sufficient preparations, and did not know how to meet the emergency. He sent out a spy to meet the foe.

The fellow, gazing from a distance, saw advancing a countless multitude of soldiers, armed with lances.

He immediately turned and galloped back to his sovereign.

" My Lord," he said, " you are about to be attacked by an army as numerous as current coin, for I saw advancing such a crowd of lances that they hide the sun from us."

" Take this robe of honor," said the monarch; " please God we shall fight to-day in the shadow of the enemy."

By this warlike answer, he was able to inspire his troops with a daring and courage which were invincible.

He who suffers himself neither to be cast down by alarm nor dismayed by danger can surmount every obstacle.

THE RIVER AND ITS SOURCE

A River one day said to its Source: " How idle and good-for-nothing you are! In spite of your incessant movement you do not contain the slightest quantity of fish! In me, on the contrary, are seen more choice fishes swimming than in any other watercourse; thus I produce joy and happiness in all the plains and their inhabitants, through which I pass! You seem to me to be a corpse, from which life has completely vanished."

The Source, indignant at these insulting words, made no reply, but began to diminish the quantity of water which she furnished to the River; soon she entirely ceased to feed it. By this means the height of the flood sank gradually, until at last water failed entirely, and River and fish disappeared together.

This fable is addressed to those who treat their friends in a similar manner and imagine that their prosperity is specially and directly due to the munificence of God.

An ungrateful man, says the poet, is one who addresses no thanks to Divine Providence for the innumerable gifts showered upon him: he is a blasphemer, as well as an ingrate, who is grateful toward no one excepting the giver of them all.

THE HUNTER AND HIS HOUNDS

A certain Hunter, who was seized with an ardent desire to make his prey a superb anqua,[1] spent large sums of money in the keeping of Hounds. By accident, one of his bitches bit his son, and the child died of the wound.

" Since the Hounds have caused his death," said the master to the servants, " let us kill them all."

" Alas ! " cried one of the poor creatures, " all of us must die for the fault committed by a single one of us ! "

A single scoundrel is sufficient to bring ruin on a whole ward.

THE FOOL WHO SELLS WISDOM

A certain Fool kept constantly passing through the streets of a town.

" Who will buy Wisdom? " he cried in a loud voice. A passer-by met him on his way, accosted him, and presented him with some small pieces of money.

" Sell me a little Wisdom," he said.

" Here it is," replied the other, cuffing him heartily. Immediately afterward he put into his hands a long thread.

" If you wish in future to be wise and prudent," said the Fool to him, " always keep as far away from fools as the length of this thread."

We should avoid all connection and communication with fools and cranks.

---

[1] A fabulous bird, a species of vulture or gigantic condor.

THE DICER

A Dicer one day lost at play all that he possessed, even to his clothes. Sitting at the door of a wine shop he burst into tears.

One of his friends happened to pass, and noticed the state he was in.

"Have you anything the matter with you that you are so mournful, my friend?" he inquired.

"I have nothing," replied the other.

"Nothing?" went on the other. "Then there is no reason for weeping."

"It is really because I have nothing that I weep," replied he.

Numerous are the applications of this profound fable.

THE LAMB AND THE WOLF

A tender lamb was in the fold, when suddenly a Wolf entered for the purpose of devouring her. Throwing herself at the feet of the Wolf, she said, weeping: "God has put me in your power; sound therefore your horn in order to grant me one moment's delight; my desires will then be perfectly satisfied, for my parents have told me that the race of wolves are the best players on the horn." The Wolf heard this silly proposal, and set himself to cry out with all his might and main; when lo and behold, the dogs were waked up and attacked him. He took to flight, and did not stop until he reached a hill, where he said, lamenting: "I certainly deserve this mishap, for who has made me a musician, when I have never been anything but a butcher?"

This fable proves that many good people are deceived by attending to silly proposals, and afterward, like the Wolf, are sorry for it; and that many others undertake, either in word or deed, things for which they are not adapted, and consequently fall into misfortune.

THE INSECTS, THE BEE, AND THE ANT

The Insects betook themselves one winter to the dwellings of the Bee and the Ant.

"Give us some food." they said, "for we are dying of hunger."

The others answered: " What do you do in summer time? "

" We rest on the spreading trees," they replied, " and we cheer the traveller with our pleasant songs."

" If that be so," was the reply, " it is no wonder that you are dying of hunger; you are therefore no proper objects of charity."

This fable shows that the foolish virgins ask charity, and those who are wise refuse to give, because there comes a time when not charity but justice is to be rendered.

During the time of this life, which is our summer, we must gather, by wisdom and industry, the spiritual food, without which, we shall be made, at the day of judgment, to die of hunger in hell.

THE TWO COCKS

Two Cocks were fighting in the middle of a street; he who defeated his comrade and flung him to the ground was inflated with pride at his victory.

He flew off, and taking his station on a high place, began to swagger up and down and to crow, elated with victory. While he thus exhibited his vanity an eagle unexpectedly swooped down upon him and carried him off.

This fable shows that he who rejoices over the defeat of his adversary, or plumes himself upon victory over a foe, brings upon his own head, without knowing it, torments and sufferings which will compel him to deplore his own lot.

THE ASSEMBLY OF THE BIRDS

The Birds gathered together and elected the Peacock and crowned him King, on account of his great beauty.

Then the Dove came to him and said: " O excellent King, if the Eagles harass us, how will you be able to bring help? "

This fable shows that beauty is not the sole attribute to be sought for in a king, but that he is required to show on every occasion, courage, military valor, and ripe wisdom.

THE FOX AND THE CRAB

The Fox and the Crab lived together like brothers; together they sowed their land, reaped the harvest, thrashed the grain and garnered it.

The Fox said one day: "Let us go to the hill-top, and whoever reaches it first shall carry off the grain for his own."

While they were mounting the steep the Crab said:

"Do me a favor; before you set off running, touch me with your tail, so that I shall know it and be able to follow you."

The Crab opened his claws, and when the Fox touched him with his tail, he leaped forward and seized it, so that when the Fox reached the goal and turned round to see where the Crab was, the latter fell upon the heap of grain and said: "These three bushels and a half are all mine." The Fox was thunderstruck and exclaimed:

"How did you get here, you rascal?"

This fable shows that deceitful men devise many methods and actions for getting things their own way, but that they are often defeated by the feeble.

THE GOATS AND THE WOLVES

All the Goats gathered together and sent a message to the nation of the Wolves. "Wherefore," said they, "do you make upon us this ceaseless war? We beseech you, make peace with us, as the kings of nations are wont to do."

The Wolves assembled in great joy, and sent a long letter and many presents to the nation of the Goats. And they said to them:

"We have learned your excellent resolution and we have rendered thanks to God for it. The news of this peace will occasion great joy in the world. But we beg to inform your wisdom that the shepherd and his dog are the causes of all our differences and quarrels; if you make an end of them, tranquillity will soon return."

On learning this, the Goats drove away the shepherds and their dogs, and ratified a treaty of peace and friendship with the Wolves.

The Goats then went out and scattered themselves without fear among the hills and valleys, and began to feed and render thanks to God. The Wolves waited for ten days, then they gathered themselves together against the Goats, and strangled them every one.

This fable shows that hatred and aversion between nations

and families, or between individuals, is deeply rooted in the heart of man, and that peace and friendship are not established among them, excepting with the greatest difficulty.

THE LION, THE WOLF, AND THE FOX

The Lion, the Wolf, and the Fox, having made an alliance, went forth to hunt, and captured a ram, a sheep, and a lamb.

When dinner time came the Lion said to the Wolf, " Divide the prey among us."

The Wolf replied : " O King, God apportions them thus : the ram is for you, the sheep for me, and the lamb for the Fox."

The Lion flew into a violent rage at this and gave the Wolf a blow upon the cheek that made his eyes bulge out. He retired in bitter tears.

Then the Lion addressed the Fox, bidding him apportion the prey.

" O King," he answered, " God has already apportioned it. The ram is for your dinner, we will join you in eating the sheep, and you shall sup upon the lamb."

" Little rogue of a Fox," said the Lion, " who taught you to apportion things with such equity ? "

" The starting eyes of the Wolf taught me that," replied the Fox.

This fable shows that many wicked men see the error of their ways, and amend, so soon as kings and princes cause robbers and malefactors to be hanged.

THE WOLF AND THE ASS

The Wolf having come upon an Ass who was in prime condition wished to eat him.

Then the Ass said : " I beseech you, Mr. Wolf, cure me of a wound which I have in the foot ; an abominable nail has pierced it, and produces intense suffering. Afterward, you can eat me, for God has destined me to be your food."

The Wolf accordingly went behind the Ass for the purpose of extracting the nail ; but at that moment the Ass flung out a kick with all his strength, which struck the Wolf and smashed his teeth. The Wolf, weeping bitterly, reflected :

" It is right that I suffer this disaster, for being by nature a butcher, no one can make a blacksmith of me."

This fable shows many people are filled with sorrow and regret, from attempting to practise arts and accomplishments which they have never learned, and which are unsuited to their life.

THE FOX AND THE PARTRIDGE

The Fox having caught a Partridge was preparing to eat it. But the latter said:

" Blessed be God, who calls me to his kingdom, and delivers me from the evils of this world. But do you, Mr. Fox, render thanks to God for this feast upon me, which will be your great reward."

The Fox sat down, looked up to heaven, and opened his mouth, saying:

" I thank thee, gracious God, for the excellent feast thou hast prepared for me."

As he spoke, the Partridge slipped from his jaws, and flew away. Then the Fox said: "Fool and dotard that I am! I should have eaten first, and thanked God afterward."

This fable warns us not to count on things that are promised, and not to thank anyone until we have actually received a favor.

THE FOX AND THE SPARROW

The Fox held a Sparrow in his mouth and was on the point of eating it, when the latter said:

" You ought first to give thanks to God, and then you can eat me, for at this moment I am on the point of laying an egg, big as that of an ostrich. It is a priceless egg, but let me go, that I may lay it, and afterward you may eat me. I swear that I will put myself at your disposal."

As soon as the Fox dropped him, he flew off and lighted on the branch of a very high tree. Then the Fox said to him:

" Come, now, do as you have decided, and return when I ask you."

" Do you think I am as senseless as you are?" asked the Sparrow, " that I should return at your pleasure? How could you possibly believe me, or imagine that such a little body could lay such a disproportionately large egg? Listen to the advice

I give you: Don't you credit extravagant statements, or go to sleep under a tottering wall."

The Fox answered: "God will judge you for the trick you have played me."

"Some falsehoods," answered the Sparrow, "are praiseworthy; God highly rewards the lie that delivers one from death or danger, and which saves another's life."

The Fox then concealed himself near by, and began to plot and peer for the capture of the Sparrow; but the latter dropped dung into his eyes, saying: "O fool, listen to another piece of advice: Do not strive after that which you cannot attain, and in the quarrels of husband and wife, or of brothers, say not a single indiscreet word of which you may afterward repent."

THE SYRIAN PRIEST AND THE YOUNG MAN

A Syrian Priest, good and wise, and an Armenian were engaged in a dispute. The Young Man, at last enraged, said to the Priest:

"I will drive this stone down your throat, in order that your thirty-two teeth may choke you."

The Priest returned hastily to his house, lost in astonishment, and said to his wife:

"In the name of God, wife, light a candle, and count how many teeth I have."

She counted them and said:

"They are just thirty-two in number."

The Priest at once returned to the Young Man and said:

"How did you learn the number of my teeth? And who told you?"

"Sir," replied the other, "I learned the number of your teeth from the number of my own."

This fable shows that from my own bad qualities I am able to guess yours, for all faults are common.

THE CONVERTED CAT

The Cat, having put on the cowl and become a monk, sent word to the mice and said:

"It is an abominable thing to shed blood. As for me, I will shed no more, for I am become religious."

Then the mice replied: "Although we saw in you the whole
Order of St. Anthony, or of our holy Father St. Mark, we could
have no confidence in your hypocrisy."

The Cat covered herself with a dust rag, and smeared herself with flour. The mice approached her, saying:

"Wretch, we see through your dust rag!"

Then she pretended to be dead, and lay in the path of the
mice, who approached her and said:

"Miserable cheat, although your skin be made into a purse,
we could not believe that you had given up your habitual
knavery."

This fable shows that when you have once found out a person of dishonest, treacherous, and evil character, you should not
trust him, even if he tries to do right, for he cannot change his
nature.

THE FOX AND THE WOLF

The Fox deceived the Wolf, telling him that if he delivered
a letter to the heads of the village, they would give him food
to bring back. When the Wolf reached the village the dogs
fell upon him, biting and wounding him. When he returned
in a sad plight the Fox said to him: "Why did you not show
your letter?"

"I did show it," was the reply, "but there were a thousand
dogs, who did not know the handwriting."

This fable shows that there are many people ignorant, though
brave, with whom it is best not to dispute or to mix, but pru-
dently to keep away from them.

THE HORSE AND HIS RIDER

The Horse complained to his Rider, saying that it was unjust
that a fair and powerful creature, such as he was, should be
a slave and carry so weak a thing as man.

His Rider replied: "I feed you, I shelter you with a roof,
and I show you where water and grass are to be found."

"But you take away my liberty, and put a hard bit in my
mouth. You weary me with long journeys, and sometimes
expose me to the dangers of battle," answered the Horse.

"Take, then, your liberty," said his master, removing the
bridle from his head and the saddle from his back.

The Horse bounded off into the mountains, where grass and water abounded. For many weeks he enjoyed ease and plenty. But a pack of wolves, seeing him in good condition, pursued him. At first he easily outstripped them, but he was now heavy with much nourishment, and his breath began to fail. The wolves overtook and threw him to the ground.

When he found his last hour was come he exclaimed mournfully. "How happy and safe I was with my master, and how much lighter and easier were his bridle and spur than the fangs of these blood-thirsty enemies!"

This fable shows that many people do not estimate duly the blessings of their condition, and complain about those duties, the performance of which is the sole condition of their life and safety.

THE ROSE AND THE BUTTERFLY

A Rose growing in a garden of Tiflis saw in summer time a Butterfly of many colors fluttering in a neighboring flower-bed.

"Poor creature," said the flower, "how short your life is! You are here to-day and gone to-morrow. But I remain on my stalk, spread my leaves in the sun, and scatter scent on the air without change."

"I have the power of going into many gardens," replied the Butterfly. "You are only a prisoner; I can get under shelter when it rains, seek the shade when the sun is hot, and if my life is short, it is a merry one. Besides, your life is short also, and a storm at any moment may throw you to the ground and scatter your red petals in the dust."

The Rose tossed her head in a burst of rage. "I am at least beautiful and fragrant while my life lasts; but you are no more than a worm with a pair of wings."

There would have been more angry words between these two had not the lady of the house come that moment and plucked the Rose, while a bird from the bough of an oak-tree swooped down and carried off the Butterfly.

This fable shows that pride and vanity make people very often fancy themselves superior to others, while all are really of no importance, being subject to the same condition of decay and death.

THE ARCHER AND THE TRUMPETER

The Archer and the Trumpeter were travelling together in a lonely place. The Archer boasted of his skill as a warrior, and asked the Trumpeter if he bore arms.

" No," replied the Trumpeter, " I cannot fight. I can only blow my horn, and make music for those who are at war."

" But I can hit a mark at a hundred paces," said the Archer. As he spoke an eagle appeared, hovering over the tree tops. He drew out an arrow, fitted it on the string, shot at the bird, which straightway fell to the ground, transfixed to the heart.

" I am not afraid of any foe, for that bird might just as well have been a man," said the Archer proudly. " But you would be quite helpless if anyone attacked you."

They saw at that moment a band of robbers approaching them with drawn swords. The Archer immediately discharged a sharp arrow, which laid low the foremost of the wicked men. But the rest soon overpowered him and bound his hands.

" As for this Trumpeter, he can do us no harm, for he has neither sword nor bow," they said, and did not bind him, but took away his purse and wallet.

Then the Trumpeter said: " You are welcome, friends, but let me play you a tune on my horn."

With their consent he blew loud and long on his trumpet, and in a short space of time the guards of the King came running up at the sound, and surrounded the robbers and carried them off to prison.

When they unbound the hands of the Archer he said to the Trumpeter: " Friend, I have learned to-day that a trumpet is better than a bow; for you have saved our lives without doing harm to anyone."

This fable shows that one man ought not to despise the trade of another. It also shows that it is better to be able to gain the help of others than to trust to our own strength.

THE WOLF, THE FOX, AND THE SHEPHERD'S DOG

A Fox was once carrying home to his young a leveret which he had caught by stealth. On his way he met a Wolf, who said to him, " I am very hungry, and I hope you will not refuse me a taste of your prey."

" In the name of God," cried the Fox, " eat your fill; but leave me a fragment for the supper of my little ones."

The Wolf, however, swallowed the dainty morsel at a mouthful. Although the Fox was very angry he said in a humble voice: " I am glad that your appetite is so good. Farewell. Perhaps some day I will gain for you another meal of equal sweetness."

When they parted the Fox began to plot how he might revenge himself upon his enemy the Wolf. Now it happened that a Shepherd's Dog came to the Fox for advice. He asked him how he should destroy the Wolf, who every night kept robbing his master's folds.

" That is an easy matter," replied the Fox. " You must put on a wolf's skin, so that when the Wolf sees you he will make up to you without fear, and then you can seize him by the throat and strangle him."

The Wolf also came to the Fox for counsel.

" The Shepherd's Dog," he complained, " barks when I approach the fold, and the sticks and stones of the shepherds often give me a severe mauling. How shall I be able to kill him?"

" That is easy," said the Fox; " put on a sheep's skin, enter the fold with the flock, and lie down with them. At midnight you can strangle the Dog unawares, afterward feast as much as you like."

Then the Fox went back to the Dog and told him to look out for the Wolf disguised as a Sheep.

When night came the Wolf entered the fold dressed like a sheep, and had no fear, for he saw no dog, but only a wolf at the door. But the Dog saw the fierce eyes of the Wolf and flew at his throat. Meanwhile the shepherds heard the noise, and as they saw a wolf mangling a sheep, they laid on the Dog's back with their heavy staves until he died, but not before he had strangled the Wolf.

This fable shows how unwise it is to seek help from people without principle.

THE MAGISTRATES

—

BY

MIRZA FETH–ALI AKHOUD ZAIDÉ

[Translated by Epiphanius Wilson, A.M.]

DRAMATIS PERSONÆ

SEKINÉ-KHANOUN, a young lady of eighteen, sister of the late Hadji-Ghafour.

AZIZ-BEY, the lover and *fiancé* of Sekiné-Khanoun.

ZOBEIDE, paternal aunt of Sekiné-Khanoun.

ZEINEB-KHANOUN, mistress of the late Hadji-Ghafour.

AGA-ABBAS, brother of Zeineb.

AGA-SELMAN, son of the sieve-maker, advocate of Sekiné-Khanoun.

AGA-MERDAN, son of the confectioner, advocate of Zeineb.

AGA-HASSAM, a merchant.

AGA-KERIM, chief of the courtiers.

GOUL-SEBAH, servant of Sekiné-Khanoun.

THE PRESIDENT OF THE TRIBUNAL.

AGA-REHIM,
AGA-DJEBBAR,   } Assessors of the Tribunal.
AGA-BECHIN,
AGA-SETTAR,

THE INSPECTOR OF THE MARKET.

HEPOU,
CHEIDA,   } witnesses for Zeineb.
QOURBAN ALI,
HANIFE,

BEDEL,
QUHREMAN,   } soldiers, witnesses for Sekiné-Khanoun.
GHAFFER,
NEZER,

THE CHIEF OF THE BAILIFFS.

ECED, domestic to the President of the Tribunal.

NASSER, a lackey.

A seven months' old infant.

THE MAGISTRATES

ACT FIRST

Scene I—The Scene is laid in the House of the Late Merchant, Hadji-Ghafour

Sekiné-Khanoun, sister of Hadji-Ghafour, is discovered standing before the window; she calls to her servant, Goul-Sebah.

SEKINÉ-KHANOUN. Goul-Sebah! Goul-Sebah!

GOUL-SEBAH [*entering the room*]. Here I am, madame. What do you wish?

SEKINÉ-KHANOUN. Have you not heard of the trouble which my shameless sister-in-law is bringing upon me, Goul-Sebah?

GOUL-SEBAH. No, madame. How could I hear about it?

SEKINÉ-KHANOUN. She has given notice to the President of the Tribunal that she objects to his paying over to me the money which my brother had placed in his hands for me. She claims that this sum should revert to her. Good heavens! Goul-Sebah, was ever such a case heard of? I do not know what sin I have committed against God, but things always fall out unluckily for me.

GOUL-SEBAH. Whatever put such ideas in your head, madame? Why should things fall out unluckily for you?

SEKINÉ-KHANOUN. As you are aware, Goul-Sebah, I am desperately in love with Aziz-Bey. For two whole years did the unhappy youth in vain beseech my brother to give him my hand; my brother would not consent, because Aziz-Bey is the son of a heretic, and an officer of government. But now that my brother is dead, and I am free to dispose of my hand as I choose, I wish to enter into possession of

27

the money which he has left me, to provide for my wants in peace, and to fulfil the vow of my heart. And lo and behold, this shameless sister-in-law has protested against the payment of the legacy! We must therefore have all the worry of a lawsuit.

GOUL-SEBAH. Is it not a fact, madame, that your sister-in-law has no right to the legacy left by your brother?

SEKINÉ-KHANOUN. She certainly has none. What right could she have? She was not his lawful wife, that she should inherit his fortune. She has not even a child who could be co-heir to it! I do not really know why she has protested.

GOUL-SEBAH. Do not trouble your head about it, madame. Please God, nothing will be done against you. But make one promise to your servant; I will pray God to bring out your business well, and to grant that you may soon reach the goal of your desires.

SEKINÉ-KHANOUN. What is your desire? What promise do you wish me to make to you?

GOUL-SEBAH. Promise me, when this affair is settled, by the favor of God, and you have come into possession of your fortune, promise me to defray the expenses of my wedding and to give me a husband. What could I desire beside that?

SEKINÉ-KHANOUN. Very well. Do you pray to God that our lawsuit may be quickly ended, and I will give a husband to you also. But start at once, and go to the house of Aziz-Bey, and tell him to come to me; I wish to see what he says about all this. The President of the Tribunal has induced me to ask an advocate to plead my cause. But I have no one in this country excepting Aziz-Bey, and a paternal aunt—and she is, of course, a woman, and what can a woman do for me?

GOUL-SEBAH [she goes out and at once returns]. Madame, here comes Aziz-Bey himself at the very nick of time. [Sekiné-Khanoun closes the window and Aziz-Bey enters the room.]

Scene II

AZIZ-BEY [*abruptly*]. See what a mess you have led me into,
Sekiné.

SEKINÉ-KHANOUN [*with surprise*]. I! What mess have I led
you into? But, tell me, what has happened that you seem
so vexed and gloomy?

AZIZ-BEY. Listen to me, Sekiné. You know that two years ago,
just as I left school, I fell sick with love for you, so that
I had no longer strength to leave the house, although your
brother ill-treated me, and made every effort to separate
us two. During this whole time, I have proved constant,
and have put up with his harshness. My love, so far from
being cooled, has grown from day to day, and in the hope
that sooner or later we should be united, I have patiently
endured all sorts of outrage and persecutions. Meanwhile
the moment of our union seemed to be near, and my
thoughts became somewhat more cheerful, and I enjoyed a
little more peace of mind—and now I learn that I am again
to be plunged into misfortune!

SEKINÉ-KHANOUN. What do you say? Speak more plainly,
that I may understand your meaning. I do not comprehend you.

AZIZ-BEY. How is it you do not comprehend? Are you not
aware that yesterday, Aga-Hassam, the merchant, has sent
the wife of the head of the Traders' Company, that of the
mayor, and that of Bagis, the lawyer, to the house of your
aunt, to demand your hand of her? Your aunt has given
her word in assent.

SEKINÉ-KHANOUN. But my aunt talks nonsense! Who pays
any attention to her words?

AZIZ-BEY. I can stand this no longer. You must send at once
and call for your aunt, and let me with my own ears hear
her declare that you shall never be the wife of Aga-Hassam, or else I must decide to kill Aga-Hassam this very
day, and may I succeed in doing so! What is this Hassam?
A shopkeeper! He wishes to step into my shoes, to pay
court to my *fiancée*, and to cross my path, does he! By
God, I will cut his heart out with this dagger.

SEKINÉ-KHANOUN. Very good. I will send to my aunt, and

beg of her to come at once. Then I will tell her that I am not, and never will be the wife of Aga-Hassam. When my aunt arrives, you must go into this room, and you will hear what she says with your own ears.—Goul-Sebah!

Scene III

GOUL-SEBAH. What is it, madame?

SEKINÉ-KHANOUN. Goul-Sebah, go and ask my aunt to come here. [*Goul-Sebah goes out.*]

Scene IV

SEKINÉ-KHANOUN. Well, but come now, whom shall we take for our advocate?

AZIZ-BEY. Advocate? For what purpose?

SEKINÉ-KHANOUN. Alas, he asks me for what purpose! Have they not told you, then, that my sister-in-law disputes the legacy, and wishes to involve me in a lawsuit?

AZIZ-BEY. Yes, I have heard it said, but at present my head is whirling round. First let your aunt come, and when she goes away, I will find an advocate. [*At this moment a footstep is heard, Aziz-Bey returns to the other room, and Zobeide, aunt of Sekiné-Khanoun enters the apartment.*]

Scene V

SEKINÉ-KHANOUN. Good-day, my dear aunt.

ZOBEIDE. Good-day, Sekiné. How are you? Are you quite well?

SEKINÉ-KHANOUN. Ah! how can I be well, when I have allowed you, aunt, to promise me in marriage to Aga-Hassam? I have neither father nor brother, and am altogether dependent on myself for the management of my life.

ZOBEIDE. Are you not ashamed to speak thus? What! not a blush! Has not all been done in your interest? You need a husband; you must take him who is given to you. It is not proper that young girls should speak in this style before their elder relations. It is shameful! Fie upon you, Sekiné!

SEKINÉ-KHANOUN. Not at all. I have spoken just as I choose; I will no longer surrender my liberty, and no one shall force a husband upon me.

ZOBEIDE. Very good. You do not, then, wish to marry?

SEKINÉ-KHANOUN. No; I certainly do not wish to marry.

ZOBEIDE [smiling]. There are many girls who say no, like you; but later on they come to reason.

SEKINÉ-KHANOUN. In the name of God, aunt, do not make fun of me; it is absurd to wish me to marry Aga-Hassam; you may as well give up that idea altogether.

ZOBEIDE. It is not possible for you to recede, my dear niece. You would make enemies for me of all the leading people of the country.

SEKINÉ-KHANOUN. They may go to the devil for all I care. Aga-Hassam is loathsome to me; the very sight of him makes me sick.

ZOBEIDE. Why is that?

SEKINÉ-KHANOUN. He is a low fellow.

ZOBEIDE. He may be a low fellow to everyone else, but to us he is of the first water. He is successful in business, is very rich, and his connections are among the leading people of the province. Where will you find a better husband?

SEKINÉ-KHANOUN. Even if Aga-Hassam were to load me with jewels from head to foot I would never be his wife. Go and tell him to give up all idea of this.

ZOBEIDE. Never. Who, pray, are you, that you presume to go back on the word which I have given? Aga-Hassam sent to me the leading ladies of the land. I am no child, and I, of course, consented to their offer; I had your interest in view, and gave my word to them. Do you wish me to appear in the eyes of the world as an imbecile? I have, I believe, both name and rank; I have a position of dignity, and am an honorable woman.

SEKINÉ-KHANOUN. And so I am to be made unhappy for my whole life in order that your reputation and your honor may suffer no damage! You have laid a strange duty upon me, aunt. By Heaven, I swear that I will never, never marry Aga-Hassam, even though the whole world be brought to ruin. It is I who tell you this, and you must explain matters to him, and make him abandon this pro-

posal. If you do not, I will send for him myself, and I
will meet him face to face and give him such a tongue-
lashing as he never had before. I will treat him worse than
a dog, and send him away with a flea in his ear.

ZOBEIDE [*covering her face with both her hands*]. Oh! Oh!
My God! Oh! how the whole world is become topsy-
turvy. The young girls of to-day have neither shame nor
reserve. Sekiné, I have never before met a girl of such
effrontery as you exhibit. I myself have been young, I
have had older relatives about me, but from respect toward
them I would never have dared to raise my head in con-
tradiction to them. It is because of this effrontery of yours
that plague and cholera cease not to waste this province.

SEKINÉ-KHANOUN. No, it is owing to the baseness of certain
degraded people that plague and cholera are raging here.
This miserable wretch has heard of my fortune of 60,000
tomans, and this is the reason why he sent and asked
for my hand. If this were not so, why did he not seek
to win me by the avenue of love and inclination? If he
desired to espouse me for my own sake, why did he keep
his mouth shut, and refrain from breathing a word during
my brother's lifetime.

ZOBEIDE. He might have had no desire to wed you in your
brother's lifetime. But you do well to remind me of the
60,000 tomans. Are you not aware that unless you marry
Aga-Hassam he will cause you to forfeit this sum of
money?

SEKINÉ-KHANOUN. Why, and in what way will he cause me
to forfeit it?

ZOBEIDE. In what way? Why, he will go to your sister-in-law,
and make common cause with her. His kinsmen and family will support her claim and confirm her declaration, and
you will be compelled to abandon your rights. The reason
is palpable; it lies in the greed and devilish trickery of
those people whose minds are set on nothing else but the
absorption of other people's fortunes, great and small.
And what do you know about such matters as these? Who
will listen to your arguments or pleas?

SEKINÉ-KHANOUN. Very good. Let us admit that my rights
are to be invaded and my pleas disregarded. Still, I do not

understand how a mistress, a domestic servant, can pretend
to the legacy that belongs to me. We shall soon be told
that there is neither right nor justice in this country, and
that everyone can do just what he likes, and as he understands it to be best for himself!

ZOBEIDE. Ah, my child, is there any safeguard from the trickery of mankind? What rights had the wife of Hadji-
Rehim in the fortune of her husband? Nevertheless 12,000
tomans in cash and a bathing establishment were stolen
from Aga-Riza, the son of Hadji-Rehim, to make a gift
for this vile woman. By all sorts of rascalities the advocate of this woman forged a deed of gift, and pretended
that Hadji-Rehim in his lifetime transferred to his wife
12,000 tomans, in specie, and a bathing establishment.
Five or six persons were produced as witnesses, and in
spite of his cries and lamentations, the money and the *ham-
mam* were stolen from poor Aga-Riza, who utterly failed
to obtain justice? You are quite unaware of the diabolical
wiles of law officers in this country; no one can escape
from the manœuvres of these people, no one can see
through these manœuvres and false statements. Do you
think that I have promised your hand to Aga-Hassam to
please myself? Not at all. I have seen that there was no
course to take, and I said to myself that we must accept
the situation with a good grace; and that this was the best
thing to be done.

SEKINÉ-KHANOUN. Even though all my fortune should be
swallowed up to the last penny, I will never be the wife of
Aga-Hassam. Go, then, and explain this to him; tell him
that your niece refused her consent.

ZOBEIDE. Do not speak in this way, Sekiné. I see your plan.
You wish to become the wife of Aziz-Bey, and to mingle
the blood of our race with heretics; to bring in those people, and to set them at the head of our family; to do despite to the spirits of our ancestors, and to cover yourself
with disgrace. Never, up to this day, has such a thing been
seen in our family. How can the daughter of an honest,
God-fearing merchant become the wife of an unbeliever?
How is it possible?

SEKINÉ-KHANOUN. How do you know that I desire to espouse

Aziz-Bey? I wish to espouse neither him nor anyone else. I wish to remain in my own house. Be quick, then, and give my message to Aga-Hassam.

ZOBEIDE. You are a young girl, you have not reached years of discretion, and cannot see your own interests. I have not the slightest intention of going to find Aga-Hassam, and telling him that my niece is unwilling to marry him. I have promised you to him, and he left after receiving my word on it; you may spare yourself further talk on this matter. [*Zobeide rises and goes out.*]

Scene VI

AZIZ-BEY. You see now what real trouble I am in. I shall go off at once.

SEKINÉ-KHANOUN. Where will you go?

AZIZ-BEY. To this villain, Aga-Hassam, to punish him as he deserves. I can no longer restrain myself.

SEKINÉ-KHANOUN. What is the matter with you? Do not go; remain here. You will otherwise commit some blunder. I intend sending someone from me to this wretch, to tell him to come here, and I will compel him myself to abandon these designs of his.—Goul-Sebah! [*Enter Goul-Sebah.*]

Scene VII

SEKINÉ-KHANOUN. Goul-Sebah, go to the home of Aga-Hassam, the merchant, take him aside, and tell him that a woman asks for him on a most important errand; but do not mention my name. [*Exit Goul-Sebah. Then Sekiné-Khanoun turns toward Aziz-Bey.*]

Scene VIII

SEKINÉ-KHANOUN. By heavens, Aziz-Bey, you are a child whose lips are still wet with your nurse's milk! Go and look at yourself in the glass and see how red your eyes are from rage. How is it you have so little force of character? This base fellow cannot take me by force.

AZIZ-BEY. You are right; but what can I do when my heart is overflowing. [*Footsteps heard without. Aziz-Bey re-*

turns to the other chamber. Sekiné-Khanoun veils her face and seats herself. Enter Goul-Sebah with Aga-Hassam.]

Scene IX

AGA-HASSAM. Good-day, madame.

SEKINÉ-KHANOUN [*pleasantly*]. Good-day, sir. Do you know who I am, brother Hassam?

AGA-HASSAM. No, madame, I do not.

SEKINÉ-KHANOUN. Really! Well, Aga-Hassam, I must inform you that I am Sekiné, the sister of Hadji-Ghafour.

AGA-HASSAM [*in astonishment*]. Indeed! I have heard of you. Can I do any thing for you? I am your humble servant and your slave, your domestic, your lackey.

SEKINÉ-KHANOUN. No, Aga-Hassam, let me beg you to be neither my slave nor my servant; be my brother, both in this world and in the next, and give up all idea of marrying me. It is for the purpose of making this simple request that I have called you here; this is all I have to say to you.

AGA-HASSAM [*in confusion*]. But, madame, why do you not permit me to be your slave? What fault have I committed?

SEKINÉ-KHANOUN. You have committed no fault, and it is best that I should speak plainly to you. I am informed that you sent to my aunt to ask for my hand; but it is quite useless for her to give her consent to your demand. I may as well tell you that I am not the person to suit you in this matter; abandon, therefore, your purpose. From henceforth do not name me in connection with this subject again.

AGA-HASSAM. And pray, madame, why is this? Give me the reason. Let me understand why I am not worthy to offer you my services.

SEKINÉ-KHANOUN. The reason I need not explain. All I have to ask of you is to leave me alone.

AGA-HASSAM. But really, madame, I must know what fault I have committed which makes you repulse me.

SEKINÉ-KHANOUN. You have not committed a single fault, my brother. But I am to-day mistress of my own actions, and I do not desire to become your wife. I do not love you; nothing can force the heart to love.

AGA-HASSAM. It is very wrong of you to speak in this strain, madame. Do not repeat such words.

SEKINÉ-KHANOUN. I understand what you mean. Well, do your worst. Spare me, or spare me not, it matters not to me, vile wretch!

AGA-HASSAM. Ah! you will repent of this later on. But think again for a while, and consider whether you have nothing more to say to me.

SEKINÉ-KHANOUN. I have considered the whole question, and I have but one more observation to make. Leave me! and do whatever you will. There is no one more despicable than you are.

AGA-HASSAM [enraged]. Are you mad? I intend to lead you such a dance that everyone will talk about it; even to the day of your death you will remember it. [He rises.]

SEKINÉ-KHANOUN. Begone! Begone! He who fears you is lower than you are. Do your worst against me. Begone! —What does he say? Does he fancy that anyone is afraid of him? [Aga-Hassam withdraws, and Aziz-Bey comes back into the room.]

Scene X

SEKINÉ-KHANOUN. Come in and let me think over matters. One stone frightens away a hundred crows.

AZIZ-BEY. I am going to tell the whole affair to Chah-Zade, the King's son, and ask him to settle it offhand.

SEKINÉ-KHANOUN. The Prince Royal cannot stop the lawsuit. In any case we must have an advocate.

AZIZ-BEY. The Prince Royal cannot stop the lawsuit; but he can defeat the artifices of a rascal like Aga-Hassam. I must inform him of the affair. My father has long been devoted to his service, and he is well disposed toward me; he has promised to give me employment and to establish me in an office, and to give me my father's fortune.

SEKINÉ-KHANOUN. That is all very good, but let us first secure the services of an advocate; afterward you can go and tell the whole story to the Prince Royal, and he will see what is best to be done.

AZIZ-BEY. Very good. Whom would you like to have for an advocate? [At this moment Goul-Sebah enters the room.]

Scene XI

Goul-Sebah. Madame, a certain individual who professes to have important business to discuss with you is waiting at the door. He asks if there is anyone who can serve as his representative with you.

Sekiné-Khanoun. Certainly, Aziz-Bey is here. Tell the man to come in; we wish to know what he wants. [*Goul-Sebah goes out.*]

Scene XII

Aziz-Bey. Do you think it wise that the newcomer should see me with you?

Sekiné-Khanoun. Do people know who you are? Probably you will be taken for one of my family. [*Aga-Kerim enters the room. Sekiné-Khanoun veils herself.*]

Scene XIII

Aga-Kerim. Good-day to you both.

Aziz-Bey. Good-day, sir. Be seated, if you please; you are welcome.

Aga-Kerim [*seating himself and turning to Aziz-Bey*]. My young master, kindly tell me your name.

Aziz-Bey. My name is Aziz-Bey.

Aga-Kerim. It is a fortunate name. But Aziz-Bey, may I speak to you on a certain matter in the presence of Sekiné-Khanoun?

Aziz-Bey. You may address your remarks directly to Sekiné-Khanoun. Do not think that she is frivolous like other young ladies; she delights in conversation, and will not be at all bashful in answering your questions.

Aga-Kerim. She is right. But let me first of all inform you, Aziz-Bey, that I am Aga-Kerim, the chief of the courtiers, and that I was a close friend of the late Hadji-Ghafour. I happened to drop in on business a moment ago, at the house of Aga-Merdan, the son of the confectioner. By chance Aga-Hassam, the merchant, was also there. He greeted me, sat down, and spoke as follows: " I am told, Aga-Merdan, that you are the advocate of Zeineb, the widow of Hadji-Ghafour. I take your side in this lawsuit, and I have something to say to you in confidence." I saw that they wanted to have a private talk, so I withdrew. I learned, however, that they were plotting against Sekiné-Khanoun, and I therefore came to warn her, merely from a feeling of gratitude toward Hadji-Ghafour.

SEKINÉ-KHANOUN. I am delighted to find, Aga-Kerim, that you have not forgotten the claims of friendship, and that in the present emergency you have remembered the sister of an old friend.

AGA-KERIM. Ah yes, madame, friendship is a valuable thing in these days. I have seen how things stood, for this Aga-Merdan is a rogue and a scheming rascal whose equal is to be found neither in earth nor in heaven. I therefore decided to come, and in a friendly spirit to warn you beforehand of their intrigues, for if they are permitted to carry them out, there will be no cure for the consequences.

SEKINÉ-KHANOUN. But, Aga-Kerim, what can Aga-Merdan do against me?

AGA-KERIM. What can he do? I am told that he is the advocate of your sister-in-law, and intends to sue you at law in her name. He is very clever and resourceful in affairs of this sort; you would be no match for him. It is very difficult to get ahead of him.

SEKINÉ-KHANOUN. What can he do in this lawsuit? My brother has no child to inherit his fortune. On the other hand, a woman who has been no more than temporary wife can make no claim to the heritage. However clever Aga-Merdan, or anyone else, may be, what injury can they do me in a case which is so clear?

AGA-KERIM. You have had very little experience in affairs of this sort. Aga-Merdan will find means to accomplish his ends. You must not let him take you at a disadvantage in the struggle.

SEKINÉ-KHANOUN. But how can we help being taken at a disadvantage?

AGA-KERIM. Well, tell me in the first place who your advocate is, so that I may see him, and make him acquainted with some of the tricks of Aga-Merdan. If he is intelligent he won't let himself be caught napping.

SEKINÉ-KHANOUN. We do not know whom to take for our advocate.

AGA-KERIM. How is that? You don't know whom to take, and have not appointed anyone to defend you in this case?

SEKINÉ-KHANOUN. No, we do not know whom to choose; we are just on the point of considering the question.

AZIZ-BEY. Could not you, Aga-Kerim, name someone to whom we could intrust our case?

AGA-KERIM. No, I know no one who would be able to hold his own against Aga-Merdan. I thought you had your advocate already on hand.

AZIZ-BEY. No, we have not appointed anyone. We were merely on the lookout for a man of great ability whom we could intrust with the defence of our interests. But think again; cudgel your brains. Have you no idea of anyone?

AGA-KERIM. No, I can think of no man who is of great ability. There are plenty of advocates, but there is none of them who could cope with Aga-Merdan. But stay; there is someone, if he would consent to be your advocate, for he has retired for some time from business of the kind. He alone would be able to hold his own with Aga-Merdan.

SEKINÉ-KHANOUN. Who is he?

AGA-KERIM. He is Aga-Selman, the son of the sieve-maker. Intrust your case with him if he will undertake it.

SEKINÉ-KHANOUN. Who would be able to see him and speak to him about it?

AGA-KERIM. It is not necessary to delegate anyone to see him. Send for him, and speak to him yourself here. Perhaps your arguments may persuade him to accept the case; the discourse of a woman has so much influence.

SEKINÉ-KHANOUN. Aga-Kerim, could you not see him yourself, and send him to us?

AGA-KERIM. No, madame. I have fallen out with him about a trifling matter. Send somebody else to fetch him.

SEKINÉ-KHANOUN. But how can you in this case give him certain information which you wish him to have?

AGA-KERIM. If you had another advocate, I should deem it necessary to instruct him in these matters; but in the case of Aga-Selman it is superfluous. He is clever enough to make slippers for the devil himself. Although I have quarrelled with him, I cannot deny his merit. God grant that your lawsuit may succeed.

AZIZ-BEY. I shall go and fetch him myself. [*Aziz-Bey and Aga-Kerim rise from their seats and prepare to go out.*]

AGA-KERIM. God preserve you, madame.

SEKINÉ-KHANOUN. Thanks for your kind visit.

AGA-KERIM. I shall never forget your goodness. [*Aga-Kerim goes out with Aziz-Bey.*]

Scene XIV

SEKINÉ-KHANOUN. Goul-Sebah! bring in a lounge, and lay a cushion on it. [*Scarcely has Goul-Sebah brought in the lounge and placed a cushion on it, when a sound of footsteps is heard in the vestibule. Aziz-Bey enters the room with Aga-Selman. Sekiné-Khanoun takes a seat at the back of the stage; Goul-Sebah stands by her side.*]

Scene XV

AGA-SELMAN. Good-day, madame!

SEKINÉ-KHANOUN. Good-day, sir. You are welcome, Aga-Selman, and your visit gratifies me exceedingly. Have the goodness to take a seat. [*She points with her finger to the lounge. Aga-Selman seats himself at the foot of the lounge and Aziz-Bey takes a place by his side.*]

SEKINÉ-KHANOUN [*in a melancholy voice*]. Aga-Selman, I am the sister of Hadji-Ghafour. I hope that you will treat me as your daughter, and will not refuse me your support in this day of misfortune.

AGA-SELMAN. Speak, madame, tell me what is your desire?

SEKINÉ-KHANOUN. You know, Aga-Selman, that seven or eight months ago everyone forsook the city and fled in every direction because of the cholera. Hadji-Ghafour was a man full of confidence in God; he declared he would not leave, but as a precaution he took to the President of the Tribunal and placed on deposit with him, in exchange for vouchers, and in the presence of witnesses, a sum of 60,000 tomans, laid up in strong-boxes, " If I should happen to die," he said, " you must give this money to my legal heir." The President of the Tribunal took charge of the money, and then, like everybody else, he quitted the city. All our neighbors also left. No one was at home but my brother and I, with a woman whom he had espoused in temporary marriage. It happened that my brother fell sick. No one was left in the town but some soldiers whom the government had left to guard the houses of the inhabitants, and to carry the dead to the cemetery. On that day four soldiers came to our house, and my brother said to them: " I am dying, and I have no other heir in the world but my sister here. After my death take me away to the cemetery." Then my brother departed to the other world. Meanwhile my sister-in-law, who is no more than a mistress to whom no legacy can fall, pretends to be the heiress of my brother, and institutes a suit against me. Her advocate is Aga-Merdan, the son of the confectioner, and I hope that you will be willing to undertake the task of defending me.

AGA-SELMAN. Madame, I have retired from practice, and do not intend henceforth to be anyone's advocate.

SEKINÉ-KHANOUN. This business will not take long, Aga-Selman; it will soon be finished; it is matter for a single session. If witnesses are required to testify to the words of my brother, there are the soldiers—you can summon them as witnesses. I hope that you will undertake my case out of mere good-will toward me.

AGA-SELMAN. Do you know the names and addresses of these soldiers?

SEKINÉ-KHANOUN. Yes. Aziz-Bey will write the information on a sheet of paper and will hand it to you.

AGA-SELMAN. Since you depend upon me, I accept the case; but on condition that it is not to turn out a long one, for if it is likely to last for any period, it will not be possible for me to devote myself to it.

SEKINÉ-KHANOUN. It is matter for a single day, and in recompense for your trouble I will give you a fee of 500 tomans.

AGA-SELMAN. That is scarcely necessary, madame. I engage in this business purely out of regard for you, and without motives of self-interest.

SEKINÉ-KHANOUN. I know it, Aga-Selman, but I offer you this sum as pocket-money for your children.

AGA-SELMAN. Allow me now to retire, madame; I must go and find the soldiers and ask them to come and testify at the trial. As for you, make out a brief and send it to me.

SEKINÉ-KHANOUN. Very good, I will prepare and send it to you. But I would remind you, Aga-Selman, that Aga-Merdan is said to be very crafty; leave nothing undone to defeat his tricks.

AGA-SELMAN. Keep your mind easy, madame, his tricks will avail nothing against me. Aziz-Bey, make a note of the names and addresses of these soldiers and send the particulars to me.

AZIZ-BEY. Yes, yes; they will be at your house in less than an hour. [*Aga-Selman rises and goes out. Aziz-Bey and Sekiné-Khanoun remain alone.*]

Scene XVI

AZIZ-BEY. As for me, I am going to tell the whole story to the Prince Royal.

SEKINÉ-KHANOUN. Sit down. First of all write the names and addresses of the soldiers, and send them to Aga-Selman; then you can leave me. [*Aziz-Bey sits down to write.*]

ACT SECOND

Scene I

The action passes in the house of Aga-Merdan, son of the confectioner.

AGA-MERDAN [*discovered seated alone*]. I do not know what can have happened that Aga-Kerim is so late in coming. He must have been planning that Aga-Selman may be Sekiné-Khanoun's advocate, and this is probably what has detained him. If this affair succeeds, as I predict, beside the fact that I shall gain no small sum of money, my reputation will be spread through the whole city and will rise sky high. That is to say, that this lawsuit is an inexhaus-

tible mine of wealth to the man who can direct it and
make it turn out aright. Thank God, I am not troubled
about that. [*While he speaks the door opens, and Aga-
Kerim enters the room.*]

Scene II

AGA-KERIM [*gayly*]. Good-day. Congratulate me; I have arranged everything.

AGA-MERDAN [*with a smile*]. Really? Is it credible?

AGA-KERIM. Yes, on your soul it is. I have praised you so
highly to the widow of Hadji-Ghafour that if you had
been there you would not have believed your ears. " To-
day," I said to her, " there is no one of more consideration
with the President of the Tribunal than Aga-Merdan. He
is never deceived, and all he says comes to pass. At the
palace among the advocates he is the only one recognized.
This is so true of his reputation that on certain occasions
he has public and private audiences with the Prince Royal.
For knowledge of affairs he is the Plato of the century.
Follow his advice implicitly, and do not be anxious about
anything. It is only under his direction that you will be
able to enter into possession of Hadji-Ghafour's fortune;
for, excepting through him, you have no right to the legacy!" The woman was well satisfied, even delighted, as was
her brother, Aga-Abbas. Meanwhile they are coming to
see you, in order that you may dictate to them the line they
are to take.

AGA-MERDAN. Very good, very good. But, tell me, have you
been equally successful in securing for Aga-Selman the
defence of the other party?

AGA-KERIM. Yes. Aga-Selman is at this very moment with
Sekiné-Khanoun, and as soon as he is at liberty he will
come here.

AGA-MERDAN. It is wonderful, Aga-Kerim. By God, you work
miracles with your tongue. But, tell me, is the widow of
Hadji-Ghafour pretty?

AGA-KERIM. Why do you ask?

AGA-MERDAN. Why, because I want her to fall in love with
me, and marry me. Why should she not be my wife?

AGA-KERIM. How can I tell you whether she will love you or not? Your age is a little advanced and the woman is young.

AGA-MERDAN. No, Aga-Kerim, as sure as death, I am not so advanced in age. I am exactly fifty-one.

AGA-KERIM. I shouldn't have believed it; I thought you were seventy.

AGA-MERDAN. Seventy? Not on your life. You know I was born the year of the great earthquake at Tebriz.

AGA-KERIM. You are married already.

AGA-MERDAN. I do not wish to marry her because I am in want of a wife. But this is how I consider the matter: If we succeed in carrying off all this fortune from Hadji-Ghafour's sister, and transferring it to this woman, why should it go to another husband? Let me marry the woman, and the fortune becomes mine at the same time. This is also in your interest; what advantage will you otherwise gain from it?

AGA-KERIM. Yes, but in that case what matters whether she be pretty or plain? It would be much better that she should be a monster, if in that way she would become enamored of you, and consent to marry you. But she is not plain, and I do not believe she would find you to her taste.

AGA-MERDAN. Do you mean that I am not likely to please her, and to be accepted by her?

AGA-KERIM. Come now, do not you know this yourself? Your face is certainly not particularly captivating.

AGA-MERDAN. Of course I cannot truly say what effect I produce on you. Let me look at myself a little in the glass. [*He looks at himself in a wardrobe mirror.*] By God, Aga-Kerim, what do you find to criticise in my appearance? Do you mean that my teeth are gone? They fell out through an inflammation, and not from old age. It is true that my jaws are slightly wrinkled, but this is not seen, the beard hides it.

AGA-KERIM. Good for you. That is sufficient. Now sit down; she will soon be here.

AGA-MERDAN. Wait a while; let me put on my cashmere robe, button my surtout, and comb my beard. Then I will come and sit down. [*He begins to dress himself.*]

AGA-KERIM. Is all this necessary? Do sit down.

AGA-MERDAN. Certainly it is necessary. Our women always
veil themselves from the eyes of men, but they are extremely fond of gazing at us. If the widow of Hadji-
Ghafour sees me in full dress she will have more consideration for me, and my words will have more influence on her mind. It is even possible that I may prove
captivating to her. [*He dresses, combs his beard, and seats
himself. At this moment the door opens, and the widow
of Hadji-Ghafour enters with her brother, Aga-Abbas.*]

Scene III

AGA-ABBAS. Good-day, gentlemen.

AGA-MERDAN. Good-day to you both. You are very welcome,
and your visit gives me great pleasure. Be good enough
to sit down. [*The widow of Hadji-Ghafour, wearing a
veil, sits down, and so does her brother.*] I am going to
address my remarks to you, Aga-Abbas; Madame Zeineb
will hear, and will answer when necessary. Six months
ago Hadji-Ghafour died. It is necessary that the root
of the matter be made clear, and without mystery. Everyone knows that Zeineb-Khanoun was not the legal wife of
Hadji-Ghafour; she cannot, therefore, pretend to receive
whatever of fortune there is by right of inheritance. But
having learned this circumstance, I sent Aga-Kerim to you
to inform you that if you wish to take my advice, and govern yourselves according to the measures I shall take, I can
find a way to bring all this fortune into the hands of Zeineb-
Khanoun. As you know, the sister of Hadji-Ghafour is
an orphan, she has neither relatives nor family to abet
her. The young lady has indeed a lover, but this young
man is no match for me. You have accepted my proposals, and have forbidden the President of the Tribunal
to deliver to the sister of Hadji-Ghafour the sum which
the latter had deposited into the judge's hands until you
have shown cause why. The President of the Tribunal
has held the money, and has next notified you and the
sister of Hadji-Ghafour to employ counsel, and to bring
your case before the Tribunal, in order to state the object

of your petition. I am the man whom you have empowered to act for you. But it is necessary that madame should listen attentively to all that I am going to say, and that she comport herself in accordance with my advice; if she wishes the affair to turn out in accordance with our desires.

AGA-ABBAS. Certainly. Nothing can be done without this. Come, then, detail to us the conditions which you would impose upon Zeineb.

AGA-MERDAN. First of all, Zeineb-Khanoun must deposit with me a fund of 500 tomans to meet certain unavoidable expenses; the remainder of the dues will be paid afterward. Zeineb-Khanoun has herself declared to Aga-Kerim that at the death of Hadji-Ghafour there were a thousand tomans left in the strong-box, and that she carried them off, without the knowledge of the dead man's sister.

ZEINEB-KHANOUN. I make no objection to your demands on this point; tell me your other condition.

AGA-MERDAN. It will be also necessary, madame, that you be satisfied with one-half of the legacy; that is to say, that of the 60,000 tomans half goes to you and the other half, some 30,000 tomans, is to be divided between Aga-Kerim and me, as comrades, friends, and associates.

ZEINEB-KHANOUN. Good gracious, Aga-Merdan, but this is exorbitant!

AGA-MERDAN. It is by no means excessive, Madame. You have no right to this inheritance; the 30,000 tomans are therefore my free gift to you.

ZEINEB-KHANOUN. What do you mean? I have no rights? For years I have trudged up and down the house of Hadji-Ghafour; all the closet keys were in my hands; I had all I desired, and it was I who controlled the expenses. So long as Hadji-Ghafour lived his sister could not dispose of a single franc of his. What has happened that I am to be thrust on one side, and that this adventuress is to come and carry off all the money; that she is to drink it up, and spend it in order to have a wedding with a young scamp?

AGA-MERDAN. Such reasons as these are not listened to by the Tribunal.

ZEINEB-KHANOUN. What! not listened to? Ought not justice to be considered in a lawsuit? For ten years and more this fortune remained in my hands, and now I am to be stripped of it!

AGA-MERDAN. Yes, indeed, and you ought to be stripped of it. Listen to me. Surrender one-half of this inheritance, for in reality you have no right to a single penny of it. Aga-Abbas is well acquainted with the matter, and he knows what I say is true.

AGA-ABBAS. Yes, we accept the condition. What conditions beside these do you impose?

AGA-MERDAN. My third condition is that Zeineb-Khanoun shall declare in presence of the President of the Tribunal that she has by Hadji-Ghafour a child now seven months old, and still at the breast; this child she shall present before the Tribunal.

ZEINEB-KHANOUN. Oh, oh, Aga-Merdan, this is very, very hard. How can I dare to tell such a lie? That I have a child seven months old!

AGA-MERDAN. It is not hard at all. While Hadji-Ghafour was living you were *enceinte*. A month before his death you brought into the world a little boy—now seven months old. Is there any difficulty in stating that?

ZEINEB-KHANOUN. I look upon you as my father, Aga-Merdan, and I will never contravene your counsels; but this condition is too hard. Will not people say to me, knowing I have never had a child, "Where is your child? Where is your child?"

AGA-MERDAN. Don't distress yourself on that score. The child is all ready. You have brought him into the world. The babe has been in your arms, and in the arms of Hadji-Ghafour. There are even people that will testify to that effect. Don't distress yourself about these matters; simply make your statement, and others will confirm it.

ZEINEB-KHANOUN. In the name of God, Aga-Merdan, impose upon me some condition that I can fulfil; this is really too trying. How can I perpetrate such a falsehood? I'd never dare to talk in that way.

AGA-MERDAN. You are talking nonsense, Zeineb-Khanoun! I know what you mean by all this. Why would you not dare to say it? Why are you ashamed to do so? Everybody knows that it is the business of women to produce children. What shame is there in it? You have perhaps never been *enceinte,* and you have never borne a child. Let it be so; but he who wants to catch a fish must put his hand into cold water. It is quite necessary that you make this declaration. There is no other way of succeeding.

ZEINEB-KHANOUN. What end do you wish to gain by this, Aga-Merdan?

AGA-MERDAN. I wish by this means to have the fortune of Hadji-Ghafour secured to you, and in order to arrive at this result, there is no other expedient possible but this one. You cannot inherit from your husband in your own name. Your child, on the other hand, is heir at law. When the existence of your child is proved all the fortune reverts to him. I will then have myself without difficulty appointed his guardian; then in five or six months, I will give it out that the child is dead, and in that case the inheritance will be legally transferred to you. You will take half of it and give me the other half. God is the best foster-father.

ZEINEB-KHANOUN. O you for whom I would give my life, can such a lie be uttered?

AGA-MERDAN. If the sister of Hadji-Ghafour had anyone to maintain her cause do you think that she would fail to defeat us? But to-day she has no one to oppose us, and plead her cause for her. If she had married Aga-Hassam, the merchant, the business would have been very difficult for us. But now, Aga-Hassam, himself, and all his influential kinsfolk have become enemies of this young lady; they desire that this fortune should not be hers. The girl is deserted and left with her lover, who is good for nothing.

ZEINEB-KHANOUN. Well, well! and this child of whom you speak, where is he?

AGA-MERDAN. You are going to see him this moment.—Aga-Kerim, go and take the child from the arms of his nurse there in the chamber. Bring him in for madame to see. [*Aga-Kerim goes out to fetch the child.*]

Scene IV

ZEINEB-KHANOUN. Is she a wet-nurse?

AGA-MERDAN. No, it is his own mother who has him at the breast. But she becomes his nurse now. [*Aga-Kerim returns, carrying the child in his arms. Aga-Merdan takes it and gives it to Zeineb-Khanoun.*]

Scene V

AGA-MERDAN. This is your child. You see his eyes and brows are exactly those of Hadji-Ghafour.

ZEINEB-KHANOUN. My God, one might take it for his portrait! But I fear that at the trial my tongue will refuse to tell this lie.

AGA-MERDAN. The cause of your fears, Zeineb-Khanoun, is that you are not persuaded that you yourself are not the mother of this child. You must, before everything else, bear well in mind that this is your child, or else you will lose countenance at the hearing, and will stand before the judge with closed mouth. Have no fear, and give me your word that you will make the declaration as I dictate.

ZEINEB-KHANOUN. Yes, I promise you, if I am able.

AGA-MERDAN. You will be able, please God. It would be fine, in truth, if your sister-in-law should carry off the whole inheritance, and squander it with a scamp, trimming his mustache with it.

ZEINEB-KHANOUN. Yes, by God, you are right. But one thing troubles me. Will not the advocate of Sekiné-Khanoun discover my falsehood?

AGA-MERDAN. Ha! ha! ha! See how frightened she is of him! Fear nothing. He won't say a single word to expose you. Go now and get your application to the judge drawn up. All must be ready by to-morrow. As for me, I have another matter to attend to. Another person is looking for me; I have a thousand suits in hand. Take Aga-Kerim with you, and give him the 500 tomans; he will bring them to me.

AGA-ABBAS. The money is ready. We have brought it. Aga-Kerim had told us to do so beforehand.

AGA-MERDAN. Very good; leave it with me and retire. [*Aga-Abbas puts down the sum of money in a purse before Aga-Kerim. At the moment when Zeineb and Aga-Abbas rise to depart Nasser, the valet of the Prince Royal, approaches Aga-Merdan.*]

Scene VI

NASSER. Good-day, gentlemen. Aga-Merdan, the Prince Royal begs that you will come to his house this evening and spend an hour with him. He requires your services in an important affair.

AGA-MERDAN. Tell your master in reply that I am at his service. [*The lackey retires. Soon afterward, Eced, the servant of the President of the Tribunal, arrives.*]

Scene VII

ECED. Good-day, gentlemen. Aga-Merdan, my master invites you to dine with him this evening at the home of Hadji-Semi. He has pressing business on which he wishes to consult you.

AGA-MERDAN. You may tell your master that I will be there, and consent merely to please him. [*Aga-Abbas and his sister retire.*]

Scene VIII

AGA-KERIM. I do not understand where this messenger of the Prince Royal and this servant of the judge came from.

AGA-MERDAN. I felt that the woman might be troubled with regard to the conditions which I imposed upon her. This is the reason why I bribed these individuals to deliver such messages in her presence. I did so in order that she might imagine me to be the friend of the Prince Royal and the boon companion of the President of the Tribunal, in order that she might recover her spirits. I was afraid that otherwise she would not dare to make her allegations at the hearing of the case, and so we should be non-suited.

AGA-KERIM. By God, your idea was a happy one, but at the hearing of the case we must keep our eye on her. If possible we must manage that she gives her evidence after I have brought on the witnesses. You will promise her as her share 500 tomans; fifty in cash, and the balance later. The witnesses shall each have thirty tomans; fiften in cash, and fifteen afterward. We will give up this sum after winning the lawsuit, in order that the inspector may not poke his nose into our business; but you know that the affair cannot be made to succeed without his aid, he is so crafty. You know he has already on one occasion detected our game. We cannot cheat him.

AGA-KERIM. Very good. I will go and see about it. [*He rises from his seat to retire.*]

AGA-MERDAN. By the by, just stop one moment. I have an idea which I wish to communicate, and do not forget the hint. When you see the widow of Hadji-Ghafour, give her to understand, in one way or another, that she must not call me " father." As sure as death you must attend to this. I don't like the woman to address me by such a name as father, as if they thought it pleased me. What need can there be to call me by this title?

AGA-KERIM. Well! Well! Do not swear any more. I know what you are driving at. Let your mind be easy. I will tell her not to call you her father again, but to call you her lord. [*Aga-Kerim leaves, and on his departure, Aga-Selman enters.*]

Scene IX

AGA-SELMAN. Good-day, Aga-Merdan.

AGA-MERDAN. Ah, good-day! Come now, how are things getting along?

AGA-SELMAN. I am intrusted with the defence; it is all arranged. But, tell me, what do you think is now to be done?

AGA-MERDAN. I think we would do well to prepare the witnesses, and to take them to the court-room. What honorarium have you been promised?

AGA-SELMAN. They have promised me only 500 tomans; their witnesses, they say, are all ready, the course of the trial plain, and there is nothing either obscure or mysterious in it. I have expressed my satisfaction.

AGA-MERDAN. You have done well; but you know that there is not much profit in defending a good cause. The widow of Hadji-Ghafour sacrifices 30,000 tomans, these 30,000 tomans will be for us two and for Aga-Kerim. Have you ascertained the names of the witnesses? Have you learned their addresses?

AGA-SELMAN. Yes, I have learned and noted all these things. These witnesses are four soldiers: Bedel, Quhreman, Ghaffer, and Nezer—all of Nerdji Street.

AGA-MERDAN. I must send and fetch them, and impress upon them to testify exactly opposite to what they saw. But, first of all, you must go and find them, and beg them, on your part, to bear faithful testimony. As soldiers are willing but poor, much the same as wretched beggars, these men will ask you what present you intend to make them after the trial. " My children," you must answer them, " in an affair like this, it is not good to ask for a fee. You ought to give in your testimony solely for the sake of pleasing God, and he will fully reward you on the day of the resurrection."

AGA-SELMAN. Very good.

AGA-MERDAN. You cannot guess even approximately what will be the testimony of these soldiers?

AGA-SELMAN. Oh, yes, I know that. They will declare that two hours before the death of Hadji-Ghafour they betook themselves to his home, and that he said to them: " I am dying; and have no one in the world surviving me but a sister. Bury me as soon as I am dead."

AGA-MERDAN. Very good; but they will have to change that, and say that Hadji-Ghafour had a little son one month old. Exert yourself now, and go after these soldiers. [*Aga-Selman rises and leaves.*]

Scene X

AGA-MERDAN [*alone*]. Thanks be to God, events are turning out excellently. This is the time when Aga-Kerim is to bring his witnesses. [*At this moment the door opens, and Aga-Kerim enters the room with the Inspector of the Market and four other individuals.*]

THE MAGISTRATES

Scene XI

THE INSPECTOR. Good-day, Aga-Merdan.

AGA-MERDAN [*to Aga-Kerim, without turning or recognizing the Inspector*]. Good-day, you have found the Inspector?

THE INSPECTOR. No need to find him, for he was never lost. That was an odd question of yours, Aga-Merdan. I see that you do not yet recognize me.

AGA-MERDAN [*first of all leading aside Aga-Kerim*]. Go and fetch Aga-Selman, and make him point out to you the soldiers he spoke of, then bring them to me. [*Turns toward the Inspector.*] My lord, present these gentlemen to me and inform me what sort of men they are.

THE INSPECTOR. Here is Hepou, a professional gambler, who arrived here from Ardebil yesterday; the next is the famous Cheida, of Quzvin, who keeps a bank during the day, and dissipates during the night; then follows Qourban-Ali, of Hamaden, who is Jack-of-all-trades during the night, a hosier in the bazaar by daylight, and lodges with me at night.

AGA-MERDAN. God be praised, they are all honest people, of good standing. But the profession of Hepou is slightly open to suspicion. There will be some distrust roused by his presence.

THE INSPECTOR. Do not be alarmed. Hepou is an old fox who will fool anyone. Do you wish him to appear as a distinguished merchant he will present himself before you, and you yourself would not recognize him. You are doubtless unaware of the fact that he is of a race whose skill has been tested. He is the son of Heides-Qouli, whose foot was cut off. One day, Heides-Qouli was seen in the city of Eher. He traversed on foot two posts during the night, and reached Tebriz, stole from the house of the defunct governor a casket of pearls belonging to the latter, and returned to Eher the same night; at dawn, he was found asleep in the corridor of the caravansary. Everyone was astounded at this feat. It was only on account of the credit he got for it that he was not put to death immediately on detection. They merely cut off his foot and let him go.

AGA-MERDAN. This, then, is the son of Heides of the docked
foot? Very good; but we will change his name. All
these men are well acquainted with legal procedure, are
they not?

THE INSPECTOR. Let your mind be easy on that point; they
are all educated; by my life, they could make slippers
for the devil. There is none like them; every day
they meet together and offer the Lord's Prayer in the
mosque.

AGA-MERDAN. Very good. Do they know what sort of testimony they are expected to give?

THE INSPECTOR. No, you will have to teach them that yourself.

AGA-MERDAN. Good. They must depose as follows: One
evening at sunset a week before the death of Hadji-Ghafour, we were going all four of us to pay a visit to the
houses of the dead. In passing before the house of Hadji-
Ghafour we saw him standing at his gate and holding in
his arms a babe in long clothes. We saluted him, and
asked him how his health was? " Whose child is that? "
we said to him. " It is my own," he answered, " he was
born three weeks ago. He is my only son; I have no other
child."

THE INSPECTOR [turning to the witnesses]. Do you understand, boys?

HEPOU. Yes, we understand.

AGA-MERDAN. Can you repeat the story as I told it?

HANIFE. Undoubtedly so; there are no far-fetched expressions
to puzzle us.

AGA-MERDAN. Very good, my friends. May God bless you!

CHEIDA. How in the name of everything, Aga-Merdan, would
God bless such a transaction as this?

AGA-MERDAN. Why not? My dear friend, if you were acquainted with the whole affair you would certainly say
yourself that God would bless it. The unhappy widow
of Hadji-Ghafour has been for ten years mistress of his
house and fortune. Would it be just that a sickly wench
should carry off all this money, and proceed to enjoy it
with a base loafer, a heretic, and for the sole reason that
the latter is to have criminal relations with her? Accord-

ing to the words of your doctors, the Sunnites are excluded from the court of heaven.

CHEIDA. Now, by God, but you speak the truth!

THE INSPECTOR. Come now, Aga-Merdan, fix the fee to be paid the boys.

AGA-MERDAN. What? Has not Aga-Kerim done so? I said that I would give thirty tomans to each of those gentlemen. You know, yourself, what your share is to be.

THE INSPECTOR. Yes, but you must advance to the lads the half of their fee.

AGA-MERDAN. Most willingly, if you will now retire. Aga-Kerim will bring your fifty tomans for yourself, as well as half of the fee to be paid to each of these young men.

THE INSPECTOR. Very good. God protect you. [*The Inspector retires with his followers, then the door opens again, and four soldiers enter with Aga-Kerim.*]

Scene XII

THE SOLDIERS. Good-day, sir.

AGA-MERDAN. Good-day, my lads. Be good enough to take a seat. You are extremely welcome. Excuse the trouble which I have given you.

ONE OF THE SOLDIERS. Don't mention it, sir; it is ours to be grateful for the honor of entering the house of a man so honorable.

AGA-MERDAN. A well-educated man is well received anywhere. Have you lunched?

THE SOLDIERS. No, we arrived before luncheon time.

AGA-MERDAN. Aga-Kerim, send someone to the bazaar to purchase for the boys four portions of rice of kebah, likewise of ice and citron cup. See there be an extra supply of kebah, for they are very hungry. You'll like a great deal, won't you?

A SOLDIER. Why take all this trouble, my lord? We will repair ourselves to the bazaar, and eat a bit there.

AGA-MERDAN. What trouble is it, my dear friend? It is lunch time, why should you wish to leave my house fasting and famished? Please God, my plan is best.

THE SOLDIER. My lord, what do you desire of us?

AGA-MERDAN. Nothing much, my lad; I only wish to ask you a plain question.

THE SOLDIER. Speak, my lord—two if you like.

AGA-MERDAN. Did you bear to burial Hadji-Ghafour?

THE SOLDIER. Yes, my lord, it was we who buried him. Why do you ask?

AGA-MERDAN. Ah, I congratulate you on your generous conduct. Your company is always a great honor, not only because you are the defenders of Islam, but also because you do good service to all people in their days of distress. While the cholera prevailed there remained scarce a living soul in the town; you alone did not quit it, making in advance the sacrifice of your lives. May the Thrice Holy Majesty of God reward you worthily for this! But did you ever see Hadji-Ghafour when he was alive, my son?

THE SOLDIER. Yes, my lord, we saw him alive.

AGA-MERDAN. In that case, you must also at his side have seen his little son in long clothes, who was then a month old.

THE SOLDIER. No, my lord, we never saw him.

AGA-MERDAN. Perhaps he was at that moment in his mother's arms?

THE SOLDIER. No, my lord. We asked Hadji-Ghafour how many children he had, sons or daughters, big or little, and he answered that only a sister would survive him.

AGA-MERDAN. That is possible; he did not count his son because the latter was only a baby, one month old. But this babe was then in the arms of his mother; other people have seen him there; and I believe that you have also seen him. There is no harm done; it is all right. But in this case what testimony will you give? For, as you know, there is a lawsuit between the heirs as to the rights of succession.

THE SOLDIER. We will testify of what we have been informed. The advocate of Hadji-Ghafour's sister has already questioned us on this point, and we have corroborated his account.

AGA-MERDAN. Ah, I understand why you speak thus; it is because the discourse of this wretched renegade has produced an impression on your mind. Therefore you deny the existence of the child. He has doubtless promised you for this twenty tomans, and has advanced you ten.

THE SOLDIER. No, my lord, he did not promise us a penny, and even when we asked for a little present he told us that a witness ought to be disinterested, and that we ought to expect our recompense from God alone.

AGA-MERDAN. Oh, the accursed rogue! See how mean, grasping, and close he is! He won't let anyone profit by a penny excepting himself, and while he tries unjustly to obtain evidence in his favor, in a suit for 60,000 tomans, he grudges to spend twenty or thirty tomans on such kind young fellows as you! By God, there is not in the whole world another wretch like him! May God punish him by utter ruin! His work is unjust, and his conduct ignoble, and he himself a skinflint and a robber.

THE SOLDIER. How is his work unjust, my lord?

AGA-MERDAN. Because he evidently wishes to deny the existence of the little seven months' old child of Hadji-Ghafour. He wishes to cast out this child, and deprive him of his patrimony, in order that the sister of Hadji-Ghafour may get it. But God will not favor this action; he will prove that the child is still alive, and that his existence cannot be overlooked. Can such a thing be denied? I am the defender of this poor little orphan. I have sworn to give thirty tomans to whoever will testify in favor of this child, and as I know and believe that you have seen him I have this sum ready here, in cash. But what good is it after all, since you say that you have no recollection of the child? Yet perhaps if you were to see him now, your mind might recall him.—Aga-Kerim, go into the house, take the child from the arms of its mother, Zeineb-Khanoun, and bring him here. [*Aga-Kerim soon returns with the little boy, whom he has found in the next room.*]

Scene XIII

AGA-MERDAN. Consider well, my lads, how is it possible that you have not seen this little boy? Would it be humane to let another person swallow up the heritage of this little orphan who cannot speak to defend himself, and that the unhappy creature be abandoned to sigh and mourn in the streets and behind doors. Perhaps in the excitement of all this trouble you have paid no attention to this child. There are times when people seem to lose their heads.— Aga-Kerim, take from the closet the offering of this young child, and bring it here. [*Aga-Kerim immediately takes from the closet four packets wrapped in paper and lays them within Aga-Merdan's reach.*]

AGA-MERDAN. My dear friends, beside the reward which God will most certainly give you, this little orphan has made to each one of you an offering of thirty tomans enclosed in these four sheets of paper. He is not like that cursed Aga-Selman, who would impose upon you a dishonest action, yet from avarice gives you nothing as a recompense.

A SOLDIER [*suddenly turning to his comrades*]. Tell me, Quhreman, am I mistaken, for it seems to me that I do recall hearing the voice of a little child, while we were at the house of Hadji-Ghafour.

QUHREMAN. Yes, I remember it; there was a woman seated in the corner of the house and she held in her arms a little child in long clothes.

GHAFFER. Why, of course! I remember that Hadji-Ghafour said to us: "This is my wife, and this little child is my son; his mother brought him into the world a month ago."

NEZER. Well, now, to think how we have forgotten this incident! It is true, there are days when people lose their wits Yes, indeed; did not Hadji-Ghafour ask us to watch over his house, his wife, and his little child, until the inhabitants returned, for fear that the villains of the town should do them some harm?

ALL THE SOLDIERS [*in chorus*]. Yes, he commended to our care his wife and his child.

AGA-MERDAN. May God bless you, my lads! I knew well that you would recall it to mind. Accept, then, the offering of this orphan, and spend it as you choose. After the trial is over, please God, ten tomans more will come to each one of you. A good and sincere action is never lost. My lads, bear witness before the Tribunal exactly as you have done here, and afterward pocket your money.

ONE OF THE SOLDIERS. But, my lord, we have promised to Aga-Selman to testify in his favor. Must we meanwhile inform him that we cannot be his witnesses?

AGA-MERDAN. No; you need not say anything to him. Let him think all the time that you are his witnesses, and that he himself brings you before the Tribunal; when there, deliver your testimony just as you have now done. Aga-Selman has no rights over you, and he can make no claim upon you. If he asks why you speak so, you must answer that it is because you know what the truth is, and are bearing witness to it. Then, you shall pocket your money. The rice has come; go into that room and do me the favor to rest yourselves. But I have one thing to ask of you; no one must know that you have been summoned, and have come here. It is solely for the sake of pleasing God that you will keep this secret, but I promise in return for your secrecy to give to each one of you a Bokhara hat.

THE SOLDIERS. Have no fear on this point, my lord.

AGA-MERDAN. Aga-Kerim, lead these good fellows into that room that they may take their repast; afterward you may dismiss them.

Scene XIV

AGA-MERDAN [*alone*]. So far, so good. Let us start for the court. I am going to get the assessors on my side, and to prepare them to act, so that to-morrow, at the time of deliberation, they may give me the necessary assistance.

ACT THIRD

Scene I

The scene is the Tribunal. The President is seated on a cushion, in the place of honor, having Aga-Rehim on his right, and Aga-Djebbar on his left. By their side are seated the ordinary assessors of the Tribunal, Aga-Bechin and Aga-Settar. On a lower bench is Aga-Merdan, advocate of Hadji-Ghafour's widow, lolling easily upon his seat.

AGA-BECHIN [*addressing the President of the Tribunal*]. Have you detected, my lord, by your intelligence and wisdom, the wiles of that woman who came yesterday to lodge a complaint? She stole three tomans from her husband; she was herself bruised with blows, and had artfully smeared her face with blood, and torn her hair—then she lodged a complaint against her husband.

THE PRESIDENT. Did I not tell you that this woman inspired me with suspicion? We must clear the matter up.

AGA-BECHIN. Yes, my lord, I wish merely to remark how marvellous is your sagacity! None in the whole court doubted the sincerity of this woman, but you at the first glance made us suspicious, and you were quite right.

THE PRESIDENT. In such cases my opinion is often in accordance with the facts.

AGA-BECHIN. One is quite right in the opinion that governments are guided by Divine wisdom. What is this suspicion but a direct inspiration from God?

AGA-REHIM. You seem very much astonished at it, Aga-Bechin, but the most Holy Majesty of God chooses for their merit, and places at the head of their contemporaries, those of his servants whom he has distinguished by special favor. Now, the most Holy Majesty of God has distinguished the President of the Tribunal with quite extraordinary gifts in regard to the knowledge of affairs. Would you like to know what this really is? It is not inspiration; it is, to my mind, a special gift of grace from God.

AGA-DJEBBAR. Yes, you have the choice of the two opinions, either of which may be maintained. Is it not so, Aga-Merdan?

AGA-MERDAN. Undoubtedly. It is certainly so.

AGA-REHIM. Aga-Merdan, how is the little boy of Hadji-Ghafour getting on?

AGA-MERDAN. Very well, thank God. His mother understands it all, and he will come as soon as he is summoned to appear.

AGA-DJEBBAR. He must be fully seven months old, is he not?

AGA-MERDAN. Yes, exactly seven months.

THE PRESIDENT. How is this? Does a son survive Hadji-Ghafour? They told me that he had no child.

AGA-BECHIN. But he had one, my lord; you have been misinformed. He left a little boy who is as beautiful as a crescent moon. Yesterday, as we returned from prayer, we saw him on the doorstep in the arms of his nurse.

AGA-MERDAN. He and Hadji-Ghafour are as much alike as two halves of an apple.

AGA-SETTAR. Do you recall, my lord, the features of Hadji-Ghafour?

THE PRESIDENT. Yes, it is not so long since he died.

AGA-SETTAR. Well, when you see the face of this child you would think at first sight that you beheld that of Hadji-Ghafour.

THE PRESIDENT. I did not know that. It is very good. But tell me, Aga-Merdan, if there is a son of Hadji-Ghafour living, it is a waste of time to open the case. It is evident that the fortune of his father ought to revert to this child, and in such a case the other relatives and collateral heirs have no claim upon it.

AGA-MERDAN [*in a tone of perfect humility*]. My lord, if I recounted to you the reason on which their claims are based, you might doubt of my sincerity. But Aga-Bechin will tell you the whole story.

AGA-BECHIN. Permit me to relate the whole affair, my lord. Hadji-Ghafour left a sister, Sekiné-Khanoun. This woman is infatuated with a young man, whom she loves to madness, and wishes to wed. But the rogue does not so take it; he reminds her that he has nothing and expects no fortune to come to him. What would he do with her? Meanwhile the damsel works tooth and nail to get into her own hands the inheritance left by Hadji-Ghafour, and so to bring about a marriage with this youngster. Her aunt wishes to marry her to the merchant Aga-Hassam, who is a rich and distinguished man; she refuses. She has chosen an advocate, and set up witnesses in support of her plea that Hadji-Ghafour left no child, and that the 60,000 tomans that constitute his heritage ought to come to her. The woman is half-witted if she imagines that she can carry off the heritage of Hadji-Ghafour by means of such tricks and artifices. This is an absurd idea, and she is giving herself a great deal of useless trouble.

THE PRESIDENT. Very well. The affair is not so complicated or involved as to detain the court long; we shall probably be able to decide and pass sentence in two hours. The two parties must support their claims by testimony and proofs.

AGA-MERDAN. Yes, my lord, the witnesses are all ready.

AGA-SETTAR [to the President of the Tribunal]. There were brought here yesterday, my lord, two little abandoned orphans. " We will look out," you said, " for a servant of God, pious and charitable, and confide the children to him." I believe you would do wisely by placing them in the care of Aga-Merdan. He will care for them as if they were his own, for he is always on the search for an opportunity of doing good.

THE PRESIDENT. Very good. Do you consent to this, Aga-Merdan?

AGA-MERDAN. With all my heart, my lord. I will care for them as if they were my own children.

THE PRESIDENT. May the Master of the Universe recompense you as you deserve! [The door opens during these preliminaries and Aga-Selman enters with Aziz-Bey, in company with four soldiers. Shortly afterward Aga-Abbas and Zeineb-Khanoun, the widow of Hadji-Ghafour, arrive also, accompanied by their four witnesses. Zeineb-Khanoun sits down at one side of the hall, enveloped in a long veil. Aga-Selman, Aziz-Bey, and Aga-Abbas stand up on the other side of the hall.]

Scene II

THE PRESIDENT. Aga-Selman, it is said that Hadji-Ghafour left a son. Can you prove to the contrary?

AGA-SELMAN. I have witnesses, my lord, who will depose that in the hour of his death, Hadji-Ghafour declared to them that he had no other heir but his sister, Sekiné-Khanoun.

THE PRESIDENT. Let the witnesses make their statement.

AGA-SELMAN [turning to the soldiers]. Make your statement.

THE FIRST SOLDIER. My lord, one day before the death of Hadji-Ghafour we went, my comrades and I, to pay him a visit. We asked him whether he had any children, sons or daughters, and he replied: " I have no one in the world but my sister, Sekiné-Khanoun."

THE PRESIDENT. Swear by the name of God that this is just what you heard.

THE FIRST SOLDIER. I swear by the name of God that this is just what I heard. [Aga-Merdan becomes quite pale, and seems thunderstruck, as does Aga-Selman.]

THE PRESIDENT [turning to the other soldiers]. And you, what did you hear? Speak in turn.

THE SECOND SOLDIER. I call God's name to witness that this is just what I heard.

THE THIRD SOLDIER. I call God's name to witness that I also heard the same.

AGA-MERDAN [in a voice trembling with anxiety]. But at that moment did you not perceive a little child in the arms of Hadji-Ghafour's wife?

THE FIRST SOLDIER. It was elsewhere we saw the little child. Would you like us to state where?

AGA-MERDAN. It is well. Keep silence. [Turning to the President of the Tribunal.] My lord, I have witnesses who saw an infant one month old in the arms of Hadji-Ghafour, on the very day of which the soldiers speak. " Whose child is this? " they asked Hadji-Ghafour, and he said to them in reply, " It is my son." The witnesses are yonder, before you. [Beckons witnesses to advance.] They are all educated, honorable, and pious people.

AGA-SETTAR [*in a tone full of kindness toward Aga-Merdan*]. Verily, Aga-Merdan, the father of this young man was a certain Hadji-Cherif.

AGA-MERDAN. Yes, may God have mercy upon him! He belonged to a saintly family.

AGA-SETTAR. The son of such a father cannot but be an honorable man, and Hadji-Cherif was certainly a most strict man.

THE PRESIDENT [*turning to the witnesses*]. Tell me what you know about it.

HEPOU. Shall I tell all I know?

THE PRESIDENT. Yes, all that you have learned about this affair.

HEPOU. Well, my lord, yesterday Aga-Merdan asked us to come to his house, my companions and me. He gave each of us fifteen tomans to present ourselves here before you, and to declare that at the time of the cholera we saw in Hadji-Ghafour's arms his little child, then one month old. As I am a gambler by profession, I accepted the money and took it; but this money had been given to me for doing evil, and brought me no profit. That night I lost the fifteen tomans to the last penny, for I had fallen in with a sad rogue to whom Leibadj himself could not hold a candle. I know nothing more than that, my lord. I have never seen Hadji-Ghafour, and didn't even know him. [*Aga-Merdan gasps with excitement.*]

THE PRESIDENT [*to the other witnesses*]. And you, what have you to say?

THE OTHER WITNESSES [*in chorus*]. We can only repeat what our comrade has said.

THE PRESIDENT [*to his assessors*]. And you were affirming a moment ago that Aga-Merdan was a virtuous man! Your words prove your dishonesty and deceit. Praised be God in his greatness and sublimity. I do not understand what all this means.

AGA-BECHIN. No, my lord, what proves, on the contrary, that we are honest and loyal men is that we have given faith to the words of Aga-Merdan, and have believed him to be a man of honor.

AGA-REHIM [*sotto voce to Aga-Settar*]. Oh, the liar, may the devil take him! Do you hear this scoundrel Aga-Bechin, what a good excuse he has ready? The President believes him, and imagines that we are really honest and sincere. [*At this moment the head bailiff of the Prince Royal enters.*]

Scene III

THE HEAD BAILIFF [*to the President of the Tribunal*]. My lord, the Prince Royal asks whether the rights of Hadji-Ghafour's sister have been proved?

THE PRESIDENT. Yes, they have been established. But does the Prince Royal know how the proof has been effected?

THE HEAD BAILIFF. Yes, my lord. The Inspector of the Market saw through the designs of Aga-Merdan and Aga-Selman. He informed the Prince Royal, who took the necessary measures for defeating their machinations. Meanwhile the crime of these two individuals has been proved, and I have received orders to lead them into the presence of the Prince Royal.

THE PRESIDENT. Is Aga-Selman also implicated in this plot?

THE BAILIFF. Yes, he was the secret accomplice of Aga-Merdan. [*The bailiff seizes Aga-Merdan and Aga-Selman and carries them off.*]

Scene IV

THE PRESIDENT. Aziz-Bey, you are to-day the protector of Sekiné-Khanoun. Go and tell her that in two hours I will take with me the sum of money left by Hadji-Ghafour, and bring it to her, and place it in her hands before the most honorable witnesses.

AZIZ-BEY. It is well, my lord; I will go.

Scene V

AGA-BECHIN [*striking his hands together*]. By the death of the first-born, is it possible to utter fabrications such as those of this Aga-Merdan? O my God, what dishonest people have you created in your world! By his impostures, this wretch wished to set up a son to Hadji-Ghafour! Gentlemen, have you ever seen such audacity? Ah, you may

now treat me as a fool, Aga-Djebbar, and may say that I
am exceedingly simple and guileless to believe what the
first-comer tells me.

AGA-DJEBBAR [*turning his face and speaking sotto voce*]. Ah,
the liar! May the devil carry him off! Oh, yes, you are
simple and guileless—that is well known. [*Then in a
loud tone:*] Let us adjourn, gentlemen. Let us abridge
the fatigue of the President; he has gone through much
exertion to-day. Why prolong this talk? [*The President
of the Tribunal leads the way out lost in thought. Then
the others rise and leave.*]

OTTOMAN POEMS

—

[*Metrical Translation by E. J. W. Gibb, M.R.A.S.*]

OTTOMAN POEMS

FROM THE 'ĀSHIQ PASHA DĪWĀNI

ALL the Universe, one mighty sign, is shown;
God hath myriads of creative acts unknown:
None hath seen them, of the races jinn and men,
None hath news brought from that realm far off from ken.
Never shall thy mind or reason reach that strand,
Nor can tongue the King's name utter of that land.
Since 'tis his each nothingness with life to vest,
Trouble is there ne'er at all to his behest.
Eighteen thousand worlds, from end to end,
Do not with him one atom's worth transcend.

'Āshiq Pasha.

FROM THE ISKENDER–NĀMA

Up and sing! O 'anqā-natured nightingale!
High in every business doth thy worth prevail:
Sing! for good the words are that from thee proceed;
Whatsoever thou dost say is prized indeed.
Then, since words to utter thee so well doth suit,
Pity were it surely if thy tongue were mute.
Blow a blast in utt'rance that the Trusted One,
When he hears, ten thousand times may cry: "Well done!"
Up and sing! O bird most holy! up and sing!
Unto us a story fair and beauteous bring.
Let not opportunity slip by, silent there;
Unto us the beauty of each word declare.
Seldom opportunities like this with thee lie;
Sing then, for th' occasion now is thine, so hie!

Lose not opportunities that thy hand doth find,
For some day full suddenly Death thy tongue shall bind.
Of how many singers, eloquent of words,
Bound have Death and Doom the tongues fast in their cords!
Lose not, then, th' occasion, but to joy look now,
For one day thy station 'neath earth seek must thou.
While the tongue yet floweth, now thy words collect;
Them as Meaning's taper 'midst the feast erect,
That thy words, remaining long time after thee,
To the listeners' hearing shall thy record be.
Thy mementoes lustrous biding here behind,
Through them they'll recall thee, O my soul, to mind.
Those who've left mementoes ne'er have died in truth;
Those who've left no traces ne'er have lived in sooth.
Surely with this object didst thou come to earth,
That to mind should ever be recalled thy worth.
" May I die not!" say'st thou, one of noble race?
Strive, then, that thou leavest here a name of grace.

Ahmedī.

FROM THE ISKENDER–NĀMA

ONCE unto his Vezīr quoth the crownèd King:
" Thou, who in my world-realm knowest everything!
With my sword I've conquered many and many a shore;
Still I sigh right sorely: ' Ah! to conquer more!'
Great desire is with me realms to overthrow;
Through this cause I comfort ne'er a moment know.
Is there yet a country whither we may wend,
Where as yet our mighty sway doth not extend,
That we may it conquer, conquer it outright?
Ours shall be the whole earth—ours it shall be quite."
Then, when heard the Vezīr what the King did say,
Quoth he: " Realm-o'erthrowing Monarch, live for aye!
May the Mighty Ruler set thy crown on high,
That thy throne may ever all assaults defy!
May thy life's rose-garden never fade away!
May thy glory's orchard never see decay!

Thou'st the Peopled Quarter ta'en from end to end;
All of its inhabitants slaves before thee bend.
There's on earth no city, neither any land,
That is not, O Monarch, under thy command.
In the Peopled Quarter Seven Climes are known,
And o'er all of these thy sway extends alone!"

Ahmedī.

FROM KHUSREV AND SHĪRĪN

THE spot at which did King Khusrev Pervīz light
Was e'en the ruined dwelling of that moon bright.
Whilst wand'ring on, he comes upon that parterre,
As on he strolls, it opes before his eyes fair.
Among the trees a night-hued courser stands bound
(On Heaven's charger's breast were envy's scars found).
As softly moved he, sudden on his sight gleamed
A moon that in the water shining bright beamed.
O what a moon! a sun o'er earth that light rains—
Triumphant, happy, blest he who her shade gains.
She'd made the pool a casket for her frame fair,
And all about that casket spread her dark hair.
Her hand did yonder curling serpents back throw—
The dawn 'tis, and thereof we never tired grow.
He saw the water round about her ear play;
In rings upon her shoulders her dark locks lay.
When yon heart-winning moon before the King beamed,
The King became the sun—in him Love's fire gleamed.
The tears e'en like to water from his eyes rolled;—
Was't strange, when did a Watery Sign the Moon hold?
No power was left him, neither sport nor pleasure;
He bit his finger, wildered beyond measure.
Unconscious of his gaze, the jasmine-breasted—
The hyacinths o'er the narcissi rested.
When shone her day-face, from that musky cloud bare,
Her eyes oped Shīrīn and beheld the King there.
Within that fountain, through dismay and shamed fright,
She trembled as on water doth the moonlight.

Than this no other refuge could yon moon find
That she should round about her her own locks bind.
The moon yet beameth through the hair, the dark night,
With tresses how could be concealed the sun bright?
To hide her from him, round her she her hair flung,
And thus as veil her night before her day hung.

Sheykhī.

FROM KHUSREV AND SHĪRĪN

WHEN Ferhād bound to fair Shīrīn his heart's core,
From out his breast Love many a bitter wail tore.
On tablet of his life graved, shown was Shīrīn;
Of all else emptied, filled alone with Shīrīn.
As loathed he the companionship of mankind,
In wild beasts 'midst the hills did he his friends find.
His guide was Pain; his boon companion, Grief's throe;
His comrade, Sorrow; and his closest friend, Woe.
Thus wand'ring on, he knew not day from dark night;
For many days he onward strayed in sad plight.
Although before his face a wall of stone rise,
Until he strikes against it, blind his two eyes.
Through yearning for his love he from the world fled;
From out his soul into his body Death sped.
Because he knew that when the earthly frame goes,
Eternal, Everlasting Being love shows,
He fervent longed to be from fleshly bonds free,
That then his life in very truth might Life see.
In sooth, till dies the body, Life is ne'er found,
Nor with the love of life the Loved One e'er found.

Sheykhī.

YAZIJI–OGLU

The Creation of Paradise

HITHER come, O seeker after Truth! if joy thou wouldest
share,

Enter on the Mystic Pathway, follow it, then joy thou'lt share.

Hearken now what God (exalted high his name!) from
naught hath formed.

Eden's bower he hath created; Light, its lamp, he did prepare;

Loftiest its sites, and best and fairest are its blest abodes;

Midst of each a hall of pearls—not ivory nor teak-wood rare.

Each pavilion he from seventy ruddy rubies raised aloft—

Dwellings these in which the dwellers sit secure from fear
or care.

Round within each courtyard seventy splendid houses he hath
ranged,

Formed of emeralds green—houses these no fault of form
that bear.

There, within each house, are seventy pearl and gem-incrusted
thrones;

He upon each throne hath stretched out seventy couches
broidered fair;

Sits on every couch a maiden of the bourne of loveliness:

Moons their foreheads, days their faces, each a jewelled crown
doth wear;

Wine their rubies, soft their eyes, their eyebrows troublous,
causing woe:

All-enchanting, Paradise pays tribute to their witching air.

Sudden did they see the faces of those damsels dark of eye,

Blinded sun and moon were, and Life's Stream grew bitter
then and there.

Thou wouldst deem that each was formed of rubies, corals,
and of pearls;

Question there is none, for God thus in the Qur'ān doth declare.

Tables seventy, fraught with bounties, he in every house hath
placed,

And on every tray hath spread out seventy sorts of varied fare.

· · · · · · · ·

All these glories, all these honors, all these blessings of de-
light,
All these wondrous mercies surely for his sake he did pre-
pare:
Through his love unto Muhammed, he the universe hath
framed;
Happy, for his sake, the naked and the hungry enter there.
O Thou Perfectness of Potence! O Thou God of Awful
Might!
O Thou Majesty of Glory! O Thou King of Perfect Right!

Since he Eden's heaven created, all is there complete and
whole,
So that naught is lacking; nothing he created needs repair.
Yonder, for his righteous servants, things so fair hath he
devised,
That no eye hath e'er beheld them; ope thy soul's eye, on
them stare.
Never have his servants heard them, neither can their hearts
conceive;
Reach unto their comprehension shall this understanding
ne'er.
There that God a station lofty, of the loftiest, hath reared,
That unclouded station he the name Vesīla caused to bear,
That to his Belovèd yonder station a dear home may be,
Thence ordained is Heaven's order free from every grief and
care.
In its courtyard's riven centre, planted he the Tūba-Tree;
That a tree which hangeth downward, high aloft its roots are
there:
Thus its radiance all the Heavens lighteth up from end to end,
Flooding every tent and palace, every lane and every square.

Such a tree the Tūba, that the Gracious One hath in its sap
Hidden whatsoe'er there be of gifts and presents good and
fair;
Forth therefrom crowns, thrones, and jewels, yea, and steeds
and coursers come,
Golden leaves and clearest crystals, wines most pure beyond
compare.

For his sake there into being hath he called the Tūba-Tree,
That from Ebū-Qāsim's hand might everyone receive his
  share.

Yaziji-Oglu.

RUBĀ'Ī

Cup-bearer, bring, bring here again my yester even's wine;
My harp and rebec bring, them bid address this heart of mine:
While still I live, 'tis meet that I should mirth and glee enjoy;
The day shall come when none may e'en my resting-place
  divine.

Sultan Murād II.

GAZEL

Souls are fluttered when the morning breezes through thy
  tresses stray;
Waving cypresses are wildered when thy motions they survey.
Since with witchcraft thou hast whetted keen the lancet of
  thy glance,
All my veins are bleeding inward through my longing and
  dismay.
"Why across thy cheek disordered float thy tresses?" asked
  I her.
"It is Rūm-Eylī; there high-starred heroes gallop," did she
  say.
Thought I, though I spake not: "In thy quarter, through thy
  tint and scent,
Wretched and head-giddy, wand'ring, those who hope hope not
  for stray."
"Whence the anger in thy glances, O sweet love?" I said;
  then she:
"Silence! surely if I shed blood, I the ensigns should dis-
  play."
Even as thou sighest, 'Avnī, shower thine eyes tears fast as
  rain,
Like as follow hard the thunder-roll the floods in dread array.

'Avnī.

FRAGMENT OF GAZEL

TORN and pierced my heart has been by thy scorn and tyranny's
   blade;
Rent by the scissors of grief for thee is the robe that my
   patience arrayed.
Like the mihrāb of the Ka'ba, as shrine where in worship to
   turn,
Thy ward would an angel take, if thy footprint there he surveyed.
They are pearls, O mine eye! thou sheddest her day-bright
   face before;
Not a tear is left—these all are dried by the beams by her
   cheek displayed.

                                            'Avnī.

GAZEL

To obey Fight hard for Allah is my aim and my desire;
'Tis but zeal for Faith, for Islām, that my ardor doth
   inspire.
Through the grace of Allah, and th' assistance of the Band
   Unseen,
Is my earnest hope the Infidels to crush with ruin dire.
On the Saints and on the Prophets surely doth my trust re-
   pose;
Through the love of God, to triumph and to conquest I
   aspire.
What if I with soul and gold strive here to wage the Holy
   War?
Praise is God's! ten thousand sighs for battle in my breast
   suspire.
O Muhammed! through the chosen Ahmed Mukhtār's glori-
   ous aid,
Hope I that my might may triumph over Islām's foes ac-
   quire!

                                            'Avnī.

GAZEL

Who pleasure seeks must oftentimes experience sad pain, in
  sooth ;
He must a beggar be who doth desire to win domain, in
  sooth.
Whene'er I sigh, up rise my tears, they, boiling, fast o'erflow
  my eyes ;
Winds surely must full fiercely blow, with waves to fill the
  main, in sooth.
My heart's domain now thought of thee, now grief for thee,
  alternate rule ;
This realm to wreck and waste to lay those two sublime Kings
  strain, in sooth.
Spite zeal and prayers, Truth sure is found within the cup
  that's filled with wine ;
So acts of rakes are free from all hypocrisy's foul stain, in
  sooth.
O 'Adenī, rub thou thy face low 'midst the dust that lines her
  path ;
For eyes with blood filled stand in need of tūtyā, health to
  gain, in sooth.

'Adenī.

FRAGMENT OF GAZEL

When I saw my love's hair, ambergris-hued, o'er her visage
  shake,
"Strange," I thought, "a moon, musk-shedding, 'midst the
  flowers its bed should make!"
How thy locks, moon-face, are fallen o'er thy cheek in many
  a curl!
As in day he lies reposing, so in strength doth gain the
  snake.
From thy cheek the rose and tulip tint and scent have stol'n
  indeed ;
Therefore through the bāzār round they bear them, bounden
  to the stake.

'Adenī.

GAZEL

AGAIN, then, doth this apple, thy chin, tooth-marks wear!
Again they've eaten peaches in thine orchard fair!
If strange hands have not reached thee, O rosebud-lipped
    one,
Doth thy rose-garden's pathway a foot-step print bear!
I cannot reach thee before rivals all throng thee round:
Less for true lover than vile dog dost thou care.
Witness that thou with my rivals the cup drain'dst last night,
Bears the sleepless and worn look thy languid eyes wear.
With whom didst thou last even carouse, that this day
Morn's zephyr about thee did so much news declare?
Beholding thy lips hurt, Āfitābī hath said:
" Again, then, doth this apple, thy chin, tooth-marks wear! "

Afitābī.

GAZEL

CAST off thy veil, and heaven and earth in dazzling light
    array!
As radiant Paradise, this poor demented world display!
Move thou thy lips, make play the ripples light of Kevser's
    pool!
Let loose thy scented locks, and odors sweet through earth
    convey!
A musky warrant by thy down was traced, and zephyr
    charged:
" Speed, with this scent subdue the realms of China and
    Cathay! "
O heart! should not thy portion be the Water bright of
    Life,
A thousand times mayst thou pursue Iskender's darksome
    way.
O Zeyneb, woman's love of earthly show leave thou be-
    hind;
Go manly forth, with single heart, forsake adornment gay!

Zeyneb.

GAZEL

Ah! thine eyes lay waste the heart, they 'gainst the soul bare
daggers dread;
See how sanguinary gleam they—blood aye upon blood they
shed.
Come, the picture of thy down bear unto this my scorchèd
breast—
It is customary fresh greens over the broiled flesh to spread.
Said I: "O Life! since thy lip is life, to me vouchsafe a kiss."
Smiling rose-like, " Surely, surely, by my life," she answerèd.
As I weep sore, of my stainèd eyebrow and my tears of blood,
" 'Tis the rainbow o'er the shower stretched," were by all be-
holders said.
While within my heart thine eye's shaft, send not to my breast
despair;
Idol mine! guest after guest must not to one same house be led.
Through its grieving for thy hyacinth down, thus feeble grown
Is the basil, that the gardeners nightly o'er it water shed.
Quoth I: "O Life! do not shun Jem, he a pilgrim here hath
come; "
" Though a pilgrim, yet his life doth on a child's face hang,"
she said.

Prince Jem.

FRAGMENT

Lo! there the torrent, dashing 'gainst the rocks, doth wildly
roll;
The whole wide realm of Space and Being ruth hath on my
soul.
Through bitterness of grief and woe the morn hath rent its
robe;
See! O in dawning's place, the sky weeps blood, without control!
Tears shedding, o'er the mountain-tops the clouds of heaven
pass;
Hear, deep the bursting thunder sobs and moans through
stress of dole.

Prince Jem.

GAZEL

He who longs for ruby lip's kiss may not calm of soul re-
    main;
He his head must yield who hopes the dusky locks' sweet scent
    to gain.
Still in heart abides not longing's flame when one her ward
    beholds;
Him who seeks her face contents not even Heaven's flowery
    plain.
Yonder sugar-lip's surrounded by her cheek's down;—where
    art thou,
O thou seeker of the rose's company without thorn's pain?
Wouldest thou delight? Then plunge thou deep beneath
    Love's ocean surge:
He who would for regal pearls dive, surely should know well
    the main.
Though the loved one mocks at Ahmed's faults and failings,
    what of that?
He who seeks a friend that's blameless must without a friend
    remain.

Ahmed Pasha.

FROM THE WINTER QASĪDA

Locust-like down from the sky the snowflakes wing their
    way;
From the green-plumaged bird, Delight, O heart! hope not
    for lay.
Like drunken camels, spatter now the clouds earth's wind-
    ing sheet;
Laded the caravan of mirth and glee, and passed away.
With lighted lamps in daytime seek the people for the sun;
Yet scarce, with trouble, a dim, fitful spark discover they.

.   .   .   .

The Moon in Sign of Bounteousness! the Shade of Allah's
    grace!
The King, star-armied! he in aspect fair as Hermes' ray—

The Khān Muhammed! at the portal of whose sphere of
  might
To wait as servants would Darius and Key-Khusrev pray!
E'en should the sun till the Last Day it measure with gold
  beam,
Nor shore nor depth could e'er it find to th' ocean of his
  sway!

Nejātī.

FROM THE SPRING QASĪDA

THE early springtide now hath made earth smiling bright
  again,
E'en as doth union with his mistress soothe the lover's pain.
They say: " 'Tis now the goblet's turn, the time of mirth 'tis
  now;"
Beware that to the winds thou castest not this hour in
  vain.
Theriaca within their ruby pots the tulips lay:
See in the mead the running streamlet's glistening, snake-like
  train.
Onward, beneath some cypress-tree's loved foot its face to
  rub,
With turn and turn, and singing sweet, the brook goes
  through the plain.
Lord! may this happy union of felicity and earth,
Like turn of sun of Love, or Jesu's life, standfast remain!
May glee and mirth, e'en as desired, continuous abide,
Like to a mighty Key-Khusrev's, or Jemshīd's, glorious
  reign!

.   .   .   .

Sultan Muhammed! Murād's son! the Pride of Princes all;
He, the Darius, who to all earth's Kings doth crowns
  ordain!
Monarch of stars! whose flag's the sun, whose stirrup is the
  moon!
Prince dread as Doom, and strong as Fate, and bounteous as
  main!

Nejātī.

FROM THE QASĪDA ON THE ACCESSION OF SULTAN BĀYEZĪD II

ONE eve, when had the Sun before her radiant beauty bright
Let down the veil of ambergris, the musky locks of night;
(Off had the royal hawk, the Sun, flown from the Orient's
      hand,
And lighted in the West; flocked after him the crows in
      flight;)
To catch the gloomy raven, Night, the fowler skilled, the
      Sphere,
Had shaped the new-moon like the claw of eagle, sharp to
      smite;
In pity at the doleful sight of sunset's crimson blood,
Its veil across the heaven's eye had drawn the dusky Night.

        .   .   .   .

Sultan of Rome! Khusrev of the Horizons! Bāyezīd!
King of the Epoch! Sovereign! and Centre of all Right!
The tablet of his heart doth all th' affairs of earth disclose;
And eloquent as page of book the words he doth indite.
O Shāh! I'm he who, 'midst th' assembly where thy praise
      is sung,
Will, rebec-like, a thousand notes upon one cord recite.
'Tis meet perfection through thy name to my poor words
      should come,
As to rose-water perfume sweet is brought by sunbeam's light.
                                                   Nejātī.

GAZEL

TRUTH this: a lasting home hath yielded ne'er earth's spread-
      ing plain;
Scarce e'en an inn where may the caravan for rest remain.
Though every leaf of every tree is verily a book,
For those who understanding lack doth earth no leaf contain.
E'en though the Loved One be from thee as far as East from
      West,
" Bagdad to lovers is not far," O heart, then strive and strain.

One moment opened were her ebriate, strife-causing eyne,
By us as scimitars, not merely daggers, were they ta'en.
Yearneth Nejātī for the court of thy fair Paradise,
Though this a wish which he while here on earth can ne'er
attain.

Nejātī.

RUBĀ'IS

O HANDKERCHIEF! I send thee—off to yonder maid of grace;
Around thee I my eyelashes will make the fringe of lace;
I will the black point of my eye rub up to paint therewith;
To yon coquettish beauty go—go look thou in her face.

O Handkerchief! the loved one's hand take, kiss her lip so
    sweet,
Her chin, which mocks at apple and at orange, kissing greet;
If sudden any dust should light upon her blessèd heart,
Fall down before her, kiss her sandal's sole, beneath her feet.

A sample of my tears of blood thou, Handkerchief, wilt show,
Through these within a moment would a thousand crimson
    grow;
Thou'lt be in company with her, while I am sad with grief;
To me no longer life may be, if things continue so.

Nejātī.

FROM THE SPRING QASĪDA

UP from indolent sleep the eyes of the flowers to awake,
Over their faces each dawn the cloudlets of spring water
    shake.
Denizens all of the mead now with new life are so filled,
That were its foot not secured, into dancing the cypress would
    break.
Roses' fair cheeks to describe, all of their beauty to tell,
Lines on the clear river's page rain-drops and light ripples
    make.
Silvery rings, thou would'st say, they hung in the bright
    water's ear,

When the fresh rain-drops of spring fall on the stretch of
    the lake.
Since the ring-dove, who aloft sits on the cypress, its praise
Sings, were it strange if he be sad and love-sick for its sake?

.   .   .   .

Prince of the Climate of Speech, noble Nishānji Pasha,
To the mark of whose kindness the shaft of thought can its
    way never make.
When poets into their hands the chaplet, thy verses, have ta'en,
" I pardon implore of the Lord " for litany ever they take.

Mesīhī.

MUREBBA'

HARK the bulbul's lay so joyous: " Now have come the days
    of spring."
Merry shows and crowds on every mead they spread, a maze
    of spring;
There the almond-tree its silvern blossoms scatters, sprays of
    spring:
    Drink, be gay, for soon will vanish, biding not, the days
        of spring.

Once again with varied flow'rets decked themselves have mead
    and plain;
Tents for pleasure have the blossoms raised in every rosy
    lane.
Who can tell, when spring hath ended, who and what may
    whole remain?
    Drink, be gay, for soon will vanish, biding not, the days
        of spring.

All the alleys of the parterre filled with Ahmed's Light
    appear,
Verdant herbs his Comrades, tulips like his Family bright
    appear;
O ye People of Muhammed! times now of delight appear:
    Drink, be gay, for soon will vanish, biding not, the days
        of spring.

Sparkling dew-drops stud the lily's leaf like sabre broad and
    keen;
Bent on merry gypsy-party, crowd they all the flow'ry green;
List to me, if thou desirest, these beholding, joy to glean:
    Drink, be gay, for soon will vanish, biding not, the days
      of spring.

Rose and tulip, like to lovely maidens' cheeks, all beauteous
    show,
While the dew-drops, like the jewels in their ears, resplendent
    glow;
Do not think, thyself beguiling, things will aye continue so:
    Drink, be gay, for soon will vanish, biding not, the days
      of spring.

Rose, anemone, and tulip—these, the garden's fairest flow-
    ers—
'Midst the parterre is their blood shed 'neath the lightning-
    darts and showers.
Art thou wise?—then with thy comrades dear enjoy the fleet-
    ing hours:
    Drink, be gay, for soon will vanish, biding not, the days of
      spring.

Past the moments when with sickness were the ailing herbs
    opprest,
When the garden's care, the rose-bud, hid its sad head in its
    breast;
Come is now the time when hill and rock with tulips dense are
    drest:
    Drink, be gay, for soon will vanish, biding not, the days of
      spring.

While each dawn the clouds are shedding jewels o'er the rosy
    land,
And the breath of morning's zephyr, fraught with Tātār musk
    is bland;
While the world's fair time is present, do not thou unheeding
    stand:
    Drink, be gay, for soon will vanish, biding not, the days of
      spring.

With the fragrance of the garden, so imbued the musky air,
Every dew-drop, ere it reaches earth, is turned to attar rare;
O'er the parterre spread the incense-clouds a canopy right
    fair:
  Drink, be gay, for soon will vanish, biding not, the days of
    spring.

Whatsoe'er the garden boasted smote the black autumnal
    blast;
But, to each one justice bringing, back hath come Earth's King
    at last;
In his reign joyed the cup-bearer, round the call for wine is
    past:
  Drink, be gay, for soon will vanish, biding not, the days of
    spring.

Ah! I fondly hope, Mesīhī, fame may to these quatrains
    cling;
May the worthy these four-eyebrowed beauties oft to mem'ry
    bring;
Stray among the rosy faces, Bulbul, who so sweet dost sing:
  Drink, be gay, for soon will vanish, biding not, the days of
    spring.

                                 Mesīhī.

FRAGMENT

Both crown and robe forsake shall I, I'll roam, by these un-
    prest, a while;
'Midst foreign lands, far off from here, I'll dwell a wayworn
    guest, a while.
O minstrel fair, both harp and lute's sweet music hushed must
    now remain;
Woe's feast is spread, ah! there the flute:—my sighs by grief
    opprest, a while.
Sometimes I'll fall, sometimes I'll rise, sometimes I'll laugh,
    sometimes I'll weep,
Blood drinking now, woe tasting then, distracted sore I'll rest,
    a while.
                                 Harīmī.

GAZEL

ONCE from sleep I oped my eyes, I raised my head, when full
in sight
There before me stood a moon-faced beauty, lovely, shining,
bright.
Thought I: "In th' ascendant's now my star, or I my fate
have reached,
For within my chamber sure is risen Jupiter this night."
Radiance from his beauty streaming saw I, though to out-
ward view
(While himself a Muslim) he in garb of infidel is dight.
Though I oped my eyes or closed them, still the form was ever
there;
Thus I fancied to myself: "A fairy this or angel bright?"
Till the Resurrection ne'er shall Mihrī gain the Stream of
Life;
Yet in Night's deep gloom Iskender gleamed before her won-
d'ring sight.

Mihrī.

GAZEL

FAITHFUL and kind a friend I hoped that thou wouldest prove
to me;
Who would have thought so cruel and fierce a tyrant in thee
to see?
Thou who the newly-oped rose art of the Garden of Paradise,
That every thorn and thistle thou lov'st—how can it fitting be?
I curse thee not, but of God Most High, Our Lord, I make
this prayer—
That thou may'st love a pitiless one in tyranny like to thee.
In such a plight am I now, alack! that the curser saith to his
foe:
"Be thy fortune dark and thy portion black, even as those
of Mihrī!"

Mihrī.

GAZEL

FROM Istāmbōl's throne a mighty host to Īrān guided I;
Sunken deep in blood of shame I made the Golden Heads to
  lie.
Glad the Slave, my resolution, lord of Egypt's realm became:
Thus I raised my royal banner e'en as the Nine Heavens high.
From the kingdom fair of 'Irāq to Hijāz these tidings sped,
When I played the harp of Heavenly Aid at feast of victory.
Through my sabre Transoxania drowned was in a sea of
  blood;
Emptied I of kuhl of Isfahān the adversary's eye.
Flowed adown a River Āmū from each foeman's every hair—
Rolled the sweat of terror's fever—if I happed him to espy.
Bishop-mated was the King of India by my Queenly troops,
When I played the Chess of empire on the Board of sov-
  'reignty.
O Selīmī, in thy name was struck the coinage of the world,
When in crucible of Love Divine, like gold, that melted I.

Selīmī.

GAZEL

My pain for thee balm in my sight resembles;
Thy face's beam the clear moonlight resembles.
Thy black hair spread across thy cheeks, the roses,
O Liege, the garden's basil quite resembles.
Beside thy lip oped wide its mouth, the rosebud;
For shame it blushed, it blood outright resembles.
Thy mouth, a casket fair of pearls and rubies,
Thy teeth, pearls, thy lip coral bright resembles:
Their diver I, each morning and each even;
My weeping, Liege, the ocean's might resembles.
Lest he seduce thee, this my dread and terror,
That rival who Iblīs in spite resembles.
Around the taper bright, thy cheek, Muhibbī
Turns, and the moth in his sad plight resembles.

Muhibbī.

GAZEL

HE who poverty electeth, hall and fane desireth not;
Than the food of woe aught other bread to gain desireth not.
He who, king-like, on the throne of blest contentment sits
    aloft,
O'er the Seven Climes as Sultan high to reign desireth not.
He, who in his bosom strikes his nails, and opes the wound
    afresh,
On the garden looks not, sight of rosy lane desireth not.
He, who is of Love's true subjects, bideth in the fair one's
    ward,
Wand'ring there distracted, mountain lone or plain desireth
    not.
O Muhibbī, he who drinketh from the Loved One's hand a
    glass,
E'en from Khizar's hand Life's Water bright to drain de-
    sireth not.

Muhibbī.

GAZEL

A FLAME that Picture's sabre in its deadliness of blow;
Like sparks upon its face the marks of damaskeening glow.
Is't strange that by thy side the bird, my heart, should rest
    secure?
Thy sabre damaskeened to it doth grain and water show!
The watered scimitar within thy grasp an ocean is,
In which the lines and marks are scattered pearls unique, I
    trow.
Thy sword a sky, its stars the marks of damaskeening shine,
My heart's blood there upon its face like break of dawn doth
    glow.
What though I call that Picture's brand a branch of Judas-tree?
For there the damask marks and grains like flowers and blos-
    soms blow.
Figānī's verse on yonder King of Beauty's empire's sword
Doth like unto a running stream of limpid water flow.

Figānī.

ON AUTUMN

O SAD heart, come, distraction's hour is now high,
The air's cool, 'midst the fields to sit the time nigh.
The Sun hath to the Balance, Joseph-like, past,
The year's Zuleykha hath her gold hoard wide cast.
By winds bronzed, like the Sun, the quince's face glows;
Its Pleiads-clusters, hanging forth, the vine shows.
In saffron flow'rets have the meads themselves dight;
The trees, all scorched, to gold have turned, and shine bright.
The gilded leaves in showers falling to earth gleam;
With goldfish filled doth glisten brightly each stream.
Ablaze each tree, and blent are all in one glare,
And therefore charged with glistening fire the still air.
Amidst the yellow foliage perched the black crows—
As tulip, saffron-hued, that spotted cup shows.
A yellow-plumaged bird now every tree stands,
Which shakes itself and feathers sheds on all hands.
Each vine-leaf paints its face, bride-like, with gold ink;
The brook doth silver anklets round the vine link.
The plane-tree hath its hands, with hinna, red dyed,
And stands there of the parterre's court the fair bride.
The erst green tree now like the starry sky shows,
And hurling meteors at the fiend, Earth, stones throws.

Lāmi'ī.

ON SPRING

FROM the pleasure, joy, and rapture of this hour,
In its frame to hold its soul earth scarce hath power.
Rent its collar, like the dawning, hath the rose;
From its heart the nightingale sighs forth its woes.
Dance the juniper and cypress like the sphere;
Filled with melody through joy all lands appear.
Gently sing the running brooks in murmurs soft;
While the birds with tuneful voices soar aloft.
Play the green and tender branches with delight,
And they shed with one accord gold, silver, bright.

Like to couriers fleet, the zephyrs speed away,
Resting ne'er a moment either night or day.
In that raid the rosebud filled with gold its hoard,
And the tulip with fresh musk its casket stored.
There the moon a purse of silver coin did seize;
Filled with ambergris its skirt the morning breeze;
Won the sun a golden disk of ruby dye,
And with glistening pearls its pocket filled the sky:
Those who poor were fruit and foliage attained;
All the people of the land some trophy gained.

Lāmi'ī.

ROSE TIME

O HEART, come, wail, as nightingale thy woes show;
'Tis Pleasure's moment this, come, then, as rose blow.
In burning notes make thou thy tuneful song rise;
These iron hearts soft render with thy sad sighs.
Within thy soul place n , like tulip, dark brand;
When opportunity doth come, then firm stand.
From earth take justice ere yet are these times left,
And ere yet from the soul's harp is breath's song reft.
They call thee—view the joys that sense would yield thee;
But, ere thou canst say " Hie!" the bird is flown, see.
Give ear, rose-like, because in truth the night-bird
From break of dawn its bitter wail hath made heard.
Their chorus all around the gleeful birds raise;
The streamlets sing, the nightingale the flute plays.
The jasmines with their fresh leaves tambourines ply;
The streams, hard pressed, raise up their glistening foam high
Of junipers and cypresses two ranks 'tween,
The zephyr sports and dances o'er the flower-green.
The streamlets 'midst the vineyard hide-and-seek play
The flowerets with, among the verdant leaves gay.
Away the morning's breeze the jasmine's crown tears,
As pearls most costly scatters it the plucked hairs.
The leader of the play's the breeze of swift pace;
Like children, each the other all the flowers chase.
With green leaves dressed, the trees each other's hands take;
The flowers and nightingales each other's robes shake.

Like pigeon, there, before the gale that soft blows,
Doth turn in many a somersault the young rose.
As blaze up with gay flowerets all the red plains,
The wind each passes, and the vineyard next gains.
The clouds, pearl-raining, from the meteors sparks seize;
And flowers are all around strewn by the dawn-breeze.
The waters, eddying, in circles bright play,
Like shining swords the green leaves toss about they.
With bated breath the Judas-trees there stand by;
And each for other running brook and breeze sigh.
The gales tag with the basil play in high glee;
To dance with cypress gives its hand the plane-tree.
The soft winds have adorned the wanton bough fair,
The leader of the frolics 'midst the parterre.
The narcisse toward the almond-tree its glance throws;
With vineyard-love the pink upbraids the dog-rose.
The water's mirror clear doth as the Sphere gleam;
Its stars, the flowers reflected, fair and bright beam.
The meads are skies; their stars, the drops of dew, glow;
The jasmine is the moon; the stream, the halo.
In short, each spot as Resurrection-plane seems;
None who beholds of everlasting pain dreams.
Those who it view, and ponder well with thought's eye,
Is't strange, if they be mazed and wildered thereby?
Up! breeze-like, Lāmi'ī, thy hermitage leave!
The roses' days in sooth no time for fasts give!

                                                    Lāmi'ī.

FROM AN ELEGY ON SULTAN SELĪM I

He, an old man in prudence, a youth in might;
His sword aye triumphant, his word ever right
Like Āsef in wisdom, the pride of his host;
He needed no vezīr, no mushīr in fight.
His hand was a sabre; a dagger, his tongue;
His finger, an arrow; his arm, a spear bright.
In shortest of time many high deeds he wrought;
Encircle the world did the shade of his might.
The Sun of his Day, but the sun at day's close,
Throwing long shadow, but brief while in sight.

Of throne and of diadem sovereigns boast,
But boasted of him throne and diadem bright.
Delight would his heart in that festival find,
Whither doth sabre's and fife's clang invite.
In feats with the sword, eke at feasts at the board,
On his peer ne'er alight did the aged Sphere's sight:
Sped he to the board's feast—a Sun beaming bright!
Swept he to the sword's field—a Lion of fight!
Whenever the war-cries: Seize! Hold! echo far,
The sword, weeping blood, shall that Lion's fame cite.
   Alas! Sultan Selīm! alas! woe is me!
   Let both Pen and Sabre in tears mourn for thee!

Kemāl Pasha-Zāda.

FROM AN ELEGY ON ISKENDER CHELEBI

High honored once was the noble Iskender;
O heart, from his destiny warning obtain.
Ah! do thou see what at length hath befall'n him!
What all this glory and panoply gain!
Drinking the poison of doom, ne'er a remnant
Of sweetness's taste in his mouth did remain.
Retrograde, sank down his star, erst ascendant,
From perfect conjunction, alas, did it wane.
Dust on the face of his honor aye stainless
Strewn hath the blast of betrayal profane.
The Lofty Decree for his high exaltation
Did Equity's Court, all unlooked for, ordain;
Forthwith to the Regions of Eden they bore him,
They raised him from earth's abject baseness and stain.
Circling and soaring, he went on his journey,
From the land of his exile to Home back again.
Neck-bounden he stood as a slave at the palace,
Freed is he now from affliction's hard chain.
Joyous he flew on his journey to Heaven,
Rescued forever from earth gross and vain.
In life or in death from him never, ay, never
Was honor most lofty, most glorious, ta'en!

Gazālī.

FRAGMENT

COME is the autumn of my life, alas, it thus should pass
away!
I have not reached the dawn of joy, to sorrow's night there
is no day.
Time after time the image of her cheek falls on my tear-
filled eye;
Ah! no pretension to esteem can shadows in the water
lay!
Oh! whither will these winds of Fate impel the frail barque
of the heart?
Nor bound nor shore confining girds Time's dreary ocean of
dismay!

Gazālī.

GAZEL

DEAD am I of grief, my Moon no love who shows, ah! where
art thou?
Reach the skies, the plaints and wails born of my woes, ah!
where art thou?
Save within thy rosy bower rests not the nightingale, the
heart;
Figure fair as waving cypress, face as rose, ah! where art
thou?
Through thy lips the rose drops sugar at the feast of heart
and soul;
Where, my Parrot whose sweet voice doth love disclose, ah!
where art thou?
Though with longing dead were Ishāq, live should he, did
once she say:
"O my poor one, wildered, weary, torn by woes, ah! where
art thou?"

Ishāq Chelebi.

ON THE PROPHET MUHAMMED

THAT thy form, O Beauty of his orchard who doth all per-
vade!
Is a cypress, wrought of light, that casteth on earth's face
no shade.
Though the gazers on the loveliness of Joseph cut their
hands,
Cleft in twain the fair moon's palm, when it thy day-bright
face surveyed.
To the mart of the Hereafter, when a man hath passed, he
gains
Through the money bright, thy love, which is of joy the
stock-in-trade.
This, my hope, that yonder Cypress in the bowers of Paradise
Shelter Zātī, and all true believers, 'neath his blissful shade.

Zātī.

GAZEL

THROUGH thine absence, smiling Rosebud, forth my soul doth
go, alas!
Earth is flooded by the tears down from my eyes that flow,
alas!
Should'st thou ask about my days, without thee they're black
as thy hair;
'Midst of darkness, O my Stream of Life, I'm lying low,
alas!
With the stones of slander stone me all the cruel rival
throng;
O my Liege, my Queen, 'tis time now mercy thou should'st
show, alas!
When I die through longing for thee, and thou passest o'er
my breast,
From my dust thou'lt hear full many bitter sighs of woe, alas!
In his loved one's cause will Lutfī surely die the martyr's
death;
Let her brigand eyes from mulct for blood of mine free go,
alas!

Lutfī.

GAZEL

If 'tis state thou seekest like the world-adorning sun's array,
Lowly e'en as water rub thy face in earth's dust every day.
Fair to see, but short enduring is this picture bright, the world;
'Tis a proverb: Fleeting like the realm of dreams is earth's
　　display.
Through the needle of its eyelash never hath the heart's
　　thread past;
Like unto the Lord Messiah bide I half-road on the way.
Athlete of the Universe through self-reliance grows the
　　Heart,
With the ball, the Sphere—Time, Fortune—like an apple doth
　　it play.
Mukhlisī, thy frame was formed from but one drop, yet, won-
　　der great!
When thou verses sing'st, thy spirit like the ocean swells,
　　they say. 　　　　　　　　　　　　　　　　　*Mukhlisī.*

GAZEL

One with Realms Eternal this my soul to make; what
　　wouldest say?
All Creation's empire's fancies to forsake; what wouldest say?
Wearing to a hair my frame with bitter sighs and moans, in
　　love,
Nestling in the Fair One's tresses, rest to take; what wouldest
　　say?
Yonder gold-faced birds within the quicksilver-resplendent
　　deep:
Launching forth the hawk, my striving, these to take; what
　　wouldest say?
Yonder Nine Smaragdine Bowls of Heaven to quaff at one
　　deep draught,
Yet from all ebriety's fumes free to break; what wouldest say?
To an autumn leaf the Sphere hath turned Khiyālī's coun-
　　tenance;
To the Spring of Beauty, that a gift to make; what wouldest
　　say? 　　　　　　　　　　　　　　　　　*Khiyālī.*

GAZEL

WITH longing fond and vain, why should I make my soul
to mourn?
One trace of love of earth holds not my heart—all is forsworn.
There ready stands the caravan, to Death's dim realms
addrest,
E'en now the tinkling of its bells down on my ears is borne.
Come then, O bird, my soul, be still, disquiet leave far off;
See, how this cage, the body, is with years and suffering worn.
But yet, to weary, wasted, sin-stained Shāhī, what of fear?
Since Thou'rt the God of Love, the helping Friend of those
forlorn! *Shāhī.*

GAZEL

O BREEZE, thou'rt kind, of balm to those whom pangs
affright, thou news hast brought,
To wounded frame of life, to life of life's delight thou news
hast brought.
Thou'st seen the mourning nightingale's despair in sorrow's
autumn drear,
Like springtide days, of smiling roseleaf fresh and bright,
thou news hast brought.
If I should say thy words are heaven-inspired, in truth, blas-
pheme I not;
Of Faith, whilst unbelief doth earth hold fast and tight, thou
news hast brought.
They say the loved one comes to soothe the hearts of all her
lovers true;
If that the case, to yon fair maid of lovers' plight thou news
hast brought.
Of rebel demon thou hast cut the hope Suleymān's throne to
gain;
That in the sea secure doth lie his Ring of might, thou news
hast brought.
Fuzūlī, through the parting night, alas, how dark my fortune grew!
Like zephyr of the dawn, of shining sun's fair light thou
news hast brought. *Fuzūlī.*

GAZEL

O THOU Perfect Being, Source whence wisdom's mysteries
    arise;
Things, the issue of thine essence, show wherein thy nature
    lies.
Manifester of all wisdom, thou art he whose pen of might
Hath with rays of stars illumined yonder gleaming page, the
    skies.
That a happy star, indeed, the essence clear of whose bright
    self
Truly knoweth how the blessings from thy word that flow
    to prize.
But a jewel flawed am faulty I: alas, forever stands
Blank the page of my heart's journal from thought of thy
    writing wise.
In the journal of my actions Evil's lines are black indeed;
When I think of Day of Gathering's terrors, blood flows
    from my eyes.
Gathering of my tears will form a torrent on the Reckoning
    Day,
If the pearls, my tears, rejecting, he but view them to de-
    spise:
Pearls my tears are, O Fuzūlī, from the ocean deep of love;
But they're pearls these, oh! most surely, that the Love of
    Allah buys!

                                                    Fuzūlī.

GAZEL

IS'T strange if beauties' hearts turn blood through envy of
    thy cheek most fair?
For that which stone to ruby turns is but the radiant sun-
    light's glare.
Or strange is't if thine eyelash conquer all the stony-hearted
    ones?
For meet an ebon shaft like that a barb of adamant should
    bear!
Thy cheek's sun-love hath on the hard, hard hearts of fairy
    beauties fall'n,

And many a steely-eyed one hath received thy bright reflection fair.

The casket, thy sweet mouth, doth hold spell-bound the *hūrī*-faced ones all;

The virtue of Suleymān's Ring was that fays thereto fealty sware.

Is't strange if, seeing thee, they rub their faces lowly midst the dust?

That down to Adam bowed the angel throng doth the Qur'ān declare!

On many and many a heart of stone have fall'n the pangs of love for thee!

A fire that lies in stone concealed is thy heart-burning love's dread glare!

Within her ward, with garments rent, on all sides rosy-cheeked ones stray;

Fuzūlī, through those radiant hues, that quarter beams a garden fair.

Fuzūlī.

GAZEL

From the turning of the Sphere my luck hath seen reverse and woe;

Blood I've drunk, for from my banquet wine arose and forth did go.

With the flame, my burning sighs, I've lit the wand'ring wildered heart;

I'm a fire, doth not all that which turns about me roasted glow?

With thy rubies wine contended—oh! how it hath lost its wits!

Need 'tis yon ill-mannered wretch's company that we forego.

Yonder Moon saw not my burning's flame upon the parting day—

How can e'er the sun about the taper all night burning know?

Every eye that all around tears scatters, thinking of thy shaft,

Is an oyster-shell that causeth rain-drops into pearls to grow.

Forms my sighing's smoke a cloud that veils the bright cheek of the moon;

Ah! that yon fair Moon will ne'er the veil from off her beauty
  throw!
Ne'er hath ceased the rival e'en within her ward to vex me
  sore;
How say they, Fuzūlī, "There's in Paradise nor grief nor
  woe"?

Fuzūlī.

MUSEDDES

A STATELY Cypress yesterday her shade threw o'er my head;
Her form was heart-ensnaring, heart-delighting her light
  tread;
When speaking, sudden opened she her smiling rubies red,
There a pistachio I beheld that drops of candy shed.
  "This casket can it be a mouth? Ah! deign!" I said;
    said she:
  "Nay, nay, 'tis balm to cure thy hidden smart; aye, truly
    thine!"

Down o'er her crescents she had pressed the turban she did
  wear,
By which, from many broken hearts, sighs raised she of de-
  spair;
She loosed her tresses—hid within the cloud her moon so fair,
And o'er her visage I beheld the curls of her black hair.
  "Those curling locks, say, are they then a chain?" I said;
    said she:
  "That round my cheek, a noose to take thy heart; aye,
    truly thine!"

The taper bright, her cheek, illumined day's lamp in the sky;
The rose's branch was bent before her figure, cypress-high;
She, cypress-like, her foot set down upon the fount, my eye,
But many a thorn did pierce her foot she suffered pain
  thereby.
  "What thorn unto the roseleaf-foot gives pain?" I said;
    said she:
  "The lash of thy wet eye doth it impart; aye, truly
    thine!"

Promenading, to the garden did that jasmine-cheeked one go;
With many a bright adornment in the early springtide's
    glow;
The hyacinths their musky locks did o'er the roses throw;
That Picture had tattooed her lovely feet rose-red to show.
    " The tulip's hue whence doth the dog-rose gain?" I said;
        said she:
    " From blood of thine shed 'neath my glance's dart; aye,
        truly thine!"

To earth within her ward my tears in torrents rolled apace;
The accents of her ruby lips my soul crazed by their grace;
My heart was taken in the snare her musky locks did trace,
That very moment when my eyes fell on her curls and face.
    " Doth Scorpio the bright Moon's House contain?" I said;
        said she:
    " Fear! threatening this Conjunction dread, thy part; aye,
        truly thine!"

Her hair with ambergris perfumed was waving o'er her cheek,
On many grieving, passioned souls it cruel woe did wreak;
Her graceful form and many charms my wildered heart made
    weak;
The eye beheld her figure fair, then heart and soul did seek.
    " Ah! what bright thing this cypress of the plain?" I said;
        said she:
    " 'Tis that which thy fixed gaze beholds apart; aye, truly
        thine!"

When their veil her tulip and dog-rose had let down yesterday,
The morning breeze tore off that screen which o'er these flow-
    'rets lay;
Came forth that Envy of the sun in garden fair to stray,
Like lustrous pearls the dew-drops shone, a bright and glis-
    tening spray.
    " Pearls, say, are these, aye pearls from 'Aden's main?" I
        said; said she:
    " Tears, these, of poor Fuzūlī, sad of heart; aye, truly
        thine!"

                                            Fuzūlī.

MUKHAMMES

ATTAR within vase of crystal, such thy fair form silken-
    gowned;
And thy breast is gleaming water, where the bubbles clear
    abound;
Thou so bright none who may gaze upon thee on the earth
    is found;
Bold wert thou to cast the veil off, standing forth with gar-
    land crowned:
  Not a doubt but woe and ruin all the wide world must
    confound!

Lures the heart thy gilded palace, points it to thy lips the
    way;
Eagerly the ear doth listen for the words thy rubies say;
Near thy hair the comb remaineth, I despairing far away;
Bites the comb, each curling ringlet, when it through thy
    locks doth stray:
  Jealous at its sight, my heart's thread agonized goes curling
    round.

Ah! her face the rose, her shift rose-hued, her trousers red
    their shade;
With its flame burns us the fiery garb in which thou art
    arrayed.
Ne'er was born of Adam's children one like thee, O cruel
    maid!
Moon and Sun, in beauty's circle, at thy fairness stand dis-
    mayed:
  Seems it thou the Sun for mother and the Moon for sire
    hast owned.

Captive bound in thy red fillet, grieve I through thy musky
    hair;
Prone I 'neath those golden anklets which thy silvern limbs
    do wear;
Think not I am like thy fillet, empty of thy grace, O fair!

Rather to the golden chain, which hangs thy cheek round, me
    compare:
In my sad heart pangs a thousand from thy glance's shafts
    are found.

Eyes with antimony darkened, hands with hinna crimson
    dyed;
Through these beauties vain and wanton like to thee was
    ne'er a bride.
Bows of poplar green, thy painted brows; thy glances shafts
    provide.
Poor Fuzūlī for thine eyes and eyebrows aye hath longing
    cried:
That the bird from bow and arrow flees not, well may all
    astound.

                         Fuzūlī.

FROM LEYLĪ AND MEJNŪN

YIELD not the soul to pang of Love, for Love's the soul's fierce
    glow;
That Love's the torment of the soul doth all the wide world
    know.
Seek not for gain from fancy wild of pang of Love at all;
For all that comes from fancy wild of Love's pang is grief's
    throe.
Each curving eyebrow is a blood-stained sabre thee to slay;
Each dusky curl, a deadly venomed snake to work thee woe.
Lovely, indeed, the forms of moon-like maidens are to see—
Lovely to see, but ah! the end doth bitter anguish show.
From this I know full well that torment dire in love abides,
That all who lovers are, engrossed with sighs, rove to and
    fro.
Call not to mind the pupils of the black-eyed damsels bright,
With thought, "I'm man"; be not deceived, 'tis blood they
    drink, I trow.
E'en if Fuzūlī should declare, "In fair ones there is
    troth,"
Be not deceived—"A poet's words are falsehoods all men
    know."

                         Fuzūlī.

MEJNŪN ADDRESSES NEVFIL

QUOTH Mejnūn: " O sole friend of true plight!
With counsel many have tried me to guide right;
Many with wisdom gifted have advice shown,
But yet this fiend hath been by no one o'erthrown;
Much gold has on the earth been strewn round,
But yet this Stone of Alchemist by none's found.
Collyrium I know that doth increase light,
What use though is it if the eye doth lack sight?
I know that greatest kindliness in thee lies,
What use, though, when my fate doth ever dark rise?
Upon my gloomy fortune I no faith lay,
Impossible my hope appeareth alway.
Ah! though in this thou shouldest ever hard toil,
The end at length will surely all thy plans foil.
No kindliness to me my closest friends show;
Who is a friend to him whom he doth deem foe?
I know my fortune evil is and woe-fraught;
The search for solace is to me, save pain, naught.
There is a gazel that doth well my lot show,
Which constant I repeat where'er my steps go."

                                        Fuzūlī.

MEJNŪN'S GAZEL

FROM whomsoe'er I've sought for troth but bitterest disdain
    I've seen;
Whome'er within this faithless world I've trusted, all most
    vain I've seen.
To whomsoe'er I've told my woes, in hope to find some balm
    therefor,
Than e'en myself o'erwhelmed and sunk in deeper, sadder
    pain I've seen.
From out mine aching heart no one hath driven cruel grief
    away,
That those my friends of pleasure's hour affection did but
    feign I've seen.

Although I've clutched its mantle, life hath turned away its
    face from me;
And though I faith from mirror hoped, there persecuted
    swain I've seen.
At gate of hope I set my foot, bewilderment held forth its
    hand,
Alas! whene'er hope's thread I've seized, in hand the ser-
    pent's train I've seen.
A hundred times the Sphere hath shown to me my darksome
    fortune's star;
Whene'er my horoscope I've cast, but blackest, deepest stain
    I've seen.
Fuzūlī, blush not then, should I from mankind turn my face
    away;
For why? From all to whom I've looked, but reason sad
    too plain I've seen.

                              Fuzūlī.

ZEYD'S VISION

His grief and mourning Zeyd renewèd alway,
From bitter wailing ceased he not, he wept aye.
That faithful, loving, ever-constant friend dear,
One night, when was the rise of the True Dawn near,
Feeling that in his wasted frame no strength stayed,
Had gone, and down upon that grave himself laid.
There, in his sleep, he saw a wondrous fair sight,
A lovely garden, and two beauties, moon-bright;
Through transport rapturous, their cheeks with light glow;
Far distant now, all fear of anguish, pain, woe;
With happiness and ecstasy and joy blest,
From rivals' persecutions these have found rest;
A thousand angel-forms to each fair beauty,
With single heart, perform the servant's duty.
He, wondering, question made: " What Moons so bright
    these?
What lofty, honored Sovereigns of might these?
What garden, most exalted, is this parterre?
What throng so bright and beautiful, the throng there? "

They answer gave: " Lo! Eden's shining bowers these;
That radiant throng, the Heaven-born Youths and Hūrīs;
These two resplendent forms, bright as the fair moon,
These are the ever-faithful—Leylī, Mejnūn!
Since pure within the vale of love they sojourned,
And kept that purity till they to dust turned,
Are Eden's everlasting bowers their home now,
To them the Hūrīs and the Youths as slaves bow:
Since these, while on the earth, all woe resigned met,
And patience aye before them in each grief set,
When forth they fled from this false, faithless world's bound,
From all those pangs and sorrows they release found! "

Fuzūlī.

GAZEL

I BEGAN love's art to study, divers chapters did I read;
Longing's texts and parting's sections a whole book would
    fill indeed;
Union formed a short abridgment, but the pangs of love for
    thee
Have their commentaries endless made each other to succeed.
O Nishānī, hath the master, Love, thus truly taught to thee:
" This a question hard whose answer from the loved one
    must proceed! "

Nishānī.

GAZEL

HAND in hand thy mole hath plotted with thy hair,
Many hearts made captive have they in their snare.
Thou in nature art an angel whom the Lord
In his might the human form hath caused to wear.
When he dealt out 'mongst his creatures union's tray,
Absence from thee, God to me gave as my share.
Thou would'st deem that Power, the limner, for thy brows,
O'er the lights, thine eyes, two *nūns* had painted fair.
O Selīmī, on the sweetheart's cheek the down
Is thy sighs' fume, which, alas, hath rested there.

Selīmī.

GAZEL

TA'EN my sense and soul have those thy Leylī locks, thy
    glance's spell,
Me, their Mejnūn, 'midst of love's wild dreary desert they
    impel.
Since mine eyes have seen the beauty of the Joseph of thy
    grace,
Sense and heart have fall'n and lingered in thy chin's sweet
    dimple-well.
Heart and soul of mine are broken through my passion for
    thy lips;
From the hand of patience struck they honor's glass, to earth
    it fell.
The mirage, thy lips, O sweetheart, that doth like to water
    show;
For, through longing, making thirsty, vainly they my life
    dispel.
Since Selīmī hath the pearls, thy teeth, been praising, sense
    and heart
Have his head and soul abandoned, plunging 'neath love's
    ocean-swell.   *Selīmī.*

GAZEL

THY veil raise, shake from cheeks those locks of thine then;.
Unclouded beauty's sun and moon bid shine then.
But one glance from those soft and drooping eyes throw,
The heart through joy to drunkenness consign then.
Were I thy lip to suck, 'twould heal the sick heart;
Be kind, an answer give, Physician mine, then.
Beware lest evil glance thy beauty's rose smite,
From ill-eyed rival careful it confine then.
O heart, this is Life's Water 'midst of darkness,
In night's gloom hidden, drink the ruby wine then.
My love's down grows upon her rosy-hued cheek,
A book write on the woes it doth enshrine then.
Thy wine-hued lip, O love, grant to Selīmī—
And by thy parting's shaft my tears make wine then.
                Selīmī.

GAZEL

THE rival entry free hath to the loved one's ward, but none
    have I;
Regard unto the very dogs they there accord, but none
    have I.
The heart doth seize the Magian's hand; the cup-bearer, his
    glass; but I—
For gentle love they grant to these their due reward, but
    none have I.
To gain regard I would complain loud as the dogs within
    thy ward,
For these have power their plight to show, their griefs re-
    cord, but none have I.
From all eternity have I to Mejnūn taught the pang of love,
How then do all the folk to him renown award, but none
    have I?
To God be praise that brightly shines the mirror of my heart,
    Shemsī,
For more or less earth's glass with dust is soiled or marred,
    but none have I.

Shemsī Pacha.

FROM THE "KING AND BEGGAR"

PARROT, sweet of voice, thy song now raise!
All thy words purify in Love's fierce blaze!
Every point of Love as whole book shows;
Every mote of Love as bright sun glows.
Drowned in one drop thereof Time, Space, in sooth;
Lost in one grain thereof Both Worlds, in truth.
Man becomes man through Love, pure, bright,
Teacher respected, guide of the right.
Through its beams everything man as chief owns,
Rays of sun into rubies turn black stones.

.   .   .   .

He who a Lover is on God relies;
On, on, upward still doth he rise.

Beside thy justice, tyranny's the code of Key-Qubād;
Beside thy wrath, but mildness Qahramān's most deadly fray.
Thy scimitar's the gleaming guide empires to overthrow,
No foe of Islām can abide before thy sabre's ray.
Saw it thy wrath, through dread of thee would trembling
    seize the pine;
The falling stars a chain around the heaven's neck would lay.
Amidst thy sea-like armies vast, thy flags and standards fair,
The sails are which the ship of splendid triumph doth display.
Thrust it its beak into the Sphere, 'twould seize it as a grain,
The 'anqa strong, thy power, to which 'twere but a seed-like
    prey.
In past eternity the hand, thy might, it struck with bat,
That time is this time, for the Sky's Ball spins upon its way.
Within the rosy garden of thy praise the bird, the heart,
Singeth this soul-bestowing, smooth-as-water-running lay.

If yonder mouth be not the soul, O heart-enslaver gay,
Then wherefore is it like the soul, hid from our eyes away?
Since in the casket of our mind thy ruby's picture lies,
The mine is now no fitting home for gem of lustrous ray.
Thy tresses fall across thy cheek in many a twisting curl,
" To dance to Hijāz have the Shāmīs tucked their skirts,"
    we'd say.
Let both the youthful pine and cypress view thy motions fair;
The gardener now to rear the willow need no more assay.
The dark and cloudy brained of men thine eyebrows black
    depict,
While those of keen, discerning wit thy glistening teeth por-
    tray.
Before thy cheek the rose and jasmine bowèd in sujūd,
The cypress to thy figure in qiyām did homage pay.
The heart's throne is the seat of that great monarch, love for
    thee;
The soul, the secret court, where doth thy ruby's picture stay.
The radiance of thy beauty bright hath filled earth like the sun,
The hall, " BE! and it is," resounds with love of thee for aye.
The cries of those on plain of earth have risen to the skies,
The shouts of those who dwell above have found to earth
    their way.

Nor can the nightingale with songs as sweet as Bāqī's sing,
Nor happy as thy star can beam the garden's bright array.
The mead, the world, blooms through thy beauty's rose, like
    Irem's bower;
On every side are nightingales of sweet, melodious lay.
Now let us pray at Allah's court: " May this for aye en-
    dure,
The might and glory of this prospered King's resplendent
    sway;
Until the lamp, the world-illuming sun, at break of dawn,
A silver candelabrum on the circling skies display,
Oh! may the Ruler of the world with skirt of aid and grace
Protect the taper of his life from blast of doom, we pray! "
Glory's the comrade; Fortune, the cup-bearer at our feast;
The beaker is the Sphere; the bowl, the Steel of gold-inlay!

Bāqī.

GAZEL

'TIS love's wild sea, my sighs' fierce wind doth lash those
    waves my tears uprear;
My head, the barque of sad despite; mine eyebrows twain,
    the anchors here.
Mine unkempt hair, the den of yonder tiger dread, the fair
    one's love;
My head, dismay and sorrow's realm's deserted mountain
    region drear.
At whatsoever feast I drain the cup thy rubies' mem'ry to,
Amidst all those who grace that feast, except the dregs, I've
    no friend near.
Thou know'st, O Light of my poor eyes, with tūtyā mixed
    are gems full bright,
What then if weep on thy path's dust mine eyes that scatter
    pearls most clear!
The Sphere, old hag, with witchcraft's spell hath parted me
    from my fond love,
O Bāqī, see, by God, how vile a trick yon jade hath played
    me here!

Bāqī.

GAZEL

YEARS trodden under foot have I lain on that path of thine;
Thy musky locks are noose-like cast, around my feet to
  twine.
O Princess mine! boast not thyself through loveliness of
  face,
For that, alas, is but a sun which must full soon decline!
The loved one's stature tall, her form as fair as juniper,
Bright 'midst the rosy bowers of grace a slender tree doth
  shine.
Her figure, fair-proportioned as my poesy sublime,
Her slender waist is like its subtle thought—hard to divine.
Then yearn not, Bāqī, for the load of love's misfortune
  dire;
For that to bear mayhap thy soul no power doth enshrine.

Bāqī.

GAZEL

WITH her graceful-moving form, a Cypress jasmine-faced is
  she?
Or in Eden's bower a branch upon the Lote or Tūba-tree?
That thy blood-stained shaft which rankles in my wounded
  breast, my love,
In the rosebud hid a lovely rose-leaf, sweetheart, can it be?
To the dead of pain of anguish doth its draught fresh life
  impart;
O cup-bearer, is the red wine Jesu's breath? tell, tell to me!
Are they teeth those in thy mouth, or on the rosebud drops
  of dew?
Are they sparkling stars, or are they gleaming pearls, that
  there I see?
Through the many woes thou wreakest upon Bāqī, sick of
  heart,
Is't thy will to slay him, or is it but sweet disdain in thee?

Bāqī.

GAZEL

BEFORE thy form, the box-tree's lissom figure dwarfed would
show;
Those locks of thine the pride of ambergris would over-
throw.
Who, seeing thy cheek's glow, recalls the ruby is de-
ceived;
He who hath drunken deep of wine inebriate doth grow.
Should she move forth with figure like the juniper in
grace,
The garden's cypress to the loved one's form must bend right
low.
Beware, give not the mirror bright to yonder paynim maid,
Lest she idolater become, when there her face doth show.
Bāqī, doth he not drink the wine of obligation's grape,
Who drunken with A-lestu's cup's o'erwhelming draught
doth go?

Bāqī.

GAZEL

THY cheek, like limpid water, clear doth gleam;
Thy pouting mouth a bubble round doth seem.
The radiance of thy cheek's sun on the heart
Like moonlight on the water's face doth beam.
The heart's page, through the tracings of thy down,
A volume all illumined one would deem.
That fair Moon's sunny love the earth have burned,
It warm as rays of summer sun doth stream.
At woful sorrow's feast my blood-shot eyes,
Two beakers of red wine would one esteem.
Bāqī, her mole dark-hued like ambergris,
A fragrant musk-pod all the world would deem.

Bāqī.

GAZEL

ALL sick the heart with love for her, sad at the feast of woe;
Bent form, the harp; low wail, the flute; heart's blood for
    wine doth flow.
Prone lies the frame her path's dust 'neath, in union's stream
    the eye,
In air the mind, the soul 'midst separation's fiery glow.
Oh, ever shall it be my lot, zone-like, thy waist to clasp!
'Twixt us, O love, the dagger blade of severance doth show!
Thou art the Queen of earth, thy cheeks are Towers of
    might, this day,
Before thy Horse, like Pawns, the Kings of grace and
    beauty go.
Him hinder not, beside thee let him creep, O Shade-like stay!
Bāqī, thy servant, O my Queen, before thee lieth low.

Bāqī.

ON AUTUMN

Lo, ne'er a trace or sign of springtide's beauty doth remain;
Fall'n 'midst the garden lie the leaves, now all their glory
    vain.
Bleak stand the orchard trees, all clad in tattered dervish
    rags;
Dark Autumn's blast hath torn away the hands from off the
    plane.
From each hill-side they come and cast their gold low at the
    feet
Of garden trees, as hoped the streams from these some boon
    to gain.
Stay not within the parterre, let it tremble with its shame:
Bare every shrub, this day doth naught or leaf or fruit
    retain.
Bāqī, within the garden lies full many a fallen leaf;
Low lying there, it seems they 'gainst the winds of Fate com-
    plain.

Bāqī.

GAZEL

TULIP-CHEEKED ones over rosy field and plain stray all
    around;
Mead and garden cross they, looking wistful each way, all
    around.
These the lovers true of radiant faces, aye, but who the fair?
Lissom Cypress, thou it is whom eager seek they all around.
Band on band Woe's legions camped before the City of the
    Heart,
There, together leagued, sat Sorrow, Pain, Strife, Dismay,
    all around.
From my weeping flows the river of my tears on every side,
Like an ocean 'tis again, a sea that casts spray all around.
Forth through all the Seven Climates have the words of
    Bāqī gone;
This refulgent verse recited shall be alway, all around.

Bāqī.

GAZEL

FROM thine own beauty's radiant sun doth light flow;
How lustrously doth now the crystal glass show!
Thy friend's the beaker, and the cup's thy comrade;
Like to the dregs why dost thou me aside throw?
Hearts longing for thy beauty can resist not;
Hold, none can bear the dazzling vision's bright glow!
United now the lover, and now parted;
This world is sometimes pleasure and sometimes woe.
Bound in the spell of thy locks' chain is Bāqī,
Mad he, my Liege, and to the mad they grace show.

Bāqī.

GAZEL

THE goblet as affliction's Khusrev's bright Keyānī crown
    doth shine;
And surely doth the wine-jar love's King's Khusrevānī hoard
    enshrine.
Whene'er the feast recalls Jemshīd, down from its eyes the
    red blood rolls;

The rosy-tinted wine its tears, the beakers its blood-weeping eyne.

At parting's banquet should the cup, the heart, with blood brim o'er were't strange?

A bowl that, to the fair we'll drain, a goblet filled full high with wine.

O Moon, if by thy door one day the foe should sudden me o'ertake—

A woe by Heaven decreed, a fate to which I must myself resign!

The fume of beauty's and of grace's censer is thy cheek's sweet mole,

The smoke thereof thy musky locks that spreading fragrant curl and twine;

Thy cheek rose-hued doth light its taper at the moon that shines most bright,

Its candlestick at grace's feast is yonder collar fair of thine.

Of love and passion is the lustrous sheen of Bāqī's verse the cause;

As Life's Stream brightly this doth shine; but that, th' Eternal Life Divine.　　　　*Bāqī.*

GAZEL

When the sheets have yonder Torment to their bosom ta'en to rest,

Think I, "Hides the night-adorning Moon within the cloudlet's breast."

In the dawning, O thou turtle, mourn not with those senseless plaints;

In the bosom of some stately cypress thou'rt a nightly guest.

Why thou weepest from the heavens, never can I think, O dew;

Every night some lovely rose's bosom fair thou enterest.

Hath the pearl seen in the story of thy teeth its tale of shame,

Since the sea hath hid the album of the shell within its breast?

Longing for thy cheeks, hath Bāqī all his bosom marked with scars,

Like as though he'd cast of rose-leaves fresh a handful o'er his chest.　　　　*Bāqī.*

ELEGY ON SULTAN SULEYMĀN I

O THOU! foot-bounden in the mesh of fame and glory's
    snare!
Till when shall last the lust of faithless earth's pursuits and
    care?
At that first moment, which of life's fair springtide is the
    last,
'Tis need the tulip cheek the tint of autumn leaf should wear;
'Tis need that thy last home should be, e'en like the dregs',
    the dust;
'Tis need the stone from hand of Fate should be joy's beak-
    er's share.
He is a man indeed whose heart is as a mirror clear;
Man art thou? why then doth thy breast the tiger's fierce-
    ness bear?
In understanding's eye how long shall heedless slumber bide?
Will not war's Lion-Monarch's fate suffice to make thee
    ware?
He, Prince of Fortune's Cavaliers! he to whose charger bold,
Whene'er he caracoled or pranced, cramped was earth's tour-
    ney square!
He, to the lustre of whose sword the Magyar bowed his
    head!
He, the dread gleaming of whose brand the Frank can well
    declare!
    Like tender rose-leaf, gently laid he in the dust his face,
    And Earth, the Treasurer, him placed like jewel in his case.

In truth, he was the radiance of rank high and glory great,
A Shah, Iskender-diademed, of Dārā's armied state;
Before the dust beneath his feet the Sphere bent low its head;
Earth's shrine of adoration was his royal pavilion's gate.
The smallest of his gifts the meanest beggar made a prince;
Exceeding bounteous, exceeding kind a Potentate!
The court of glory of his kingly majesty most high
Was aye the centre where would hopes of sage and poet wait.
Although he yielded to Eternal Destiny's command,
A King was he in might as Doom and puissant as Fate!

Weary and worn by this sad, changeful Sphere, deem not
    thou him:
Near God to be, did he his rank and glory abdicate.
What wonder if our eyes no more life and the world behold!
His beauty fair, as sun and moon, did earth irradiate!
  If folk upon the bright sun look, with tears are filled their
    eyes;
  For seeing it, doth yon moon-face before their minds arise!

Now let the cloud blood drop on drop weep, and its form
    bend low!
And let the Judas-tree anew in blossoms gore-hued blow!
With this sad anguish let the stars' eyes rain down bitter
    tears!
And let the smoke from hearts on fire the heavens all dark-
    ened show!
Their azure garments let the skies change into deepest black!
Let the whole world attire itself in robes of princely woe!
In breasts of fairies and of men still let the flame burn on—
Of parting from the blest King Suleymān the fiery glow!
His home above the highest heaven's ramparts he hath
    made;
This world was all unworthy of his majesty, I trow.
The bird, his soul, hath, *huma*-like, aloft flown to the skies,
And naught remaineth save a few bones on the earth below.
The speeding Horseman of the plain of Time and Space
    was he;
Fortune and Fame aye as his friends and bridle guides did go.
  The wayward courser, cruel Fate, was wild and fierce of
    pace,
  And fell to earth the Shade of God the Lord's benignant
    Grace.

Through grief for thee, bereft of rest and tearful e'en as I,
Sore weeping let the cloud of spring go wand'ring through
    the sky!
And let the wailing of the birds of dawn the whole world fill!
Be roses torn! and let the nightingale distressful cry!
Their hyacinths as weeds of woe displaying, let them weep,
Down o'er their skirts their flowing tears let pour—the moun-
    tains high!

The odor of thy kindliness recalling, tulip-like,
Within the Tātār musk-deer's heart let fire of anguish lie!
Through yearning for thee let the rose its ear lay on the path,
And, narcisse-like, till the last day the watchman's calling
ply!
Although the pearl-diffusing eye to oceans turned the world,
Ne'er into being should there come a pearl with thee to vie!
O heart! this hour 'tis thou that sympathizer art with me;
Come, let us like the flute bewail, and moan, and plaintive
sigh!
  The notes of mourning and of dole aloud let us rehearse;
  And let all those who grieve be moved by this our seven-
  fold verse.

Will earth's King ne'er awake from sleep?—broke hath the
dawn of day:
Will ne'er he move forth from his tent, adorned as heaven's
display?
Long have our eyes dwelt on the road, and yet no news hath
come
From yonder land, the threshold of his majesty's array:
The color of his cheek hath paled, dry-lipped he lieth there,
E'en like that rose which from the vase of flowers hath fall'n
away.
Goes now the Khusrev of the skies behind the cloudy veil,
For shame, remembering thy love and kindness, one would
say.
My prayer is ever, " May the babes, his tears, go 'neath the
sod,
Or old or young be he who weeps not thee in sad dismay."
With flame of parting from thee let the sun burn and con-
sume;
And o'er the wastes through grief let darkness of the clouds
hold sway.
Thy talents and thy feats let it recall and weep in blood,
Yea, let thy sabre from its sheath plunge in the darksome clay.
  Its collar, through its grief and anguish, let the reed-pen
  tear!
  And let the earth its vestment rend through sorrow and
  despair!

Thy sabre made the foe the anguish dire of wounds to drain;
Their tongues are silenced, none who dares to gainsay doth
　　remain.
The youthful cypress, head-exalted, looked upon thy lance,
And ne'er its lissom twigs their haughty airs displayed again.
Where'er thy stately charger placed his hoof, from far and
　　near
Flocked nobles, all upon thy path their lives to offer fain.
In desert of mortality the bird, desire, rests ne'er;
Thy sword in cause of God did lives as sacrifice ordain.
As sweeps a scimitar, across earth's face on every side,
Of iron-girded heroes of the world thou threw'st a chain.
Thou took'st a thousand idol temples, turnèdst all to mosques;
Where jangled bells thou mad'st be sung the Call to Prayers'
　　strain.
At length is struck the signal drum, and thou hast journeyed
　　hence;
Lo! thy first resting-place is Eden's flowery, verdant plain.
　　Praise is to God! for he in the Two Worlds hath blessèd
　　　thee,
　　　And caused thy glorious name, Hero and Martyr both
　　　　to be.

Bāqī, the beauty of the King, the heart's delight, behold!
The mirror of the work of God, the Lord of Right, behold!
The dear old man hath passed away from th' Egypt sad, the
　　world;
The youthful Prince, alert and fair as Joseph bright, behold!
The Sun hath risen, and the Dawning gray hath touched its
　　bourne;
The lovely face of yon Khusrev, whose soul is light, behold!
This chase now to the grave hath sent the Behrām of the
　　Age;
Go, at his threshold serve, King Erdeshīr aright, behold!
The blast of Fate to all the winds hath blown Suleymān's
　　throne;
Sultan Selīm Khān on Iskender's couch of might, behold!
The Tiger of the mount of war to rest in sleep hath gone;
The Lion who doth now keep watch on glory's height, be-
　　hold!

The Peacock fair of Eden's mead hath soared to Heaven's
    parterre;
The lustre of the *huma* of high, happy flight, behold!
    Eternal may the glory of the heaven-high Khusrev dwell!
    Blessings be on the Monarch's soul and spirit—and fare-
    well!

Bāqī.

GAZEL

CRUEL tyranny we love not, nay, to justice we incline;
Full contentedly our eyes wait for the blest command divine.
Know we truly, for a mirror, world-reflecting, is our heart;
Yet conceive not us to Fortune's ever-changeful ways supine.
To the rule of God submissive, all concern we cast aside;
We indeed on him confiding, on his providence recline.
Shall our heart anoint its eye then with the *kuhl* of Isfahān?
Pleased it with this *tūtyā:* dust that doth the Fair One's path-
    way line.
Since our heart, 'Adlī, within Love's crucible was purified,
'Midst the universe, from guile and guilt free, bright our soul
    doth shine.

'Adlī.

GAZEL

OH that a fragrant breath might reach the soul from early
    spring!
Oh that with warbling sweet of birds the groves once more
    might ring!
Oh that in melody the songs anew might rose-like swell!
That fresh in grace and voice the nightingale be heard to
    sing!
Oh that the New Year's Day were come, when, minding times
    gone by,
Should each and all from Time and Fate demand their reck-
    oning!
In short, O Bakhtī, would the early vernal days were here,
Then, 'midst the mead, ne'er should we part from brink of
    limpid spring.

Bakhtī.

GAZEL

Soon as I beheld thee, mazed and wildered grew my sad
heart;
How shall I my love disclose to thee who tyrant dread art?
How shall I hold straight upon my road, when yonder Tor-
ment
Smitten hath my breast with deadly wounds by her eyelash
dart?
Face, a rose; and mouth, a rosebud; form, a slender sap-
ling—
How shall I not be the slave of Princess such as thou art?
Ne'er hath heart a beauty seen like her of graceful figure;
Joyous would I for yon charmer's eyebrow with my life
part.
Fārisī, what can I do but love that peerless beauty?
Ah! this aged Sphere hath made me lover of yon sweetheart.

Fārisī.

MUSEDDES

Ah! that once again my heart with blood is filled, like beaker,
high;
At the feast of parting from my love I fell, and prostrate lie;
O'er this wildered heart the gloom of frenzy, conquering,
doth fly;
In the valley of distraction ne'er a guide can I descry.
  Heedless mistress! loveless Fortune! ever-shifting, rest-
  less sky!
  Sorrows many! friends not any! strong-starred foeman!
  feeble I!

In the land of exile loomed dark on one side the night of woe,
Nowhere o'er me did the lustrous moon of beauty's heaven
glow;
Yonder glared the Two Infortunes, sank my helping planet
low;
Here did fortune, there did gladness, parting from me, distant go.

Heedless mistress! loveless Fortune! ever-shifting, restless sky!
Sorrows many! friends not any! strong-starred foeman! feeble I!

Strange is't if the nightingale, my heart, in thousand notes doth wail?
Fate to part it from the rosebud, the belovèd, did prevail;
Whilst I'm on the thorn of anguish, rivals with my love regale:
Why recite my woes, O comrades? space were none to tell their tale!
Heedless mistress! loveless Fortune! ever-shifting, restless sky!
Sorrows many! friends not any! strong-starred foeman! feeble I!

E'en a moment at the feast of woes from tears can I refrain?
How shall not the wine, my tears, down rolling, all my vestment stain?
Can it be with e'en one breath I should not like the reed complain?
Sad, confused, like end of banquet, why then should not I remain?
Heedless mistress! loveless Fortune! ever-shifting, restless sky!
Sorrows many! friends not any! strong-starred foeman! feeble I!

Yonder Princess, though I served her, pitiless drave me away,
Banished me far from her city, sent me from her court's array:
When I parted from her tresses, black the world before me lay;
Helpless 'midst the darkness did I, like unto 'Atā'ī, stray.
Heedless mistress! loveless Fortune! ever-shifting, restless sky!
Sorrows many! friends not any! strong-starred foeman! feeble I!

'Atā'ī.

GAZEL

Be thou wise and thoughtful, e'en as *qalender* in mind be
    free;
Nor a faithless, graceless paynim, nor a bigot Moslem be.
Be not vain of wisdom, though thou be the Plato of the age;
Be a school-child when a learned man and righteous thou
    dost see.
Like the world-adorning sun, rub thou thy face low 'midst
    the dust;
Overwhelm earth with thy planet, yet without a planet be.
Fret not after Khizar, rather go, and, like to Nef'ī's heart,
At the channel of Life's Stream of grace drink full content-
    edly.   *Nef'ī.*

TO SULTAN MURĀD IV

Round us foes throng, host to aid us here in sad plight, is
    there none?
In the cause of God to combat, chief of tried might, is there
    none?
None who will checkmate the foe, Castle to Castle, face to face
In the battle who will Queen-like guide the brave Knight, is
    there none?
Midst a fearful whirlpool we are fallen helpless, send us aid!
Us to rescue, a strong swimmer in our friends' sight, is there
    none?
Midst the fight to be our comrade, head to give or heads to
    take,
On the field of earth a hero of renown bright, is there none?
Know we not wherefore in turning off our woes ye thus
    delay;
Day of Reckoning, aye, and question of the poor's plight, is
    there none?
With us 'midst the foeman's flaming streams of scorching
    fire to plunge,
Salamander with experience of Fate dight, is there none?
This our letter, to the court of Sultan Murād, quick to bear,
Pigeon, rapid as the storm wind in its swift flight, is there
    none?   *Hāfiz Pacha.*

IN REPLY TO THE PRECEDING

To relieve Bagdad, O Hāfiz, man of tried might, is there
none?
Aid from us thou seek'st, then with thee host of fame bright,
is there none?
" I'm the Queen the foe who'll checkmate," thus it was that
thou didst say;
Room for action now against him with the brave Knight, is
there none?
Though we know thou hast no rival in vainglorious, empty
boasts,
Yet to take dread vengeance on thee, say, a Judge right, is
there none?
While thou layest claim to manhood, whence this cowardice
of thine?
Thou art frightened, yet beside thee fearing no fight, is there
none?
Heedless of thy duty thou, the Rāfizīs have ta'en Bagdad;
Shall not God thy foe be? Day of Reckoning, sure, right,
is there none?
They have wrecked Ebū-Hanīfa's city through thy lack of
care;
Oh, in thee of Islām's and the Prophet's zeal, light, is there
none?
God, who favored us, whilst yet we knew not, with the Sul-
tanate,
Shall again accord Bagdad, decreed of God's might, is there
none?
Thou hast brought on Islām's army direful ruin with thy
bribes;
Have we not heard how thou say'st, " Word of this foul
blight, is there none?"
With the aid of God, fell vengeance on the enemy to take,
By me skilled and aged, vezīr, pious, zeal-dight, is there
none?
Now shall I appoint commander a vezīr of high emprise,
Will not Khizar and the Prophet aid him? guide right, is
there none?

Is it that thou dost the whole world void and empty now
    conceive?
Of the Seven Climes, Murādī, King of high might, is there
    none?

Murādī.

LUGAZ

THERE's an o'erhanging castle in which there flows a main,
And there within that castle a fish its home hath ta'en;
The fish within its mouth doth hold a shining gem,
Which wastes the fish as long as it therein doth remain.
This puzzle to the poets is offered by Murād;
Let him reply who office or place desires to gain.

Murādī.

SACHLI ZEMĀN   (FORTUNE THE LONG-HAIRED)

ZEMĀN the Long-haired, 'midst these lovely ones see,
A wayward, wanton Torment of the world she.
Like Fortune, she nor clemency nor grace knows;
The number of her hairs her lovers' tale shows.
The tribute from the realm of hearts her curls bore,
Seduced me have these locks that hang her neck o'er.

'Azīzī.

JIHĀN BĀNŪ   (LADY WORLD)

SHE whom they call Jihān 's a damsel moon-faced,
Who, like the World, is faithless, and doth hearts waste.
Save faithlessness, though comes not from the World aught;
The heart from that love of the soul can pass not.
Let but her mind contented be with poor me,
Then may the World divorced from me for aye be.

'Azīzī.

LĀ'L-PARA (RUBY-CHIP)

LĀ'L-PARA as her name doth one of these own,
A girl whose heart is hard as is the flint-stone.
Her mouth in very truth's a ruby bright red,
Her teeth are pearls, so too the words by her said.
Strange were it, if my heart be by her love slaved?
For sooth her rubies bear the " coral-prayer " graved.

'Azīzī.

ĀQ-'ĀLEM (WHITE UNIVERSE)

AND Aq-'Alem they one of yonder maids call,
For her the moon of heaven acteth jackal.
Is't strange if through her loveliness she famed be?
A white Rose on the earth is yonder Hūrī.
He who with that bright Moon as friend goes,
A universe enjoys more fair than earth shows.

'Azīzī.

MUSEDDES

BE mine for dress, the piercing thorn! be mine for couch, the
    hard, hard stone!
Be mine for home, grief's cot! be mine for bread, woe's tears!
    for work, pain's moan!
Be all my bleeding frame with wounds of cruel foeman's
    hatred sown!
Be these rejoiced in heart and gay who make my grieving
    soul to groan!
  Be all those glad by whom my aching heart is tortured and
    o'erthrown!
  Be those blest with their wish who say of me, " Be all
    his hopes cast prone! "

Unfaithfulness is aye the rule which guides the Sphere that
    loves to pain,
The inborn nature of the Skies is but to manifest disdain;
Within the breasts of those who pleasure seek there lurks
    some yearning vain;

O heart, blest is the practice of the thought enshrined in this
    refrain:
  Be all those glad by whom my aching heart is tortured and
    o'erthrown!
  Be those blest with their wish who say of me, " Be all
    his hopes cast prone! "

When time is past, rejoiced shall swell the hearts of all my
    comrades dear;
And through their cruelty—my choice—my foes shall mourn
    in sorrow drear.
Let all those learn this verse of me who hap to come my path-
    way near,
And let them from the tongues of that green sward which
    decks my grave this hear:
  Be all those glad by whom my aching heart is tortured and
    o'erthrown!
  Be those blest with their wish who say of me, " Be all
    his hopes cast prone! "

Within this hostel of the world my portion is the tray of dole;
My eye, the birthplace of the flame, refuseth health's most
    pleasant stole;
Fatigue, the rest of my sad heart; anguish, the present to
    my soul;
Ne'er through Eternity to gain my longing is my longing's goal.
  Be all those glad by whom my aching heart is tortured and
    o'erthrown!
  Be those blest with their wish who say of me, " Be all
    his hopes cast prone! "

O Nā'ilī, is't possible to change or alter Fate's decree?
Annulled can ever be the edict writ by pen of Destiny?
My heart is gladdened with this thought, that ne'er an hour's
    delay can be
In whetting keen and sharp that axe of pain which rust can
    never see.
  Be all those glad by whom my aching heart is tortured and
    o'erthrown!
  Be those blest with their wish who say of me, " Be all
    his hopes cast prone! "

Nā'ilī.

GAZEL

He who union with the Lord gains, more delight desireth not!
He who looks on charms of fair one, other sight desireth not.
Pang of love is lover's solace, eagerly he seeks therefor,
Joys he in it, balm or salve for yonder blight, desireth not.
Paradise he longs not after, nor doth aught beside regard;
Bower and Garden, Mead, and Youth, and Hūrī bright, de-
    sireth not.
From the hand of Power Unbounded draineth he the Wine of
    Life,
Aye inebriate with Knowledge, learning's light, desireth not.
He who loves the Lord is monarch of an empire, such that
    he—
King of Inward Mysteries—Suleymān's might, desireth not.
Thou art Sultan of my heart, aye, Soul of my soul e'en art
    Thou;
Thou art Soul enow, and Sidqī other plight desireth not.

Sidqī.

MUNĀJĀT

Allah! Lord who liv'st for aye! O Sole! O King of
    Glory's Ray!
Monarch who ne'er shalt pass away! show Thou to us Thy
    bounties fair.
In early morning shall our cry, our wail, mount to Thy
    Throne on high:
"Error and sin our wont," we sigh: show Thou to us Thy
    bounties fair.
If cometh not from Thee Thy grace, evil shall all our works
    deface;
O Lord of Being and of Space! show Thou to us Thy bounties
    fair.
Creator of security! to Thy Belovèd greetings be!
These fair words are in sincerity: show Thou to us Thy boun-
    ties fair
Iqbālī sinnèd hath indeed, yet unto him Thy grace concede;
Eternal, Answerer in need! show Thou to us Thy bounties
    fair.

Iqbālī.

MUKHAMMES

ALAS! nor dew nor smiling rose within this mead is mine;
Within this market-place nor trade nor coin for need is mine;
Nor more nor less; nor power nor strength for act or deed is
    mine;
Nor might nor eminence; nor balm the cure to speed is mine.
  Oh, that I knew what here I am, that which indeed is mine!

Being's the bounty of the Lord; and Life, the gift Divine;
The Breath, the present of his love; and Speech his Grace's
    sign;
The Body is the pile of God; the Soul, his Breath benign;
The Powers thereof, his Glory's trust; the Senses, his de-
    sign.
  Oh, that I knew what here I am, that which indeed is mine!

No work, no business of my own within this mart have I;
All Being is of him alone—no life apart have I;
No choice of entering this world, or hence of start have I;
To cry, "I am! I am!" in truth, no power of heart have I.
  Oh, that I knew what here I am, that which indeed is mine!

The Earth the carpet is of Power; the Sphere, the tent of
    Might;
The Stars, both fixed and wandering, are Glory's lamps of
    light;
The World's the issue of the grace of Mercy's treasures bright;
With Forms of beings is the page of Wisdom's volume dight.
  Oh, that I knew what here I am, that which indeed is mine!

Being is but a loan to us, and Life in trust we hold:
In slaves a claim to Power's pretension arrogant and bold;
The servant's part is by submission and obedience told;
Should He, "My slave," address to me, 'twere favors mani-
    fold.
  Oh, that I knew what here I am, that which indeed is mine!

I'm poor and empty-handed, but grace free is of the Lord;
Nonentity's my attribute: to Be is of the Lord;

For Being or Non-being's rise, decree is of the Lord;
The surging of the Seen and Unseen's sea is of the Lord.
Oh, that I knew what here I am, that which indeed is mine!

Of gifts from table of his Bounty is my daily bread;
My breath is from the Breath of God's benignant Mercy fed;
My portion from the favors of Almighty Power is shed;
And my provision is from Providence's kitchen spread.
Oh, that I knew what here I am, that which indeed is mine!

I cannot, unallotted, take my share from wet or dry;
From land or from the ocean, from earth or from the sky;
The silver or the gold will come, by Providence laid by;
I cannot grasp aught other than my fortune doth supply.
Oh, that I knew what here I am, that which indeed is mine!

Creation's Pen the lines of billows of events hath traced;
Th' illumined scroll of the Two Worlds, Creation's Pencil
graced;
Their garments upon earth and sky, Creation's woof hath
placed;
Men's forms are pictures in Creation's great Shāh-Nāma
traced.
Oh, that I knew what here I am, that which indeed is mine!

I cannot make the morning eve, or the dark night the day;
I cannot turn the air to fire, or dust to water's spray;
I cannot bid the Sphere stand still, or mountain region stray;
I cannot Autumn turn by will of mine to lovely May.
Oh, that I knew what here I am, that which indeed is mine!

From out of Nothingness his mighty Power made me appear;
Whilst in the womb I lay, saw he to all I need for here;
With kindness concealed and manifest did he me rear;
With me he drew a curtain o'er Distinction's beauty dear.
Oh, that I knew what here I am, that which indeed is mine!

God's Revelation is Discernment's Eye, if't oped remain;
The picturings of worlds are all things changing aye amain;
The showing of the Hidden Treasure is this raging main,
This work, this business of the Lord, this Majesty made plain.
Oh, that I knew what here I am, that which indeed is mine!

Now void, now full, are Possibility's store-houses vast;
This glass-lined world's the mirror where Lights Twain their
     phases cast;
The blinded thing—in scattering strange fruits its hours are
     past;
Ruined hath this old Vineyard been by autumn's sullen blast.
   Oh, that I knew what here I am, that which indeed is mine!

Nābī.

GAZEL

NE'ER a corner for the plaintive bulbul's nest remaineth now;
Ne'er a palm-tree 'neath whose kindly shade is rest remaineth
     now.
Day and night some balm I've sought for, to relieve my
     wounded heart;
Ne'er a cure within the heavens' turquoise chest remaineth
     now.
From its source, through every country, searched have I, but
     all in vain—
Ne'er a single drop, in mercy's fountain blest, remaineth now.
Empty earthen pots are reckoned one with jewels rich and
     rare;
Ne'er a scale in value's mart the worth to test remaineth now.
'Neath the earth may now the needy hide themselves, Nābī,
     away;
Ne'er a turret on the fort of interest remaineth now.

Nābī.

MUNĀJĀT

O LORD, to Thee is never a beginning, neither end;
Thy mercy's ocean, limitless, doth over all extend.
E'en though the value-weighing hand of Thine unbounded
     might
Hath wrought astounding marvels that all numbering tran-
     scend,
Yet, Lord, Thou formedst Adam in the best of symmetry;

Thou worthy of thy grace to make this folk didst conde-
    scend.
Unfathomed and unsounded lies thy mercy's ocean vast,
Which truly hath made earth beneath its surging waves de-
    scend:
O Lord, could any hurt or harm befall that shoreless deep,
Did thou a single drop therefrom to this thy servant send?
Since 'Ārif owns a Master kind in graciousness like thee,
O Lord, before another's door were't right for him to bend?
  O Lord, thus ever doth in joy thy blest device appear—
  Thy greatest glory from the works of vileness thou dost
    rear!

                                          '*Ārif.*

GAZEL

THE sun of love for thy fair cheek the heart's core floods with
    radiant light;
The soul's most secret court is filled with dazzling rays at
    thy sweet sight.
With union's joys though blest one be, or though with pangs
    of absence torn,
Are still sad wail and plaintive cry the e'er-true signs of love-
    lorn plight.
Then welcome, O thou gentlest breeze, that bear'st to him
    who dwells midst woe,
As news from yonder absent maid the sweet scent of her
    garment white.
Of gilded halls no need in sooth to libertines when wine flows
    free;
Some ruined den beseems them more, like Jemshīd's hut of
    woful site.
The sparks raised by my passioned sighs' and plainings' smoke
    are each one quenched;
For every tear that rolleth down upon my robe's a rich pearl
    bright.
O 'Ārif! this poor captive bird hath grown to love th' en-
    tangling snare;
For curling locks to careworn hearts afford a refuge sure
    from fright.

                                          '*Ārif.*

FAREWELL POEM

AH, my Joy! thou'rt gone, and my sad weeping heart hast
    borne indeed,
And my breast by bitter parting's raging fires all worn in-
    deed;
Grief for thee in hundred pieces hath my raiment torn in-
    deed;
Be thy escort on the journey tears I weep, forlorn indeed.
    Thou art gone, and longing for thee makes my heart to
      mourn indeed;
    Without thee, banquets where friends meet, all I have for-
      sworn indeed.

Wheresoe'er thy footsteps wander, be the aid of God thy
    guide;
As the pilot to thy wishes be His grace aye at thy side;
Shadow for thy crown of glory may the *huma's* wing pro-
    vide;
Ah! may ever-joyous, happy fortune on thy path abide.
    Thou art gone, and longing for thee makes my heart to
      mourn indeed;
    Without thee, banquets where friends meet, all I have for-
      sworn indeed.

O thou Source of joy and quiet unto my poor grieving breast!
Hence forever I with separation's fires am sore opprest;
Thou, Crown of my joy! my Treasure! mercy show to me
    distrest!
Now, my Lord, to whom shall Master's title be by me addrest?
    Thou art gone, and longing for thee makes my heart to
      mourn indeed;
    Without thee, banquets where friends meet, all I have for-
      sworn indeed.

Ever in thy court of service may th' inconstant heavens be!
I am fallen, soul and body, to woe's depths by their decree;
From a kindly master like thee, merciless, they've sundered
    me;
And into the dreary vale of exile have they driven thee.

Thou art gone, and longing for thee makes my heart to
mourn indeed;
Without thee, banquets where friends meet, all I have forsworn indeed.

Though I'm far now from the shadow of thy love, O Cypress
straight,
Still my prayers I may offer for thy happiness of state.
Think at times upon thy servant 'Ārif sitting desolate;
Him from near thy skirt of kindness taken hath his dark-
some fate.
Thou art gone, and longing for thee makes my heart to
mourn indeed;
Without thee, banquets where friends meet, all I have for-
sworn indeed.

'Ārif.

GAZEL

THE realm of patience thou'st laid waste, Helāgū hight art
thou, Paynim?
O mercy! thou'st the world consumed, a blazing light art thou,
Paynim?
A maiden's grace, is that thy grace, a conquering hero's voice,
thy voice;
Thou Woe, I know not, maid or youthful lord of might art
thou, Paynim?
What mean those hidden, secret sighs, and tears, and saddest
grievings, pray?
The wailing lover of some wanton gay and bright, art thou,
Paynim?
Why on the polished mirror dost thou thus so frequent cast
thine eyes?
Bewildered and distraught at thine own beauty's sight art
thou, Paynim?
I've heard that poor Nedīm hath been by cruel Paynim captive
ta'en—
That fierce oppressor of the Faith, and foe of right, art thou,
Paynim?

Nedīm.

GAZEL

O HEART! e'en though thou tell'st thy woes, yon maid will
   ne'er compassion deign:
When constancy and troth thou seek'st, dost thou address the
   barren plain?
The student of the course of tyranny is yonder wanton
   wild;
To look for faith or grace from her who enmity desires is
   vain.
That paynim glance doth hold in hand a dagger sharp of
   point and keen;
And yet, O babe, my heart, thou dost to thousands sing her
   praises' strain.
In hope that it would yield the soul a breath of favor's odor
   sweet,
How yonder rosebud-mouth effaceth all, thou dost thereto
   explain.
O Sabqatī, what wondrous science hath thy magic talent
   learnt,
That thou right royally inditest every joyous, glad refrain?

Sabqatī.

GAZEL

A ROSE-LEAF o'er the spikenard fall'n—the red fez lies on her
   dark hair;
The perspiration studs her cheeks—the dew-drops which the
   roses wear.
Since mirrored in th' o'erflowing bowl did yon cup-bearer's
   chin beam bright,
My eyes were fixed upon that wine, like bubbles which that
   wine did bear.
Behold thou, then, her braided locks, as musk, all dark and
   sweet perfumed;
Like ambergris, her tresses shed abroad an odor rich and
   rare.

Those who set forth on Mystic Path behind soon leave the
     earth-born love;
The Bridge, as home, within this world of ours, no man hath
     taken e'er.
Now, O Belīg, that steed, thy reed, doth caracole across this
     page;
Thy finger-points, the Hayder bold whom that Duldul doth
     onward bear.

Belīg.

ON A DANCING-GIRL

WHEN that beauty of a dancing-girl her castanets hath
     ta'en,
Should the sun and moon behold her, jealous, each were rent
     in twain.
Patience from my soul is banished when beginneth she to
     dance;
Leaps with her my heart; my eyesight, faltering, is like to
     wane.
When the moon looks down upon her, must it not be seared
     of heart?
Yonder moon-fair one her crimson skirt for halo bright hath
     ta'en.
In her motions and her pausings what varieties of grace!
While her lovely frame doth tremble, like to quicksilver,
     amain!
Full delighted at her motions, loud as thunder roars the
     drum;
Beats its breast the tambourine, its bells commence to mourn
     and plain.
When she cometh, like a fairy, begging money from the
     crowd,
In her tambourine, had one a hundred lives, he'd cast them
     fain.
Deck her out on gala-days, and take her by the hand,
     Belīg;
Yonder spark-like Idol hath consumed my soul with fiery
     pain.

Belīg.

GAZEL

SURGE in waves my streaming tears, e'en like a rushing flood,
    once more,
From their smallest drop, the sources of a hundred Niles
    would pour.
Overwhelm the raging billows of my tears the heart's frail bark,
Though the mem'ry of her cheek, like to the beacon, radiance
    throw.
What my pen writes down appeareth, in the eyes of brutish
    men,
Like the needle to the blinded, of discerning clear the foe.
One the beggar's bowl would be with the tiara of the King,
Were it but reversed, for then like to the royal crown 'twould
    show.
Though it be coarse as a rush-mat, is that soul the seat of
    grace,
Which doth, like the wattle basket, freely bread to guests be-
    stow.
" Yonder hair-waist I encircled," did the braggart rival say;
But her waist exists not—hair-like slight his boasting's truth
    doth show.
O thou vain one! see, what anguish to the head of Nimrod
    brought
Was by one gnat's sting, which like to trunk of elephant did
    grow.
Sāmī, it is thy intention to compare to heaven's bowers
These thy distichs eight, with shining flowers of rhetoric that
    glow.   *Sāmī.*

FRAGMENT

THINK not that with Kevser's praises hearts become of joy
    full;
Preacher, rather doth the tale of mouth and kiss the soul rule.
Thinking of her rubies red, whene'er I drink tobacco,
The *nargila's* a flask of wine, the pipe-bowl is a *sumbul.*
Know how holy is her land: who dwelleth in Edirna,
Ere he to the Ka'ba bends, doth turn him to Istambul.
                                                    Sāmī.

GAZEL

NEAR thy rubies, ne'er I bow my head to wine of rosy hue;
'Neath the shadow of the Magian priest, I ne'er the glass
   eschew.
Now it makes me exile's prisoner, now the comrade close of
   pain—
What to do I know not, what with this sad fate of mine to
   do!
E'en the Home of Peace it turneth to the cot of woe for me,
Through the longing for thy dusky mole, when Shām I jour-
   ney through.
Since 'tis needful midst the people that I still reside and
   move,
If the days ne'er suit me, I shall suit myself the days unto.
Never unto Nev-res, never, will thy sweet words bitter seem;
Speak thou, then, for I'm contented all reproach to hearken to.

                             Nev-res.

GAZEL

IF the fair one would but come in her lover's home to
   stay,
Were his eyes not filled with light by her face as bright as
   day?
Or would yonder Moon but dart that her glance as dagger
   keen,
And my rival's bosom pierce that, like flute, he breathe dis-
   may!
Fly not this poor one, Moon-face, who hath drunken deep of
   woe;
Order not that I be burned in the fire of love, I pray.
If the Grace of God the Lord to a slave should aider be,
Though he lack a single groat he'll the Sphere as monarch
   sway.
Rush the tear drops from my eyes through their longing for
   thy face;
By its power thy sun-like face doth the dew-drops steal
   away.

By the Mystic Pathway's side, if thou'rt wise, a hostel build,
For the travellers of Love, as a caravanserai.
Proud and noble mistress mine, with those eyebrows and those
    eyes,
Where a need of bow and shaft this thy lover fond to slay?
Thou hast loosed thy tresses dark, o'er thy day-face spread a
    veil—
Or in House of Scorpio is the Moon eclipsèd, say?
Should my loved one pierce my breast, right contented sooth
    were I;
Only worthy of her grace let that Moon-face me survey.
Write, O pen, that I desire, like the salamander, fire;
Thus declare, should she it will, yonder lovely Queen Humāy.
Is it then the shining moon that the world doth silver o'er,
Or the radiance of thy face that doth earth in light array?
Did the caviller dispute and thy sun-bright face decry,
Would thy lover, like the mote, to that fool the truth convey.
Lovers surely for their loves do their talents aye employ;
Is it thine thy tribute now to present, Shāhīn Girāy?

Shāhīn Girāy.

THE SONG OF LOVE'S NURSE

O Moon! sleep, sleep thou, for this night
The cry "O Lord!" upon thine ear shall smite;
Though formed, its purpose is yet hid from sight,
It shall be seen—the stars' potential might.
    Thou'lt be the roast upon the spit of pain!

O Rosebud! sleep thou, then, this little while;
The Sphere's design against thee sooth is vile,
For pitiless is it and strong in guile;
Ah! never trust it, even though it smile.
    Thou'lt have, I fear me, reason oft to plain!

O Love's Narcissus! sleep the sleep of peace!
Fall at the skirt of Fate and beg surcease;
Thy soul's eye ope—and, lo! thy fears increase!
Guard thee against the end of woe, nor cease.
    Thou'lt be as plaything by Misfortune ta'en!

Come, in the cradle of repose thee rest
A few short nights, by sorrow undistrest;
Bid care and all it brings leave thee unprest;
In place of milk, blood shall be thy bequest.
    Thou'lt need the goblet of despite to drain!

O Jasmine-breast! within the cradle lie;
Thus will not long remain the rolling Sky:
The stars do not aye in one circle hie;
See what they'll do to thee, Love, by and by.
    Thou'lt be the mill on sorrow's torrent's train!

From slumber do not thou thine eyelids keep,
If aid can reach thee, it will come through sleep;
The Sphere will give a draught of poison deep,
Then will thy work, like Gālib's, be to weep.
    Thou'lt be the *rebec* at the feast of pain!

Gālib.

LOVE'S SONG

SWEET were those moments when the heart was gay,
And the soul's realm, the court of joy's array;
Thoughts of those times now o'er my spirit stray,
For love of God! O Heavens! mercy! pray!
    The pride of both the day and night was I.

A garden fair was that my soul's repose;
Like those in Eden's bower, its every rose;
But parting comes and all of that o'erthrows,
Now in my heart naught but its mem'ry glows.
    With honor's wine then drunken quite was I.

Then to the Sphere I never uttered prayer;
Feast, music, and delight—all mine—were there;
Moved ever by my side my Cypress fair;
Unopened then my secret and despair.
    The envy of the springtide bright was I.

Now before grief and woe I'm fallen prone;
Like nightingale in early spring, I moan.
Through fire I've past and to the shore have flown,
And, like the shattered glass, to earth am thrown.
    Sipping the wine, the fair's despite, was I.

Ah me! alas! those happy hours are past;
The spring is past; the rose, the flowers, are past;
The smiles of her who graced the bowers are past;
The thirsty soul remains, the showers are past.
    Drinking with her the wine so bright was I.

I with my loved one feast and banquet made,
Wild as the whirlpool then I romped and played;
At wine-feasts I myself in light arrayed,
And with my songs the nightingales dismayed.
    Like Gālib, blest with all delight was I.

Gālib.

GAZEL

THE mem'ry of his glance hid in my breast deep laid I
    found;
It seemed as though a fawn within the lion's glade I
    found.
O heart! a parallel unto those eyebrows and that glance,
In Rustem's deadly bow and Qahramān's bright blade I
    found.
When, through my grieving at thine absence, dead of woe
    was I,
That mem'ry of thy rubies' kiss new life conveyed I
    found.
My heart's wound, through the beauty of the spring of love
    for thee,
By turns, rose, tulip, Judas-tree of crimson shade, I found.
Is't strange, O Fitnet, if my soul around do scatter gems?
Within the ink-horn's vault a hidden treasure laid I found.

Fitnet Khānim.

MUSEDDES

THE fresh spring clouds across all earth their glistening
    pearls profuse now sow;
The flowers, too, all appearing, forth the radiance of their
    beauty show.
Of mirth and joy 'tis now the time, the hour to wander to
    and fro;
The palm-tree o'er the fair ones' picnic gay its grateful shade
    doth throw.
    O Liege, come forth! from end to end with verdure doth
       the whole earth glow;
    'Tis springtide now again, once more the tulips and the roses
       blow.

Behold the roses, how they shine, e'en like the cheeks of maids
    most fair;
The fresh-sprung hyacinth shows like to beauties' dark, sweet,
    musky hair.
The loved one's form behold, like cypress which the stream-
    let's bank doth bear;
In sooth, each side for soul and heart doth some delightful
    joy prepare.
    O Liege, come forth! from end to end with verdure doth
       the whole earth glow;
    'Tis springtide now again, once more the tulips and the roses
       blow.

The parterre's flowers have all bloomed forth, the roses, sweet-
    ly smiling, shine;
On every side lorn nightingales, in plaintive notes discoursing,
    pine;
How fair, carnation and wallflower the borders of the garden
    line!
The long-haired hyacinth and jasmine both around the cypress
    twine.
    O Liege, come forth! from end to end with verdure doth
       the whole earth glow;
    'Tis springtide now again, once more the tulips and the roses
       blow.

Arise, my Prince! the garden's court hath wondrous joys in
    fair array;
Oh, hark, there midst the rose's boughs, the wailing nightin-
    gale's fond lay
Thy bright cheek show the new-oped rose and make it blush
    with shamed dismay;
With graceful air come then, thy cypress mien before the mead
    display.
  O Liege, come forth! from end to end with verdure doth
    the whole earth glow;
  'Tis springtide now again, once more the tulips and the roses
    blow.

Enow! thy lovers pain no more, of faithful plight the days
    are now;
On streamlet's banks, of mirth and joy and gay delight the
    days are now;
In hand then take the heart's dear joy, the goblet bright, its
    days are now;
O Fitnet, come, and these thy verses sweet recite, their days
    are now.
  O Liege, come forth! from end to end with verdure doth
    the whole earth glow;
  'Tis springtide now again, once more the tulips and the roses
    blow.

Fitnet Khānim.

GAZEL

Ah! through grief for thee mine eyes blood, every night and
    day, weep;
Those who know my bitter sorrow's secret pang for aye weep.
When they see me blood-besmearèd by my bosom's red wound,
Pitying my doleful plight, the garden's flowerets gay weep.
When he viewed my bleeding heart, ruth had yon physician;
Quoth he: "Doth the cure for thee, Sick of love-dismay,
    weep."
Yet to me doth yonder Torment of the Soul no grace show;
For my plight do all my friends, who me thus sick survey,
    weep.

E'en as gazeth on thy cheek, amidst his woes, Ilhāmī,
Though his face may smiling be, his heart doth blood alway
    weep.

Ilhāmī.

GAZEL

MIDST the orchard of the world though empire may appear
    delight,
Still, if thou wouldst view it closely, empire is but ceaseless
    fight.
Vain let no one be who ruleth kingdoms in these woful
    days;
If in justice lie thy pleasure—then is empire truly right.
Reacheth e'en one lover union in the space of thousand years?
Let whoever sees it envy—empire is of faithless plight.
Think, O heart, alas! the revolutions of the rolling Sphere!
If at times 'tis joy, far oftener empire bringeth dire affright.
Do not envy, do not covet, then, the Kingship of the world;
Oh! take heed, Ilhāmī, empire bides not, swift indeed its
    flight.

Ilhāmī.

GAZEL

THE trees and flowers their turbans roll of black and white
    and red;
The garden fastens on its stole of black and white and red.
With sable eve and ermine dawn and fez of sunset bright,
The sky doth all its pomp unroll of black and white and red.
The pupils of my eyes are points upon the gleaming page,
With tears of blood I've writ a scroll of black and white and
    red.
The youthful Magian's locks and breast were shadowed in the
    wine;
It seemed as though they filled the bowl with black and white
    and red.
Is't ambergris, or is it pearl, or coral, Fāzil, say,
This poesy thy reed doth troll, of black and white and red?

Fāzil Beg.

DESCRIPTION OF CIRCASSIAN WOMEN

Ah! her cheek doth rob the fair sun of its sight,
And her sweet grace envy brings to Venus bright.
Like to moons are the Circassian damsels fair;
Whatso'er the lover seeks he findeth there.
Like to tall palm-trees their slender forms in grace,
Or a ladder to the clear moon of the face.
With the two feet of the eyes doth one ascend,
But the vision of the mind too one must bend.
Since their lips and cheeks are taverns of wine,
Is it strange their eyes inebriate should shine?
Since like rubies are created their two lips,
Doubly seared the lover's heart, like the tulip's.
Since their bodies are distilled from moon and sun,
How an equal to their pure frame find can one?
Though they lovelier than Georgians may be,
Still in Georgians one will great attractions see.
Closely curtained sit they all in virtue's place;
Pure of skirt is ever this unrivalled race;
Pure and free from stain is every act of theirs;
Not a soil the vestment of their honor bears;
Marked with chastity indeed, of noble heart,
Ever seeking to fulfil the righteous part;
Bright with bounty and fidelity and sense,
How that blessèd nature glows with light intense!
Think not with this race that any can compare
Upon earth, unless it be the Georgian fair.

Fāzil Beg.

DESCRIPTION OF GREEK WOMEN

Oh! thou the Bell upon the church of pain!
Thou the Pride of all the Messianic train!
Source of being! if a mistress thou should seek,
Then, I pray thee, let thy loved one be a Greek.
Unto her the fancies of the joyous bend,
For there's leave to woo the Grecian girl, my friend.

Caskets of coquetry are the Grecian maids,
And their grace the rest of womankind degrades.
What that slender waist so delicate and slight!
What those gentle words the sweet tongue doth indite!
What those blandishments, that heart-attracting talk!
What that elegance, that heart-attracting walk!
What that figure, as the cypress tall and free—
In the park of God's creation a young tree!
What those attitudes, those motions, wondrous fair!
What that glance inebriate that showeth there!
Given those disdainful airs to her alone,
And her legacy that accent and that tone.
All those letters on her sweet tongue's tip are rolled,
And those words with many graces she'll unfold;
Strung the regal pearls of her enchanting speech,
Pounded seem they when her gentle mouth they reach;
To her tongue if come a letter harsh to say,
Then her sweet mouth causeth it to melt away;
Her mouth would fain the words conserve in sooth,
For her mouth is speech-conserves in very truth;
Speaking parrots are they surely one and all,
To their portion doth the birdies' language fall.
With a thousand graces saith her rosebud lip:
" Zee vine, O noble Lord, vill zou no sip?
When thy glass is empty, fill it full again,
To my love drink, O my Pacha, drink amain!"
To the soul add life her ways and charms so dear,
Surely thus is it a mistress should appear.
E'en the old misogynist would conquered be,
Saw he yonder maid, uxorious were he.
So symmetrical the line her body shows,
One would it a balanced hemistich suppose.
Other women seek to imitate her grace,
As their pride and frontispiece she holds her place.
What that figure tall, and what that graceful mien!
Fair-proportioned is her body ever seen.
Moving lithely, she from side to side will turn,
That the hearts of all her lovers she may burn.
That cap which on one side she gayly wears;
That jaunty step; those joyous heedless airs;

Those motions—they are just what me delight;
And her tripping on two toes—how fair a sight!
'Twere as though with fire her pathway were inlaid,
That would burn the feet of yonder moon-like maid.
Thou wouldst deem her lovers' hearts upon her way,
Burning with their love for her, all scattered lay.

.   .   .   .

Is't herself they call " Qoqona " let us see?
Or her locks?—how wondrous sweet their odors be!
As the sash trails on the ground beneath thy feet,
So will she thy feet salute with kisses sweet.
Misbeliever, thou dost sense steal from the heart;
Torment thou—I know not what a Woe thou art;
Know not I if thou be *hūrī* or *perī*,
Know not I of Mary what is found in thee;
Art thou Mary's, child of 'Imrān's, rosebud bright?
Of the dwelling of the monks art thou the light?
Envy bearing to her hinna-crimsoned hand,
Doth the red egg covered o'er with blushes stand.
With the Greek cannot thy genus e'er compare,
Deem I, be thou genius or *hūrī* fair!

Fāzil Beg.

ON THE DEFEAT OF THE FRENCH IN EGYPT
BY THE QAPUDAN HUSEYN PACHA

O THOU Nīrem, battle-waging, of the world's fierce field of
    fight!
O thou Sām, fell dragon-visaged, of the age's plain of might!
Thou art he in whom the favors of the Lord Most High unite;
Earth and ocean thou hast conquered, waging war on left
    and right!
Gold, in Islām's cause, thou pouredst like to water down a
    height;
Legions like the Nile on Egypt's shore thou madest to alight.
With thy sabre's blow right fiercely thou the foeman's head
    didst smite;
Giddy made thy sword the misbelievers' chieftains with
    affright.

Midst the earth's oak-grove a valiant lion like to thee in
  might,
Since the days of Rustem, ne'er hath passed beneath the Heav-
  ens' sight.
  "Bravo! Champion of the Epoch! rending ranks in ser-
    ried fight!
  O'er the 'Arsh hang now thy sabre, sparkling like the
    Pleiads bright!"

Lion! Alexander! had he seen that battle thou didst gain,
Crown and throne to thee to offer Key-Qubād were surely
  fain!
O most noble! thou a Vezīr to such fame that dost attain,
That the God of Hosts did surely Lord of Fortune thee or-
  dain!
Like to flame, the fiery blast scathed foemen's lives, it blazed
  amain;
Threw'st thou, cinder-like, the misbelievers' ashes o'er the
  plain.
"Conqueror of the Nations' Mother" as thy title should be
  ta'en;
Since thou'st saved the Nations' Mother, all the nations joy
  again.
Wishing long ago, 'twould seem, to sing thy splendid glory's
  strain,
Nef'ī wrote for thee this couplet—for thy deeds a fit re-
  frain:
  "Bravo! Champion of the Epoch! rending ranks in ser-
    ried fight!
  O'er the 'Arsh hang now thy sabre, sparkling like the
    Pleiads bright!"

When the misbelieving Frenchman sudden swooped on Egypt's
  land,
Thither was the army's leader sent by the Great King's command;
But at length o'erthrown and vanquished by the foe his luckless band,
Then thou wentest and the vile foe scatter'dst wide on every
  hand;

Then, when they thy lightning-flashing, life-consuming cannon
    scanned,
Knew the hell-doomed misbelievers vain were all things they
    had planned.
Hundred vezīrs, joy-attended, countless foemen did with-
    stand;
Day and night, three years the misbelievers fought they brand
    to brand;
Worn and wretched fell those at thy feet, and quarter did
    demand:
It beseems thee, howsoever high in glory thou mayst stand!
    "Bravo! Champion of the Epoch! rending ranks in ser-
        ried fight!
    O'er the 'Arsh hang now thy sabre, sparkling like the
        Pleiads bright!"

Through this joy beneath thy shade the world doth its desires
    behold;
With thy praises eloquent the tongues of all, both young and
    old.
Thou to Faith and Empire then didst render services
    untold
Hurling down to earth the foeman's house in one assault right
    bold!
O Vezīr! Jem-high! think not that flattery my words en-
    fold;
Though a poet, not with false or vaunting boasts I've thee
    extolled.
Midst the fight for Egypt's conquest firm in stirrup was thy
    hold,
Under thy Egyptian charger trod'st thou foemen like the
    mould.
From the handle of thy sword, like water, down the red blood
    rolled;
Thou the foe mad'st turn his face, mill-like, in terror uncon-
    trolled.
    "Bravo! Champion of the Epoch! rending ranks in ser-
        ried fight!
    O'er the 'Arsh hang now thy sabre, sparkling like the
        Pleiads bright!"

Those who sing thy glories, like to Wāsif, wildered aye must
 be;
Sayeth Wāsif: "None on earth like Huseyn Pacha I shall
 see."
If there be who has in vision seen a peerless one like thee,
As a dream all void of meaning, let him it relate to me.
Cannon-ball like, 'gainst the foe thou threw'st thyself from
 terror free;
Like the winter blast thou mad'st the foeman shake in front
 of thee.
Claim to manliness forsaking, even as the blind was he,
Sword in hand despairing stood he, like to one who naught can
 see;
Quick his throat thou seizedst, like the dragon direful in his
 glee,
'Neath thy sabre's wave thou drown'dst the misbeliever, like
 the sea!
 " Bravo! Champion of the Epoch! rending ranks in ser-
  ried fight!
 O'er the 'Arsh hang now thy sabre, sparkling like the
  Pleiads bright!"

Wāsif.

SHARQĪ

O ROSEBUD of joy's flowery lea!
O graceful one with step so free!
If thou wilt yield thee not to me,
 On earth the glass of mirth and glee
 To me's forbid, apart from thee.

Behold my breast, by guile unprest,
Is't not mid thousand treasures best?
Until thou tak'st me to thy breast,
 On earth the glass of mirth and glee
 To me's forbid, apart from thee.

O Rose-leaf fresh! concealed from sight
With thee till morn a livelong night
If I may not enjoy delight,
 On earth the glass of mirth and glee
 To me's forbid, apart from thee.

Yearning for union fills my soul,
Patience and peace have no control;
O wanton one! my longing's goal!
    On earth the glass of mirth and glee
    To me's forbid, apart from thee.

Seek, Wāsif, her who hearts doth snare
Yon maid with bosom silver-fair;
Until thou thither dost repair,
    On earth the glass of mirth and glee
    To me's forbid, apart from thee.

                                    Wāsif.

SHARQĪ

To whom that wine-red ruby's shown
Is captive by those locks o'erthrown;
'Tis meet like nightingale I moan:
    A lovely Scio Rose is blown.

Unmatched yon maid with waist so spare,
Unrivalled too her wanton air;
Her ways than e'en herself more fair:
    A lovely Scio Rose is blown.

The roses like her cheeks are few;
That rose—blush-pink its darling hue;
This summer ere the roses blew,
    A lovely Scio Rose is blown.

The rose—the nightingale's amaze;
The rose the nightingale dismays;
A smile of hers the world outweighs:
    A lovely Scio Rose is blown.

O Wāsif, on the rosy lea,
The nightingale thus spake to me:
" Be joyful tidings now to thee—
    A lovely Scio Rose is blown."

                                    Wāsif.

GAZEL

ALTHOUGH my heart the truth of Those who wrong them-
　　selves doth show, O Lord!
In virtue of the words Do not despair, Thy love bestow, O
　　Lord!
Beside the mead of truth and calm make aye my soul to go,
　　O Lord!
My virtue's rose to tint and scent as captive do not throw, O
　　Lord!
From vain attachments' stain wash pure and clean my heart
　　as snow, O Lord!
Against me place not Thou the loathsome pool of lies of foe,
　　O Lord!
The burning pain of exile no relief can ever know, O Lord!
Enow, if Thou the camphor-salve, the dawn of hope, did
　　show, O Lord!
Thy slave is Rāmiz; unto none save Thee doth he bend low,
　　O Lord!
Before Thy mercy's gate his tears from eyes and eyelids flow,
　　O Lord!

Rāmiz Pacha.

GAZEL

AFTER old rags longing hath the figure tall and slight of
　　Love?
Fresh and fresh renews itself aye the brocade fire-bright of
　　Love.
'Gainst the flames from thorns and thistles ne'er a curtain can
　　be wove,
Nor 'neath honor's veil can hide the public shame, the blight
　　of Love.
Through a needle's eye it sometimes vieweth far-off Hindu-
　　stān—
Blind anon in its own country is the piercing sight of Love.
It will turn it to a ruin where naught save the owl may dwell,
In a home should chance be set the erring foot of plight of
　　Love.

Will a single spark a hundred thousand homes consume at
    times:
One to me are both the highest and the lowest site of Love.
Never saw I one who knoweth—O most ignorant am I!
Yet doth each one vainly deem himself a learnèd wight in
    Love.
Rent and shattered—laid in ruins—all my caution's fortress
    vast
Have my evil Fate, my heart's black grain, the rage, the blight
    of Love.
In its hell alike it tortures Mussulmān and infidel,
'Izzet, is there chance of freedom from its pangs, this plight
    of Love?
Of reality hath made aware the seeker after Truth,
Showing lessons metaphoric, He, the Teacher bright, St. Love!

'Izzet Molla.

GAZEL

That I'm fall'n her conquered slave, yon maiden bright feigns
    not to know;
Thus pretending, she who doth the soul despite feigns not to
    know.
Though I fail naught in her service, she doth me as alien treat;
Know not I why yonder Darling, earth's Delight, feigns not
    to know.
If I dare to speak my eager longing those her lips to kiss,
Friendship she disclaims, in sooth with cruel slight feigns not
    to know.
That she whets her glance's arrow and therewith doth pierce
    the heart,
E'en her bow-like eyebrow, yonder Ban of might feigns not
    to know.
Well the loved one knows the Sphere doth keep no faithful
    troth; but, ah!
How she copies it, that Heart-ensnarer bright feigns not to
    know.
There is ne'er a refuge, 'Adlī, from the grief of rivals' taunts;
I my love conceal not, still yon maiden slight feigns not to
    know.

'Adlī.

ON THE DEATH OF 'ANDELĪB KHĀNIM

'ANDELĪB, th' adopted sister, from this transient world hath
　　flown,
Yonder midst the flowers of Eden while still in her youth to
　　stray.
No physician, neither charmer, on the earth her pain could
　　ease;
So that youthful beauty bided not to smile on earth's mead
　　gay.
With her two-and-twenty summers, cypress-like was she, ah
　　me!
But the sullen blast of autumn smote her life's bright, lovely
　　May.
For its tyranny and rancor might have blushed the vile, hard
　　Sphere,
As the sister of earth's Monarch pined in grief without
　　allay.
Though her kind friend never parted from her eye's sweet,
　　gentle beam,
Still did she to God her soul yield, and the call, Return,
　　obey.
Down the wayward Sphere hath stricken that bright Jewel to
　　the earth;
What avail though men and angels tears of blood shed in
　　dismay?
Length of days to that great Sultan grant may He, the God
　　of Truth!
And yon fair Pearl's tomb make rival His own Eden's bright
　　display!
With the dotted letters, Leylā, thou the year tell'st of her
　　death—
　　Calm among delightsome bowers may 'Andelīb her nest
　　　array!

Leylā Khānim.

TAKHMĪS

'TIS yonder Darling of my soul that wildering my sense o'erthrows;
My waving Cypress 'tis that freshness to the garden doth disclose;
The bird, my heart, my gardener is in Love's fair parterre of
the rose:
  Mine eyes' field with thy cheek's reflection as my flowery
  orchard shows;
  For long my heart the picture of thy palm-like figure doth
  enclose.

The world seems in my eyes as prison that doth my dear love
control;
Through love for thee my heart acquireth many a scar, and
that's the whole;
From hour to hour thine absence makes my tears like rushing
waters roll:
  The heart bows down through grief for thee, and constant
  weeps the life, the soul;
  The fountain of this vineyard is the stream that from my
  weeping flows.

As well thou know'st, through fire of love for thee how sad
my plight of woe,
My smiling Rosebud, wilt thou ne'er a glance of pity toward
me throw?
My sighs and wailings thou dost see, Oh, but for once compassion show:
  Through gazing on the rose and bower, my heart repose
  shall never know,
  The ward where doth my loved one dwell alone can yield
  my soul repose.

Oh, how I think upon thy box-tree form in sorrow's night so
drear!
My story would Mejnūn's and Ferhād's tales from mind make
disappear.

My groans and sighs and wails thus high do I unto the Heav-
　　ens uprear,
　　By reason of the sparks my sighings raise that steely bowl,
　　　　the Sphere,
　　Revolves each night, my gold-enamelled beaker at the feast
　　　　of woes.

From thought of yonder witching eye my heart is ne'er a mo-
　　ment free;
When flow thy tears recall not thou to mind, O Leylā, 'Omān's
　　Sea.
Beneath thy shade my own heart's blood is all that hath been
　　gained by me:
　　My tears, an ocean vast; my lashes, coral branches, O Bāqī!
　　The mem'ry, 'tis of thy palm-form that as my Judas-tree
　　　　bright glows.　　　　　　　　　　　　*Leylā Khānim.*

SHARQĪ

OUR hopes, our thoughts, are for the weal of our dear native
　　land;
Our bodies form the rampart strong to guard our frontier
　　strand:
We're Ottomans—a gory shroud our robe of honor grand.
　　" God is Most Great! " we shout in rush and charge on field
　　　　of fight;
　　We're Ottomans! our lives we give, our gain is glory
　　　　bright.

The name of Ottoman with terror doth the hearer thrill;
The glories of our valiant fathers all the wide world fill;
Think not that nature changeth—nay, this blood is yon blood
　　still.
　　" God is Most Great! " we shout in rush and charge on field
　　　　of fight;
　　We're Ottomans! our lives we give, our gain is glory
　　　　bright. ·

A sabre on a blood-red field—our banner famed behold!
Fear in our country dwelleth not, in mountain or in wold:
In every corner of our land croucheth a lion bold.

" God is Most Great ! " we shout in rush and charge on field
of fight ;
We're Ottomans ! our lives we give, our gain is glory
bright.

Then let the cannon roar, and shower its flames on every side !
For those our brothers brave let Heaven ope its portals wide !
What have we found on earth that one from death should flee
or hide ?
" God is Most Great ! " we shout in rush and charge on field
of fight ;
We're Ottomans ! our lives we give, our gain is glory
bright.   *Ref'et Beg.*

GAZEL

A TAVERN which each moment takes a life as pleasure's pay is
earth ;
A glass which for a thousand souls doth sell each drop of
spray is earth.
The world's a Magian that adores the flame of power and
fortune high ;
If thou should brightly shine, a moth about thy taper's ray is
earth.
Anon one is, anon is not—thus ever runs the course of time ;
From end to end a warning-fraught, a strange, romantic lay
is earth,
'Twixt sense and frenzy 'tis indeed right hard to draw the
sund'ring line,
Ah me ! if understanding's wise, demented sooth alway is
earth.
The desolation of the world beside its weal is truth itself ;
Just as prosperity it seems, so ruin and decay is earth.
How many Khusrevs and Jemshīds have come, and from its
bower have passed !
A theatre that vieweth many and many an act and play is
earth.
Ziyā, a thousand caravans of wise men through its realms
have passed ;
But yet not one can tell its tale, and all unknown this day is
earth.   *Ziyā Beg.*

ON A BEYT OF MAHMŪD NEDĪM PACHA

HEART! heart! how long shall last this sorrow, anguish, and
dismay?
All things upon earth's ruin-cumbered waste must needs
decay.
What was the splendor of Jemshīd? where Khusrev and where
Key?
Hold fast the goblet and the wine, let chance not fleet
away!
    " Our coming to this world is one; man must reflect, sur-
    vey;
    Care must one banish, and look out for calm and quiet aye."

Be he Khusrev, or Rustem, or Nerīmān, or Jemshīd,
Or be he beggar; be Islām or heathenesse his creed;
A few days in earth's inn a guest is he, then must he
speed:
Something to render gay that time is surely wisdom's need.
    " Our coming to this world is one; man must reflect, sur-
    vey;
    Care must one banish, and look out for calm and quiet aye."

When viewed with understanding's eye, the mote hath no
repose;
The world must thus be imaged for exemption from its woes:
Of my coming and my going it no lasting picture shows—
That a departure surely is which no returning knows.
    " Our coming to this world is one; man must reflect, sur-
    vey;
    Care must one banish, and look out for calm and quiet aye."

Events the workings of the Lord Most High make manifest;
Being the mirror is in which the Absolute's exprest;
He who this mystery perceives in every state is blest;
The exit of each one who enters earth decreed doth rest.
    " Our coming to this world is one; man must reflect, sur-
    vey;
    Care must one banish, and look out for calm and quiet aye."

See that thou grievest not thyself with sorrows all unwise;
'Tis need all pleasure to enjoy as far as in thee lies;
Alike is he who lives in joy and he whom trouble tries;
If thou be prudent, ne'er thine opportunities despise.
  " Our coming to this world is one; man must reflect, sur-
    vey;
  Care must one banish, and look out for calm and quiet aye."

Since first the banquet fair, this world, was cast in form's de-
    signs,
How many rakes have passed away! how many libertines!
As counsel meet for revellers, when he perceived those signs,
Around the goblet's rim the Magian priest engraved these
    lines:
  " Our coming to this world is one; man must reflect, sur-
    vey;
  Care must one banish, and look out for calm and quiet aye."

At length, Ziyā, shall joy beam forth, and grief an end shall
    find;
But yet, O man, these ever enter Fortune's feast combined.
This hidden mystery learn thou, by Mahmūd Beg defined,
Who has the secret of the same within this verse enshrined:
  " Our coming to this world is one; man must reflect, sur-
    vey;
  Care must one banish, and look out for calm and quiet aye."

                                                Ziyā Beg.

THE COUNSELS OF NABI EFENDI TO HIS SON ABOUL KHAIR

—

[*Translated by A. P. de Courteille and Robert Arnot*]

INTRODUCTION

N ABI YOUSOUF EFENDI was born at Roha, about the year 1632, during the reign of Mourad IV. Coming to Constantinople in the time of Mahomet IV, he there attached himself to the all-powerful favorite Mustafa Pacha, who made him his secretary. In 1684, his protector having been made Serasker, he accompanied him to Morée. From there, he undertook the pilgrimage to Mecca and to Medina, and finally settled at Halep. It was during his stay in this city, about the year 1694, that he wrote, as he himself says, the poem dedicated to his son Aboul Khair. Some years after, Baltadji Mohammed Pacha, who was much attached to Nabi, recalled him to Constantinople, and appointed him president of the State treasury of Anatolia. He exchanged this position, however, for that of comptroller of the cavalry, in which he remained until his death, which occurred the twelfth of April, 1712.

Nabi is one of the Turkish classic authors; he occupies in Ottoman literature an exalted position, not only as a poet, but also as a prose writer. Under the title of Zeili Nabi, he wrote in the purest and most stately style an appendix to the " Life of Mahomet," by Weïsi; this work was printed in Cairo in 1248. The imperial library has a copy of the complete works of Nabi. The manuscript is well written, but is filled with clerical errors. Beside the poems, it contains the letters of Nabi and his treatise on Mecca and Medina. The divan of our author is of considerable length; therein are found kàssidès, chronograms, gazels, and two poems written for his son: the " Khairiyè " and the " Khair-abâd." This divan was written at Cairo in 1257.

The manuscript which has been used to verify the text was obtained from a learned teacher named Chinaci Efendi. The translator has also referred, although with reserve, to the manuscript of the Imperial Library. The Cairo edition has not been very useful; it includes many readings, which are doubtful at best, and which have not been thought sufficiently important to note.

Those who have translated oriental poems know how difficult it is to remain exact without becoming unintelligible. The translator has endeavored to condense the text as much as possible, and has only departed from it insomuch as was necessary in order to make it intelligible. There is an obscure vagueness in Turkish poetry which passes for a kind of beauty in oriental eyes. The reader's imagination loves to wander among these brilliant clouds; but the translator, forced to express himself clearly and openly, suffers much from this element of uncertainty.

The translator's aim has been, above all, to provide for persons who are studying the Turkish language a work of a simple and elegant classic style and of moderate price, which will be a preparation for the reading of more difficult writings.

THE COUNSELS OF NABI EFENDI

CHAPTER I

ALL praise to the Most High God, Creator of all that exists; who with his all-powerful pen has traced the characters of the world. Benign Lord, whose mercy is stretched forth over all men, whose benevolent hand has graven the image of existence on the tablet of the vow, from that void which, like a funeral mound, opened and disclosed its secrets. The Lord weighed in the balance of destiny chaos and existence; the aspect of existence became brilliant, and its forms were reflected in the mirror of chaos, whose burning gulf disappeared, and the veil which concealed the world was raised. Land was extended like a mantle over the world, and above was curved the celestial dome. The four elements and heaven became as a festal cup adorned with four roses. The Lord, uniting the two sexes, lit between them the torch of love. Then appeared the three reigns of nature: the mineral, the vegetable, and the animal. The inexhaustible munificence of the Almighty continued; next came the creation of man. God placed him above all living beings; formed from the slime of the earth, he was the noblest, the most perfect of all creatures. Although he had been moulded of earth and mud, the angels were ordered to bow down before him; the ladder of the divine decisions having been placed, man ascended to the first place in creation.

In all things there are different degrees, distinctions, and divisions, everything has different properties; nature has diversified all things, all men form quite distinct classes, and from these distinctions issues perfect order. Without them, the edifice of creation would be demolished; but how can the ignorant

167

understand the mysteries therein? Water cannot have all the properties of fire; earth cannot produce the effects of wind. Gold is impotent to replace iron; sugar will never have the flavor of salt. The foot does not play the same rôle as the hand; the lancet does not serve the purposes of the sword. Hearing cannot take the place of sight; the shoulder cannot reflect as does the mind. The jeweller does not know the weaver's art, nor does the carpenter understand the labors of the shoemaker. Nations understand nothing of the actions of those who govern them, and kings, in their turn, know not all that concerns their subjects. Warmth never produces the effect of cold; dryness and humidity are incompatible. Shade does not undergo the action of the sun, and the goblet is insensible to the transports agitating Djemschid.

Therefore understand this truth: thy nature is but formed of incongruous elements. Everywhere glaring contrasts are perceived in all objects. The wisdom and the might of God have no bounds, it is a spectacle without end. All the parts of creation are thus arranged: raise thy mind's eye as high as it can reach. In this world and in the next, in the form of facts as in their reality, on all sides are encountered different degrees. In the spiritual order there are also many distinctions, like a sea with innumerable waves. He who has penetrated the farthest in the mysteries of creation has said that society is only founded on the distinction of classes. The friends of God are high-placed, but higher still are those whom he has created prophets.

It may be said that the prophets are in the place of honor on the light-giving throne as a brilliant star which irradiates its marvellous splendor to far distant worlds. But above all, and in the most exalted place, sits the king of creation, he for whom all was created, pre-eminently the elect of God, the precious pearl of the ocean of divine generosity, the luscious fruit of the garden of creation, he who opened the gate of the treasure of light, he for whom was limned the picture of this world, he of whom it is written in the beginning of the book of fates, he in whom was all accomplished, the principle of the operations of divine mercy, the last end of the omnipotence of the Lord, he who includes in himself the form and essence of all things, the dazzling light of the torch of immutable destiny, the ornament of existence's throne, the guardian of the treasures of altitude and depth, and the seal of the mystery of the two worlds.

He it is who hath approached to God as near as two arcs, or even nearer, to whom all has been revealed; who, mounted proudly on the mighty Boraq, traversed the ethereal regions; the universal ruler throwing radiance over the domain of sovereign authority; the luminous eastern star of science, the all-excelling master of the apostolate of nations, on whom descended the glorious revelation, the most beautiful among the children of men, the most perfect of beings, the most noble of all creatures, the fountain of the graces shed on mankind, the soul of the world, the centre of creation, the illustrious and glorious Mahomet, in whom the Lord delights, the origin of all bearers of that venerable name, the most perfect of all in all degrees.

The word which proclaims him the first work come forth from the hands of God has shed universal joy. His person is the seal of glory and greatness; he is the centre of all purity, the arbiter of celestial revolutions; in him is the consummation of all perfection. As a seed concealed in the depths of the invisible earth, he appeared loaded with fruit. If you trace the rounded figure of a *mim* you will form Ahmed from the word Ahad, and if you ask where is the first letter of the Prophet's name, you will find it in the second part of the word Mahomet. The Lord has raised him above all; he has overwhelmed him with graces and blessings. Benedictions upon him, on his family and his friends till the day of resurrection!

CHAPTER II

Details of the Father's Station in Life

ABOUL KHAIR MOHAMMED TCHÉLEBI, thou who art the ornament of Halep, part of my being, substance of my life, first fruit of the garden of my happiness, thou art the luminous ray of my life, thou art the essence of the blessings which make me prosper. The Lord in his bounty has given thee to Nabi, O Joseph of thy father! O noble son! thou art indeed the living proof of the truth that the son is the joy of the father.

Thou art, O light of mine eyes, the ornament of the garden-
plot of paternal existence. Since thou hast become a shade
for my head I see thee alone in this world. Thou who art
endowed with all the graces, I have received thee from the
hand of the Almighty in my declining days.

When thou didst appear on the horizon of the world as a
moon of beauty, I had already passed my tenth lustre. Thou
wert given to me when I was fifty-four, and it is in thy eighth
year that this book is written. My place of nativity is the
charming city of Edessa; but I was dwelling in Halep when I
wrote this work. Edessa! type of the eternal flower-garden,
native soil of the well-beloved of God, object of the emula-
tion of all Syria, scene of the marvellous deliverance of Abraham! I sojourned thirty years at Adrianople and at Constantinople. Thanks to God! I, a poor slave, have been honored
with many dignities. Having no longer taste for business, I
enjoyed the repose given by retreat. The water and the excellence of the climate determined me to select Halep as an
abiding place.

CHAPTER III

Of the Motives which Decided the Author to Write the Book of Counsels

LIGHT of my hopes, gift bestowed on me by the omnipotent
and glorious God! God be praised, thou art of a noble family; thy ancestors have all distinguished themselves in science.
Although their worth is not sufficiently esteemed, learned men
all occupy an elevated position. But of what use is the worth
of thy father and of thy ancestors, if thou dost not raise thyself by thy talent? Thy origin is pure, O creature of God!
He who is well born ought not to fall! All that nature has
given me of worth is found complete in thyself. Thou hast
many noble and good qualities which nothing, by the grace of
God, can mar. Thy good nature sheds afar its perfume, thou
dost manifest the traces of innate morality. The grace of God
will come to thy aid, and thy natural capacities will easily surmount all difficulties. God protect thee and prosper thee!
mayst thou long sojourn in this transitory world!

But in order that paternal advice may make a profound impression upon children, and that you may cherish it as a precious jewel and make it the subject of your meditations, after having practised my mind and grasped the pen of art, and having brought forth from my heart's mine pearls worthy to wreathe a poetic garland, I wrote in verse a book of morals which may perhaps charm the intelligent. I have adorned it with the ornaments of poetry, and I have entitled it " The Good Book."

Reverently press it to thy heart, and look upon it as a guardian amulet. Each day, O soul of thy father, hearken to the words of this jewel. Engrave them with care on thy mind, and never separate from it a single instant. Let, until the day of the resurrection, its salutary influence be exerted on thee and on all others. As long as this table shall be prepared, may young people come to seat themselves here as thy guests. And thou, as much as thou shalt relish the joy of these riches, bless the name of thy father and of thy mother. Rejoice me by the expression of thy gratitude; then remember me in thy prayers.

CHAPTER IV

Of the Ranks of Islam

O CYPRESS of the slender form gracefully swaying in the garden of creation, learn from me what is the thing most necessary to man above all his temporal occupations. He should reflect on his end, he should embellish the edifice of his religion; the five columns on which this edifice rests are themselves based upon wisdom. It is within this enclosure that peace reigns; beyond, the shocks of adversity are to be feared. There extends a delightful garden; here opens the burning abyss of hell. There, also, are the sectarians of the straight and perfect road; here, those who are lost in error.

Observe religiously the precept of prayer; acquit thyself, if thou canst, of the obligation of pilgrimage and of the tithe in alms. Show proofs of zeal and activity in the accomplishment of these duties; do not show a criminal tendency to exempt thyself from them. Be not rebellious to the orders of the Almighty; obey all his commandments. All the salutary practices taught by religion are for Mussulmen like a robe with many folds. Recite the five prayers, O pure youth, if thou didst but know what graces thou drawest down upon thyself! Each of these practices has a mysterious meaning; a long discourse would be required to detail their merits.

The Lord, generous in his gifts, has made each of them the instrument of innumerable benefits. God has no need of thy works; 'tis thou alone who dost profit from thy wealth. O generous soul! thou alone wilt gather the fruit of thy good or evil actions.

CHAPTER V

Of the First Duty of True Religion

CHARMING branch of the garden of morality, thou who rejoicest the heart and eye of thy father, confess candidly thy faith that all the mysteries of creation may be revealed to thee. Make thy heart the shrine of truth; light there the flaming torch of uprightness and sincerity. Fill thy mouth with the honey of the profession of the Mahometan faith. Let all thy words breathe submission to divine truths. The profession of faith is the seal of the salvation of believers, the ornament of the blissful gate of paradise.

It is this profession which establishes a striking distinction between the shadow of impiety and the light of faith. On it rests the foundation of true power, and on it has risen the edifice of religion. It is the column of Islamism, the water which fills the ocean of divine decrees, the key to the straight path and that which opens the gate of that devotion agreeable unto God. It is, for the tongue which utters it, like a dish of exceeding sweet savor. It is its salutary virtue which vivifies those whose hearts are dead.

CHAPTER VI

Of the Excellence of Prayer

O ROSE of the ever-blooming garden, thou, the support of thy aged father, at the prescribed time perform the ablutions and purify thyself of exterior pre-occupation! Clothe thyself as with a robe of innocence and light that thou mayst be worthy to sit among pure men. Prayer, for the faithful, is as a celestial ascension; open thine eyes to this divine rapture. Consider not prayer as an irksome task; it is an honor which God deigns to grant us. It is the support of religion; and the corner stone of the house of faith. Incline devoutly in thy adorations; be among the faithful who surround the *mihrab*. Drag thy countenance in the dust before the Lord; be a slave in thy heart; consider his majesty. Prayer said without devotion is valueless in the sight of God; each time that thou dost bow down send forth to him a thousand ardent sighs. Plunge thyself completely in these holy practices; let thy reason succumb to a mysterious intoxication.

Far be it from thee to think of the delights of paradise or the torments of hell; love with all thy heart the sovereign Master of both. Yield not to sleep in the morning; be vigilant and assiduous in praying for the pardon of thy sins.

What happiness for thee to cross thy hands on thy breast and weep in the presence of thy God! When thou dost bow down, strike the earth with thy forehead; behold the potentates of this earth, O my son! is it permitted to everyone to salute the steps of their thrones?

The intelligent man, prostrated in the dust, does not raise his head; his eyes are not dazzled by a sudden brilliancy. Canst thou not be assiduous in the exercises of thy piety, if thou dost understand how precious they are to thee? I wish to disclose to thee a secret which is not permitted to be told to children. Apply thyself with all thy strength to understand it; thou wilt succeed in grasping its meaning. When thou dost pray while standing, is it not true, O youth beautiful as the full moon, that thou dost resemble an *élif?* But when thou art inclined, one might believe thou wert a *dal:* it is the enigma of the prophets, endeavor to understand it. If thou dost prostrate thyself the rounded form of a *mim* is seen, and then thou dost indeed merit the name of man. Forget not this truth which is revealed unto thee: he who neglects prayer is not a man.

CHAPTER VII

On the Excellence of Fasting

O MOST delicious of the fruits of the paternal garden! precious pearl of the sea of life! dost thou wish to avoid the maladies which afflict the body? neglect not the fast of Ramazan. Fasting is a grace which the Lord grants to his servants; he does not leave it without recompense. Fasting is a table prepared by the divine mercy: he who practises it wears a robe of light. It demands mystery and retreat; hypocrisy should not come to profane it. Fasting is a mysterious emanation from eternity: it is a figure of spiritual royalty. The Prophet said, speaking with the breath of one who fasts, that it was more pleasing to God than the odor of musk! Fasting is the herald of the joys of paradise: to renounce these joys is to condemn one's self to despair.

Until the shades of night begin to appear, let the disk of the sun be as a seal over thy mouth. As long as the jewel of thy being shall shine, abstain until darkness delivers thee from the eyes of the ᶜᵘᵣious. What happiness for thee to have closed lips: to be beyond all agitation, with closed mouth and quiet body, to polish the mirror of thine existence, to deliver thy nature from the trammels of matter, to make it beam with a radiance full of grace, to dissipate the shadows of thy soul's sanctuary, to be resplendent as the moon of the Ramazan!

CHAPTER VIII

Of Pilgrimage, of Sacred Journeys, and of Mount Arafat

O FRESHLY blooming rose of the garden-plot of my soul, perfume that dost charm the nostrils of courtesy, undertake no other journey but that of Caaba. A useless journey is as disastrous as the fire of hell. Caaba is the noblest of all the temples and the central point of the universe. It is the seat of royalty; the ornament of the foot of the throne of the Divinity; the trunk of the tree of divine mercy; the threshold of religion and of felicity; the torch that burns in the shrine of mysterious truths and whose brilliancy attracts suppliants as the candle the butterfly.   It is the mysterious reflection of the high heavens: the abode veiled in black of Leila; the place of the adoration of men and angels, where the celestial vault inclines in reverence.

It is the site of the garden-plot of delights, all shining with an ineffable light.   It is the station of the sacred mysteries; may God forever increase their significance!   It is the throne of the rule of the Omnipotent and the threshold of the court of the All-Merciful.   It is the centre of the earth around which the heavens accomplish their revolutions.   It might be compared to a holy man, tall in stature; and the black gem to the buckle of his girdle.   The black gem is the jewel of salvation kissed with awe by the friends of God.   It is the first thing honored by the hand of the Creator; the more precious than amber, adorning the earth's surface.   The chief treasure of the secrets of the Divinity's palace, the ornament of humanity's domain, the dust at its portals is as a balm to the eyes; 'tis the abode of generosity and the happy home of purity.   The life-giving water of the well of Zemzem is all prepared for the cleansing of our sins.   The holy ground is the glory of the well of Zemzem, itself the glory of the world.

Mercy escapes from its golden funnel in inexhaustible abundance, purifying our faults.   The water of Zemzem is a pure remedy which restores health to those who languish in separation.   When thou dost arrive to the limits of the sacred territory, then visit the two walls of the *ihrâm*.   The visiting of holy spots gives new life; each band of pilgrims participates in the divine mercy.   Each breath which escapes these breasts burning with love is as a spirit messenger ascending to heaven. O felicity, O delight, O unspeakable honor, to revolve around God's throne!   Over this sacred place of processions, that it be not profaned, let thy forehead be as a tapestry!   And thy heart, like a moth, should circle around this holy candle!   Diligently visit the court of the Author of all good.   L'Arifè is a figure of the gathering at resurrection and the solemn day of the counsel of the merciful Lord.   There the crowds which cover Mount Arafat receive the certificate of the pardon of sins.

There are purified those who were burdened with crime;
there are freed the slaves of sin. These culprits form a dazzling ring whose setting is the column of divine mercy. All
that was dark becomes white as snow; the record of evil deeds
is thrown in the fire. Mina is a vast market where pardon is
given in exchange for sins. The temple of Caaba is as the
heart of the world, and its black gem is its inmost part. Exert
thyself to penetrate the mystery of thy nature, formed of slime
and water; on this question exhaust all thy faculties. If thou
dost desire to discover its central point, imitate the compass that
always turns in the same circle.

CHAPTER IX

Of the Excellence of Alms-Giving

O PRECIOUS pearl, worthiest heir of a noble family, give till
the last *para* the alms prescribed by law: they will amass for
thee a capital of salvation and blessings. Alms are due unto
God: beware of negligence in paying him. Thou with whom
the Lord has so generously shared, dost thou not hasten to
purify thy wealth? Alms are the wealth of the poor; if thou
dost retain them unjustly, thou wilt tarnish a legitimately
acquired fortune. What thou dost give to obey the law of God,
he will return to thee tenfold. If thou dost refuse, he will withdraw his benediction, and thy prosperity will vanish. Wealth
not purified by alms is soon spent, and serves as a target for the
blows of adversity. That blessed by this holy practice is as a
seed which it pleases God to fructify. The grains dispersed here
and there will grow and multiply, and thou wilt derive profit
from them both in this world and in the next.

He who created poverty and wealth made alms the share of
the poor. By an impenetrable mystery of his omnipotence, he
has assigned to thee ease and to another indigence. Retain
not unjustly the rights of the poor; pay them as soon as they
are due. Complete legal alms by voluntary ones, which are
the branches which shoot forth from the trunk of the others.
How many passages of the Sacred Book bear witness to the
excellence of their merits! Without poverty riches would have

no value, so has ordained he who has done all things. The poor are as the mirrors of the rich; thus the nature of each thing is revealed by contrasts. What couldst thou have accomplished against fate, hadst thou been poor and not rich? The sight of poverty provokes the rich to thankfulness; it gives them occasion to congratulate themselves for their prosperity.

If there were no beggars in the roads of this perishable world, how couldst thou purify thy goods by alms? If the pauper refuses thee, thou hast reason to be sad; if he accepts, thou art his debtor. Is he not the instrument of thy joy and of thy prosperity? What do I say: he is one more benefit added to all those thou hast received from God. Know that it is the liberality of the Lord which sends the mendicant to the faithful, because the profit of alms is his who donates. Thank the Lord for the gifts he has bestowed upon thee; thy glory will become more brilliant. Look upon the poor with the eye of compassion; beware from speaking harshly to them. Be affable and mild to them. Pour forth thy riches upon those who suffer from hunger; it is their right.

Let thy door be the rendezvous of the poor that thy bounty may equal thy power. Is it not better to come to the aid of the unfortunate, and assuage the pangs of the hungry, than to impose on thyself an added abstinence, and to defray the costs of repairing several mosques? There is more merit in giving water to one who thirsts than to visit Caaba annually. Glory and honor to him around whom press all those who suffer, and happy indeed is the wealth which serves to solace the misery of the poor. How worthy of envy is that powerful man who bestows bounty upon thousands of paupers! Is he not a river of blessings, whose liberality pours over all his brothers?

Do not regard the poor with disdain, nor reproach them with the gifts thou hast made. May thy benevolence rejoice children, and thy caresses console their afflicted hearts!

Blessed be the treasures destined by God for such glorious uses, that are as a saving ointment on the wounded hearts of defenceless orphans! Dry their tears with thy beneficent hand; may thy caresses make them forget the parents they have lost! When thou dost prosper in thy affairs, when Providence overwhelms thee with favors, put not thy foot in the way of ingratitude; fly from it with all the strength of thy soul!

Gratitude is often only a vain word; let it be more in thy actions than in thy speech. Thank God from the bottom of thy heart; be generous to the poor. When thou seest the servants of God without bread and without garments, close not before them the door of liberality; repulse not those who extend to thee suppliant hands.

Whoever be the guest who takes shelter beneath thy roof, spare nothing to spread before him the table of hospitality. Treat him according to his deserts; honor him according to his dignity. If he makes himself troublesome, have patience; perhaps a single word will win his heart to thee. Let not disappointment fill his eyes with tears; refuse him nothing, if it is possible. Dost not wish to deliver him from all anxiety and to second with thy efforts all his desires? If it is not in thy power to content him, at least let the mildness of thy refusal leave him without regrets. Calm his mind with goodly words; fetter his heart with benevolence. That he may not leave thee with a wounded heart, think of what thou wouldst do in his place. How many ways thou hast to show thy gratitude!

No, gratitude cannot be limited. The mind of man is as incapable of understanding its merits as he is of worthily manifesting it. If thou dost wish the sincerity of thy sentiments not to be suspected, bestow liberally of thy wealth upon the poor. Let thy bounties, pure of all ostentation, have no other witness than the Divine Majesty. Beware of making allusions to them in words of pride; the Lord will know how to raise the veil with which thy modesty has covered them. The misconduct of intoxication is better than benefits accompanied with reproaches. There are many whom shame prevents from begging; go to meet those who have a right to thy compassion. How many men are divested of prosperity and whom misfortune has thrown at thy feet! To him who remains so overwhelmed in misery, even though he solicit not thy generosity, go, extend a succoring hand; that is more profitable than the building of sumptuous palaces.

Be convinced of this truth: thou wilt receive the reward for thy good deeds. Hypocrisy soils thy bounties; they will be neither useful to thee nor to them who have received them. Better is it to aid one unfortunate than to invite the rich to luxurious repasts. Seated at thy table, they would laugh at thy expense, and would criticise thy least faults. Hospitality given thus to the opulent, what is it but prodigality? What will it reap, in this world and in the next, but the eternal tortures of hell? Except in the cases where it is absolutely necessary to avoid serious inconvenience, to conciliate the good-will of thy brothers and live on good terms with them, every time that abundance reigns with thee, call in the poor and the orphans to share with thee.

CHAPTER X

The Desirability of Knowledge

O YOUNG and growing shrub, ornament of the meadow of education, thou who dost lighten the heart and the eyes of thy father, apply thyself night and day to the study of noble wisdom; remain not like the brute, plunged in ignorance. Beware of a shameful idleness; knowledge and study are inseparable. The numerical value of these words is a proof in itself of this truth. Without study no knowledge; where one is not, the other cannot exist. Knowledge is the attribute of God; it is the most precious of all qualities. Neglect nothing to acquire it; such is the teaching of the illustrious preceptor. He also has said: Devote thyself to study from the cradle to the tomb. Exert, then, all thy strength to arrive at a city whose gate is the son-in-law of the Prophet.

Knowledge, celestial gift, is the table of divine hospitality. Mediator between being and void, it adorns the visage of existence. It is for it that the king of the domain of light exclaimed: Lord, increase my knowledge! It is the source of glory and of elevation; it gives an authority free from all taint. It holds the empire of dignity and of elucidation; it dispenses all knowledge. Vast ocean without bounds, he who claims to possess it is without wisdom. Ignorance is death, knowledge is life, said the Lord; dost thou then desire to be counted among the dead? Do not deprive thyself of eternal life; learn, with the aid of knowledge, to distinguish good from evil. Enrich thy mind with all kinds of knowledge; who knows if thou wilt not have occasion to make use of it? If thou art questioned concerning

a difficulty, is it not better to reply thereunto than to confess
thy ignorance?

God said to men: Seek knowledge even to the ends of the
earth. Blush not to take lessons from a teacher skilful in
archery; in all things it is finer to know than to be ignorant.
The unlearned, in comparison with the learned, are dunces, and
even less. How can an educated man be compared to an ignorant one? are the blind and those that see on the same level?
Whatever be his rank and power, true dignity will never be
the portion of the ignorant. Ignorance is the capital of shame
and dishonor; his lot is debasement and contempt. It is a
cursed prison, in which those who fall never see liberty again.
Ignorance is chaos, knowledge is existence, how can two such
contrary principles be associated?

Apply thyself to the study of the secrets of nature; do not
stray in the valley of philosophy. What is more precious than
knowledge? have any ever repented of devoting themselves to
it? Subjects and kings all have need of the assistance of
learned men. The nobility of knowledge has no more limits
than the attributes of the Creator. As long as these cannot
be limited, how can one fix boundaries to the others? Do not
pause at the shell of things; seek to penetrate to the marrow.
From the surface, pass to the interior: does the bird fly in the
air without wings? The outside of a house is as a place of
passage; it is within one seeks repose. Pearls are not found
on the borders of the sea; if thou dost wish to possess them,
thou must plunge in the depths.

The study of grammar, of syntax, and of literature is necessary; they are indispensable instruments to learn Arabic; but
it is not necessary to give all one's time to it: of what good is
an instrument which one does not use? It is good to acquire all
sorts of knowledge; not, however, to the same degree. It suf-
fices thee to ornament thy mind with the knowledge of juris-
prudence, of the *hâdis* and of the commentaries of the Koran.
For the rest, content thyself with theory, leave to others the
practice: fly lawsuits and contests. Abandon law for the practice of good works; enter not in the domains of chicanery: if
thou dost not understand anything of the questions of purchase
and sale, what disadvantage will come to thee of it in this world
and the next?

CHAPTER XI

Of the Knowledge of God

O MOST beautiful of the pages of the book of creatures, thou whose image adorns the mirror of qualities! hearken to this paternal counsel: Boast of thy merit to no one; do not pursue a vain science which is babbled of in public lest thou consume thy strength to no purpose. Devote thyself to some science worthy of thy Creator and of thyself. Only pass through the realm of philosophy, but fasten thy attention on the writings of the friends of God. The holy aspirations of these illustrious guides bring men to truth. How difficult is it to find a perfect spiritual director! For the present, these precepts may suffice for thee. Let thy piety be enlightened. Far be it from thee to become a hypocrite and bigot, and weary not of aspiring to perfection and of working to become a sincere adorer of God.

Do not stray in the slippery places of doubt, for there are no wise men save those who are learned in divine things. How can he who devotes himself to grammatical subtilities penetrate the divine mysteries? The Creator of love has said: Acquire knowledge; such should be the aim of the two worlds. Knowledge is the ornament of man and the last places are the share of the ignorant. Knowledge is a spiritual happiness and a gift of divine beneficence. The ignorant reject knowledge because they cannot raise themselves to the required level, for they would devote themselves to it body and soul, were it possible. Examine closely, and then decide.

The mud of deception is not able to sully the garb of knowledge and the garment of instruction. Thou knowest that it is God himself who hath put thee in this world to serve him with all thy heart. Of necessity he is the master of the house; the fool only sees the house and mistakes the master. Labor courageously night and day to obtain the grace of the abiding of God with thee. Let him be the constant object of thy thoughts and of thy meditations, and be attentive to this great spectacle beneath thy eyes. Trouble not thyself with heaven or with hell, for it is their Master only whom thou must seek. If thou dost possess him, O life of my soul, thou wilt possess two worlds.

Seek to know thyself well, if thou dost wish to fathom the mysteries of this world. Seek morality eagerly, and give thyself no respite when thou wilt have found it. Whoever knows it not is a blind man below the ox and the ass. Morality is the chief riches of an enlightened soul and heart, and the last step to the knowledge of God. He who hath not penetrated to the light of morality remains lost in the shadows of error.

If thou dost well understand the truth of things, O pearl of Aden, thou wilt be invulnerable against fear and sadness. There lies all the mystery of unity; there is the secret of eternal felicity. Light of mine eyes! how full of anguish it is to be struck with blindness in this world and in the next! Anoint thine eyes with the salve of morality; if not, the day of judgment will be that of thy condemnation. He is blind, he that does not bear witness, for whom the gates of truth remain closed. He who was the glory of prophets asked in his prayers that the truth might be revealed to him. The writings of the men of God make the mirror of the intelligence to burn: do thou apply thyself to understand their meaning. Let these teachings be the safeguard of thy soul. He who seeks God has no better guide than the *mesnévis* of the greatest Physician. The sublime truths of the " Book of Victories and of Distinctions " are a balm of purity for the mind's eye. The saints have left many teachings which aid man to know his Creator. Therein are found mystic and spiritual truths derived from the Koran. Outwardly, they are only legal decisions, but beneath is a whole order of incontestable revelations. Consecrate all thy hours to the study of these books: mayst thou possess in full the doctrine which they contain!

CHAPTER XII

Eulogy of Constantinople

O MOON that dost light the eye of hope, and dost adorn the days of thy aged father! it availeth thee more to cultivate thy talents than to break the seal of a treasure. Knowledge and instruction have no surer asylum than Constantinople, which has not its equal for the flavor of its intellectual fruit. May

God prosper this abode of all greatness, the home and school of all great men, and the seat of administration for all people! There merit always finds consideration. Every perfection, every talent, is there esteemed at its just value. There are all the degrees of honor and of nobility; everywhere else life is lost and wasted. There everything has its peaceable course, and merit has not the injustice of fortune to fear. There are found all places, all dignities, and all careers. Heaven in vain revolves around the world, it sees nowhere a city like unto Constantinople. There are seen paintings, drawings, writings, and gildings, dazzling and gleaming beyond belief. All possible kinds of arts contribute their own brilliancy and splendor. See how she gleams with a beauty all her own, as the sea languidly caresses her!

At Constantinople all arts and all professions are esteemed and honored, and one finds here talents whose names even are unknown elsewhere. Does he who is outside the house know what is within? Does he who stands on the shore see what is hidden by the depth of the sea? There also they excel in archery and the names of conquerors are immortalized on stone. Without mention of the rest, how pleasant and charming it is to fly over the surface of the sea, to reign at the same time over the air and the waves, like Solomon on his throne, and to recline luxuriously on a cushion with eyes fixed on a mirror of silver! There are combined at once music, song, and all pleasures. There, riding on the wings of the wind, the eyes perceive a great number of cities. Tranquilly resting on the breeze, one traverses the earth without fatigue. There are marvellously reflected the most gorgeous spectacles, which seem to mirror one another and give an enchanted aspect to the shores. The *quaîqs* glide lightly over the water, with their wind-filled sails like a bird's wings. How can so beautiful a sight be described? what need has it of eulogy?

Behold Saint Sophia, marvel of the world, whose cupola might be termed the eighth celestial body. Nowhere has she her equal, save, perhaps in paradise. Contemplate the imperial seat of the sultans of the world, the dwelling of the kings of time, the court of the Ottoman Empire, and the centre of the rule of the khâns. In this ever-blessed region is found all that is desirable. Whatever thou canst imagine, she possesses in the highest degree. She combines the elect of the beys, of the pachas, and the efendis, the most illustrious warriors and the most renowned wise men.

All the world's difficulties there find their solutions: all efforts are there crowned with success. The mind cannot conceive all the charms she contains. If she were not afflicted with all kinds of disease and the abominable plague, who would consent to leave this celestial abode whence care is forever exiled? If her temperature were more equal, would she not cause the rest of the world to be forgotten? Whoever has an established fortune should not establish his home in any other country. No city, no country, resembles or is comparable to her. She is the asylum of all sciences: everywhere else study is neglected for gain, commerce, agriculture, or usury, so that all vestiges of knowledge have disappeared. Money takes the place of talent in a province, and it seems as if merit could be extracted from it. In the provinces scientific men have become extinct and books are forgotten. Poetry and prose are both held in aversion, and even a Persian phrase is tabooed. The study of Arabic has vanished as snow without consistency, and the principles of grammar and syntax are entirely neglected. Luxury and presumption have intoxicated all hearts, and there is no worship but that of dignities and employments. There one finds neither virtue nor knowledge, and morality is outraged.

The ambition to secure vain honors leaves no time for the labor for perfection. How many do not lift up their voices unto the Lord except when their fortunes are threatened by reverses! It is by a special dispensation of Providence that God has withdrawn learning from the provinces. If he had not first chained them in ignorance, who could have governed such men? The seat of power belongs to the great, but pride is the part of provincials. He who is high placed is not vainglorious; but these wretches are filled with arrogance. They constantly compare their dignity and importance to that of the representatives of authority.

But what would it be if they possessed learning? They would not deign to look at their fellows. They know not their value, and take no account of their worth.

Nothing teaches the inferiority of the provinces more than the sight of Constantinople. In the gatherings of the capital he who passes elsewhere for a wisest man of the century is but a blockhead; the strong-minded loses his assurance, and the fine talker has no longer a tongue. They who boasted so loudly of their rank and nobiiity are only admitted to the most commonplace circles. The arrogant, who knit his brows so disdainfully, eagerly seeks the door-keepers. He who bore a title so pompously cannot even obtain the honor of kissing the hem of a robe. He who occupied the first place is not even deemed worthy to remain at the door. What city can be compared to Constantinople? Is not the prince above him whose homages he receives? After the capital, there is no place so charming as Halep. Halep! honor of the province, illustrious and flourishing city; the resort of Indians, Europeans, and Chinese; object of the envy of the whole universe; the market of all merchandise; haven of joys and wealth, with thy delicious waters and climate, thy vast plains and magnificent buildings.

CHAPTER XIII

On Flight from Avidity and Avarice

O NEW copy of the collection of mysteries, rosebud of the garden of graces! discover thy needs to no one, bend not thy back under the load of a favor received. Open not thy mouth to request; let not servile and entreating speech soil thy lips. Cupidity always engenders a bad reputation: the true secret to gain the esteem of others is to moderate thy desires. Hast thou not received the portion assigned to thee by destiny? What is the water of life, if it is not consideration? Should we not always show it? Be animated by generous feelings, beware of baseness, and do not demand all that thou seest. What is there so desirable in thy brother's hand that thou shouldst so unceasingly covet? Has he not need of the gifts of the Lord, as thou hast? and is he not also the debtor of his universal beneficence? Is he not able to show thee favor, a weak mortal, and has he not sufficient wealth to share with thee? God never reproaches us with the benefits he grants: but is the hand of man other than an instrument? Although in all things the first causes must be considered, what are these causes without that which directs them? Seek not the creature to the exclusion of the Creator; lose not thy trouble. Confide in the generosity of the Lord; the portion he has allotted thee will return in spite of thyself. How sweet it is to repose in the shade of a modest retreat and to content one's self with the gifts of Providence! Lay not a bold hand on the object of thy covetousness; God knows what is necessary for thee. Let thy heart, satisfied with the Creator's gifts, accept with gratitude all that he grants thee! In his high wisdom, he knows all thy needs and he will provide for them at the seasonable time. Pious legacies do not belong to thee; the universal Dispenser will exhaust other sources to enrich thee. Money cannot appease hunger nor can it serve for the nourishing of thy body. If thou didst amass pyramids of gold or of silver, could they take the place of bread, or of oil, or of rice? Why trouble thyself concerning thy subsistence? Does not God provide for his servants' needs? All that is not given willingly loses its worth: were it a rose, it has no longer a perfume.

If thou art offered anything, O soul of thy father! sully not thy eyes and thy heart with cupidity: be courageous, and abase not thyself by looks which beg on all sides. However, thou canst accept with simplicity what a friend offers. In thy turn, thou wilt evidence thy gratitude by some present. Let thy promises remain always inviolable: be a religious observer of thy word. Know that a promise is a sacred obligation, and that to fail therein is to be covered with shame. Beware lest by lying words thou plantest the tree of promise on the roots of bad faith.

CHAPTER XIV

On the Bad Effects of Pleasantry and Jocularity

O THOU who dost aspire to repose in this world and in the next, who dost seek the way of peace of soul, abandon not thyself to pleasantries and jokes! This habit plunges into trouble all those who contract it. Sacrifice not thy friend to a play on words; throw not to the wind the rights of bread and salt. Pleasantry breaks the ties of intimacy, and its results are sad and painful. However brilliant it may be, it inflicts none the less deep wounds. How can the name of pleasantries be given to those burning arrows aimed at a friend's heart?

How many sallies, impregnated with venomous spleen, have filled with anger and rage those whom thou dost love! True wit is that which is appropriate, brief in expression, full of sense, innocent and inoffensive, like a blooming rose of the heart's garden, whose charms attract from afar all the nightingales. Its perfume, breathed with delight, drives from the heart all thoughts of hate. It charms the ear like good tidings, and all who hear it are filled with joy. It is carried from city to city, and passes into a proverb from age to age. Nothing is more charming than such a pleasantry; if it is otherwise, it were better to refrain from making it.

Beware of fault-finding and backbiting: a shame for all wise men. No pleasure nor profit can be found therein, and a very great sin is committed in yielding to it. The confidence of thy friends is lost; and thy name is detested where it is uttered. Fault-finding and backbiting render one as odious as does calumny. May God preserve thee from this scourge; mayst thou live in purity of heart and tranquillity of body!

CHAPTER XV

Of the Nobility of Generosity

O THOU who dost enumerate carefully the advantages of success, and dost consider the spectacle of refusals and welcomes, throw not a look of indifference on thy neighbor! Turn with interest to the unfortunate. Observe the rights of thy neighbors with justice; let the expression of thy countenance wound no one. Be not so parsimonious with thy food that thou canst not share it with others. Provide for their needs as much as possible. Let all the weak take refuge in the shadows of thy generosity! Do not entertain sentiments of hate and enmity against anyone; do not acquire the habit of tumult and agitation. Beware of anger, rage, and revenge; show to no one a countenance furrowed with discontent.

Live on good terms with all the world and be always of an equable disposition. Do not annoy thy inferiors, nor impose upon them the constraint of cold formalities. Let not the expression of thy countenance grieve anyone; captivate everyone with thy good-nature. Let no one be a victim of thy injustice, never return evil for evil. Be not a burden on thy friends, do not make thyself insupportable by thy bad disposition. Let no soul be in anguish for thee; rather labor to elevate those who are desperate. Bring no lawsuit against anyone, that God may preserve thee in turn from litigants. Do not compromise thy honor in this world and in the next for strange interests. Be neither guardian, counsellor, nor trustee.

Fly the domain of chicanery; do not rush into profitless agitation with lowered head. He who enters into quarrelling and strife with others brings down upon himself trouble and anxiety. Never follow the road of disputes and strife, for they provoke the flames of hatred! Raise not a finger to do evil: let one of thy hands be always busy in doing good. Carry not thy complaints to the door of the prince; refer to God's tribunal him who hath wronged thee. However great be thy weakness and impotence, will the Lord therefore be less zealous for thy defence? Resigned and modest, be without care and without anxiety.

CHAPTER XVI

Eulogy of Good-nature

O PRECIOUS pearl of the sea of life, chosen model of the beauty of virtues! practise modesty, have always a dervish's heart. Content thyself with little, practise humility: •shoot forth roots in the garden-plot of the roses of prosperity. Mildness, politeness, and good deeds will win to thee all unprejudiced men. Is it fitting for good-nature to knit the brow and contract the forehead? Kindness and urbanity of character brighten the mirror of the heart. As truly as a smiling countenance is an indication of the mercy of God, so is a sullen face a cause for reprobation.

Bad morals, reprehensible habits, and ill-humor lead to eternal damnation. How insupportable are the manners of whom-

soever is given to haughtiness! Presumption is a diabolical
fault unknown to the court of angels. Have no intercourse
with the vainglorious; fly from him. If thou be forced to
sit near him, show humility. The wise men, although with
apparent moderation, have said: Be proud with him who is
proud; but as thereby there may be cause for discord, hasten
to avoid it by thy humility. Pride and presumption in human
nature are an inevitable malady and incurable wound. He
who falls into this abyss cannot prosper; the hurt of his misfortune becomes incurable.

Suffer not thyself to be intoxicated by honors and dignities;
expose not thus thy brow to the wrath of the lord. Grandeur
and eminence are fitting in God; but what can they accomplish
in a slave? Let all thy ways be submissive: never reach forth
thy hand to do wrong to another. If pride and haughtiness
appear in thee, God will raise up enemies for thee even among
thy kindred. Let us suppose that thy rank lifts thee to heaven,
thou art none the less the last of the slaves of the Lord. Repulse no one from thy door harshly; give neither thy hand nor
the hem of thy robe to be kissed.

However high placed thou mayst be, do not exact servile
homage. It is thou who shouldst prostrate thy countenance
on the ground: is it fitting for a slave to have his hand and
his garment kissed? Do not conceive a false opinion of thy
own worth; as much as possible, do not take precedence.
Many candidates aspire to precedence, and perhaps they will
obtain it before thee. Boast to no one of thy rank and importance, for fear of becoming a burden to him. Salute others
with mildness and modesty; oblige no one to remain standing.
If thou art treated with honor, there is nothing better; if otherwise, dispute not. If modesty and good form reign in thy
conduct, doubtless consideration will be shown in turn to thee.
Modesty is the ornament of the countenance of faith; effrontery is pernicious in this world and the next. Let morality
perfect good-nature in thee; then see how many joys there are
in modesty!

Morality is the ornament of man; without it, he is but the
slave of Satan. Because he was without it, the envious one
was driven from the throne of celestial mercy. At the last
judgment, on the day of the final catastrophe, thou wilt not

be able to lift thy head nor turn thy eyes. But the judgment
of God is omnipresent; his eye embraces all that is. In the
eyes of his omniscience there is no difference between this
world and the world to come. The Creator is beyond the
vicissitudes of fortune; no change can affect him. Knowing
that he is omnipresent and all-seeing, how dost thou dare to
break the laws of morality?

Show not to the foolish the depths of thy heart; hearken
unto the prophets, practise their teachings. Did not the Apostle of God receive the order to act with wise dissimulation?
Without it, thou wilt have no repose, says the Glory of the
World, the Spring of all Wisdom. It is for thee as a protecting
arm; without its aid, how many quarrels and disputes! It is
the surest rampart against all the troubles of the world. Do
not turn like the wind in all directions; like the sun, do not
shine on the doors of all. Do not reveal thy secrets to strangers;
open not to fools the gate to thy private affairs. Give not thy
confidence to the first comer; do not retail in public what re-
gards thee alone. Do not believe that all men are sincere, but
do not look upon them all as hypocrites. Be not blinded by
the praises that thou dost receive; be not loath to overcome
thy passions. How could these praises lavished on thee be
free from hypocrisy?

For myself I see no difference between the stings of the wasp
and the flattering words of the foolish. If they have nothing
to hope from thee, they will never gather in thy house. On a
festival day, do not go to anyone's house without an invitation, nor to the homes of any save the honorable. Let the
gatherings that thou dost frequent be composed of pious men.
Let them not be meetings of corruption and perversity. While
thou must acknowledge an invitation, wilt thou not be out
of place where thy honor is compromised? When thou art in
an assembly, abuse neither speech nor silence; use in turn thy
tongue and thy ear. Let thy words like pearls be as brief as
possible. Govern thy speech according to this motto: brevity
and clearness. Man has only one tongue and two ears; speak,
then, little and listen much.

However, if a garrulous person evinces stupidity the silent
man ends by becoming burdensome. Speak neither too little
nor too much; keep a correct medium. Be neither stupid nor

importune. He who holds the scales of good education said: to speak too much availeth a man nothing. Do not recite in public the praises of God; prayer should be hidden in solitude; before others it is only hypocrisy and importunity; a terrible chastisement will be its just award.

Never reply harshly; when thou speakest to anyone let it be with sweet courtesy. Reproach no one face to face with his hidden faults; lend to his discourse a friendly ear. Never expose the ignorance of anyone. Why cover with confusion a creature of God? Take care not to strike with the weapon of slander; an eternal penalty will be its punishment. The penetration of him who has given thee the jewel of knowledge has shown him that ignorance was well for thy brother. Such is the providential dispensation of the Creator; so has ordained the justice of his omnipotence. Let these words be the ornament of thy mouth; woe unto thee if thou dost not heed them!

Renounce injustice and violence; never utter harsh words that wound the heart. Be generous, whatever happens, O soul of my soul; let thy tongue outrage no one! To wound thy brother to the heart is the worst of sins, the greatest of all iniquities. Labor with ardor to raise up those who have fallen; wouldst thou desire to overthrow the throne of the Lord? Will the avenging God suffer a temple to be ruined from dome to foundation? Light of mine eyes! be convinced that there is no pardon for such a sin.

CHAPTER XVII

Of Lying and of Hypocrisy

O THOU who dost hearken unto my teachings, who dost take lessons in the school of experience, never contract the habit of lying and of hypocrisy which sap the foundations of concord. Give no access in thy heart to deception; be simple, ingenuous, and without cunning. Lying and deception are pollutions which only produce deception and confusion. Forerunners of the works of Satan, they throw their authors in eternal chains. Justly abhorred by men, they only produce disastrous results.

What is more horrible than never to open the mouth for good, and to excite discord by false allegations? It is a speech passed into a proverb that the perfidious die in grief. Infamy is the only good that they can acquire; their life is consumed in sadness and grief. Perfidy, bad faith, lying, hypocrisy, perversity of mind, and corruption of heart; all these are the qualities of the damned, but they become not the true faithful. The great teacher of religion said: The true Mussulman is he whose hand and tongue are not to be feared. O thou who dost seek happiness, should not the reputation, life, and riches of all believers be regarded a sacred repository?

CHAPTER XVIII

Forbidding the Practice of Astrology and Chiromancy

O THOU who dost aspire to a solidly founded happiness, who seekest the ways to obtain the favors of Providence! be not addicted to the sorceries of chiromancy and astrology; they draw down misfortune on those who practise them; they precipitate them to ruin: instead of the gold they hoped to receive, they draw forth a vile metal. Since immutable destiny has ordained all that can come to pass, forget the future to think only of the present. Why be troubled in advance by what is not yet, and sow needlessly in thy heart the seeds of anguish and trouble?

Believe not the lying words of chiromancy, for God above knows what is concealed. Even if this were a science, the man who teaches it is of no worth; his knowledge is null, his words false, his mind diseased. Do we not see what happens to these diviners and astrologers; is there a single one who prospers? Might we not say that misfortune is the satellite of all these sorceries? Leave, then, loans, and enjoy thy ready money. What wilt thou do when thou shalt have been plunged in all these agonies? Believe my words, and may God preserve thee from so disastrous a blindness.

CHAPTER XIX

Of the Defilement of Drunkenness

O PRECIOUS pearl of the jewel casket of my soul, thou whose image is stamped on my heart! be not seduced by the rosy cup; it debases man in the eyes of his fellows, renders him odious to all, and deprives him of his honor and respect. Have no connection with this mother of all vices, who engenders all sorts of calamities. What a shame to pass for a debauchee, to be known everywhere for thy passion for wine! Beware of drunkenness, of that stupefaction which causes the loss of reason. Since the all-wise Creator has forbidden this excess, be submissive to his decision. Sully not thyself with the crime of revolt, have no cause to blush before thy Creator. Fear to fall in the snares of sin; if that occurs, entreat for pardon.

When thou dost visit an assembly, publicly reproach no one. Do not jostle those who are drunk; do not throw stones at those without reason. Why grieve these senseless persons, when thou thyself art able to share their misfortune? Why molest them? Some time, doubtless, a like mishap will befall thee. Avoid reproaching others for their blindness in sin, and declaring thyself free from stain. O soul of thy father, know well; when thou dost accuse thy brother, thou dost render thyself guilty. Must thou attack with violence the errors of others, and turn thy eyes from thy own conduct? Repentance always follows sin, for adversity is the consequence of crime. One day, in a gathering, at the house of Djelal eddin Roumi, someone said boastingly: " I have never seen the color of wine, never have I tasted liquor." " It were better still not to drink it after having seen it," answered this holy sage, the pole of good conduct, the king of the domain of grace, shocked at this proud presumption.

Suffer not thyself to be weakened by the assaults of drunkenness, do not deliver thyself up to the seductions of hashish and opium. Bendj [1] and esrar [1] are still more destructive; he who consumes them is a dunce. These drugs make a man the laughing-stock of other men: he is an ape in human form.

[1] Drugs.

Obscure not the light of thy soul's jewel; cover not with darkness the eye of thy intelligence. Wrap not opium in a shroud
during the Ramazan, so that thy body may become as the tomb
of one dead. This poison makes man wicked and immoral;
perverts him, corrupts his heart, alters his features, and be-
wilders his tongue. When intoxication arrives, he hugs himself with delight; when it is dissipated, he is beside himself;
he is a corpse in the form of one living: the brilliancy of his
cheeks is blighted. Even though there appeared no exterior
effects, who would not blush to be called *Teriaki?*

CHAPTER XX

Of the Vanity of Adornment

O THOU who art as the veil behind which hides seductive
beauty, thou who canst not be captivated by the wish for noto-
riety, fasten not thy heart on ornaments and adornment; do
not love inordinately pearls and precious stones. Doubtless
the sight of these objects rejoices the eye, but they are not
suitable for men. For him, gold is the source of all benefits;
for woman, it is the ornament of the body. Leave finery, then,
to women, make a generous use of thy riches. Be not with
thy sparkling garments like unto a gilded box of perfume.

Do not pride theyself on the splendor of thy raiment, but
content thyself with a modest outfit. Although moral purity
is indeed estimable, still the fabrics which cover thy body
should be spotless. Do not torment thyself with the search
of all manner of tissues for thy adornment. All who see
anyone arrayed after that fashion shrug their shoulders in
passing him. Whatever be the costume adopted by thy equals,
adopt it thyself. Let thy garb be conformed to theirs, however different thy fortune may be. Let the carpets and fringes
of thy hangings, and all the objects thou dost use, be not distinguished by inordinate luxury. If thou art able to wear
sable, is not the fox's fur as useful? It is nothing, after all,
but the skin of a dead animal; nothing is less precious in the
eyes of wise men. Luxury in furs and raiment throws man

into ruinous expenses; he gets into debt to keep up his pomp, and adds to his troubles and anxieties.

Do not dissipate thy goods inconsiderately: prodigality is detested by God. A wise man, to teach the value of wealth, used this just and reasonable comparison: To acquire riches, to accumulate a capital which keeps us in ease, is as difficult as to tear a cliff away from the earth and carry it to the summit of a mountain; to spend our money is as easy as to let it roll to the base. Appreciate after that, which of the two requires the more trouble, and weigh all thy actions in a just scale. Suspend from thy ear the pearl of my words. O soul of thy father, beware of debt! Debt changes a man completely; were he a Plato, it makes of him a Medjnoun. His body is in perfect health, his morals are diseased; he bears on his neck the yoke of his creditor. Debts make a fool of a wise man; they enervate the most heroic hearts, their day of reckoning is like that of death, and they lead to prison as death to the tomb. What is that, then, when a harsh creditor throws every day trouble into the heart of the debtor, when usurious interests, increasing the capital, make his body bend under an unsupportable burden; when the creditor, invoking the aid of the law, calls to his assistance false witnesses; when, crushing his victim under the feet of violence, he dishonors him in the eyes of everyone until that moment when, unable to vindicate himself, the end of life draws near?

O light of mine eyes, may Almighty God preserve thee from the scourge of debt! Better is it a thousand times to sell thy raiment and carpets, to go to rest fasting and in tatters, than to have creditors and lose thy peace in litigation. Lend to no one at usurious interest; it becomes the source of disputes. The fear of God is rare in this world: people are always ready to conceal and deny the truth; the most incontestable rights are unceasingly contested; all are busy in denying or taking oaths. A delay is demanded, then another. The money which is refused thee is eaten up by the expenses of justice. Is thy debtor the relative of some personage? claim thy money if thou dost dare; even at the hour of payment he goes to see that personage, warms his zeal by some present, and says to him: " What, lord, thou art here, and yet such an one would force me to pay!" Immediately this oppressor mounts his horse, and goes to the cadi and mufti; then thou wilt be threatened with the wrath of the judges, and thou wilt be continually urged to renounce thy pretensions. If all these artifices have no effect, thy adversary will stir up the waves of lying, will raise up false witnesses, will produce legal deeds and manufactured *fetvas*. Whatever thou mayst do in the vain hope of winning thy cause, he will do all to make it of no avail. Such is the custom of our times. Woe to him who lends his money to another!

THE ASCENSION OF MAHOMET

—

[Translated by A. P. Courteille and Robert Arnot]

INTRODUCTION

IN the journal of Antoine Galland, the celebrated translator of the "Arabian Nights," we read on page 29 of M. Charles Schefer's edition: "Thursday, January 14: I purchased for his excellency (M. de Nointel) a book entitled 'The Marvels of Creatures,' written in old Cufic characters with sixty-six illustrations representing different fabulous actions of Mahomet for the establishment of his pernicious doctrines, such as his ascension to heaven, his descent to hell, etc.; I bought it for twenty-five piastres."

This manuscript to which Galland, although he was of small experience in such matters, gives so singular a title, was brought to France and presented to Colbert by the Marquis de Nointel. Colbert, who prided himself on his knowledge of the treasures of his library, commissioned François Pétis de la Croix, the elder, to prepare a notice of his new acquisition. The learned Orientalist, after a minute examination of the manuscript, recognized the fact that it would be impossible for him to decipher it. He, therefore, contented himself with giving a detailed description of the curious miniatures with which the manuscript is ornamented, and introduced it with the following note: "Translation of the inscriptions in the Turkish language which give the subjects of the sixty-four illustrations of the book 'Leilet el Mirage,' written in curious script, in the library of Monseigneur Colbert, by La Croix, Interpreter and Secretary to the King. 'The Night of the Ascension' treats of the Mahometan faith and of the story of Mahomet. This is assumed with some justice, not only on account of the Turkish and Arabic inscriptions which it contains, but also on account of the words that have been deciphered in the queer script in which it is written. For instance, the profession of faith of the Mahometans in the forty-

fourth and forty-fifth illustrations, which is painted in minia-
ture capitals, can be easily read. Its script is fundamentally
Arabic and is ancient; not that which we ordinarily call ancient
Arabic, of which there are several books from five to six hundred years old; but another ancient script called Cufic, used by
the people of Cufa, to distinguish them from the other Arabs,
several figures of their letters resembling that Chaldaic script
which was originally Syriac."

THE ASCENSION OF MAHOMET

A LL praise and thanksgiving to the Almighty, the Everlasting, who has created and disposed the 18,000 worlds,
he who has no equal, the sole pre-eminent Being, the
sovereign Lord, the most high God. May his glory shine forth
forever! May his holy name be hallowed! There is no other
God but he. A hundred thousand prayers and blessings upon
the Friend of the most high God, the chief of the 124,000
prophets, Mahomet the chosen of God! May the celestial
graces fall in abundance on the children and the four companions of the Prophet of God (on whom be benedictions!). May
the Lord deign to favor them all!

Now you must know that the title of this work is "The
Book of the Ascension." We have translated it from that
book known as "The Way of Paradise" into the Turkish
language, that a greater number of readers may derive profit
from it. Since it is completely translated, we hope, by the
grace of God, that many intelligences may be thereby enlightened.

Imam Bagavi (may the divine mercy rest doubly on him!)
in his book entitled "The Beacon Lights" has narrated an
Arabic tradition, the substance of which is as follows:

Enis Ibn Malek tells concerning the Prophet that, on the
night of the ascension, Gabriel came to him, leading Borak, all
saddled and bridled. When the Prophet (blessed be his name!)
prepared to mount him, Borak was restive. Whereupon Gabriel exclaimed, Never hath a nobler before God than Mahomet
mounted thee, O Borak! At which words Borak sweated from
fright.

Moreover, one of the Prophet's companions, named Malik,
gives the following story of Oumm Hani, the sister of Ali:
One night, the Prophet (on whom be blessings forever!)

lodged in our house. In the morning he arose, and said to us: There happened to me many strange adventures last night. What were they, O Mahomet? we asked. I will tell you. Listen to me. Know that last night Gabriel and Michael came to me, each accompanied by 66,000 angels, and leading with them an animal called Borak, saddled and bridled. Smaller than a mule and larger than an ass, his face was like that of a human being, while his tail and hoofs were like those of a cow. (In another book we read that his tail and hoofs resembled a goat's.) He had the rump of a horse, and carried an emerald green saddle, a harness of pearls, and turquoise stirrups. Gabriel approached me and said: O Mahomet, almighty God, who hath overwhelmed thee with his gifts, and hath granted thee innumerable favors, hath decreed that this night thou shalt ascend to heaven to contemplate there the works of his omnipotence, and to receive the graces which he desireth to bestow on thee.

Hardly had I heard these words, continued the Prophet, when I sprang up to perform my ablutions. Gabriel presented to me in a ewer of red hyacinth the water of the Kaoucer, which flows in paradise, and when I finished my ablutions, he poured on his wings the water I had used. Why dost thou thus? I asked. That the most high God may not cast me into hell-fire on the day of the resurrection, he answered.

When I left the house, Michael, leading Borak by the bridle, and other angels carrying 66,000 luminous banners, around each of which were seven divisions of angels—when they saw me they all bowed down, and I, returned the greeting. Then I mounted Borak, the distance between the strides of whom when I made him tread the earth was as far as the eye could reach; and when I turned the bridle toward heaven, he soared in the air like a bird. We all repaired to the Holy House at Jerusalem, and entered the Mosque el Aksa. There I beheld all the prophets, with Abraham, Moses, and Isaac at their head. Advancing, they greeted me, and exclaimed: Rejoice, O thou whom the Almighty hath loaded with gifts; for all that thou dost ask of the Lord this night will be granted unto thee.

Then Gabriel made the call to prayer. Abraham the prophet said to me: O Mahomet, do thou perform the functions of imam; for we should all pray under thy direction. Then I, as imam, prayed; and immediately afterward, implored the blessing of God for my followers, and all the prophets raised their hands to heaven, crying Amen!

O Mahomet, arise, for we must continue our journey, said Gabriel, and arising, I saw before me a ladder of light, resting on the earth and reaching to heaven. Gabriel bade me mount the ladder, and I obeyed, while repeating the invocation, In the name of the merciful and pitying God, and many others. Thus without trouble I arrived within sight of heaven, where I saw a sea so immense that none knew its extent save the Lord of all. O Gabriel, I said, what is this sea? It is that which is called the Sea of Kaoucer, he answered; which is suspended in space by the divine omnipotence, and no one save almighty God knows its extent.

When we had traversed this sea and pursued our journeys by the order of God, we reached the first heaven. I saw that it was made of an enamel the color of turquoise, with a thickness which it would take 500 years to cross. Gabriel knocked at the gate, and had no sooner called the angel intrusted with the guard of the gate than he asked, Who art thou? Gabriel, bringing Mahomet with me. Apostle of God, said the angel, has the time of thy coming then arrived? And opening the gate of heaven with great demonstrations of joy, he saluted me, and I him; then he added: Be welcome, O Mahomet, enter and honor with thy presence the celestial world. I entered and I perceived seven choirs of angels ready to receive the commands of him who guarded the gate, and who all saluted me. There I saw a personage whom I did not know. It is Adam the prophet, said Gabriel, greet him.

I therefore went to salute him, which salute he returned, saying to me, Be welcome, O Mahomet, thou art come at a seasonable hour. May prosperity be with thee forever! Then I saw that Adam (on whom be blessings!) glanced to his right, and smiled with a satisfied air; then looked to his left, and became anxious and tearful. What aileth Adam? I asked of Gabriel. At the right hand of Adam, answered he, are the souls of the prophets, of the saints, and true believers. While contemplating them his heart is joyous, and he smiles. On the contrary, at his left are the souls of the infidels, of the perverse and incredulous. The sight of them is painful to him, and he weeps.

I passed beyond, and saw a white cock, whose head was under the throne of God, and whose feet clutched the earth. Who is that cock? I asked Gabriel. 'Tis an angel, said he, who counts the hours of the day and night. When the hour of prayer comes, he crows and recites the *tesbih;* and when the cocks on earth hear him, they crow in their turn and recite the *tesbih.*

Farther on, I saw an angel, who was half snow and half fire. Who is that angel? I asked of Gabriel. 'Tis the angel whose voice is so sonorous that when he recites the *tesbih* men say, It thunders! He had two *tesbihs* in his hands.

Farther on, there was a white sea. What is this sea? I asked of Gabriel. It is, said Gabriel, that which is called the Sea of Life.

We pushed forward, and at length we reached the second heaven. I saw that it was of white pearls. Its breadth was that of a 500-years' journey. Gabriel knocked at the gate, and a voice asked, Who art thou? I am Gabriel, and with me is Mahomet, the chosen Prophet of God, he replied. Immediately the angel, filled with joy, opened the gate of this heaven. We entered and saluted the angel, who returned our salute, and said: Rejoice, O Mahomet, for the Almighty grants thee great graces to-night! Twenty choirs of angels, ready to receive the orders of him who guarded the gate, surrounded us, and saluted.

Farther on, I came near unto a gigantic angel. Who is that angel? I asked. It is he who rules the concerns of all creatures. At a distance I beheld an angel who had seventy heads, and moreover, seventy tongues in each of his heads. With each of these tongues, he was reciting seventy kinds of *tesbih.* Passing beyond this place, I saw two personages. Who are they? I asked. One, said Gabriel, is Jacob the prophet, and the other is the prophet Zachariah. I saulted them, and they said to me: O Mahomet! be welcome! Thou dost honor with thy presence the celestial world. May the gifts of the most high God make thee to prosper!

Going on, I saw a white sea, on the shores of which a multitude of angels recited the *tesbih.*

At length we reached the third heaven, where Gabriel, knocking at the gate, had no sooner called than the angel who was the sentinel of the gate asked, Who art thou? I am Gabriel, and Mahomet is with me. I saw that this heaven was of red hyacinth. Then the angel said to me, Be honored, O Mahomet, with the gifts of almighty God! There were thirty choirs of archangels under the orders of this sentinel of the gate, and 30,000 angels beside were ready to obey each archangel. All saluted me, which I returned, and then they wished me well. Going on, I saw two personages in a delightful spot. The countenance of one of them was as the full moon. Who are those persons? I inquired. They are, said Gabriel, the prophets Jacob and Joseph. I approached them, and exchanged greetings, whereupon they said: Welcome, O Mahomet! The Lord hath promised us that we should behold Mahomet; a hundred thousand thanksgivings to him for that we have gazed upon thy blessed face! All that thou shalt beg of him to-night, he will grant unto thee.

Withdrawing from them, I perceived two more persons. I questioned Gabriel, who answered, One is David the prophet, and the other is Solomon the prophet. I greeted them, and they returned the salute, saying, O Mahomet! enjoy the gifts of the Lord, and forget us not! Then they added: Thanks to God, we have seen thy ever-glorious face! And they wished me well. Passing on, I saw on the shore of a vast sea a gigantic angel seated on a throne. He had seventy heads. A multitude of angels seated on thrones surrounded him, and all were reciting the *tesbih*.

Farther on, we arrived at the fourth heaven. Gabriel knocked on the gate and called. The angel who guarded it opened it joyfully, and said to me, bowing down, Welcome, O Mahomet! Be thou honored with the gifts of the most high God!

Journeying farther, we reached the fifth heaven, which is made of gold. When Gabriel had knocked at the gate and called, the angel joyfully opened it, and saluted me, saying, Be thou welcome, O Mahomet, thou wilt be honored with the gifts of the Lord! And he wished me well. After an interval, I beheld together the prophets Ishmael, Isaiah, Haroun, and Lot. I greeted them, and they said to me: Whatever thou dost beg this night, O Mahomet, God will grant it unto thee without excepting anything; ask of him the salvation of the souls of all those who follow thy laws.

Pursuing my way, I came to a sea of fire. On the day of the resurrection, said Gabriel, this sea of fire will be thrown into hell, and those who dwell in hell will be tormented by this fire.

We passed this place, and reached the sixth heaven, which is made of pearls. Gabriel knocked at the gate. The guarding angel opened it, greeted me, and said, Be thou welcome, O Mahomet; thou dost crown us with joy by coming to visit the celestial world; be thou crowned with the graces of the Lord! And he called down upon me the blessings of God. Sixty choirs of angels, standing around him, recited the *tesbih*.

Farther on I saw a *keuchk* on which stood a person entirely veiled, and surrounded by a great multitude. Who is that? I asked. It is the prophet Moses (on whom be blessings!) answered Gabriel. I went to him, and saluted him. He saluted me in his turn and said, O Mahomet, be thou welcome! Happy is thy arrival! Proceed, said Gabriel to me, ascend higher. At these words, Moses began to weep. Wherefore dost thou weep? asked Gabriel of him. Alas! I imagined that my place and rank were above all; and here is Mahomet, coming after me, who surpasseth me by far; his followers will be more numerous than mine, and they will enter before them into paradise. Then the august voice of almighty God spoke to Moses in these words: O Moses! I have made thee illustrious among all by speaking to thee face to face; I have delivered thee from the malice of thine enemies. Why not return thanks unto me for the gifts thou hast received from me? I passed on, and I saw the prophet Noah and the prophet Edra. I exchanged salutations with them, and they loaded me with benedictions: Be thou welcome, O Mahomet! they said, with demonstrations of joy.

Pursuing our journey, we arrived at the seventh heaven. Gabriel, going before me, knocked at the gate and called. The angel who guarded it opened with joy, and we entered. Then he said to me: Welcome, O Mahomet! who dost honor us with thy visit! Mayst thou be honored in thy turn! There were seventy choirs of archangels under the command of the angel who guarded this heaven made of light. There remained vacant not the smallest space; the angels occupied the whole heaven. We passed through this place and came to a vast *keuchk*, before which was erected a great chair of emerald green. A person with a white beard, seated in this chair, was leaning on the *keuchk*. Who is he? I asked. It is thy ancestor, the prophet Abraham, said Gabriel. I went to salute him. He returned the salute, saying, O pre-eminent prophet, be welcome! May God bless thy coming! Gabriel said to me: Behold thy residence and that of all those who follow in thy footsteps. Then he added, Enter that house and visit it, for every day 70,000 angels come to visit it. I also saw a band of creatures, half of whom were in white tunics, and the other half in white tunics striped with black. They are those who follow thee, said Gabriel. Then, addressing those who wore white tunics, he said, Enter with your Prophet. And he permitted them to enter, but he refused entrance to those garbed in the tunics striped with black and white.

Passing on, I saw a sea as black as ebony. On beholding it, my sight became as it were obscured with gloomy shadows. In this sea, I saw an innumerable throng of angels. I inquired of Gabriel: Why is the water of this sea black? No one save the Lord of all knows the nature of this sea, he answered. On the shore I saw a gigantic angel, his head touching the base of the throne of God, and his feet resting on the earth, and able to ingulf in his mouth the seven strata of the earth. At some distance I saw another angel of gigantic proportions, having seventy heads as large as this entire lower world. Each of these heads possessed seventy tongues. Night and day he recited the *tesbih* in honor of the Most High. Near him was an angel so enormous that if the water of all the earth's seas had been poured into one of his eyes, it would not have sufficed to fill it. Farther on was an angel bearing 10,000 wings. Beside him was a sea, in the waters of which he plunged only to come forth immediately shaking himself. Every one of the drops which fell from his dripping wings became an angel by the creative power of God. Not far distant was another angel with four heads: one resembling that of a man, another like that of a lion, another still resembling the head of the bird houmaï, and another like that of a bull.

Proceeding, we attained the *sidret-el-mountehâ*. That which is thus called is a large tree, some of whose branches are of emerald, others of pearls, with foliage similar to elephants' ears. Its fruits are of considerable size. From the foot of this tree gush four springs which flow into as many canals. Two of these canals are open to the skies, but the two others are covered. Of the first two, one is the Nile flowing through the city of Misr, and the other is the Frat, which flows through the city of Koufa. As to the other two whose beds are subterranean, one is the Selsebil, which flows through paradise; and the other pours into the basin of the Kaoucer. The water of these two rivers is whiter than milk and sweeter than honey. Angels coming toward me, greeted me, and brought three goblets, which they presented to me. In one was milk, in another wine, and in the third was honey.

I took the one containing milk, and drank it. Seeing that I did not touch the others, the angels said to me: Thou hast done well to choose the milk and to drink it, for all those who follow in thy footsteps will go forth from this world with faith. I was overjoyed at these words. Then Gabriel said, I shall not go farther. And, pausing at this place, he returned to his own form. I saw him stretch his 600 wings, with one shoulder in the east and the other in the west. I said to him, What form is this, O Gabriel? It is mine, he replied, that in which I was created.

As the wisdom and knowledge of the creatures who dwell on the surface of the earth do not go beyond the *sidret-el-mountehâ*, they have given him the name of Gabriel, which signifies, the lotus of the last boundary. Then he added: O Mahomet, approach now as near as it is permitted unto thee to approach, and prostrate thyself.

I therefore advanced, and when I reached that point nearest to the throne, I prostrated myself to the earth, and I saw the supreme Lord with the eyes of my heart. At that moment I heard the voice of God saying to me: Lift up thy head, and glorify my name! Raising my head immediately, I cried, *Etlaiyât lillahi ouessalaouât ouettaïbat,* which means, Let all be for God, whether it be the praises, homages, and *tesbihs* uttered by the tongue, or acts of devotion, such as alms, tithes, and offerings performed with the aid of temporal goods. After which I heard these words: *Esselâm aleïka eiuânnebi oue rahmet ullah oue berekâtouhou,* which, being interpreted, is, Mayst thou be delivered from the terrors of the next world and from its chastisements! Mercy, benedictions, and prosperity be upon thy head! Then I said: *Esselâm aleïna oue ala ibâdillahissâlihina,* which signifies, May the salvation which cometh from God and his divine mercy be with me and with his faithful servants! At the same time, all the angels, seeing that I had been accorded the honor of approaching so near to the divine Majesty, exclaimed:

Ach' adou en lâ ilaha illâllahou oue ach' adou enne Mahometan abdouhou oue reçoulouhou, that is, We bear witness that the supreme Lord is the only living God, and that there is no other God but he. Furthermore we testify that Mahomet is his servant, and his chosen Prophet!

Then the Lord said to me: O Mahomet, I impose upon thee fifty prayers to be said within the space of a day and a night; go and prescribe these fifty prayers for them who follow in thy footsteps.

I bowed down before the divine Will, and, retracing my steps, I betook myself to the prophet Moses (on whom be blessings forever!). He asked me: Mahomet, what hath the Lord required of thee? O Moses, I answered, he hath required fifty prayers to be said in the space of a day and a night.

Mahomet, he continued, thy followers will never recite those fifty prayers. I, who went before thee, have known and proved many men, and I have received many blows from the people of Israel. Go, then, and proffer another request. It may be that the Lord God, out of his great mercy, will excuse thee from some of these fifty prayers.

I therefore returned and groaned in entreaty before the throne of God. Mahomet, said a voice, I remit ten of the fifty prayers. Thou shalt therefore only recite forty.

Again I turned back to Moses, and told him what the Lord God had said.

Go once more, he answered, pray and lament; perchance God will make another concession.

I went and prostrated myself, bewailing my fate. The Lord,

hearkening favorably unto me, remitted another ten prayers and only demanded thirty of me. Moses, on my return, said, O Mahomet, turn again to God, who will surely make another concession. Thirty prayers are yet too many. I went, I entreated, I presented my request. I obtained the remission of another decade, and was ordered to say twenty only.

It is still too much, said Moses, when I had rejoined him. Thy followers cannot acquit themselves of the obligation, and will be deemed rebellious before the Lord. Seek again; doubtless thou wilt obtain what thou askest.

I went, I implored, and God excused me from ten more prayers; there remained now but ten. I came back to Moses. O Mahomet, ten prayers are still too many; it is to be feared that the faithful cannot say them. All that thou dost ask this night, God will grant unto thee. Arise, therefore, and ask again. I went, and entreated, moaning, and God excused me from five more prayers. When I returned to Moses, he said: If thou shouldst return, the Lord God would not desire to send thee away disappointed in thy hopes, but he will doubtless come to the rescue of thy followers.

I rejoiced to have obtained so great favors, and was satisfied.

Then the voice of the Almighty said to me: O Mahomet, to him of thy followers who will recite in the ardor of faith these five prayers, I promise to give the recompense due to fifty. Nor is this all; should one of the faithful form the resolution to perform a good work, I will order the angels to inscribe ten good deeds on the record of his life. If, on the contrary, he commit an evil deed, I will command it to be inscribed as one only. I will blot out the sins of those who do penance with a sincere heart, and to those who shall fast during thirty consecutive days I will grant for each day the reward of ten, which will make a total of 300 for the thirty days. Whoever will fast six days in the month of Schevval, I will grant him for each day the recompense of sixty days, so that he shall receive the reward for 360 days of abstinence. And to all these I will grant paradise at their deaths.

I said unto the Lord God: My God, thou hast given sovereignty over all to Solomon, the miraculous rod to Moses, and to Isaiah the power to bring the dead to life.

The Voice of Voices replied: O Mahomet, I have raised thee above all. Moreover, I have suffered all thy followers to approach me, and I will grant them participation in my mercy. And the voice of the Most High pronounced unto me 90,000 utterances: 30,000 on laws, 30,000 on the spiritual life, and 30,000 on the essence of truth. Then I was given this commandment: Proclaim unto all the 30,000 utterances concerning the laws; tell those on the spiritual way to those whom thou desirest, but not to those whom thou wilt reject; repeat not importunely to anyone the words on the essence of truth.

Having passed beyond, I saw 700,000 (seventy *touman*) curtains, some of light, others of fire, and of hyacinth; some of pearls, and others of gold. Each one has seven choirs of angels for guardians. I had no sooner reached a curtain when an angel, advancing, took me by the hand and made me cross it. Having traversed in this manner 70,000 curtains, I perceived the arch, the celestial throne. It was so large that in comparison with it heaven and earth with its seven strata are as nothing. God created the arch of red hyacinth. A multitude of angels circled around it, reciting the *tesbih* night and day in honor of the Lord of all. I saw also, ranged in circles around the arch 700,000 tents, each one of the dimensions of this lower world, and the distance from each tent to the next was a space the breadth of which was a 50,000-years' journey. In each tent were fifty choirs of angels all adoring God; some standing, others seated, and others bowing their foreheads to the ground while they were reciting the *tesbih*. I passed through the tents, and was preparing to take off my sandals, intending to ascend the arch, when I heard the voice of the Almighty saying:

O Mahomet, remove not thy sandals, that their contact may bless my throne.

I ascended the arch, and prostrating myself to the earth before the Lord God, I cried, Glory and praise to thee forever! Then I returned.

Now must be told how the Prophet (on whom be blessings forever!) visited paradise and hell.

In his book entitled "The Beacon Lights," Imam Bagavi (may the mercy of God be with him!) has quoted this *hadis*

written in Persian, and which is as follows: " Paradise is conquered by difficult tasks, such as prayer, fasting, pilgrimage,
and holy wars. To enter it we must bind ourselves to spiritual
exercises and be exact in all the practices of the true religion.
Hell, too, is gained by the toils of concupiscence and by all
kinds of desires."

The Prophet (blessings upon him!) also says: When the
Lord God, after having created Paradise, had adorned it with
all kinds of delights, Gabriel was commanded to go to journey through it. Gabriel examined it, and saw that God, by
an effort of his omnipotence, had prepared for his servants
a multitude of delights which no eye had ever seen, and no
ear had ever heard described. O my God! he exclaimed, whoever hears the description of paradise, will have no rest until
he will have attained it.

Then it was that the Almighty surrounded the four sides of
paradise with irksome tasks; such as fasting, prayer, pilgrim-
ages, holy wars, moderation of desires (contentment), and
watches consecrated to adoration. It was ordained by the
supreme Will that no one should enter paradise unless he had
passed through these arduous trials. Gabriel knowing this,
said: If it is thus, no one will have access to this abode of
delights.

Likewise, when God had created hell, he called to Gabriel,
Go, Gabriel, and visit hell also. Gabriel beheld in hell all kinds
of punishments and tortures which no one could ever describe.
O my God! he said, no one will ever enter this hell.

Therefore the Lord surrounded the four sides of hell with
all kinds of inordinate desires, with the passion for wine,
unlawful intercourse with women, unbridled love of lucre,
tyranny, and the exaggerated search for pleasure. At this
sight, Gabriel exclaimed, My God, I see well indeed that no
one will escape this hell.

Now let us return to the subject. When the Prophet returned, after having been granted access to the throne, Gabriel
received this commandment from the Lord:

Guide my friend Mahomet that he may see the marvels of
the paradise I have prepared for believers; then let him also
contemplate the various punishments of hell that I have arranged for the wicked.

Whereupon Gabriel said unto me: O Mahomet, thou must first visit the basin of Kaoucer, which was created for thee; then we shall see paradise.

We proceeded then immediately to the Kaoucer. On the edge of this basin I perceived a great quantity of *koubbèh*, that is domes, some of pearls and others of red hyacinth or of emerald. The slime of these waters is of musk and the pebbles which carpet the bottom of the basin are of red hyacinth. The extent of the basin of Kaoucer is that of a month's journey. The waters are whiter than milk, sweeter than honey, and more highly perfumed than musk. All around the basin, and more numerous than the stars in heaven, there are golden vases and goblets of silver, of hyacinth, of emerald, and of pearls for those who wish to quench their thirst. Whoever drinks of this water never again feels the pangs of thirst.

In the Word (the Koran), the supreme Lord thus expresses himself: "*Ana ateïnakal kaoucera fe salli li rebbika ouenhar inna châniyaka houa bilabtar*," which, being interpreted, means: "O Mahomet, I have given thee beside many goods the basin of Kaoucer. Pray, then, in honor of thy Benefactor, and sacrifice victims unto him. Whoever saith unto thee that thou art *abtar* [maimed] will be so himself, and not thee."

The Prophet had by Khadija a son named Abd Allah, who died at an early age. A person called As, having been to see the Prophet to tender him his condolences, was returning to his home, when he met on the way some infidels of the tribe of Koraïchites. As, they said to him, where hast thou been? I have been to see that *abtar* to tender him my condolences, he answered. Now it is a custom among the Arabs to call *abtar* he whose son dies at an early age; indeed the meaning of this term is really who hath no offspring, no end. When the Prophet (on whom be blessings forever!) learned that the heathens had treated him as *abtar*, he was thereby much grieved. Then Gabriel brought him this *surate*.

O Mahomet, the supreme Lord giveth thee the basin of the Kaoucer; evidence thy gratitude by prayers, supplications, and offerings. Whoever doth treat thee as *abtar* will merit himself that epithet; he will be honored neither in this world nor in the next. As for thee, we will raise thee to such a degree of veneration that until the day of resurrection thy name shall be invoked after mine in prayer.

When the Prophet heard these words of the sovereign Lord, his heart was filled with joy. Gabriel also said: O Mahomet, the first to drink of the water of the Kaoucer will be those who threw in their lot with thee when thou didst go from Mecca to Medina, and who accompanied thee to this city, leaving behind their wives and children. Next will come those who have renounced the pleasures of this world, the small, the humble, the poor, and thy companions who were esteemed of no account. On the four sides of the basin will be stationed Abou Bekr, Omar, Osman, and Ali. Whoever hates one of thy companions, will not be given to drink of this water.

Afterward Gabriel said, O Mahomet, now thou must visit paradise. When we reached its gates, Gabriel knocked. Who art thou? asked the angel who guarded the gate. Gabriel, and with me is Mahomet the chosen Prophet of God.

Immediately the angel joyfully opened the gate and welcomed us. In a garden created by the Lord of All for those who follow in my footsteps, I saw a multitude of houris. Some were seated on thrones, and others sportively clasped each other's hands. Birds fluttered around and finally alighted on the heads of these houris. On a certain day (the day of Azineh, Friday) they mount goats and go to visit each other, and spend their time in laughter and amusements; then they separate after an exchange of good wishes.

I saw also a *keuchk* in the centre of the gardens. A multitude of houris were laughing and dallying on the lawns which surrounded it. To whom does that *keuchk* belong? I asked. To Omar, answered the houris, among whom I recognized Romeïca, the wife of Talka.

Is it indeed thou whom I see here, O Romeïca? I said.

It is I indeed, O Prophet. The Most High hath shown mercy unto me, and hath granted me the grace of entrance into paradise.

When the Prophet was asked for details concerning the dwellers in paradise, he answered: These fortunate beings are of the stature of Adam, whose height was sixty cubits, and of the age of the prophet Isaac, who was thirty years of age

when he was on earth; they are as handsome as the prophet
Joseph, and in their bearing they are like unto the prophet
Jacob, on whom be blessings forever! They have neither hair
nor beards, and their eyes are anointed with *surmeh*. In their
hearts there exists neither envy nor hate. They are no more
susceptible to pain than to old age, and they are subject to
none of the necessities of human nature. As for the houris,
whatever the number of the tunics they wear, they are all
transparent; one beneath the other; their flesh is seen under
the tunics, and their bones beneath the flesh, and even the marrow of the bones appears distinctly. Nor do the houris entertain sentiments of envy. Each follower of the true faith has
also a tent entirely of gold, sixty *igadj* (300 miles) in diameter.

Gabriel next said to me: O Mahomet, now that thou hast
seen the dwelling place of thy friends, it is time to visit the
spot destined for the enemies of the most high Lord.

Then did I see that hell was a terrible and horror-inspir-
ing region. At the gate stood an angel of sinister and terrify-
ing mien. Who is that angel? I asked Gabriel. His name is
Mâlik, he replied. He is the prince of hell whose entrance
he guards. Since his creation, he has never smiled, nor has
he exchanged with anyone whomsoever the slightest colloquy.
I saluted him, but he did not return the salutation.

It is Mahomet, said Gabriel. Immediately Mâlik offered
me apologies, saying: Rejoice, O Mahomet, on account of the
gifts of the Lord, who hath desired thee to behold the works
of his omnipotence, and who hath generously loaded thee with
so many benefits.

O Mâlik, said I, breathe once upon the fires of hell. Mâlik
blew once, and Gabriel and I stood stricken with terror.

I saw in the middle of hell a tree which shaded a space
500-years' journey in dimension. Its thorns were like lances,
and its excrescences resembled the heads of *dio* (demons).
Gabriel said to me: This tree is the *zakkoum*, whose fruit is
more bitter than poison. The dwellers in hell taste it only to
reject it at once.

At the foot of this tree I saw a band of reprobates whom
the angels were torturing by cutting off their tongues, which
were always renewed and cut off anew. Who are these
wretches? I inquired of Gabriel. They are, he replied, those

leaders who have not ceased to say to others: Drink no wine, commit no impure actions, and beware of wicked and perverse deeds, while they themselves, not practising their own precepts, commit all kinds of reprehensible acts.

I also saw another company of persons whose flesh the angels were cutting off and forcing them to eat.

And who are they? I asked. They are those, answered Gabriel, who mocked Mussulmen to their faces, and said evil of them in their absence, without fearing the day of the resurrection.

Again I saw a group of men whose abnormally enlarged stomachs prevented them from moving an inch. Who are they? I asked. They are the greedy, who were insatiable in their thirst for gain. Some more I saw whom the angels were tormenting by pricking them with lances. Who are those yonder? I inquired. Those, he answered, who, denouncing Mussulmen to their oppressors, used violence to take possession of their goods; and not content with that, by practising slander among Mussulmen, breed rivalries, wrangling, and discord. Farther on was a band of men suspended by chains in the midst of the flames of hell. And who are they? They are those, said Gabriel, who prayed hypocritically when they were on earth that they might be honored as pious and virtuous persons. They had no other aim but temporal advantages, and thought not of the rewards of the future life nor did they reflect upon the day of the last judgment.

I saw also a number of women suspended by their hair in hell. From their nostrils whirlwinds of flame gushed forth. Who are those women? I asked. They are the immodest ones, said Gabriel, who allowed their hair to be seen by strangers, who, enticed by this sight, coveted these women. And thereby sprang up between them criminal relations, for they had lost all fear of the last judgment.

Beyond were some women whose feet and hands were bound. Serpents and scorpions swarmed over them, stinging and biting them. Who are these women? I asked. They lived in impurity, Gabriel answered, without ever praying, or performing ablutions, nor do they request anyone to teach them the laws of ablutions. Neither have they ever learned in what prayer consists. Again I saw some women hung by their tongues in the midst of hell-fire. And who are these? They left their husbands no repose by their unceasing scolding and bickerings. They went out from their homes without permission and committed shameful actions.

[The Prophet (may salvation attend him!) said that paradise would be the reward of the women who obey the commandments of the Lord of All, and who trouble not their husbands with scolding and quarreling.]

At some distance, I beheld a group of people whom the angels were tormenting by pouring poison down their throats. What have these people done? said I. They consumed the goods of orphans without thought of the day of the last judgment.

Next I saw a multitude of women suspended by their breasts, who were being tormented without mercy or respite. I sought to learn who these women were. They brought into the world, said Gabriel, the fruit of their criminal deeds; then, by pretending that they were legitimate, these mothers gave to them the inheritance of others, and bestowed on them wealth which was not lawfully theirs.

Farther on, I perceived some with grindstones hung around their necks. They were bound hand and foot, and angels tortured them unrelentingly. Who are these? I inquired of Gabriel. They paid not the tithes of their wealth. Full of indulgence for their desires, they thought not of this great day, and through the avarice which filled their souls, they could not resolve to purify their wealth by alms.

Again I beheld a band of wretches, with blackened faces, their necks and hands loaded with chains, and who were undergoing frightful tortures. I asked their crime. They always greeted the great with flattering compliments, answered Gabriel.

At some distance was a group of men whose tongues protruded from their mouths. Their heads were as those of swine, and they had legs and tails similar to those of asses. They are, said Gabriel, those who bore false witness, as they possessed not the fear of the Most High.

Some also I saw who were slain and brought to life alternately, while they were asked, What good hast thou ever done?

Some, too, were enchained by their necks. Angels poured

poison in their throats and cruelly chastised them. Who are those unfortunates? I asked. Those who drank wine, answered Gabriel, and died unrepentant.

I also saw at the gate of hell a certain number of chests, filled with serpents and scorpions writhing out only to return. Gabriel, questioned by me, replied: These are the haughty, with hearts full of pride and harsh in their deeds, whom these serpents and scorpions will torment until the day of the resurrection, and who will suffer eternally.

The Prophet (upon whom be blessings forever!) says: O ye who follow my way, weep without ceasing through fear of hell, and do ye those deeds which shall earn for thee happiness in the next world; for terrible are the agonies of hell! Its depth is equal to the distance between heaven and earth. When the Lord God created hell, he ordered the angels to keep it burning for a thousand years in succession, when it became red. When they had kept it burning for another thousand years, it became white. Still another thousand years it was kept burning, and it became black. As for the infidels who enter hell, their skin is of the thickness of forty cubits; their teeth are as large as Mount Ohod. Everyone occupies a space equal to the distance which separates Mecca from Medina. The reprobates, in the very heart of hell, weep so that their countenances have furrows like canals, and when their tears are exhausted, blood commences to flow from their eyes.

When I returned, after having successfully visited paradise and hell, I received from the Lord God the following commandment: O Mahomet, now that thou hast seen the marvels of my omnipotence, go, tell them to those who follow in thy footsteps. Promise paradise to the faithful, and seek to warn the infidels, the hypocrites, and the vicious by inspiring them with the fear of the tortures of hell. As for thee, do thou persevere with patience in the holy practices of the true religion; be thou mild in thy speech and kind in thy deeds. Invoke my name before all thy actions, for I am nearer unto thee than is thy soul itself. Even if the infidels invoke my name, I will not leave them without hope. O Mahomet, let not thy heart be puffed up with pride, for I love not those who are intoxicated with vanity.

After the Lord God had spoken to me, Gabriel made me

mount on his wings, and so brought me to the mount of Kâf.
I saw that this mountain, which is entirely of emerald, completely surrounds the earth. Gabriel, by the command of God,
showed me two cities on the summit of Mount Kâf, one situated to the eastward, and the other to the west. One was called
Djabalaça and the other Djabalaka. Each of them had a thousand gates; and from one gate to the next there was a distance
of an *igadj*. All the houses were exactly the same size. While
the mosques were situated far from the dwellings, the cemeteries were at their very doors. Who are these people? I asked.
Followers of the religion of Moses, answered Gabriel, and said
unto them, Here is Mahomet, whereupon they all cried out,
Praise to the most high Lord of all, who hath granted us a
sight of thy blessed countenance! And they all without an
exception embraced my faith at once. Then I inquired why all
their houses were the same size. It is because, answered they,
there is no jealousy or envy among us, and therefore no desire
to excel each other. But what is the reason, I again asked, of
the distance of the mosques from your residences, while the
cemeteries are within a stone's throw? If we have built our
mosques at some distance, said they, it is to remind us that
heaven will be our future reward, whereas we have our cemeteries near by that we may be unceasingly reminded of death.
Then they added, O Mahomet, we pray, we observe the fasts,
we practise charity toward each other, we entertain no wicked
sentiments in our hearts, we conceive no projects of hate nor
of revenge, nor do we encourage spite; honoring our fathers
and mothers, we avoid all that will give them pain; we beware
of all wicked deeds. Now give us advice, and enlighten us
with thy precepts. I answered thus: Live always in the
fear of almighty God, suffer not your hearts to be puffed up
with pride, and humbly submit yourselves to the yoke of
the law.

All having unreservedly resolved to put my words into
practice, I arose and we went to visit them all individually,
and they swore allegiance to the true faith.

May the Lord of all accord them the grace of good works,
and the scrupulous practice of the true religion; may he deliver them from the torments of hell, and make them participate
in the joys of paradise. Amen and amen, O Ruler of all worlds!

THE MARVELS OF THE FOURTH HEAVEN

The Prophet (may grace and blessings be upon him!) said also: I reached the fourth heaven, which was created of pure silver and which is called Aziloun. It has a portal of light adorned with a lock of light. [According to another description, it was made of pearls.] Compared to it, the seven strata of the earth are as a ring in the midst of a vast plain. On the fastening of the gate are engraved these words: "There is no other God but Allah; Mahomet is His Chosen Prophet." At this gate was stationed an angel [named Azraël according to one story, and Moucâil according to another]. After we had knocked on the gate as before and answered the question he put to us, he opened the gate. I saw there innumerable marvels, eight only of which will be mentioned in this book:

First. Moucâil, the angel who is stationed at the gate, exercises a supervision over all that exists, and he has under his command 400,000 angels. His *tesbih* is as follows: Glory be to the Creator of darkness and light, of the dazzling sun, and the silver moon! Glory be unto the Lord God, the Most High!

Second. I saw there my brother Moses, blessings be upon him forever! [According to another account, this interview took place in the sixth heaven.] Gabriel having bidden me by a sign to do so, I approached, and saluted him. He arose, pressed me to his heart, and kissed me between my eyes, saying, Glory be to Allah, who hath permitted me to behold thy countenance, and hath given me the honor of seeing thee. Then he gladdened me by the tidings of a great number of marvellous gifts of the Lord, and said:

This night thou wilt be brought even unto the feet of the sovereign Majesty, to that sanctuary where no creature hath access. Forget not when thou art there the feeble and the faithful; ask a share for them of all that may be granted to thee; endeavor to obtain for them as many mitigations of the lawful commandments as possible. I hearkened unto him, and overheard him as he recited this *tesbih*: Glory be to him who guides whom he wills in the right way, and leads astray whom he wills! Glory be to the All-Merciful, the All-Pitiful!

Third. As I went away, Moses began to weep. When I asked him the cause of his tears, It is because, he said, there has been sent after me a young apostle whose followers will enter paradise in greater numbers than mine.

[According to another account, he thus explained the motive of his tears: The children of Israel regarded me as the most honored of all the sons of Adam by the most high God, and now is this young man more honored than I, and the favor of which he is the object will be necessarily shared by his followers. He will be the first of the prophets in the eyes of God, and his followers will be the first of all nations.]

The Lord God having summoned the angels, all approached on their knees and began to recite this *tesbih*: Glory be to the All-Merciful and All-Pitiful! Glory unto him from whom nothing is hidden! Glory unto the supreme Master of all worlds!

Is it thus that they worship? I asked of Gabriel.

Yes, he answered, and pray to God that thy followers may be granted the grace to do likewise. I asked, and the Lord God, hearkening unto my prayer, commanded this posture in the *namâz* (orison).

Fourth. I beheld in this heaven Meriem-Khatoun, the mother of Moses, and Acièh, the wife of Fer'oun. All three came toward me. Meriem had for her use 70,000 *keuchk*, all of emerald. The mother of Moses had 70,000 *keuchk* of white pearls, and Acièh had 70,000 of red hyacinth and 70,000 of red coral.

Fifth. An angel was seated on a throne, with moody air and contracted brows. At each of the four corners of this throne were 700,000 steps of gold and of silver. All around there was such a multitude of angels that God alone could know their number.

On the right of the throne I saw resplendent angels, all clothed in green, breathing exquisite perfumes, pronouncing words which charmed the ear, and whose countenances were of such dazzling beauty that the eye could not gaze upon them. On the left I saw the angels of darkness, with faces and garments of black, of discordant speech, and exhaling a pestilential odor. As they uttered the *tesbih* flames leaped out from their mouths. Before them were spears, maces, and piles of fire-arms whose aspect could not be borne. The angel who was seated on the throne was covered from head to foot with eyes as brilliant as Venus and Mars. He had as great a number of wings. He held in his hand a leaflet, and before him was a small board on which he fastened his eyes and never raised them. There was also before him a tree whose leaves God alone could number, and on each leaf was written the name of a mortal. The angel had also a sort of basin at his disposal. Sometimes he plunged his right hand therein and drew out an object which he handed to the luminous angels on his right, sometimes he seized the object with his left hand and delivered it to the angels of darkness.

At the sight of this angel, my heart was filled with awe, a trembling seized my whole body, and I felt my strength abandoning me. I questioned Gabriel, who said: It is Azraël, whose face no one can behold; he who destroys joys and who sunders all ties. Then, addressing him directly, Gabriel said, Behold, O Azraël, the Prophet of recent times, Mahomet, the friend of the All-Merciful. Azraël raised his head, smiled, and arose to do me honor.

Be thou welcome, he said. The Most High hath created none more worthy of reverence than thou; thy people are also the most favored of all in his sight. As for me, I feel more compassion for thine, than for their fathers and mothers. Thou hast rejoiced my heart, I answered, and thou hast freed my soul from its anguish. Nevertheless, there remains one care. Why do I see thee so full of sadness and grief?

Apostle of God, he replied, since almighty God appointed me to this ministry I fear that I shall not worthily fill the office and that I shall be unable to render account for it. And what, then, is that bowl? I asked. It is the entire lower world from Mount Kâf to Mount Kâf; it occupies no more space than that in my eyes, and I wield there a supreme power. And that small board? It is that which marks the appointed hour of every creature. And this leaflet? It is the record of all that happens. And that tree? On its leaves are inscribed the names of all creatures, happy or unhappy, with their felicity or their misery. If anyone be sick, his leaf becomes yellow. When the moment of his death comes, this same leaf falls on the tablet, where his name is blotted out. Then I stretch forth my hand and seize his soul whether it be in the east or the west. If it be the soul of one blessed, I give it to the angels on my right, who are the angels of divine mercy. If it be the soul of a reprobate, I consign it to those on my left, who are the angels of damnation.

And what is the number of all these angels?

I know not; only every time I receive the soul of one dying there are present 600,000 angels of mercy and 600,000 angels of damnation, who observe to which category the soul belongs, and those who have assisted once at this function will never return to witness it again until the day of the resurrection.

Angel of Death, I said, is it indeed thou who dost seize the souls of all dying?

Since I was created I have never moved from this place where thou dost see me now, but I have in my service 70,000 angels, each of whom has likewise under his orders 70,000 angels. When I desire to seize a soul, they go to conduct the soul of the dying one into his throat, whence I receive it, stretching forth my hand from this throne.

I entreat thee, said the Prophet, to consider the weakness of my followers and to take them only with gentleness and care.

I call Allah to witness, said Azraël, he who hath created thee the seal of prophets and his chief friend, that the Creator (everlasting glory to him!) in person urges me 70,000 times night and day to take the souls of the followers of Mahomet gently, and to let all my dealings with them be as considerate as possible. Assuredly I have more affection for them than their own mothers.

Sixth. I also saw there a sea whose waters were whiter than snow. Gabriel, questioned by me, told me that it was called the Sea of Snow, and if a drop of its waters escape the heavens and earth would perish with cold.

Seventh. I saw the blooming temple *beïti ma'mour*. [According to others, the *beïti el ma'mour* was situated on the *sidret-el-mountehâ* above the seventh heaven. However this may be, this is the description of it given by the Prophet.] It is a mansion of red hyacinth with two portals of green emerald. Ten thousand lustres of red gold hung from the ceiling, adorned with hyacinths and gems every one of which shed forth more light than the sun. At the door of this temple was placed a pulpit of gold and a minaret of white silver, whose height was that of a 500-years' journey. Since the temple was created, and so it will be until the day of the resurrection, every day 70,000 angels coming under the arch bathe in a sea of light; they make the circuit like pilgrims clad with the *ihrâm*, repeating *Lebbeïk, lebbeïk* (We are here, we are here); and once they have performed this duty their turn will never come again until the day of the resurrection.

Then Gabriel, taking me by the hand, led me to the blossoming temple and said to me, Apostle of God, perform here the functions of imam, and let the angels take thee for a model. I said a prayer of two *rik'at,* and I served as model for the angels who people the seven heights of the heaven. At the sight of this multitude surrounding me there came to my mind that my followers might unite in the same manner. He who penetrates all secrets and hidden things made a commandment of the desire nestling in my heart: O Mahomet, there should be among thy followers a meeting of this kind and which will be a day of reunion, *yeomi djum'a.*

[In certain commentaries it is said that on the day of reunion the angels who people the heavens meet at the blossoming temple. Gabriel recites the *ezân* upon the minaret, Esrâfil pronounces the *khotbèh* in the pulpit; Mikaïl fills the office of imam, and the angels of the seven heavens follow his directions.

When the prayer of the day of reunion is finished, Gabriel says: O ye angels, bear witness that I yield the recompense for my *ezân* to the *muezzin* of the followers of Mahomet. Esrâfil, in his turn, says that he yields to their *khatib* the reward of the *khotbèh,* and Mikaïl abandons to them the recompense for the *imamat,* while the angels do as much for all the faithful who join in common prayer. Then the most high God, speaking to the angels, says: Do ye think to show me what generosity is, I who am the Creator of generosity! Be ye witnesses that I remit all the sins of the followers of Mahomet, and that I deliver them from hell!]

Eighth. There, it is said, the Prophet saw the sun, which, according to a tradition, is 160 times the size of the terrestrial globe. According to Ibn-Abbas, its breadth is that of a 60,000-years' journey. When God created the sun, he made for it a golden barge, on which he placed a throne of red hyacinth, with 360 steps, on each one of which were 1,000 angels. The sun was placed on the barge, which is placed on a throne by 360,000 angels. Every day they guide the barge on the sea of the fourth heaven from sunrise to sunset; then they devote themselves to the adoration of the Most High. The next day, 360,000 other angels come to take the places of those who did this service the day before; and so will it be until the day of the resurrection without the recurrence of the same angels' turn. The Lord God has said: The sun goes to its fixed point.

According to certain commentaries, the fixed point of the sun is beneath the arch, to the foot of which this star is brought back every night, and where it is prostrated before the Most High until the dawn. At that moment, obedient to the divine command, it comes forth from the east, and so it will be until the approach of resurrection day. It will then receive the command to rise in the west. This tradition is preserved in the book of the deceased Imam Talebi, entitled " Araïs " (" The Betrothed ").

Then, said the Prophet, I reached the fifth heaven.

Without pausing, we proceeded forward. As soon as we had reached the fourth heaven, Gabriel, always at his post, passing before me, knocked at the gate, saying: Open! Who is there? he was asked. I, Gabriel, he replied, accompanying Mahomet, the king of apostles. Be ye welcome! exclaimed the angels who guarded the gate, and who, opening the gate, approached us. This heaven was of gold entirely red. Here was an angel named Salsaïl. He advanced to meet us, and Gabriel saluted him, whereupon Salsaïl said to me : Receive our congratulations, O Mahomet! Thou who art in so great favor with the Lord God, thou who art the greatest of all prophets! It is for thee to intercede for thy followers, O well-beloved of the Lord, for thee whose happy star has made thy followers the most fortunate of all!

I saw innumerable choirs of angels standing to receive the commands of Salsaïl. All recited unceasingly the *tesbih*, nor did they grow weary night or day. Here, too, I saw David, whom I saluted. He returned the salutation and said to me, Welcome, O apostle of truth, venerable brother, august prophet! With David I also saw Solomon in this heaven. As soon as they saw me they came to meet me, and exchanged salutations. Here I saw seated on a throne an angel whose luminous brilliancy filled the heaven. So imposing and majestic was his appearance that none can look upon his countenance. His head almost touched the arch, while his feet reached down below the earth. The entire universe was for him as a plain where each particular man is as a porringer.

Before him also was a large tablet on which he constantly fixed his eyes. Opposite the angel was a gigantic tree whose boughs were covered with green leaves, and two awe-inspiring spears were suspended before him; one white, and the other black. Entirely absorbed in his ministry, the angel paid attention to no one, and his harsh and frowning features gave him an altogether terrible and forbidding expression. At the sight of him, my soul was seized with awe, my heart grew cold, and my body trembled. Who, then, is that angel? I asked of Gabriel. At what task is busied this being of such imposing mien? Behold, said Gabriel, him who slays the sons despite their fathers' cries, who makes children orphans, and causes the rich to weep even as the poor; he who dissolves all unions, and turns laughter into tears; Azraël himself, who bears away all souls, and leaves lifeless those who were replete with life.

I then approached him, and saluted him, but so occupied was he, that he did not glance toward me.

Brother, cried Gabriel to him, turn to this side; doff thy fierce expression, for here is the prophet of recent times, the friend of Allah, and the prince of apostles. He raised his head and saluted me, saying: Pardon me, O imam, for during the long time that I have been busy in accomplishing my work, I have not lifted my head a single time. Tell me, I said, what is that tablet, what is that tree, and what are those spears?

O Mahomet! he answered, this tree causes the death of all those who live on earth. Every one of them has his leaf on this tree, although the slime of which they were moulded was taken from the earth. Every one of them also has his name written on the leaf which is assigned to him as well as on this tablet. In whatever part of the world he is when his existence reaches the fatal hour, his leaf dries and falls at once. At the same time his name is erased from this tablet and disappears, even as he himself is wiped out and departed from the life of the earth. It is then that I take possession of his soul so inevitably that no one can find a way to escape his destiny. As for myself, I never have one minute of distraction and let nothing escape me, and never do I hearken unto the entreaties of anyone. If it be the soul of one of the elect, I seize it with this white spear. If it be, on the contrary, the soul of a reprobate, I use the black lance. If the soul be that of a faithful follower of thy creed, O Mahomet! I assist him to ascend to heaven in light; but if it be that of an infidel, I suffer it to fall in torment down to hell amid encircling gloom.

Having again resumed our journey, we soon reached a lofty castle, to the summit of which the eye could not attain, and the surpassing beauty of which the intelligence was powerless to grasp to its full extent.

THE ROSE AND THE NIGHTINGALE
(Gül and Bülbül)

—

BY

MOHAMMED FASLI

*[Metrical Translation by J. von Hammer-Purgstall and
Epiphanius Wilson]*

THE ROSE
AND THE NIGHTINGALE

I

BLESSED is the phrase that praises Allah's name;
It is the very rosary of God's word;
For through it blooms the rose-bed of the soul;
And through it sings the bosom's nightingale.
Each single letter has the rose's hue,
And thus adorns the rose-field of our faith.
B is the bloom of the creation's rise,
The rose that stands on plains of Paradise.
S is the sultan, ruling over M;
The dew-drop sparkling on the lip of buds.
A is the cypress of God's kindliness,
The buds of sanback, buds of promise true.
The L leads on to leaves of happiness,
Like the curled locks that deck the grove of truth;
The H is like the eyes of hyacinths;
Fresh as the rosebud when it starts to blow;
The R is like the nation of the rose,
Hither and thither tossed by morning wind.
The H is the mild breeze that sweeps the plain,
And is a symbol of eternal grace;
What is the N but Eden's Nenuphar
The dot rests on it like a pistil point.
The J is, as it were, a jasmine flower,
Bending above a violet full in bloom.
The double mark that stands above the L
Is dew upon the leaf of hyacinths.
The points are nothing else but drops of dew,
That rest on tulip, rose, and violets.

The vowels of the sentence breathe their sounds
Like breezes scenting glades of Gulistan;
Emblems of peace are seen on every side,
Like to the peace of Eden in the world;
So do we come at last to Gulistan,
And on the new-blown roses gaze with joy.
And you, oh Fasli! to the rose-bed come,
And sing your ardent passion for the rose.

II

THE PRAISE OF GOD, THE WONDERS OF GOD, AND HIS MARVELLOUS WORKS

THOU didst with fire make red the rose's heart,
And kindle passion in the nightingale;
Thou didst lend sweetness to the open air,
And scatter in the East the scent of musk;
To thee the spring-time owes her living crown;
The groves of roses owe their fame to thee.
'Tis thou didst paint the rose's gallery;
And China's flowery land had birth from thee.
The festival of roses is from thee;
The rose guests owe their genial hours to thee;
Thine is the burning aloe of the East;
Thine, the loud warbling of the nightingale;
From thee, the rose her glowing color takes;
From thee, the nightingale her melody;
The tulip's bosom glows with love for thee;
Delight in thee perfumes the cypress boughs;
Great nature's heart is opened at thy smile;
And by thy grace the vernal waters flow.
Thy wrath bows down the violet to the dust.
'Tis at thine indignation that it wilts.
Thou lightest tapers in the forest glade,
And sometimes in thy flames the tulip dies;
And the narcissus, like a beggar crouched,
Thou dost ennoble with thy crowns of gold;
Yet, 'tis their voices and their tongues that praise
With melody, thy name in woodland glades.

For thou alone on earth art harmony;
And aught beside is but an idle dream.
The world's life is illusive, nothing more
Than the reflection on a mirror's face;
Things are no more than words to being brought,
And names the sole realities of life.
The sun of beauty casts its light abroad,
And all it touches kindles into life.
Thy power astounds the human reason; makes
The mind to totter and the brain to reel.
No human wit thine essence comprehends;
Reason and intellect before it fail.
No man can grasp thy nature, nor can plumb
With intellectual glance thy truth's abyss.
Men's understanding is a cradle-child;
And only by thyself canst thou be known.
O God, I was conceived and born to sin,
And to the passion that degrades my soul;
Fast held, enamored by the beautiful,
Grief was my portion for my earliest years;
In empty brains did sensual longing burn,
And wine bedrenched me like an empty skin.
Eager I yielded to the goblet's charm,
And lingered like a drunkard over cups;
Draught after draught, I took the ruddy wine,
And threw the pleas of virtue to the wind.
And all of life's religion I renounced,
And turned from all devotion's practices;
Yet what would profit oft-repeated prayer
To one like me who stand aloof from God?
If to the mosque I sometimes turn my way
'Tis only to behold the beauty there.
I lift mine hands in prayer toward the place
Where the fair women of the assembly sit.
Oft at the Portal Beautiful I wait,
To mask my sins by such religious guise.
Sad is the plight in which I find myself;
O Lord, forgive the evil I have done.
For under thy control, O Lord most high,
Are works of good and works of evil set.

Were it obedient for a thousand years,
The world could never see thee as thou art
And sins committed for a thousand years
Could not impair one jot thy worthiness.
And I, who can do nothing of myself,
How could I, Lord, obedient prove to thee
Yet in thy unity do I believe,
And with a heart sincere observe thy law.
Show me the pathway of the unity,
That in it I may lead myself aright.
Grant that mine eyes may still reflect thy face;
My heart receive the light thy knowledge yields.
Leave not my soul in darkness absolute,
But cast the light of grace upon my path.
Drive from my breast the instincts that degrade,
And fill it with the radiance of thy love.
Oh, make mine eyes reflect thee constantly;
My tongue forever speak of thee alone;
My heart be filled with love of thee, and lit
With all the splendor of thy unity.
Let me behold thy secret state unveiled,
And manifest to me thyself alone.
For why should human glances seek the light
And turn toward the countenance of God?
Make me with wine of love inebriate,
And of my nothingness, thy creature form.
I call for the delirium of love;
And naught but thee, Jehovah, do I seek.
Therefore the name of God is on my lips;
And still I cry, "There is no god but God."
I care not that my soul perdition see
So long as I behold the great Amen.
Grant only that my soul be filled with truth,
And my heart led along the path of light.
Sincerity my rule I do ordain,
And gratitude the watchword of my life.
Of secret falsehoods shall my heart beware;
Of pride and rancor's desolating flame.
Oh, change my being; open wide to me,
Poor as I am, the treasury of thy grace,

And quench the flame of anger in my soul.
Kill in me avarice, and concupiscence;
Let pleasure never dominate my life,
Nor chastity be wanting in my heart.
Inflame me not with wrath's pernicious fire,
But quench it in the steady stream of thought.
Send me not forth on paths of cruelty
And give thy justice to direct the world.
Make truthfulness my guardian; and let me see
The dear Kaaba stone of my desire.
Contentment be my storehouse as I haste
Upon my journey to the wished-for land,
And when the vision dawns upon my sight,
Grant that I never more may leave thy law.
Grant that my habits ne'er may master me,
But custom ever change at my command.
May I be ne'er abandoned by thy grace,
May my obedience ever perfect be;
And bend my wishes to the mood of prayer,
That they may burst in flowers of happiness.
Cast, when I kneel, my intellect to earth,
That thus my prayer may never be disturbed.
When I am set on honor's lofty seat,
Give me the strength to bear prosperity.
Keep me untainted by hypocrisy,
And in thy service make my mind sincere.
Grant daily growth to my obedience,
May it be nourished on the Prophet's lore,
And let my tongue flow ever in thy praise.

IV

HYMN OF PRAISE TO THE LORD OF LORDS, TO THE GLORY
OF HIS CREATURES, AND TO THE PROPHETS

He, the first cause of all created things;
The bloom of planetary elements;
In all the treasures of his mighty heart,
Is the great light that lights existences;
And in the order of celestial things

He is the circle's first and utmost line;
And he, the all-respected, all-beloved,
Mahomet, Mustapha, and Mahmoud named,
Sprung from the house of Haschim, Koreish' stem,
First published to the world the Monuments.
From out God's secret treasure-house he came,
Like to the light of morning in the East,
To be on earth the prophets' guide, to be
The great director of the pure in heart.
When on the world his features cease to shine,
It seems as if the sun was veiled in heaven;
And when his grandeur does not rear itself,
The very heavens no longer soar aloft.
Without the shadow of his mightiness,
The throne itself would totter in decay.
When he is wroth, he in confusion throws
The water's torrent and the dust of earth;
His dazzling existence could not fail,
But both the worlds of heaven and earth were gone.
The world and all therein exist for him;
Angels and men and demons of the air;
And the nine heavens their being owe to him;
For him the heavens their revelations make;
He is the world's foundation, cause, and end,
And he preserves the beauty of the world.
His law remains the age's guiding light;
And in his countenance does Allah shine.
Mankind in guilt and dire perplexity
Had wandered blindly from the way of truth.
Until the loving-kindness of his law
Recovered them, and brought them to the path.
Before the splendor of his law arose,
The human race was separate from God.
Mahomet showed the path that led to God;
He was the polestar in the arch of night;
The leader of the pilgrims on their way;
The refuge of the rulers of the world:
For when Mahomet on the earth appeared,
He shone the candle of intelligence.
Mahomet, called the prophets' prince to be,

Was first in excellence of holiness.
Mahomet rules the future of the world;
In him existence is not bound by space;
Mahomet is the source of light to all;
The guide and guardian of the universe.
Adam was once the glory of the world,
But he is Adam's greater counterpart.
'Twas he that rescued Noah from the flood;
And so preserved the good of all the earth.
Enoch ascended into paradise,
But he, an earthly creature, mounted heaven.
While Abraham was eminent for love,
Mahomet only keeps the throne of love.
And while on Sinai does Moses stand,
Mahomet holds the highest place in heaven.
'Tis true that Jesus waked the dead to life;
Life to the dust was by Mahomet given.
Though Joseph was of comely countenance,
Mahomet is the Saviour beautiful.
God to King Solomon great wisdom gave,
The prophet's wisdom was Mahomet's dower.
Though David was God's caliph on the earth,
Truth in Mahomet is epitomized.
Endless the pomp of his nobility,
And endless is his honor and his power.
When to his mighty power he gave free course,
He ripped the curtain of the moon apart.
And see what mighty miracles he wrought;
" I have been poisoned," said the lamb to him.
Like the dim cypress that in summer springs,
He cast no shadow on the ground he trod;
But light invested him from head to foot,
And people saw his pathway shadowless.
Shadows from out the realm of darkness come,
And never shadow yet has beamed with light.
Yon full-orbed moon casts light, not shadow down,
Yet on the cornfields flings the shadowed trees.
So like a shade-tent did the people cast
Their shadows on him in the sunlight clear.
His beauteous eye, the window of his soul,

Was raven black amid the dazzling light.
He saw, at once, in all directions, all,
Before, behind him, near him, or far off.
For in that eye was light as sunbeam clear,
And by it was the sun itself eclipsed.
Vain were it all his miracles to count,
Though I should labor to the judgment day;
Though I should speak them with a thousand tongues,
Ten thousand yet unsung I should omit.
Only his passage to the highest heaven
Can yield full witness of his excellence.

V

How He, the Master of Both Worlds, on the Night of
His Celestial Journey Rose From the Bosom of the
Earthly Multitude to the Summit of the Divine
Unity

'Twas night, and yet, as in the light of day,
The earth lay bathed in splendor brilliant.
For like a company of princes ranged
The happy stars were shining overhead.
And the full moon her silver radiance poured;
'Twas the great feast time of the Ramazan.
On such a night the moon was throned in heaven
Above the thousand star specks of the world;
A queen surrounded by nobility.
His house was flooded by the moonlight clear.
And from the moon, now fourteen nights in orb,
Came Gabriel, the messenger of heaven.
He said: "Oh thou who like the moon on earth,
And like the sun in purity of light
Art eminent, and lord of honors here,
Accept the thousand greetings that I bring,
For with this greeting God a summons sends,
To the enjoyment of his majesty.
This journey, then, with longing keen begin,
For the All-Wise desires thee at his side.
Forsake the crowd to meet the unity

And taste the presence of all purity.
The angels all are ranked below thy seat,
Thou art the princely ruler of the heavens."
As Ahmed listened to the messenger
He praised the Lord of heaven with fervent prayer.
Calmly he mounted on the cherubim,
And rose in haste toward his celestial friends.
He moved like some fresh morning wind that blows,
Toward the sanctuary of Zion's hill.
Soon he, the master of all grace, arrived;
And, as the leader of the spirits pure,
He stood in heaven, and through the stars he passed,
While constellations honored his approach.
As in the primal heaven he sat enthroned,
The moon was waxing to her fullest orb.
With deep obeisance did the queen of night
Welcome the visit of the prophet form.
Thence to the second heaven he bent his way;
The heaven of Mercury blessed him as he came.
There on heaven's page were pointed out to him
The dazzling wonders of creation's work.
To the third heaven at last he soared aloft,
And Venus welcomed him with kindly grace.
Deep bliss his ardent breast with rapture filled,
As lutes of love their dulcet notes resound.
In the fourth heaven o'er radiant meads he trod,
His shadow lent a lustre to the sun.
Peacefully fell that shadow on the star,
Filling with light the spot that welcomed it.
At the fifth heaven he glanced, and lo! he saw
That Mars had drawn his falchion, full of fear,
Yet with submissiveness the man of God
He welcomed, greeting with obeisance due.
On the sixth throne elate sat Jupiter,
Once happy, festive, lord of heaven and earth.
By him the Prophet was received with smiles
And prospered on his way with happiness.
Saturn, the ruler of the seventh ring,
Received him in the circle of his light.
" I come," the Prophet said, " from dark to light;

Repulse me not, I pray thee, from thy door."
Thence he ascended by the sunlit path,
To that clear region where the stars are fixed,
And in the radiance of his approach,
Great joy was caused through all the region high.
And as his gracious shadow there was cast,
He found himself upon the meadow plain,
Whose carpet spreads before the throne of God.
And he who was the first in highest heaven,
Heard in that radiant place a voice, that cried,
" Oh, tread my plains, for in thy steps is peace."
O'er the whole region did he wend his way
And stood at last before the Tree of Life.
Before the Tree of Life he paused a while;
For there his guide had bidden him to repose.
Thence to the throne of his dear God he passed,
The God unlimited by time or space.
All the dark memories of the world were lost,
For there the light of the one God beamed forth.
And there he took his station next to God,
Higher than prophet or t'.an seraphim.
His inmost soul was lost in ecstasy.
For God within that circle sole exists;
God infinite and absolute is there,
In the full splendor of his attributes.
There is the light of life divine revealed,
Clear as a spotless diamond in heaven.
There saw he what no eye before had seen,
And heard what yet had reached no human ear.
For speech in heaven is wordless, and the heart
Speaks out aloud, yet with no uttered sound.
From thence he was permitted to return
To the waste hill land of his native home.
He traversed heaven and blessed it with his face,
Returning on his way to earth again.
And when he reached his couch, he found that all
That boundless journey through the infinite
Had happened in the twinkling of an eye.
The prophets greeted him with loud acclaim,
And spread the joyous news of his return,

And all who heard it, turned their minds to God.
All were transported with celestial joy.
All rendered thanks of gratitude to Heaven.
The hearts and souls of all were filled with light,
Plunged at the moment in the Sea of Truth.

VI

A BLESSING ON THE PROPHETS, THE MEDIATORS OF THE
PEOPLE, WITH A PRAYER OF INTERCESSION AND A GREET-
ING TO HIS COMPANIONS

ALL hail to thee, thou messenger of God!
My heart goes out to thee, and ye, who stand
As mediators in the path of truth,
Weigh well the good and evil of the heart.
Prophet, my spirit is with rapture filled.
Be gracious to me, listen to my cry,
For when thou pleadest for sinners all the band
Of followers pay their homage at thy feet.
For in the bygone days there was revealed
A rule of right and wrong, and in the scale
Of justice all was cast. The world for thee
Has hoped, O mediator, all the world.
Become thou, then, a mediator for me,
And make me with the peace of Eden blest.
Why fear I when my guilt is infinite,
If infinite the grace that thou canst give?
For my infirmities are without bound,
And in transgression am I swallowed up.
My sins, my sins are multitudinous
And I have failed to see the end of God.
Now at thy footstool do I prostrate lie,
I touch thy hands, I supplicate thy face,
For if thy kindness will not intercede
What is the intercession of this sigh?
And if thy tenderness refuse support
My soul must wander in the maze of grief,
And yet I hope thy interceding prayer
Will win some respite to my tortured soul;

'And I call myriad blessings on thy head
And upon all who follow in thy train,
On all who travel on the path of good;
To all the leaders of the saintly band;
On those the four elect ones, on all friends;
On the primordial powers of either world.
Upon the sovereign king of wisdom's realm,
On Ebubeker, who is lord of truth,
Then upon him who is the one just lord,
Omer, the noblest, purest among men;
Next upon him, the Koran's faithful scribe,
Upon the lordly Osman, Haffan's son;
On Ali, friend of me and friend of all;
To whom all realms of knowledge were revealed.
Next on the pair, for whom my vision thirsts—
On Hassan and on Huscin, princes both,
Noblest in purpose and in dignity;
On Omar, Hamsa, Abbas, whom I greet,
With myriad salutations, while I lay
A thousand gratulations at their feet.

VII

WHAT WAS THE OCCASION OF THIS POEM AND THE ARRANGEMENT OF THE NARRATIVE

UPON a morn, a glorious morn of June,
When eastern light, with many colored charm,
Tinted the gentle birth throes of the year;
And streams with ardent longing ran their race,
And cloudless azure floated o'er the world,
The rose and tulip oped their petals wide,
Within a garden fair as paradise,
Where sand and soil were clothed in dazzling green.
All earth was blushing in the morning ray,
As if a second Eden had arisen.
The tulips ranged along the mountain walls,
Held up their chalices with eager hands.
And all the flowers were waking out of sleep,
And day was changing watch with vanished night.

Narcissus flowers had filled their golden cups,
Stanching their thirst in draughts of diamond dew.
Each rose within the garden seemed a king,
And every floweret was a belted knight.
The nightingales were sighing in the grove,
And deep delight the stream and forest filled.
The cypresses were bending in their dance,
And all the world was radiant with joy.
Within the garden stood a company
Of friends, on joy and recreation bent;
For great and small, either by night or day,
In pleasure banquets to that garden came.
But I within the wood remained aloof,
And wandered, lost in solitary thought.
Then came to me a man of a refined
And gentle aspect, and of noble race.
For many a year this friend of mine had laughed
And wept with me, in pleasure or in pain.
Then said he, " Friend of mine, arouse thyself."
Nor dally here in listless indolence,
For spring has tinted bright the dewy world,
And God's enchantments fill the garden glade;
On the world's leaf he writes the message clear:
" Oh, come and see God's monument on earth!
Why tarriest thou? Behold this circling realm!
How beautiful is earth—'tis paradise.
For vernal life revives the blooming year,
And if thou live the thought must raise thy heart."
I, as I heard these pleadings of my friend,
By his benignant influence was swayed.
Into the garden as he led the way,
I entered; there a grove of roses stood.
We crossed a level area, where we saw
The scene adorned with flowering elder-trees.
The place was noble, for the hillside shone
With the fresh loveliness of Eden's bower.
Such scenes unlock the heart and make it glad,
And over all they spread the balm of peace.
The fresh blown roses hung on every side;
From every copse the nightingales were heard.

And in this place of beauty marvellous
A thousand words passed swift 'twixt friend and friend,
And kindly greetings rose, and hearts were soothed
With genial conversation; poesy
Lent to the converse of the band her charm,
And prose and verse alternately they quote;
Mesnevi's tale was subject of debate;
And meaning and expression were discussed.
Then with my friend I held a colloquy;
And, in a kindly mood, he said to me;
" The nightingale is singing loud to-day,
And thou, whose heart is drinking in delight
From the soul utterance of the nightingale,
How comes it thou art silent in the world?
Thy breath and utterance should impart new life;
Thy word give healing, from thy mouth should come
The stream that yields refreshment unto men.
Why art thou dumb and lifeless; without song?
Write thou a volume with poetic grace
Replete, and show the compass of thy power;
God gave to thee the poet's destiny.
Whence is thy mood of careless indolence?
He in whom mind is more than fleshly might
Alone can frame a song that moves the heart.
Write, then, a book which shall transmit thy name
Down to the records of remotest time.
For certainly, the name of him whose mind
Dwells on the beautiful shall never die."
Now as I listened to this kind advice,
A keen ambition seized upon my soul.
I answered: " Friend, thy counsel I approve;
Thy words have made me opulent in soul;
I lend my ear to all that thou hast said,
For he who would gainsay thee is a fool.
But, though with ample skill and wit enough
I might a book in one short week compose,
The world would scorn imagination's work,
Although my power of utterance be supreme."
Then all the circle to my plea demurred,
Laying a thousand fetters on my heart.

"But," I continued, " 'tis for daily bread
We toil, and scarce the pen can meet the need;
When with my brain as pilot I proceed,
A thousand cares for corporal wants molest;
Entangled thus, invention fails my mind,
And all my spirit's best emotions die."
"Stay," said my friend, "this argument is vain,
Vain are these timid pretexts. Courage take.
Is not the nightingale in prison bars
Forever wont to pour her dolorous chant?
And in its cage the cheerful popinjay
Learns to repeat the words of human folk,
And chatters with untiring gaiety,
And warbles in a rapture of delight."
"My friend," I answered, "in these times of ours
The world is nothing but the slave of gold;
Honor and office is the aim of all,
While merit follows like a slave on foot.
How sordid is the spirit of the world!
True fame alone from generous wisdom springs.
Where can we find the scholar exquisite?
Alas! the world is full of ignorance;
Who cares to-day for books of verse or prose?
Who dares to tread the path of poetry?
There may be magic in the song you sing,
But the dull world is dull to every note."
He answered: "What does all this babbling mean?
No man of purpose can this plea allow.
Think'st thou the world as empty as thou say'st?
Leave off repining, and, with courage bold,
If thou hast jewels, bring them to the mart;
The buyer is not difficult to find.
If thou hast merit wherefore this delay?
How canst thou heedless waste the fleeting hour?
Merit will always win the praise of men.
But bring thy beauty boldly into view.
The Shah will first of all make recompense;
He knows to treasure up the worth of words;
A critic he, in poetry and prose,
Expert, munificent as well as wise.

To him thy poem must thou dedicate,
Thy poem rare and writ in double rhyme.
And in this work thy name along with his
Shall live unto the very judgment day."
Soon as the Shah was named, I felt in vain
Were all excuses, and I answered him:
" Friend of my soul, I will the work begin.
I swear it on my head, this very day!
Yet in what style shall it accomplished be?
That I may execute a splendid work."
He said: " My dearest friend, what other theme
But the rose legend can suffice for thee?
The legend of the beauty of the rose,
The legend of the lover nightingale.
Tell us the lot, the plight of bird and flower,
And all they did and were; set this to rhyme
In that fine book of thine, and with the skill
Of thine unerring genius, tell the tale."
Moved by these words, I took my pen in hand
And went with eager longing to the task.
The legend of the nightingale I wrote,
And dedicated it to him who rules
The land, and with the Shah's name in the front
I made a book that all the world has praised.

VIII

PRAISE OF THE PEARL OF LORDSHIP, THE HEAVEN-GREAT
PRINCE, WHOSE PITY AND WHOSE PURPOSE EXTEND
FROM HEAVEN TO EARTH

THE Shah, our heavenly highness and our king,
Is as an angel or a Jupiter;
Face of the moon and beauty of the sun
Are his; his fortune and his blood are peers.
A prince is he of high and happy line,
Of fair renown and intellectual power.
The very glory of the Osman house,
Elected as the Sultan of the land,
Is Shah Mustapha Ben Suleiman, born

A very shah from royal ancestors.
He is the man, who by his skill to guide,
Has filled the earth, the age, with happiness.
Worth is alone the banner and the crown
Which win, by merit, throne and diadem.
Worthy successor of the Osman kings
Among the sultans, like a monument
He stands, a sun of bright prosperity.
Shah of the moon and mirror of success.
He in the shining jewel case of bliss
We style the pearl of lofty destinies,
A shah who is so filled with rectitude,
That he is the Nuschernan of his time;
So brilliant he in generosity
That he eclipses Hatim Tais' renown.
His justice is the ruler of the world,
Which by his grace is nourished and upheld.
His righteous mind gives happiness to all,
His loving-kindness is their highest gain.
He visits with severity the bad,
But on the good he heaps his favors high.
And as he grace and wrath in men perceives
He takes the goblet or he draws the sword.
He is a hero of full gallant mien,
Whose aspect is the dread of Rusteman.
As blows across the mead the autumn breeze
And the reeds quake, so quake the hearts of foes.
When Gog and Magog thunder forth their threats
Their vanquished power is driven back again;
And when the lands with panic fear are struck,
The armies of the foe are trod in dust.
And Tahmas trembles at his gleaming sword
As Euas once before great Timur quailed.
The Persian's head was ruddy with his gore;
No wine ran ever in a redder stream.
His royal heart had then divided cares,
To terrify his foes, and heal his friends.
Fear of the Shah dissolved the foeman's rage,
His pity melted friendly hearts in love.
The fear of him made Rusteman grow weak,

And fly, with bloody spoils behind him trailed.
And while his loving-kindness calmed the world
He won the love alike of young and old.
And while his might and power waxed eminent
He brought the hearts of all to beat with his.
As the high cypress flings a shadow round,
His presence crushed in agony his foes;
Before his greatness and his loftiness,
The spirit of earth's peoples ebbed away.
And were the doughty Dschemschid living yet,
He'd give himself in slavery to the Shah.
When Skender first his gleaming grandeur saw
He wished to be the slave of such a king.
Were Feridum to see his greatness now,
He would have promised fealty to his house.
And on his threshold Cæsar would have dropped,
Like to a slave, his laurel-covered sword.
O clemency, thou hast the whole round world
Led captive by thy rule of righteousness.
Through all thine age of sighs and bitter tears,
Thou only art beloved by night and day,
And in that age, great Alexander sees
The wolf and lamb together take their food.
No robber now in ambush waits to kill,
Our only ambush is in woman's looks;
And no man beats his breast for grief and woe,
But beats a drum tap in the mood of joy.
How shall I estimate thy happy peace!
The happy splendor of thy sanctity!
Were all the trees and bushes turned to pens,
And every leaf were changed into a book,
And the seven seas were darkened into ink,
And every space was written o'er and o'er,
By thousand writers, only one exploit,
Out of one thousand, would recorded be.
And as we here would offer up our prayer,
Let our petition be on justice based.
For thou, as is the sun among the stars,
Art potentate o'er all the climes of heaven;
Sagacious Padishah and Lord of Light

Art thou; for wisdom has enthroned thee Shah.
May God decree full length of years to thee,
And bring a just dishonor on thy foes.
Thee may God's grace conduct to happiness;
And fill the earth with thy transcendent name.
Long mayst thou wear the crown upon thy brow,
And may thine enemies be brought to naught.
God grant long life to all the royal house
And give the land joy, rain, and industry.
May age and peace and happiness arrive,
And all thy reign with endless glory shine.
Who to this prayer of mine responds Amen
May misfortune ever plague his life!

IX

THE BEGINNING OF THE FASCINATING NARRATIVE AND OF THE HEART-RAVISHING FABLE

SPEAK, Nightingale, thy accents utter clear,
And from thy secret haunt reveal thyself;
Thou knowest full well the meaning that lies hid
Within the rose-bed of the inmost mind.
Long hast thou tarried, silent as a bud;
Breathe out the meditation of the Rose,
Let thy voice warble in the voice of love
A song instinct with love's own melody.
So sweet that Sohre, when thy lay is heard,
The lute shall fling in anger to the ground.
And thus the Nightingale in Gulistan
Began, with song, her legendary tale.
Once, in the ancient days that long are past,
Over a country pleasant above all,
There lived a shah, the reigning king of Kum,
And he was gracious, mild, and liberal.
Good fortune followed every step he took;
And he was fair in manner as in face.
In every action was he moderate;
And all his deeds were welcome to the folk.
Pure was his mind, his lineage starred by fame;

He drew all hearts by ruth and tenderness;
He was a monarch of a high descent;
They named him Springtime, for his look was spring.
The earth he cheered, as if with vernal showers,
His presence was a breath of paradise;
Far famed for grandeur and for graciousness,
For strictest justice bore he wide renown.
His sovereign word flew wider than the wind,
And poured its torrents like a foaming stream,
Refreshing by its very righteousness,
Like balmy eastern breezes, earth and time.
For when he spoke, men heard no other sound,
But his. So sang the happy Nightingale.
And no man from the scabbard drew his sword;
Even the sword-lily vanished from the heath;
And never pointed weapon made a wound,
Except the thorns that pierce the bulbul's breast.
And not a crown was ravished against right;
And the east wind the tulip's circlet spared.
Though earth were mantled with a host of green,
A leafy company that none may count,
'Twere easier far to number forest leaves
Than count the flowers that in his palace grew.
Like to a guard-troop, helmeted with gold,
Narcissus flowers were ranged in countless bands;
With lips and beakers blushing ruby red,
The lovely flowers as cup-bearers attend;
The lilies stand full-armed like sentinels,
Mail clad in steely green, with flashing sword.
There many cypresses toss high their heads,
And verdant banners thickly cover them.
From the high walls a shower of thorns is shot,
As lances hurtle, and lay lions low.
Ambassadors in crowds, from east and west,
Bring crowns to him, and eager tribute yield—
Jewels that blaze like planets of the sky,
And gems the prize of fortune's brightest hour.
Within his grove he has a stately rose.
The grace of God is watching over it;
And he is happy in a daughter fair,

Who, like the rose-bush, beautifies the world.
Her name is Rose, though she is still a bud—
A bud in beauty's garden fresh as morn:
Round were these buds, like ruddy lips that called
For kisses with a passionate desire;
Such was the beauty that belonged to them,
That all the world enamored gazed on them.

X

DESCRIPTION OF THE ROSE'S BEAUTY IN EVERY MEMBER

GRACEFUL indeed are all the Rose's tints,
Above, beneath, they move with equal charm,
And all their life expresses beauty's self;
And each is dowered with equal loveliness.
Her restless-streaming and dishevelled locks
Were long life to the heart of those who loved.
And she was beauty's sum and monogram,
By whom to earth descended human bliss;
And many a heart within those meshes lay,
And pined as mine did, from a thousand wounds.
Her figure was like boughs from paradise,
The lotus at the sight obeisance made;
Her figure kills all other trees, and puts
The cypress and the plane-tree out of mind.
Never did cypress wave with such a grace;
For soulful was that figure of the Rose.
The constellations' signet crystalline
Shines out like Alexander's looking-glass.
Venus in Sagittarius is she,
Where sun and moon together cross the sky.
And so her countenance a tablet is
On which the Lord has written—" A child of light,"
And in her eyebrows, rising o'er her eyes,
We see the double moon that comes in Mars.
Joined like the double arches of a bridge
Are those twin bows of beauty and delight.
Without that portico of loveliness,
The house of beauty would to ruin fall.

And those two arches lead into the house,
Where beauty's self is fostered as a child.
How skilfully the magic bow is strung,
The double bow with but a single span!
And every glance that from this bow is shot
Flies to the mark and makes the red blood flow.
That eye—enchantment's self is resting there,
And sorcery's fountain springs beneath that brow.
Whoever looks upon those lustrous eyes
Must cry " Now God be with you, lady fair."
For like Narcissus flowers the eyes adorn
The happy beauty garden of the face.
Twin stars of flame are they, which archers shoot,
Like arrows, from the strong and bended bow.
Two Turks, who in the court of Shinar's plain
Fall drowsy, after drinking, to the floor.
The glance that subjugates the heart of all
Is like a dagger by the acid worn,
Which keener grows with every wound it deals;
For every arrowed glance the heart's blood draws.
The sidelong glances are as skirmishers—
A band of lancers rushing into fight.
Each waving ringlet is a teazing bolt,
That gives unrest, not comfort, to the soul.
Her nose is like a shadow's streak of cloud,
In which the signature of beauty lives;
It is a jasmine, budding and unblown,
Set in the beauty garden of the face.
A finger, which, by power of sorcery,
Has cut the circle of the moon in twain.
Her cheeks, what are they but two roses fresh,
Which with the great archangel converse hold?
Two ruddy pages in which boys have read
Their earliest lesson in the lore of love?
Nay, they are likest to the rising sun,
From which the earth illumination draws.
The little mole upon the lady's cheek
Is but a foil to set her beauty off;
'Tis but a sign of noble ancestry,
A seed of beauty on a field of flowers.

There never fails on every countenance
Some line or feature that commands the whole;
No mole can such pre-eminence assert;
It is her eyes that captivate our gaze.
The ears with pearls that not a blemish own
Reflected on the sea their beauty show;
They are two roses upon which the dew
Of dazzling pearls is radiantly set.
The lips which quite eclipse the world's delights
Are like the holiness which Mary showed,
They are like rubies which attract men's souls
And touch their spirit e'en without a word.
And if I should make known those lips' delight,
What shall I say in reference to the mouth?
'Tis true that God created worlds from naught.
But I am uncreative, vain my words.
The tongue is like a singing nightingale
Which nests above a murmuring waterfall;
It is a bird whose words are brilliant
As are the rubies in a jewel case.
A wise interpreter whose words are true,
Revealing all the secrets of the heart,
The teeth are nothing but the dewy pearls,
Which glitter on the rosebuds of the grove.
They are the precious stones that form a link
Between two rows of ruddy carbuncle;
They are the jewels in a jewel case,
Which in concealment have their radiance hid.
Their sugared sweetness every sweet excels;
And even honey doubly sweet outvie.
The chin is like a beauty apple hung,
With ever-changing charms it wins the eye;
The apple is the fairest fruit of all.
The Rose's chin is more desirable,
And as the quince that hangs unplucked, she says,
" I am the fruit of beauty; pluck me not."
The dimple on the chin is like a well;
And he who falls therein must captive bide.
The chin is like to beauty's tambourine,
On which the dangling locks their soft blows ply;

And when their sporting pattering they begin
It is the march of beauty that they sound.
Her neck is like a taper camphor white
And darkened with the film of falling locks.
Without is light, within a burning fire,
A flame of pride and yet of fickleness.
Most it resembles some white cloud of heaven,
A silver column set in beauty's hall.
And we may well divine her arms are like
The handles of some vase in silver wrought.
By the trumpeter of these fair arms
A thousand heads have fallen in blood and wrath;
Hers are the whitest arms in all the land,
White as the hand of Moses once became,
Her arm rests in a sleeve it fills with light;
Like to a crystal, which itself is clear.
The hand is matchless both in charming shape
And in the light which beauty gives to it.
The Lord has given this hand the bracelet fair
Of fascination that surrounds the wrist.
Under that hand, by its desired caress,
The country and the people rest subdued.
Nor does the henna dye those fingers red,
But naturally the tips are coralline.
For each fair finger is a silver pen
Which writes the winning verses of the heart.
The hand is like the moon; the fist, the sun.
The fingers are the pleasant beams they cast.
And as the almighty Scribe their outline formed,
So wrote he beauty in each finger nail.
For like a rose-leaf is each finger nail,
A rose-leaf that adorns the Rose's stem;
And as each nail is like the moon at full,
Each fragment cut from them a crescent seems.
Her bosom is a tablet crystal clear,
A waterfall that gleams in Paradise.
'Tis the most glorious and the purest light
That ever broke in waves from height of heaven.
The feet are silver pillars, pedestals
Supporting beauty's palace, firm and fair.

They soar like arrows to heaven's highest throne;
They stand twin graces ever side by side,
And like an anchor is the steady foot,
Holding in heaven the white moon's argosy.

XI

THE SHAH PROVIDES A TEACHER FOR HIS DAUGHTER ROSE

As in daytime does the moon appear,
In beauty tender, yet but half revealed,
So did the father see his daughter's face
Grow fair, and thanked his God by day and night.
He watched her beauty with an anxious eye,
And prayed it might to full perfection come.
And brought a teacher, who might lead his child
Along the path where knowledge could be plucked.
He wrote upon a book of pages old
As flame the precious lore which she should scan.
Into her hand he placed the precious book;
It was a new adventure for the Rose.
And from the ancient tutor she began
To read the lines of learning's alphabet.
Page after page the volume was explored,
But all was dull and comfortless to her.
She learned the history of Gulistan,
She learned by heart the annals of Bostan,
It soon had mastered all Vaharistan,
She read the booke of history in Divan,
Yet full of grace, her mind by no means dull,
She had no skill in writing prose or verse.

XII

MORNING AND EVENING IN THE ROSE GARDEN

UPON a morning when the glittering ray
Flooded the meadow green where bloomed the Rose,
And when the sun upon the world's high throne
Showed the Rose the radiance of his orb,

The sun saw joyfully that his daughter dear
Was in her freshest beauty full bedecked.
He knew that she was worthy happiness,
That she was worthy of her princely lot.
Another was sovereign of a realm that brought
Quiet and happiness throughout the world,
His castle was a fortress green in hue,
Green was the hue of its foundation stones;
Inside was decked with high magnificence,
There tulip beds and cypress boughs abounded.
The master who had raised this lofty pile
Had given to it the name of Rosary;
By those who knew the beauteous city well
It very often bore another name.
And every grove and gelder-rose and mead
Had each its proper and especial title.
And in this city did the ruling king
Give to the Rose the highest post of state,
And that the city might be full of grace
He gave to it the Rose to be its flower;
And going with great joy into the grove,
She sat upon the throne in honor there;
And straightway all the world was filled with glee,
And all the world by balmy winds was swept,
The fragrance of whose odors filled the world.
And by their charm lapped it in ecstasy;
In calm felicity the hours went by,
And stream and soil in blessed peace reposed.

XIII

THE ATTENDANTS OF THE PURE ROSE, AND A DESCRIPTION OF HER NOBLE COURT SERVICE

Of rose gardens the Bulbul is the muse,
And thus begins her clear and thrilling song:
The Rose of simple mind and tender mood,
With frank heart, and with disposition kind,
Has chosen for the servants of her house
A band of trusty followers true of heart.

The first was guardian of the sherbet cup;
Comrade of laughter, tears, and genial hours;
Each morning she the rose-water prepared,
The crimson-tinted wine that scents the glade.
'Twas the delight and joy of the Divan,
And shared the name and honors of the dew.
Another was the cheerful cup-bearer.
Ruby his belt, and his cup a carbuncle;
With rosy cheeks he was conspicuous,
For loveliness of lip the painter's choice.
His inmost bosom was the home of love,
And tinged blood-red with passionate desire.
He drank the wine that fed his passion's fire,
And never failed the wine cup to his hand.
He was the chief at each Rose festival,
And the guests called him by the Tulip's name.
Another was the garden's eye, and seemed
The very lamp and eyelight to the grove.
So full of contemplation was his face,
So full of meditation's sober glance.
The radiance of his eye was in its orb,
And wise men saw that it was crystal clear.
This was the prophet of the sinless glance,
Who stood the president of the Divan.
Five golden coins he found, and in his hand
He bore them on the petals of his cup:
He handed round the goblet night and day,
And late and early was he drunk with wine;
So long as wine was flowing, at his board
He would not close his eye till dawn of day.
The eye-glance of the close in sooth was he,
And in the rose-bed is Narcissus called;
And since he holds his goblet in his hand
The gold Cup is he among flowerets named.
Sword-Bearer was another waiting-man;
The guardian of the spacious Rosary;
He bore his naked sword behind the Rose,
And night and day he closely guarded her.
A fencer of incomparable skill
Was he, in short, the prefect of the burg.

A valiant Cerberus and dragon he,
Whose sword and dagger never left his hand.
He was in very truth a trusty slave,
And wide and free his reputation spread.
In the rose garden his acquaintances
Had styled him the Free Lily of the glade.
And there was still another, free as he,
Whose form had grown as lofty as his mind;
Towering he stood, with high and graceful head,
He was the very emir of the grove.
Tall as a column did he seem to rise,
And as an arrow straight his course he took;
And so in Gulistan by day and night
He watched as porter at the entrance gate.
By night and day his faithful watch he kept,
Upright to stand was what he most desired;
He recked not that his day-long post was hard,
While on one foot he stood before the gate;
He was a man of stature eminent
A mighty man, and Cypress was his name.
There was another, like a messenger
Becapped, who pilfered crowns for livelihood;
No parallel of his this world has seen;
He ever seemed to outstrip all rivalry.
Soon as he burst from out the western post,
He reached within a twinkling to the east.
He was so light, that while his course he took,
No cloud of dust arose beneath his feet.
A youngster was he, boisterous in play,
And East Wind was his title in the world.
Another was of purest character,
And simple in his mind, and frank in mien;
His inmost bosom was a well unstained,
And fair as were his cheeks, that all admired.
And yielding was his tender heart to love;
His artless nature moves another's smile.
And, while his heart was thus so pure and clear,
He was the mirror-holder to the Rose;
And winning was he from his babbling flow;
And men had ʻiven to him the name of Brook.

Another was a thief, as full of tricks
Of knavery as a dusky Indian.
Well could he snare his victim in a gin;
He was a robber full of pranks and tricks.
He could the thread spin out with marvellous skill
And hang suspended by a single hair.
His subtility was endless, and more crooks
Were in it than in woman's curling locks.
His heart was full of trickeries and feints,
And as a flower his name was Hyacinth.
And each of these are ranged around the Rose
As escorts at the throne of king and queen.
And in the rose garden from time to time
The Rose refreshment seeks in cups of wine.
The Rose alone of all the flowers around
Was decked with satisfying grace, and hence
Fit opportunity she gained, in which
She might for brighter happiness prepare.

XIV

How in the Morning the Mirror-holder of the Tender-
cheeked Rose Holds the Mirror, and How the Rose
is Proud of Her Beauty

It was in the bright morning of the day,
And lo, her face was in the mirror shown;
And in the radiance gleamed her lovely face,
For it was mirrored in the placid brook.
And in a thousand ways the Rose was ware
That all the world believed how fair she was.
She raised herself above her cloak of night,
And freshly in the streaming sunlight waked;
To lay her fair attire in fullest view
She set herself upon a ruby throne;
Radiant indeed her beauty there appeared;
'Twas red on red in brilliancy shone.
She sat like monarch 'mid his people throned;
All other kings were dust upon the road.
But that her beauty may be manifest,

Needs must she cast her image on the glass.
And lo! the Brook before her ran his course,
And laid the glittering mirror at her feet.
And when she saw herself reflected there,
So lovely, she was rapt in wonderment.
And when she saw herself so fresh and bright
And lovely, she was touched with vanity;
And blushing red in her own charms delight,
" Ah, God," she cried, " there is no god but God!
What beauty hast thou given to me, O Lord,
What excellence among the flowers is mine!
What gracious eyebrows arch above mine eyes!
Like to a canopy they set them off.
How diamond-like and gray those orbs appear!
Their gaze might stir the pulses of the dead.
How lustrous are those amber locks! Their light
Must strike amazement to the minds of man.
And oh, how dazzling are these cheeks of mine!
For after these the moon itself is dim.
And what a beauty mark that little mole,
Which more becoming makes the tender cheek!
Who now will value eyes that fiercely scowl,
And the fell glances that like swords they wave?
But here are eyelashes that twinkle fast,
Like friends that stand together ranged in war.
And then that mouth, whose breath is sweet enough
To bring the mantling life-blush to the dead."
The bolt of self-love pierced her to the heart,
And she was pride-struck by her loveliness,
" And oh," she said, " is houri in the world,
Or peri, so delightsome to behold?
Was ever one with beauty so bedecked,
As I am in the universe beheld?
Such beauteous charm as God has given to me,
To none in this life has he given e'en this.
And can my beauty now be paralleled,
And is not this my face without compare?
The world admits that ne'er in time before
Has such a prize of beauty been revealed;
I am the beauty that has never like,

The only fair with whom not one can vie."
Thus she extolled herself to honor's height,
And made the claim of beauty absolute,
Then called the Eastern Wind, her messenger,
And said, " O faithful bearer of my words,
Assist me in my dire perplexity,
And lighten up for me the night of doubt.
Traverse the realms of Syria and Kum,
And glancing over all the plains you cross,
(Either in Occident or Orient,
Where evening darkles, or where morning glows),
See if in any spot you chance to reach
Aught fairer you can find in face than me;
If anywhere there's beauty like to mine,
And whether there's perfection reaching mine.
Make thou my beauty known to all the world,
That he who listens may with passion burn.
Let people of the time be made aware,
All beauty has been consecrate to me;
That mortals have not had it as their dower
In shape so faultless as belongs to me;
The fair must learn to estimate their charms
Aright, and know how few they do possess,
And that I only may true beauty claim;
The rest are slaves, while I alone am queen."
The herald East-Wind, as he heard her word,
Kissed low the ground before the monarch's feet.
" Thou art indeed the only beautiful,
My Queen, the beautiful, the Queen of Light.
Who will refuse to say that this is true,
Excepting him whose sight is lost to him?
Who to thy beauty's question answers ' No '?
All estimate thy grace as bright and pure,
And own the whole wide world is filled with light
From thy great beauty, as from dawn of day.
I'll make my circuit through the farthest nook,
From the bright Orient to the cloudy West."
He spoke, and started straightway on his course,
Blew a loud blast, and travelled with the wind;
Like to the flocks of birds he shaped his course,

And saw the beautiful in every place;
He quickly travelled o'er the land of Kum,
And soon on Persia's confines found himself.
Soon to the realms of India did he cross,
Next to Manchuria, and to China's plain.
And here on beauty's track he found himself,
And heard of one called Beauty's King Supreme.
Into his presence eagerly he went,
And, blowing softly, saw him face to face;
So o'er the whole wide world he passed, and saw
Naught far or near in beauty like his friend.
By day and night he traversed hill and dale.
Now hear what at the last befell to him.

XV

The East Wind Finds the Nightingale, and They Discuss the Beauty of the Rose

Thus the betrothed of that lorn lover sang,
In verses such as these his song of pain:
" There was a wanderer, the slave of want,
Who had full many a wrong endured of love,
His bosom had its pain, his heart its rage;
He was a dervish, cowled like any monk.
By day he gave full voice to his complaint,
And in the night-time watched the skies of heaven.
His sole existence nowadays was love,
For love alone had claimed him for its slave.
And in his day of trial was his dust
In love compacted, and in love absorbed:
With love his very essence was compounded,
In love the letter of his life was writ.
And now without an object in his life,
He was in love's consuming fire inflamed.
At times he sang aloud a song of love,
While sighs of bitter sorrow tore his breast.
He sang Ghasele, winsome youth and fair,
Who drew the souls of many a neophyte
By his pure mind and by his brilliant charms;

A noble stripling gay, and soft of heart.
His voice brought cheerfulness to every heart,
His music banished sorrow far away,
And when his flute-like tones swelled out amain,
In every soul he kindled passion's fire.
His breathing tones sent gladness through the land,
And those who heard him plainly understood.
In short, he was a tender juvenal,
In all things ready for some enterprise.
Though beggared now, forlorn, and sick for love,
He was a noble in descent and birth,
Who to the winds his lands and lineage threw,
And gave himself to melancholy thoughts.
His coronet and throne capricious spurned,
And to the power of love surrendered all.
For he indeed for very love was crazed,
And as a doting maniac roved the world.
His talk was nothing but the voice of love,
And he was named the Wandering Nightingale.
With rapid foot the East Wind sped his way
Like a bird messenger o'er all the world;
And lo! there reached his ear a strain of love,
In tones of lamentation dolorous.
Arrested by the song, the East Wind stood,
Long listening with delight to that refrain;
For such a *chanson* made his heart to swell,
And seemed like summer fragrance in the air.
Forward he hasted to behold the wight,
Who was so love-struck, and so woe-begone;
And said: " Thou art indeed plunged deep in love,
And from love's goblet drunken with desire.
Thy voice infuses passion in the soul,
Why is it that thou kindlest thus our blood?
Whence didst thy song its powerful spell obtain,
That thus it sets on fire the human breast?
Who art thou, by what name mayst thou be called?
And from what master didst thou learn thy lay?
Whence came to thee this chosen lot of thine?
What inspiration is it makes thy soul?
What means the ecstasy that rules thy strain,

And gives thy voice its overmastering charm?
Thou whom such gifts transcendent glorify,
How is it thou art fallen thus so low?
Why do thy brows this mournful cowl disgrace,
And thou, why art thou seated in the dust?
Love in thy very countenance is writ,
And love's wound plainly has transfixed thy heart.
Art thou in love? How has thy passion fared?
Now is the time to tell, so tell me true."

Now as these words the Bulbul listened to,
She roused in Gulgul joy and love's delight.
" Thou seest here," said he, " a mendicant,
With tearful eyes, that plead to pity's soul.
'Tis love has lessoned me in sorrow's school,
But never have I learned what is my name.
Thou askest me the place from which I come,
Love is my origin and native land.
My foot turns backward still to beckoning love;
'Tis love inspires and gives me genius;
For I am one whose mind is crazed by love;
And in the world I wander lost for love.
Heedless I hurry by, nor care for rest,
Yet travel cannot give the balm I crave.
And often to my love I give full rein,
Until I am not master of my mind;
And at the will of love, am driven adrift,
And therefore ever wait I love's behest;
In short, this love pang quite o'ermasters me,
And takes away from me the power of choice.
Now I am brainless, footless, purposeless,
Tossed like a plaything at the whim of Fate.
I am constrained by love, and driven along
Hither and thither like an autumn leaf.
I have no other impulse in my soul,
Where love and love alone predominates.
The shame of love is more than honor's meed
To me, and more than fortune's smile.
The very gloom of love is sweet to me,
For what were worldly bliss without this flame?

The hand of pleasure has made smooth and clear
The mirror of my heart with Love's own glass.
Love is no shame, for love is happiness;
True shame in worldly happiness is found."

Soon as the East Wind heard these words of love
He murmured loudly, thrilled with deep delight.
Thus spoke he: "O thou, all afflicted one,
Who from the love pang of thy secret wounds
Groanest and sighest, like a man in love,
Tell me where is the lady of thy love?
Toward whom does thy soul's intuition turn?
Who is the Leila that enchains thee thus?
Who is it that has burdened thee with grief?
Where is the Schirin that thus plagues Ferhadan?
Who is the Afra of thine ardent flame?
Say to what king thou wouldst devote thy blood?
For whom is it thou sufferest loss of rest?
And whose compassion dost thou supplicate?
What light in all the world has fame enough
To keep thee moth-like hovering in its flame?
And of what rose art thou the nightingale,
That thou shouldst be the slave of music's sound?"
Thus spoke the warbler: "Gracious are thy words,
And therefore will I make my chanson plain.
From the first moment that I was conceived,
Love with my inmost essence was entwined,
And in my mother's womb it came to me
That love should be my only intellect.
And that great painter Nature made for me
The only form of beauty to be love.
And since my life was in my spirit locked,
Only by love can I my soul unlock.
And without hindrance or reserve, so far,
I have outpoured, unchecked, my song of love.
Yet know I not for whom I burn, for whom
By night and day I suffer in this flame.
However may this flame continuous glow,
I know not yet how it was kindled first.
So runs my life; a solitary wight

I live in ignorance of her I love,
Of her who lit in me this flaming torch;
To whom I ever lift this suppliant hand.
Restless, ah me, these weary sighs I heave,
Yet do not know the queen for whom I sigh.
This bitter plight is all the life I know,
Of all things else I am in ignorance.
Now tell me, what thy current's course may be,
Whence comest thou, and whither dost thou wend?
What message is it thou art sent upon,
And who it is thou seekest in this land?
What is the object of thy wandering search,
And who thou art, and what thy name may be?
What was the first beginning of thy life,
And in what country was thine origin?
Thou bringest fragrance of the truth sincere,
And needst must be a creature trustworthy;
Thy breath gives life to every human soul,
And in thy fragrance is a human soul.
The breath of health is certainly thy dower,
Before it even the dead might come to life."
The East Wind to these golden words gave ear,
Then answered: " Stranger, amiable and good,
I, in return for all that thou hast told,
Will tell my story with the strictest faith.
I also, like Abdallah strenuous,
Am in the same perplexity with thee.
I think a child who is with beauty dowered
As fickle and unstable as the wind;
It is desire that sends me wandering,
And yields to me the essence of my life.
Like to a vortex runs my eddying course;
And without head or foot I drift away.
Nor can I stop a while and take repose;
Desire is all the power to act I know.
My origin is pleasure and desire,
Which in the howling desert gave me life.
And for my outward lot, my happy friend,
I in a grove of roses have my home.
And am a servant to the sovereign Rose,

And wait upon her pleasure constantly,
My breath refreshment brings to all the flowers,
And cheers the rose parterre with cheerful light."
Then said the Nightingale: " O happy friend,
Thy breath brings health and purity to me!
But what is that you call a rose garden?
And prithee tell me who this princess is?"
Then said the Wind which fosters life in things:
" Gladly I tell, and thou shalt joyful hear.
There stands a place within the realms of Kum.
'Tis called the rose parterre, the Rose's realm;
There, in a climate genial, this burg
Is equally renowned with paradise,
Of paradise with Eden's beauties blent;
And flowers, fresh flowers are ever blooming there.
The waters gleam like springs of paradise;
The dust is fragrant as the purest musk;
The watered plain is like the mirror stream
That flashes over Eden's happy realm;
The dust is naught but amber all unpriced;
This home of healing is a paradise.
Within 'tis filled with all things beautiful,
And siren strains incomparable resound.
Well may it bear the name of paradise,
For every glade with glowing houris shines.
The Rose is queen and ruler of the town,
Which holds the lordship over all the world.
Unique for beauty is the reigning Rose,
And her charm beautifies all other worlds.
She is the princess of things beautiful,
The moon of beauty in the arch of heaven.
All spheres celestial lie below her feet
When she sits throned on cushions of delight.
Be she by me both praised and idolized,
Whose sight might lap you into ecstasy!
The bloom of love gives radiance to her eyes;
Enchantment fills the meshes of her hair.
Her brows are beauteous as the crescent moon;
Her mole is like a glittering star of eve;
The eye, when angry, like a dragon gleams;

It draws the dagger against all who love.
No courage can endure the terror spread
By the arched brows that overstand her eyes.
The flash, so soon as it is felt by man,
Confounds his senses, and defeats his wit.
Those eyes can rob the very soul of life;
The whisper of the mouth alone restore it.
He who their beauty looks upon, declares
'Tis God who sends a blessing on this face;
In short, she only does the ideal show,
As being the only beauty in the world.
And I have wandered in a hundred realms,
And never have I found the match of her.
For beauty is in her so eminent
That she is the perfection of the world.
She is the padishah, the queen of light,
And as a slave to such a queen I bow;
I swiftly speed her errand when she bids,
And flash along my journey like the wind."

When Bulbul had these words attentive heard,
Straight to the earth he groaning fell for grief;
For in his heart the love-fire had been lit
And blazed like tapers in a holy place;
Endurance now was overcome by love;
He flung himself with cries into the dust.
His breast was filled with passionate desire,
And in the pain itself he found delight.
The dew of ardent passion filled his eye,
And pangs of love his inmost bosom tore;
He cried aloud with anguish, sighed, and groaned,
His eyes were wet with tears unworthy love.
Then said he to the East Wind anxiously:
" Why should this sudden flame consume my life?
What is the arrow that unfeeling fate
To my bared bosom has this instant shot?
What is the goblet whose enticing draught
Has robbed me of my senses while I drank?
How shall I reason of the dazzling light
That flutters round my spirit like a moth?

What is this lightning flash, whose sudden blaze
Kindles a world of terror in my soul?
What blast is this that carries me away
And strikes my very being as it flies?
What stranger guest is this who comes to me
And takes away my reason by his word?
Peace like a bird escapes from out my hand,
And all my soul in utter ashes lies.
The old distress has taken the strength of new,
And yonder beauty overwhelms my heart."

XVI

The Witty East Wind Counsels the Wandering Nightingale

The East Wind calmly on the vagrant gazed,
Whose heart and soul were lit with raging flame,
And said, " Now tell to me, thou shameless one,
Where are thy courtesy and manners fled?
Whence can a beggar claim such dignity,
That he in love could ask a princess bride?
What spurs and flogs thee on to such extremes?
Beware, or thou will lose at last thy wits.
Compare her loftiness with thy estate;
What can a beggar want of royalty?
The Rose is winsome in a thousand ways,
The Nightingale is but a singer clear;
Although a thousand times thy love thou sing,
Hope not the Rose's fragrant charm to win.
Whence dost thou gain such fitting dower of worth,
As makes thee fit to mate the balmy Rose?
Abandon passion, with its torments sore,
And shun this emptiness of wild desire.
For even should'st thou live a thousand years,
Ne'er wilt thou reach the level of the Rose.
And though thou cry Gulgul a thousand times,
Thou never wilt arouse the lady's heart.
Refrain, then, further to torment thyself,
Nor strike on iron cold thine idle blows."

Now when the Nightingale had heard these words,
He burst into a passionate lament;
And said: " Although I but a dervish be,
Yet still the wounds that pain my heart are fresh.
A beggar am I in my outward guise,
But I am none the less love's padishah.
Love makes me independent in the world,
Such beggary as mine is worth a crown.
I love the Rose, and shall forever love,
And a fakir may sometimes love a shah;
Sense is indeed the guide of sober life,
But sense is never fostered by true love;
The lover in his acts is privileged,
As is the drunkard and the beggar-man.
He who would moderation value first,
Can never taste the luxury of love.
The lover who is shamefaced and reserved
Can never see the beauty which is coy.
Until the lover scorns the public blame
He gains no trust nor kindness from his love.
Though I have no enjoyment of the Rose,
'Tis joy enough for me to speak of her.
Though no return reward my passion's pain,
Yet love itself is fair enough for me,
And he who knows the harmony of love
Will think enjoyment less than absence is.
Who lives in full fruition of his love
Is always fearing it will fly away;
He who contentedly has watched its flight
Is happy hoping it will soon return.
Absence to me is love and dignity,
Although fruition be denied my heart.
I live in agony's o'erflowing stream
And love's fruition willingly renounce."
The East Wind saw that it was vain to try
The ardor of this beggar wight to quench,
For counsel did not profit him a jot.
His love kept burning like an aloe-flower,
And all his words were emphasized by sighs,
And his heat withered him like foliage parched.

And so he left him, and pursued his way
Into the precints of the rose garden;
There at the ruler's feet he kissed the ground,
And said to her, " O righteous queen of light,
Let it be written with exactest care,
That above all the Rose is beautiful,
Though I through many realms have travelled
I have not found a beauty like to thine."

XVII

How the Lamenting Nightingale Comes to the Garden of the Rose

Beset with pain and sorrow of the heart
And overmastered by a longing keen,
The Nightingale began to utter loud
His love forlorn in notes of bitterness;
An ardent longing throbbed within his throat,
And he was stabbed by keen misfortune's thorn.
Struck by love's pang, like tree that feels the axe,
He fell at last inanimate to earth;
Fainting from wounds of love and pulseless limbs,
There lay he down as if by absence slain.
From songs despondent thus his love desponds,
And pining grown as thin as is a hair.
At last the truth was wrought into his soul
That inactivity but adds to ill.
So up he rose, and in fit garments clad,
Set out upon his way to see his love.
Love seemed to spread out pinions for his flight,
O'er field and hillock bearing him along.
By the discreet direction of his friend
He travelled day and night in ardent love.
He reached the post town of United Hearts;
Thence straight he travelled to the rose garden.
And now at last arrived at Gulistan,
There breathed on him the fragrance of his love.
And on the outside of the garden fence
There came a friend who waited sedulous,

A traveller, who without an hour's delay
Was hurrying from this garden to the sea.
The stainless Brook, whose spirit shone in light,
The pilgrim wandering to see the world.
Straight from the garden of the Rose he came,
His bosom clad in spotless fluttering folds,
And when the Nightingale beheld him come,
With eager greeting he drew near to him.
The Brook a low obeisance made to him,
And scanned the new-comer with eager eye.
He saw it was a beggar stood before him,
A beggar sick and all distraught with woe.
'Twas love had brought him to that low estate
And he was branded on the brow by love,
Then said the Brook, " O thou by love distraught,
And bowed to earth by love and suffering,
Why wearest thou this lorn and lifeless air?
Does now no heart's blood warm thy inmost veins?
Who branded this love-token on thy face?
Who is it laid on thee the name of love?
Where is the Mecca of thy heart's desire,
Which claims thee and demands thee for itself?
And what has made thee drunken by its draught?
What cedar with its shadow blighted thee?"

The Nightingale replied: " O kindly one,
See what I am, and do not question me.
I am enamored of a pictured face;
And there are many thousands such as I;
I am a beggar, and my love a queen.
I am all destitute, but she is rich;
She is with beauty radiant as the sun,
And I am duskier than a sunbeam's mote.
In beauty's garden does she bloom a Rose,
And I am naught but the poor Nightingale.
I by no name am known, but she speaks out,
And by her very graces names herself."

So spoke the Nightingale, and down he fell,
With dolorous cries of grief and notes of woe.

Then he began a song of love forlorn,
With trills and runs of a many a circling tone.
"And love," he said, " intoxicates my sense,
Through ardent longing for that ruby mouth.
The lightning flash of love that struck my heart,
Laid ruin in the chambers of my breast.
The heart's endurance can no longer stand,
It has been worn away by pangs of love.
For love to ashes has reduced my life;
Love only leaves to me the power of song;
And love has filled my inmost heart with fire,
'Tis love that draws the sweat-drops of the heart,
For love has banished me from house and home;
My soul in sickness languishes through love.
And love has wearied out my tuneful throat;
The secrets of my soul hath love betrayed.
The torch of love has fallen upon my heart,
My soul is set on fire by force of love;
For love has taken my heart to be its friend;
But like a halter is this love to me.
I am become a laughing-stock through Love,
And love has set my name among the fools."

Now as these accents by his friend were heard,
His heart with tender sympathy was touched.
His heart with generous indignation burned,
And to the pain of fierce desire he woke.
He said: " Poor wretch, inebriate of love,
Afflict thyself no more, for God is kind.
For happier fortune has he destined thee,
For it was he who gave thy love her charm;
Thy breath of music penetrates my soul,
And I will straight conduct thee to the Rose.
Gaze once upon her beauty e'er thou die;
And in her joys thine ardent passion breathe."

The Nightingale was gladdened by these words
And joy that moment lighted up his mind,
" O sir," he said, " is this but sleep and dream?
The fragrance of fruition hits my sense.

Thou who has given me bliss, be happy thou,
And fortunate in either universe.
Thou who dost help me to my dearest wish,
May all thy purpose lead to happiness.
The best loved news dost thou convey to me;
For guerdon, thou may'st take my very soul.
I give to thee my soul, I give my life,
O bring me to the jewel of my love."

He answered: " Patience and not haste be ours;
And often in delay is safety found.
Thou, dervish, must restrain thyself a while,
For overhaste is slower in despatch.
I bring thee to the bower of loveliness,
To Cypress, who is porter of the gate.
I hope by such expedient that the Rose
May entertain thee as a man of truth."

So spoke to him the friend of purity
And showed him where the Rose's meadow lay;
The Nightingale his footsteps followed fast
Until they reached the garden of the Rose.

XVIII

How the Nightingale Entered the Rose Garden Through the Kindly Offices of the Cypress

He saw a lofty building fair bedight
Like the green castle of the firmament,
A castle emerald-bright in radiance.
It twinkled like a marshalled host in arms;
Pure was the water, earth was sweet as musk.
An air of sanctity and plenty reigned.
Whoever came to this from Edentown
Might think his resting-place was paradise.
How could it fail to be a paradise
For him who hoped to find his love therein?
When the sad Nightingale beheld the place
Breathless and lost in wonder did he stand.

Above him was the arch of azure sky,
And at his feet the lovely river ran.
Then said the river: " Take good heed, and see
Thou give some respite to thy burning heart;
Meanwhile I stand me here, and as a man
I introduce thee to the portal's guard."

This said, he greeting to the Cypress sent.
Right quick the Cypress was his word to heed.
Low in the dust his countenance he laid
And with his tears bedewed the thirsty ground.

He said: " O Cypress, loftiest of mien,
Thou sittest at the footstool of the great,
I have a courteous word to speak to thee.
Open thy lips to me, I beg of thee;
For if thou lend me for a while thine ear,
I know my prayer at once will be fulfilled.
Here with a stranger destitute I come,
To show how the road lay to this place.
He is a man both kind and dutiful,
Of purest disposition and intent;
A dervish, and a man of loving heart.
But he is lorn and sick from pangs of love,
In outward guise he seems like a fakir,
But in the realm of science he is prince.
A genial friend, a comrade tender-hearted,
Of blameless mind and sympathetic soul,
A poet full of spiritual light
Is he, and in imagination young."

XIX

How the Wandering Nightingale Alone in the Night Abides With His Sighs and Weeping Till Morning

'Twas night, when in the azure sky above
The stars as sleeping closed their sparkling eyes,
When friends and foes alike in slumber lay,
Yet, at the music of the Nightingale,

Awoke, for Bulbul then all sleepless sate
And uttered to the world his dolorous chant,
While thinking on the beauty of the Rose.
For vivid passion wakened in his heart,
And with his sad and melancholy voice
He 'gan to mourn above his well-beloved.
And thinking on his melancholy plight,
And on his desolation all forlorn,
He thus began his sad and mournful lay:
" O queen who dwellest in a careless realm,
O thou who art the moon of beauty's heaven,
Half of all beauty's bloom belongs to thee;
Thou the Rose-bloom of beauty's paradise,
Oh, listen to the message that I bring,
As I begin to utter my lament.
For love of thee I sicken to my death;
And all my understanding fails in me;
Some secret pang my patience has destroyed,
I am distraught in this fair world of thine,
My fettered heart is struggling in a snare,
And all my soul is manacled in woe.
And through the dolor of my dazzled sight,
I am as faint as is the new-born moon.
Some power, as in the chase, my spirit hunts;
E'en now the gleaming knife is at my heart.
For, oh! the beauty of thy cheek has cast
Fire in the dreary dwelling of my mind;
And all the perilous lustre of thine eye,
Like a sharp sword, is levelled against me.
My suffering has cleft my heart in twain,
And in dire desolation ruined me.
I melt to nothing in the grief of love,
And plunge deep buried in a flood of woe;
For I am overcome with passion's wound,
My inmost being heaves in pain and blood;
I am consumed, and absence tortures me.
And like a mote I hover in desire.
My love pain burns me like a heated iron,
My eye is like a beaker filled with wine;
Oh, help me, for endurance can no more;

Oh, spare me further buffets of disdain.
My strength is all unequal to this load,
And all my feebleness is free from guilt.
O slender Rose, and wilt thou that thy bird
Should still descant of absence and neglect
With thorn-pierced bosom ever hid from thee?
Now beauty in the lightest slumber lies,
And deeper sorrow checks my prayers to thee.
O Rose, beware thou of the gale of sighs,
For, like the morning wind, it mars the Rose.
On this distracted heart some pity take,
Be merciful and heal me of my pain."
So sang the silver-throated nightingale,
So sang he, with his soul aflame in love.
But there was naught that noted or allayed
His pain, and tears were still his sole relief.
No one gave heed to his sad cantilene,
And no one knew the meaning of his woe.
To him the world in utter darkness lay,
He was encompassed by a trackless maze,
On one side were the shadows of the night,
And on the other was the force of fate.
The world in dreariness and sorrow lay,
The very stars were dimmed in slumber deep,
And darkness would not yield before the light,
And not a sign of morn was on the hills.
And long and lonesome were those darkling hours
Of agony, while refuge there was none.

XX

The Sleepless Nightingale is Tormented in the Dark Night, and Mourns Aloud

While he was thus oppressed with many a woe,
Thus he addressed his *chanson* to the night:
"What means, O night, this dark and murkiness,
Which so torments with terror every soul?
Is it from absence from the loved one come,
That now the moon withholds her welcome beam?

Is all the radiance of the sunlight quenched?
And all the circling Pleiads put to flight?
Has my lament extinguished Saturn's ray,
So that his rings no longer flash their beams?
Has Jupiter his happy seat forsaken
Because of the unhappiness of earth?
Is it that Mars has fallen by the sword,
That therefore all the heavens are clothed in black?
Why does the sun refuse to show his face?
Is he, the fount of light, to darkness turned?
Has Anahid, in hopeless apathy,
Flung to the ground her lute of poesy?
Is Mercury, heaven's letter-writer, grown
Black as the ink that dries upon his pen?
Why does the world this face of darkness wear?
Is it that my lament has brought it gloom?
Why is it morning fails to show itself?
Surely my *chanson* has not held it back.
Why is the night so slow in its advance?
Is it that day brings absence from my love?
Surely the day of resurrection dawns,
When all the stars fall down upon the earth!
Who has thus closed the window of the moon?
And broken the golden lampstand of the sun?
Is it the operation of my sighs
That tinges all the earth with dismal hues?
And has the dart of light forsaken heaven?
And does the sky wear mourning for my woe?
The constellated eagle stops his flight.
Or has he flitted to the realms of gloom?
Has Vega fallen, with a broken heart,
Down from her pinnacle of happiness?"
When he had uttered loud this lone complaint,
He with his spirit thus soliloquized:
"Why is it that the ruler of the world
Has set me in this valley of distress?
For neither to my mother nor my sire
Have I been aught but minister of pain.
Oh, better were it I had ne'er been born,
And all my blood had flowed away like milk!

So that, before I closed my eyes in sleep,
Death's sword had doomed me to forgetfulness.
Or while I yet in cradle bands reposed,
My life had early passed away from me.
Oh, that the mother's milk that wet my lips
Had turned to poison in that very hour!
Oh, that an arrow swift had struck my heart,
And parted at a stroke the thread of life!
Oh, that some poison-fanged and treacherous snake
Had bitten me to death upon my bed!
Oh, that some vulture fierce had carried me
To its lone eyrie in the heights of Kaf!
And when the soft hand of a mother dear
Arrayed her infant in the richest robes,
Oh, that some sturdy robber of the road,
For love of all my gold and finery,
Had without pity drawn his rapier keen
And from my shoulders struck my head to earth!
Why does the world refrain from setting me,
As its great foe, 'mid perils and mishaps?
Why is it this calamity of woe
Has failed to cleave my bosom unawares?"
As thus he sang aloud his dolorous lay,
The moon came out upon the clearing sky,
And when he looked on heaven's expanded field,
Thus he addressed the goddess of the night.

XXI

The Nightingale in His Amorous Pain Anxiously Addresses the Radiant Moon

He sang in agony, " O radiant moon,
That fillest all the welkin with thy light,
Dost thou in some bright sun thy mansion find,
Whence thou derivest thine enraptured beam?
And hast thou thence a borrowed splendor gained,
With which to fill the world thou gazest on?
The darkness that is dense and hideous
Turns at thy coming into splendor clear.

Leave me not comfortless this whole night long,
But guide me to my darling's wakeful bower.
To me, a wanderer on the rough highway,
Be guide and leader on a path direct.
And, when thou movest in thine orbit blest,
Let thy light flow like some enchanting lay.
Thou art indeed the glowing sun of night,
Flinging o'er heaven the light flecks of thy face.
Oh, cast thy radiance on this friend of thine,
Who wanders with no sunshine in his life.
Be to the poor, who consolation need,
The balm for every wound 'neath which they faint.
One glance of thine has power to dissipate
The fevered pangs of sufferance in the poor.
Needy and friendless and of all forlorn,
Fit object he of thy consoling aid.
And since his sorrows are beyond compare,
And with no changing breath he bears thee love,
And since his love to thee is reckoned crime,
Do thou absolve him of his guiltiness.
For if thou turn thee from a beggar's path,
Before the people thou shalt blush with shame.
When men rebuke him, and blot out his name,
Or make his name forgotten by his kind,
If thou at last become averse to him,
There is no hope of pity for his soul."
While the poor lover thus his mourning made,
The welkin sparkled with the glance of day.

XXII

The Lovesick Nightingale Accosts the Risen Morning in a Clear and Fitting Manner

" O light of morn, that beautifies the world,
By force of truth and of sincerity,
Thy heart is lit by the pure light of truth,
And open to the world as day itself.
Let thy pure joy illuminate my heart,
Make thyself known to yonder moon of heaven;

'Tis she that sheds her rays upon this world,
When thou hast flashed thy beams upon her disk;
Oh, tear away this veil of gloom from me,
And call to me the mistress of my heart.
Say to her: 'Sore is yonder poor man's heart;
He journeys o'er the world with silent lips.
To this poor wanderer in the way of love
Must thou show pity and compassion due,
For want has torn the mantle from his back,
And love has laid him prostrate on the earth.
He sees before him nothing but the grave,
And never turns his glance aside from it.
Oh, do not tread the helpless in the dust,
Dam up the flood of wrath that threatens him!
When this poor man the needed morsel wants,
The beggar still can boast a wallet full.
He has nor wealth nor influence, my queen,
Yet lacks he not accomplishment, my queen;
And gold and silver failing, 'tis enough
To see thy tears and sympathetic glance.
Be gentle, then, to this accomplished man,
And give assistance to a bard inspired.
The prince who acts with kindness to the poor
Proves by his deeds his loving gentleness.' "
While in this wise the nightingale discoursed,
The sun stood beaming in the arch of heaven,
And as he marked it, from the moon he turned
And fixed his contemplation on the sun.

XXIII

THE DESPONDING NIGHTINGALE ADDRESSES THE WORLD-ADORNING SUN, WHILE HIS INMOST HEART GLOWS WITH ARDENT DESIRE

He said: " O lord of light in heaven above,
Thou art the lightener of the angel realm,
Thy lustre fills with radiance all the world,
And reaches to the garden of the Rose.
'Tis by thy diligence that all things are,

And are from elemental atoms formed.
Thou art the eye and lamp of all the world,
Light to men's sight, and lustre to the stars.
Unless the moon derived her light from thee,
She were in darkness to the judgment day;
And but that thou dost gaze upon the morn,
The gloom of night would never leave the east.
Thou art indeed the morning gate of love,
Spreading thy light in footprints of the morn;
Oh, let my ardent passion shine on her,
And fall with suppliant words before her gate.
Go humbly to the place where she abides,
And fling thyself before her fairy feet.
Oh, speak to yonder moon about my love,
And say to her, Fair regent of the heavens,
For thy great beauty lies thy lover low,
And like a shadow trodden in the dust.
For him there is no daylight in the world,
So sorely absence keeps him prisoner.
The night of absence wounds him to the quick,
Oh, give him but a glimpse of thy fair face.
Oh, change the loneliness of one long night
For the delightsomeness of cheerful day.
Let him, who is with passion deep consumed,
Look with his longing eye upon his love.
This wretched one is prisoner of thine,
Have pity on the wandering devotee.
Suffering and despite is his only wealth,
And he is despicable all for thee.
He stands unnoticed in the world's wide house,
Stretch out thy hand to welcome the despised;
The window-sill and threshold of thy house,
Shall then his Sacred Stone and Mecca be.
He watches through the night till morn arise,
And speaks aloud thy name in his distress.
Early and late he thinks alone of thee;
Early and late his heart is set on thee.
His prayers he utters in thine ear alone,
He turns to thee alone his anxious eye.
Thou art his creed, all others he forswears;

Thou art the sect and ritual that he loves.
The creed that he professes is thy love.
Offend not, then, the Mussulman's belief.
Grant, queen, the prayer of thy fond devotee,
O Queen, propitious be to his desire."
'Twas thus he spake aloud his inmost thought,
But vain was all his pleading and his pain.
And so he turned him from the sun and moon,
Like Abraham, and made appeal to God.

XXIV

THE NIGHTINGALE, IN HIS DISTRESS, TURNS FROM SUN AND MOON AND ADDRESSES A PRAYER TO GOD

HE turned to the Creator with his prayer
Of pain, to Wisdom and Omniscience,
And cried: "O God, who art the Lord of all,
Who easest sorrow, and who hearest prayer,
Thou knowest the hidden secrets of the world,
For thou art Ruler both of heaven and earth.
Thou knowest well the plight in which I lie;
And that my burden ever greater grows;
No human mind can tell what I have borne,
How I am bowed beneath a load of shame;
How I have been the slave of luckless woe,
And have succumbed to the sharp stroke of grief.
I burn in passion's longing and distress,
But thy grace reigns in blest tranquillity;
I cannot ope my heart to anyone,
For utterance crushes me, and wearies me;
For I am friendless in a stranger's house,
Hopeless in absence from my well-beloved.
Nothing is constant to me, saving grief
And obloquy. Was ever such a lot?
And no one sorrows over my distress,
My eye alone distils these pearly tears;
No friend is partner of my obloquy,
My gloom of sighs involves myself alone.
No one has sympathy with my dread lot,

Nor heeds the wounds upon my bleeding breast.
If I should die, there would no mourners be,
Excepting this impassioned heart of mine.
I tread the valley of astonishment,
O God, when shall I reach the house of joy?
Oh, by this heart, that runs to thee for help,
By the deep sighs that burn me as they rise,
By the loud beatings of my whispering heart,
By the belovèd Rose in which I trust,
By all the beauty of some distant scene,
By all the rapture of heroic love,
By the high honor of my well-beloved,
By the lorn lot of him who loveth her,
By the black weeds that my devotion speak,
And by the tears that fill my eyes like blood,
By the misfortune and the wrath I feel,
By him who separates me from my love,
Yea, by the honeyed sweetness of her lips,
And by my own sincerity of soul,
By the unhappiness of him who loves,
And by his unstained rectitude of heart,
By that which to the lover causes woe,
And by the night-long pain in which he pines,
By all the light that glorifies the moon,
By all the radiance of this world of ours,
By daylight and the pomp of noonday suns,
By the thick darkness of the midnight hour,
By earth below, and by the heavens above,
And by the hustling crowd on judgment day,
By Adam's early days of innocence,
By him who is the lord of purity,
By Seth, by Noah, and by Abraham,
By Gabriel, who brought the message down,
By Moses, who as prince and preacher spoke,
By Jesus and the light that Mary shed,
By all the love that great Mahomet won,
By his forbearance and his majesty,
By his young people and his dwelling-place,
By his great might that nothing could subdue:
By the prevailing virtue of God's name

And by his nature's unity divine,
Consume me not with separation's flame,
Give me enjoyment's happiness supreme;
Oh, softly warm her frozen heart for me,
And soften it with gentlest influence;
Pour out thy balm of pity in her heart,
That so my pain at last may be allayed.

XXV

THE BEAUTEOUS ROSE HEARS THE VOICE OF THE NIGHTIN-
GALE, AND WHILE SHE FEELS AN INWARD DELIGHT IN
IT, SHE PUTS ON AN AIR OF RESERVE AND DISDAIN

AND while the Nightingale his lay prolongs,
And offers up his orisons to God,
The Rose in slumber suddenly perceived
A wondrous strain of music in the air;
Upon her listening ear there stole a strain
Which gave the joy of passion to her heart.
And as she heard the amorous Nightingale
She asked: "What sound of music do I hear?
How does the spirit of life pervade the song!
Who is it that is uttering the lay?
Ah, what a songster, a musician, he!
A songster and a hierophant in one.
Has Venus come from heaven to visit us,
And pour such floods of melody on earth?"
And then that she might hear the truth aright,
She called Narcissus to investigate.
And soon as he appeared at her behest,
She said, " O thou, our circle's watchful eye,
I heard but now a burst of music rare.
Who is it that can boast such gift of song?
The soul so fondly feeds upon that sound,
That it is rapt in utter ecstasy.
Go forth and seek and hither bring me word,
What craftsman is it that so sweetly sings?
Did he descend from heaven, like the dew?
Or did he spring, like tulip, from the mead?

Go, question make, and learn whence came the sound,
And what the singer's name and place of birth.
Dear friend, inquiries strict and searching make,
And bring to me the answer that you find."
Then said Narcissus: " 'Tis with vast delight,
I go to learn what you have asked of me;
So soon as I his countenance behold
I shall his character at once discern."
So at that very hour Narcissus went,
To fetch her information of the bird.
He found at last the outcast miserable,
That with the Cypress tree stood hand in hand,
And night and day his dolorous chanson poured,
And told his ardent passion to the world.
He questioned graciously the Cypress tree,
And learned the true condition of the bird.
He learned the Nightingale was amorous,
And deeply troubled with the pang of love.
And to the Rose returning, told her all—
His name, and in what mournful plight he lay.
He was a wretch, he said, of reason reft,
Consumed forever with the flame of love.
An exile, whom his passion had inspired
To rove in distant land from shore to shore.
He now had come at last upon his way
To lay his heart submissive at her feet.
A creature full of virtuous qualities,
And all accomplished in the tuneful art.
Soon as the Rose had heard this narrative,
Her heart was filled with secret joyfulness.
And as her beauty kindled with desire,
Her gracious charm was clouded o'er with wrath.
Then spoke she: " Wherefore hies the beggar here?
He stuns my ear with his unchecked lament.
When will this shameless arrogance have end,
Which clamors like a tocsin through the night?
What will his daring lead him next to do?
Perchance he wishes to abide with us.
What is the cause for all this loud lament?
Who is it with a sword thrust draws his blood?

What bird does this poor wanderer call himself?
I do not know the language that he speaks.
His rhapsody but stuns my ear with pain,
And yet the song he sings is kind to me.
What does the bird of evil fortune here?
There is no room with us for such a fowl.
Who is the shameless beggar that is come
To take at night a post so near the queen?
Since he arrived among us with his din
My head is giddy and my sense is gone.
He hinders me from slumber all the night,
Now tell me how this clamor to chastise.
Why does he call upon me day and night,
Reckons he not his passion's hopelessness?
Surely this fool and beggar does not hope
In the rose garden to approach the Rose?
Love has not paled his cheek; unheated iron
Is not more dark than are those cheeks of his.
Bid him begone, and leave our flowery home,
Nor hope to cast his amorous eyes on me.
Bid him o'ercome this passionate desire,
No further sing in vain his tale of love.
The wanderer may not in his mood presume
To approach from far the empress of the world.

XXVI

The Prudent Narcissus Remonstrates With the Garrulous Nightingale

As the world's bride these words of anger spake,
Narcissus went the Bulbul to rebuke,
And said: " What means this elegy of woe?
How is it thou hast fallen on lot so black?
What wit, what manners, canst thou boast to have
Who weepest in this paradise of heaven?
Thou, in the lap of misery born and bred,
Has added shamelessness to suffering.
Thy utterances have wakened up the flowers,
And robbed of sleep the eyelids of our queen.

How is it fitting that a beggar-man,
Should join a princess in delight of love?
Our Princess Rose is from her chamber come,
And filled with mighty anger at thy words.
She says: ' The varlet must bethink himself,
And ne'er again so boldly speak my name.
He has his secret to the world proclaimed,
And made my name a byword among men.
My name, through him, all babbling tongues shall speak,
Who makes me figure as his night-long prize:
Now let him check the clamor of his song,
Or I will meet him with avenging wrath.
Let him consort with those who share his lot,
Else will my anger fall upon his head.
My name no longer on his lips be found,
And from his memory let my image fade.
For now he is arousing naught but wrath,
And evil will befall him at the last.' "
'Twas thus Narcissus freely spoke to him
And with a sigh the Nightingale replied;
And, while he dared no longer sing aloud,
His silent sighs were rising in his heart.
He sickened under separation's pang,
He stood aghast, amazed, and faint in heart;
And now Narcissus backward took his way,
And left him lying like a lifeless clod.
His heart was raging with a furious heat,
Wrapt in the flaming whirlpool of its pangs.
The pain of separation made him dumb;
And all unconscious to the ground he fell;
Long time he lay as he were drunk with wine,
As if his love were quenched in longings vain.
At last his senses came again to him,
As he looked forth, his eyes were drowned in tears.
He then resolves he will renew his lay,
If only he be equal to the task.
So all the day in solitude he sighs,
And patiently endures his hapless plight.
Yet keeps he silent and no longer sings,
And no man knows the suffering he endured.

XXVII

THE EAST WIND MEETS THE WANDERING NIGHTINGALE AND
BRINGS HIM TIDINGS FROM THE TENDER ROSE

ONE balmy morning when the night had fled
And made surrender to the light of day,
When buds had oped their eyelids once again,
And nodded in the wind o'er all the earth,
The Nightingale in utter misery sat,
A wretched outcast in a cheerless world.
His song had but increased his pang of woe,
And now his silence tortured him the more.
And suddenly the East Wind comes to him,
The East Wind, nourisher of nature's life;
As his eyes fell upon the Nightingale,
Within his mind a pang of pity smote,
And hand in hand with him the Cypress moved.
He found no balm to heal the bird of woe.
The bird, deep stabbed by separation's blade,
For his friend's fate he could not find escape.
Nor would he trample on the pining wretch,
Whose life seemed feeble as a fleeting shade.
Then came he near and gracious greeted him,
The bird made answer with a burst of sighs.
"Welcome, good sir," the East Wind said to him,
"What breeze has brought thee to a haven here?
Why is it that thou pinest thus in song?
Does absence from thy loved one cause thy woe?
How wasted and how lean thy countenance!
Thou art forespent by all thy sufferings;
Thine eyes are swimming in the tears of grief,
Thy heart is bleeding from its passion's pain.
What can have thus disturbed thy being's depth?
Thank God, that thou art now before a friend!
Thou in the Rose's palace dwellest now,
Why art thou not as happy as the Rose?
Since thou art not defrauded of thy hope,

Good fortune surely must have smiled on thee.
Here thou art dwelling in a lonesome realm,
Why shouldst thou manifest such grief and woe?
What pleasure canst thou find in dolorous song,
Oh, say, poor wretch, what pleasure canst thou find?"
The lean-faced bird made answer with a sigh,
And said: "O friend, companion of my grief,
Though in the rose garden I now abide,
I am no less a singer of laments.
For still the door that leads to her I love
Is shut upon me, as thou well canst see.
Still like a pilgrim I am stranger here,
And still my Mecca's light is closed to me.
The knife of grief is fixed within my breast,
And absence from my love has laid me low;
Absence has robbed me of the food of life,
Absence has cast a gloom o'er my delight.
Still in a friend I see nor trust nor stay,
And a friend's presence still new torture gives.
Though outwardly I am in good estate,
Still am I distant from my dear delight.
I cannot yet enjoy my best beloved,
And patient resolution fails in me.
I see no sunlight in whose rays to trust;
But myriad griefs and sorrows meet my gaze.
O'er my distress all human pity sleeps
And my great heap of anguish mounts to heaven.
And no one pleads my cause before my love,
That she should show compassion on my plight.
Thus by my ardent passion worn away,
By night and day I linger in distress.
Oh, if that graceful creature knew of me,
She would show less of cruelty to me.
Then Pity's face would stand before her eyes,
She would not sacrifice my life to pain.
Oh, help me, thou who art my only hope,
Take by the hand and guide the fallen one;
Tell her how fares this miserable wight
And make me pledged to show thee gratitude.
Oh, give her knowledge of my pining pangs, .

And of the many sufferings I endure,
Let fires of ardent longing warm thy tongue,
So that her heart be filled with ruth for me."

XXVIII

The Soul-nurturing East Wind Takes Knowledge of the Nightingale and Sees Traces of Pity in the Beauteous Rose

THEN said the East Wind that gives courage new:
" Torment thyself no more, unhappy one,
Thy sadness and thy mourning pierce my heart;
And I am messenger from yonder queen;
I will refuse thee nothing in my power,
And I will work for thee with all my might.
I will thy sufferings relate to her,
And bear her message how it fares with thee.
The lofty dame must take some note of thee;
I will support thy cause as I have strength.
Perchance my word will influence her mind
And cause her to compassionate thy lot.
Take courage!" So he spake and forth he went,
Repairing to the palace of the Rose.
Right eagerly he hastened to the Rose
And threw himself before her on the ground.
And said: " O lofty sun of loveliness,
O moon, O heaven o'erflowing with delights,
May God thy gracious beauty still increase,
And give fulfilment to thy every wish!
May he thy honor never bring to blight,
And with full many a year thy life prolong!
A stranger poor, no traitor, but true man,
A suitor in the passion of his mind,
Is come to thee as if he were thy slave,
For he has fallen deep in love with thee;
The breath of love which burns him to the heart
For him life's goblet sweet with poison taints.
He is thy very slave in heart and soul,

Devoted to thee through all pain and want;
In thy disdain he finds his sustenance,
And in the pain thou givest his delight.
He mourns night long complaining to the world,
How he is tortured by his love for thee,
Helpless by day, enfeebled, and unnerved,
He passes drunk with grief, through town and plain;
The hand of love represses now his song,
The bolt of sorrow now has laid him low.
From song to song he speeds along in love,
Weak as the new moon in the light of day,
He loves thy pity and thy graciousness,
Still freshly hurrying on the path of love.
Oh, that thou wouldst, bright sun of loveliness,
Show to him all the glories of thy grace!
Since only smile of thine can make him rich,
And cause the beggar-man to reign a king.
Does the tall cedar droop from weariness,
From shadowing the soil beneath it spread?
And must the sun with lessened radiance beam,
From shining in the beggar's lowly hut?
Does loftiness its dignity forego
When Solomon converses with a fool?
The watery stream that vivifies the world
Is ever in its current downward turned.
Think pitifully on his valiant life,
Whose spirit ever was to goodness given.
Now is the poor down stricken to the earth,
Oh, let him find his rescuer in thee!"
The Rose replied, when she had heard his speech,
" Go to this beggar-man, this tempest tost
And tell him, since he loves so ardently,
And swears himself so ardently my slave,
My grace he must a little longer wait
And patient in his constancy abide.
Suffer he must till healing be in train,
For love to any man is smart enough.
Love is by absence ofttimes perfected;
And ofttimes by fruition brought to naught.
He who would end the sufferance of love

Must first the rule of selfishness forswear.
The lover has no will to please himself;
His will he yields in all to the beloved.
And if the well-beloved for absence wish,
How can he in fruition's flame be warmed?
And if she wishes to remain far off,
How is this possible if he be near?
When he who loves puts pleasure before all,
His beauteous flame desires him to depart.
Can anyone whose love is pure and high
For any time abide at peace in it
While he is thinking only of himself
And hurts his well-beloved through selfishness,
So that if he but graze her sandal's tip
She in hot anger turns away from him?
For wounds are but the ornaments of love,
And all the rest is passion dissolute."
Hearing these words, the morning wind in haste
Departed to the Nightingale, who mourned.
For when he heard the message of the Rose
His self-control and understanding fled.
Straight he began to cry aloud for grief,
And beat the bushes of the rose garden.
Sad song and sighing in his bosom raged,
As passion in the glades of Gulistan.
The day and night were all the same to him,
For in love's frenzy lay he night and day.

XXIX

DESCRIPTION OF THE MORNING AND OF THE COLLOQUY OF THE LOVELY ROSE WITH HER NOBLES AND CHIEF MEN

UPON a morning when the rising sun
His jewelled cup had taken in his hand,
And heaven's arch shone with passionate desire,
And dawn was like the glow of ruddy wine,
And morning, sipping at the golden cup,
Like to some wild disordered reveller seemed,

The Rose, who saw the temper of the day,
That morning was a bright and lovely thing,
And all the landscape round with passion burned,
And morning's glory seemed with dalliance gay,
Felt a desire within her flowery grove
For high enjoyment in a merry feast.
Therefore she order gave that on the lawn
A throne of verdure should be raised for her,
And that the sweet and placid morning dew
Should fill the Tulip's goblet with her wine.
The dwellers in the grove acceptance gave
And hastened to obey the queen's command.
And in accordance with her high behest,
The flame of revelry was kindled round.
The Rose herself presided o'er the rout,
And at her feet the faithful Cypress stood,
And all the guests regaled themselves on dew,
And Tulip lackeys filled each crystal bowl.
And as Narcissus took the goblet up
A wave of ardent longing swept the throng.
The Hyacinth unbound her waving hair,
The Musk breathed out her tribute to the feast.
The lilies laughed and out they thrust their tongues,
Waking the feast with silvery melody.
Dumb with astonishment at such a scene,
The wry-necked violets stood and blinked their eyes.
The mad Brook hurried by the surging crowd,
With shouts re-echoing the noisy rout,
And gushing forth with impulse of desire
The joy that in his bosom overflowed.
The Wind blew blandly like a breath from God,
And never stopped upon its restless course.
His touch was like caresses of desire,
His murmur an enchantment of delight,
So at full flood the tide voluptuous flowed,
The revel's din was echoed through the world.
They drank full beakers of delight that day,
And hugging tipplers crowded all the glade.
The flowers drank all that nectar amorous,
And with rent garments lay inebriate.

The tulips seized the wineglass every one,
Voluptuous ecstasy their bosoms filled.
The Cypress, by the fumes of wind inflamed,
Begin to dance and sport in dalliance gay,
Not even the wind could tell which way he ran,
For now his murmuring tongue with drink was dumb.
Two draughts the violet at the beaker took,
Then bowed his head in drowsy slumber lost—
The rose garden was all in ruin laid,
And on their swords the lilies threw themselves.
The Nightingale, as fitted lover true,
A stranger feeble, a tormented one,
Is wholly sunk in amorous desire;
And drunken with the very wine of love,
As from the thicket he beheld the feast,
Like wine his tears of bitter anguish flowed.
Tears were his wine, his eyes the goblet bright,
His sorrow's song the reed-pipe of the dance,
And all the while he gave himself to grief,
Turning aside from such strange festival.
Then he began to sigh and make lament
And utter all his sorrows to the world.
His very form was fashioned like a lute,
From which is stricken note by note the strain.
His bosom throbbed like some sweet sorrow lute,
His voice was like some lute's desponding lay,
He fluted his love anguish in the crowd,
As if his heart gave voice to its desire.
He sighed and sobbed with his loud " Lack-a-day,"
And burned like incense in some shrine of love.
And while the Rose in pleasure's throng was gay,
Poor Bulbul pined in his misfortune's gloom.
The Rose drank deep amid her favorites,
Poor Bulbul languished in his song of pain;
And so went by full many days that brought
Joy to the Rose and sorrow to the bird.

XXX

The Far-wandering Nightingale Finds No Healing for His Pain, and at Last Writes a Letter to Make Known His Plight

For a long time bewailed the Nightingale
His agony in many a tender trill,
And yet the Rose came never into view,
And never saw one sparkle of the truth.
He never saw her in his view appear,
She never mentioned with her voice his name.
The bird continued in his constancy,
And her approach was ever far away.
She had no true acquaintance with his grief,
Though patience still was torture to his breast.
Then said to him at last the fool of love,
" Why is it that I do not write to her?
I cannot speak to others my lament,
I will to her myself my plight explain;
I will the sufferings which o'erflow my heart
And all my agony recount to her.
My eyelashes shall serve me for a pen
And from mine eyes I will my ink distil;
The tears which drip like blood beneath my lids
Are ink enough to write my love letter."
With pain he took the pen into his hand
And wrote his letter with a bleeding heart.
Praise formed the exordium of this love-letter,
Praise both of God and of the prophets blest.
Then said he : " O beloved of my heart,
Thou uncompassionate of those who love,
Is there no end to thy prevailing charm?
Is there no end to my surpassing pain?
Is thy hard-heartedness persistent still?
And is thy love enchantment without bound?
Is it indeed the custom of the fair
That their great beauty should be pitiless?
Oh, leave thine hardness, prayers of love regard,
Look on the desolation of my heart.

If lovely things were ever obdurate,
Still might they with their hardness feel desire;
Let not this soul in ardent passion faint,
And this cleft bosom perish in its fire.
From keen desire by night and day I mourn,
My bosom and my eyes are wrought with grief.
The sword of agony has pierced me through
And altered quite the habit of my mind,
For patience I no longer have the strength,
Nor can I longer separation bear.
Oh, pity me, mine own, for I am weak,
I am o'erwrought and without strength to-day.
The sword of separation cleaves my breast
And tints me with the tulip's ruddied eye.
My tears are like the Oxus of mine eyes,
Pale as the lime the color of my cheeks.
Have pity on me in my feebleness—
My strength and force have ebbed away from me.
Have pity on me. Patience dies in me,
The sword of absence penetrates my soul.
No longer patience can endure the strain,
And on thy head my blood will be avenged.
Reject me not, O Rose, but pity me,
Is not the Rose the Nightingale's delight?
The beauty of the Rose's charm appeared
Long since through coming of the Nightingale.
Oh, look not angry on thy paramour;
What is he but the mirror of thy charms?
For still through Medshnun's rapture wild and strange
Was Leila's flawless beauty long renowned.
And if no moth had ever been consumed
The taper ne'er had known the adoring wing,
And the more love the pining lover feels,
So much the more his love should pine for him.
And when the lover still persists in love,
The one beloved should never turn away.
Oh, thou hard-hearted one, be not incensed,
But hear the prayer of one who dies for thee,
For through thy hardness and thy self-content
Thou hast to nothing brought thy worshipper.

Let it be granted I am not thy peer;
No grace would be in pity if I were.
O queen, with thy compassion make me glad,
And free me from the fetters of despair."
And when the Nightingale his letter closed,
His next reflection was on sending it.
" How shall I light upon a messenger
To bring this letter to my best beloved? "
At last he found a fitting messenger
To take his love epistle to the queen.

XXXI

THE NIGHTINGALE DESPATCHES THROUGH THE JASMINE THE LETTER WRITTEN OUT OF THE FULLNESS OF HIS HEART

IN those times dwelt in Gulistan a youth,
Lovely and silver-bright and kind in mien.
He was a letter-carrier fast and safe,
And stood as messenger before the queen.
This youthful letter-carrier, silver-bright,
Whose manners were as radiant as his face,
Skilful and sure in bearing a despatch,
Held ever in his hand a written roll.
The jasmine's starry radiance was his,
The ardor and the stature of a tree,
His elegance adorned the garden glade,
And Sandbach is the name they gave to him.
The Nightingale his orders gave to him
And poured his secret in a faithful breast,
And said to him, " O generous friend of mine,
May the Most High have mercy on thy soul!
Why shouldst thou not bring tidings to the queen
Of all her slave has dreamt about her charms?
If thou this letter wilt convey for me,
All that I have in future shall be thine,
Since yonder distant loveliness through thee
May show itself propitious to my prayer."
The Sandbach the commission undertook,
And said: " 'Tis well; cheer up. I only hope

Thy letter that is written by thy hand
May carry no misfortune to the queen."
He took the folded missive in his hand,
And his foot followed on his hand's despatch.
Low bowed he when he reached the Rose's seat,
And gave the love-letter into her hand.
The Rose received from him the *billet-doux*,
And read the running letters of its page.
And when she understood the note's intent,
And how the wistful bird in torture pined,
Then said she: " Tell me how the poor man fares.
Does he still mourn, and for compassion cry?
Does separation still his bosom tear?
Does his heart bleed, as bleeds the tulip's heart?
Give my heart's greeting to the wretched one,
And wish him healing of his misery.
May he no longer mourn if fate permit,
And be his heart no more consumed in woe.
I will henceforth be faithful unto him,
And bend myself to succor his distress;
Since he has separated been from me,
Consumed within the furnace of his pain,
I will henceforth with greater tenderness
Assuage the fiery ardor of the wight.
And for a proof I feel in honor bound
To send an answer to these words of love."
Then straight she took into her hands a pen,
And wrote an answer to the Nightingale.

XXXII

The Dainty Rose Sends Through the Tall Jasmine Sandbach an Answer to the Letter of the Distracted Nightingale

The letter thus began, " Now praise to God,
A thousand greetings to his prophets be!"
Then she continued: " O thou wanderer wild,
O sick at heart that knowest no medicine,
'Tis love that has encumbered all thy life

And bound thee up in this distraction's coil.
How is it that the misery of thy love
And separation has so altered thee?
How should my absence so affect thy heart,
And what concern is my heart's love to thee?
Does separation's knife thy spirit wound,
And has concupiscence thy heart inflamed?
And are thy eyes still wet with bitter tears,
And sorrow, does it desolate thy soul?
What ails thee, friend?   Art thou not well in health?
Or art thou always languishing in pain?
Art thou of me so fiercely amorous
That thou thus hastenest to enjoy my love?
I see, poor wretch, that misery drives thee so,
That I from sympathy must faithful be.
'Tis time that I obedient to thy need
Should be, and thou shouldst take me for a friend.
That I should yield my beauty to thy hand
So long as thou art worthy of the gift.
Thou hast so long been separation's slave,
Thou now should be fruition's honored king.
Long hast thou drunk dark separation's draught.
Now pledge me in enjoyment's nectary cup.
He who is bold upon the path of love
Deserves to see his loved one face to face.
Be happy, then, thy pain is ended now,
The day of full fruition has arrived."
While thus the pen went over the lettered page,
She closed the brief epistle with a kiss,
Then gave it to the messenger, and so
Let him who wept and sorrowed now rejoice.
Into his hand the letter Sandbach took,
The letter that should cheer the Nightingale,
And said: " I bring to thee good news of joy,
No more the wretch may sighing pass his hours,
Now has happiness awoke from sleep
And on the joyless now has joy bestowed."
With eagerness he gave to him the note.
" The Lord is very merciful," he said,
" For after absence oft fruition comes.

Cease, then, the clamor of thy lack-a-day."
Soon as the Nightingale the tidings heard
He was beside himself from keen desire.
He kissed the letter, read it with his eyes,
Then opened it and closed it up again.
He said: " The letter is an amulet,
A written patent from the grace of God,
A letter of reprieve in God's own name,
Of liberation from despair and grief."
And as the Nightingale the letter read
The cry of ardent passion burst from him,
A flood of inspiration seized his soul—
He worshipped every cipher one by one,
He thanked the Lord with loud hilarity,
And with a burst of gladness praised the pen
The soul of all those letters gave to him,
Fresh life supplanting now the death of love.
His keen desire inspired his throbbing throat,
And he could nothing sing but of the Rose.

XXXIII

DESCRIPTION OF THE NIGHT AND OF THE REPROOF WHICH
THE TREACHEROUS HYACINTH GAVE IN ANSWER TO THE
POOR NIGHTINGALE

It was a night in which the rose garden
Was clear illumined as with light of day,
When tints of darkness interblent with light
Went wandering over beds of hyacinths.
The moon stood high upon the dome of heaven,
And round her was the company of stars.
Upon this night the Nightingale discoursed
In dulcet notes the ardor of his soul.
He sang at first in his delight and joy
His song in every tone the poets knew.
Upon this night a hyacinth came by,
A vixen full of tricks and treachery.
In her dark night attire she forward sped,
To wander through the glades of Gulistan.

Then suddenly she heard a tuneful note;
Like Anka's echo came the storm of song.
Forward she came and saw the pilgrim poor,
Who moaned as if he consolation claimed.
Close to the minstrel she ensconced herself,
And looking up to Bulbul, greeted him.
And said to him, " Pray tell to me thy name.
Why is it that thou clamorest so loud? "

He said, " I call upon the one I love.
Through love I did forget how loud I cried."
Quoth she, " To whom has love devoted thee?
Who is it that thy heart and spirit love?"
Quoth he, " I am the bondsman of my love,
For one in love is thrall and pupil too."
Quoth she, " What bond and emblem bearest thou?
Whence dost thou come?   What is thy native land?"
Quoth he, " Love hath no ensign and no home,
No special dwelling-place in any realm."
Quoth she, " Explain to me this pain of thine,
Tell me the secrets of thy loving heart."
Quoth he, " I have no other guide but love."
And here he stopped and spake no other word.
Quoth she, " What is the character of love?
And does it bring the lover aught of gain?"
Quoth he, " Love brings its slave to nothingness,
It forfeits every gain, but wins delight."
Quoth she, " And what is, then, the end of love?
Does he who loves find rest his home at last?"
Quoth he, " The goal of love is suffering's lot,
The heart through love finds all its end in pain."
Quoth she, " The wise man never longs for pain,
More perfect he who shuns disquietude."
Quoth he, " Who suffers not is not a man,
For manhood must be based on suffering,
And he who suddenly in pain is plunged
Befits him then to suffer patiently."
Quoth she, " In pain, then, thou dost take delight,
Then cease thy sighs and study self-control."
Quoth he, " And hadst thou medicine for thy pain?"

Quoth he, " I need none till my heart be broke."
Quoth she, " And over whom dost thou lament?"
Quoth he, " My only one, my darling queen."
Quoth she, " But tell me what her name may be?"
Quoth he, " Alas, I have forgot her name."
Quoth she, " Bethink thee, till it come again."
Quoth he, " Do lovers have the power of thought?"
Quoth she, " What makes thy speech so riddling dark?"
Quoth he, " My love's hair has entangled me."
Quoth she, " Give up this passion for thy queen."
Quoth he, " But that were to give up my soul."
Quoth she, " Thy mistress is not true to thee."
Quoth he, " Enough to me is her disdain."
Quoth she, " Fruition of her cannot be."
Quoth he, " Without her I am bound to die."
Quoth she, " Begone and leave this rose garden."
Quoth he, " To leave this spot is leaving life."
Quoth she, " No pity is outpoured for thee."
Quoth he, " Yet pity still be praised by me."
Quoth she, " And dost thou hope for bliss at last?"
Quoth he, " Does not the sun shed light over all?"
Quoth she, " Thou liest beneath the sword of pain."
Quoth he, " So be it. I have naught to say."
Quoth she, " This separation costs thy blood."
Quoth he, " My blood, yes, and my soul as well."
She saw that this poor wretched stripling still
An answer made to every jibe of hers.
The hyacinth with jealous passion glowered,
Her face grew black through bitterness and wrath.
Quoth she: " 'Tis palpable to me at last,
This oaf is amorous of the Rose herself,
And can it be that in the rose garden
So dissolute a rover should appear?
What is his business here in Gulistan?
What is he doing in our garden realm?
He must at once be banished from the place,
So that he tread no more our glorious glade.
It is a burning shame, in truth, that one
So beggarly should at our threshold lie."
And so excited was the hyacinth

That long she pondered trick and guile and ruse.
Well versed was she in crooked ways of guile,
And took delight in devious intrigue.
And now she tried some method to devise
By which to purge the bowers of Gulistan.

XXXIV

The Insidious Hyacinth, Her Mind Darkened With Envy, Contrives That the Nightingale is Expelled From the Rose Garden

Just when the sun of full fruition dawned,
An obstacle that instant rose to sight.
Oft the possessor of a faithful friend
Is rescued from the clutches of despair,
The Rose is circled round with many a thorn,
And where the treasure lies do serpents coil.
And where a friend appears to cheer the heart
A foeman also rises to oppose,
A cruel foe had thus appointed been
To take his stand as guardian of the Rose.
The royal watchman of her Majesty,
Her careful master at her beck and call,
Tyrannical, in nature envious,
Evil in mind, rejoicing to give pain.
Whose nod was dreadful as the cast of spears,
Whose eyelashes were terrible as darts.
He ever stood with dagger at his belt
And in his hand the deadly partisan;
Like Mars on guard within some prison-house,
Armed was he on each limb with knife and spear,
And he who merely offered him his hand
Was ripped and mangled to the very quick.
His every deed was full of rancorous wrath,
And in the rose-garden his name was Thorn.
The hyacinth fell in with him that day
In her attempt to oust the Nightingale.
And by the thorn she thought to bring him bane,
And kept this secret in her darkling breast,

That from the pleasant shades of Gulistan
Bulbul might banished be for evermore.
The hyacinth, in many an intrigue versed,
Thus full of rage approached the deadly thorn,
And said: "O thou, what dost thou rage for now?
Hast thou no sense of honor and no pride?
For in this rose garden a rover stands,
A lover of the Rose, a noisy wight,
A wanton fool, inspired by jealous whim,
Who desecrates the Rose's queenly name.
But he is shameless, without reverence,
And talks the whole night long of naught but love.
Can it be possible, that such as he
Is taken up with passion for the Rose?
That he by sighing and by songs of love
Should take the fair name of our queen away?
That he should choose her name to be the theme
Of common babble in the market-place?
The Rose through him will now be scandal's theme,
And round the world will men revile the Rose.
This vagabond hath thus behaved himself
And many a lying vow has breathed to her.
I fear that by his reckless impudence
Her noble name at last may suffer loss.
Soon as the thorn these treacherous tidings heard
Each hair upon his head became a sword,
And the assassin thorn spake full of wrath:
"God blame thee for a worthless loon! And why
Didst thou not long ere this the vagabond
In fetters bind, a prisoner on the spot,
And put the chain of serfdom round his neck,
And lock him fast within the prison hold?"
She answered: "Though I have not fettered him,
Yet have I reasoned with him many times.
My council yet was bootless to the churl,
He answered every word with repartee."
The thorn replied: "Point out the wretch to me,
The sot and the seducer of the town.
His gore shall tinge my poniard scarlet bright,
For I shall plunge it in his dastard blood."

So saying, from his seat out sprang the thorn
And drew his dagger in a burst of rage.
The very moment he the Bulbul found
He dealt him many a wound with flashing blade,
And said to him: " Audacious beggar, thou
Who knowest neither modesty nor ruth,
What brought thee to the harem of our Queen?
Think of her rank and of thy base estate,
Thou who each night dost shout thy lack-a-day
Dost thou not feel some shame?   Away with thee,
Away with all this hubbub and this cry.
Is this a prison, or a lady's bower?
How comes it that without a blush of shame
Thou callest o'er and o'er again her name?
Show thyself here no longer, beggar vile,
Go hide that sottish countenance of thine.
Or else without or hinderance or delay
I with my dagger will thy bosom cleave."
With that the thorn transfixed the Nightingale,
Giving him pangs of sufferings manifold.
And now the Nightingale with cries of pain
And thousand lamentations leaves the grove.
He left the grove, the rose garden of love,
And sang his sorrow to the break of morn.

XXXV

THE RUTHLESS THORN GIVES ADVICE TO THE SOFT-CHEEKED ROSE

THE thorn, his thoughts on hate and vengeance fixed,
Soon as he had outraged the Nightingale
Went straightway hurriedly to see the Rose,
And gave her counsel in a long address.
And said to her, " How did it happen, Rose,
That such an oaf could make his love to thee,
And that the very lowest of the low
By his addresses could affront thy name?
Thou art the pearl, the princess. Can it be
A nameless beggar should draw nigh to thee?

That night and day by his persistent song
He causes all the grove to prate of thee?
Is it that thou his daring would approve
And smilest on his ardor and desires,
And givest ear to such a rogue as this
And listenest to the words he says to thee,
So that the beggar in thy favor proud
Shameless inflates himself and boasts his crime?
He is a man of boundless arrogance,
And of audacity untamable.
Do not encourage him, my gracious queen.
The beggar knows the truth about himself.
I, with my sword, have pierced his breast with wounds
And gladly stretched him bleeding on the ground.
And that I did not out of fear for thee,
But out of reverence for this pleasant grove."
Soon as the Rose these words of fury heard,
Pained to the heart, her rage o'ermastered her.
She said: "What has this beggar done to thee,
That thou shouldst thus transfix his soul with pain?
He is a harmless wretch in dire distress,
In sorrow and perplexity involved.
He came with all his melodies of love
Two days ago a guest in this fair grove.
Shame that thou thus hast wronged and injured him!
Sure no one has this guest repulsed with scorn.
Does it befit the soul magnanimous
To outrage and bring scorn upon a guest?
Tell me what harm he ever did to thee,
This pilgrim foreigner and hermit pure,
That thou hast undertaken thus to cleave
His bosom with that cruel blade of thine?
Was it because he sang with flowing heart?
A song of sorrow gives our souls delight.
He was the minstrel of our happy lawn,
And won the flowers to raise their chalice higher.
Not lawlessly my fetters he endured.
Then what disgrace for me can be in this?
For beauty and accomplishment complete
Have always made their orisons to love.

And beauty's self is perfected through love,
And beauty without love endures eclipse.
When love entwines itself round beauty's form
It gives no stigma to the thing it holds.
And nothing can the crown of beauty mar,
Though thousand thousands babble out her name.
Was Joseph in Egyptian lands disgraced,
When he was object of the people's love?
Go, leave the poor man in tranquillity,
Harass him not, be pitiful to him.
Thou must not him with cruelty oppress,
But treat him after this with kindliness."
When the thorn heard the Rose's reprimand,
Like needles on his head uprose his hair.
What he had heard was not what he desired,
And trouble overspread his countenance.
And now the royal audience was o'er,
He went to visit Spring, the garden's king.

XXXVI

The Hard-hearted Thorn Slanders the Lovesick Nightingale Before the Monarch of the Spring

He hurried to the palace of the shah,
And standing on his feet before the throne,
He said: " My sovereign to the end of time,
May thy prosperity unbroken be!
There lingers in the rose garden a rogue
By day and night, a rogue incurable
Who by the Rose infatuated lives,
And drunken with love's goblet is distraught.
Nor night nor day he ceases his complaint
As he relates the beauties of the Rose,
Nor night nor day can I o'ermaster him.
The beggar still with fire poetic burns,
He has nor shame nor self-respect in life,
And finds alone in drunkenness delight.
The Rose herself is fettered by his lay,

And sympathizes with this amorous sot.
Now the affair has reached the final stage,
And he has gained the notice of the Rose."
Soon as the monarch had heard the thorn's address,
Perturbed, he thus addressed the listening slave:
"Where is this beggar, pale and passionate?
Let him be seized and in a cell confined."
And so he sent his hunter to the grove,
A hunter of inexorable heart.
And said to him, "Go seek the beggar-man
And put him without pity into chains."
Soon as the firman of the king went out
They quickly scoured the glades of Gulistan,
And sought amid the rose-garden parterres
For traces of the tuneful Nightingale.

XXXVII

THE WOUNDED NIGHTINGALE SEES THE VIOLETS, HIS COM-
PANIONS IN ADVERSITY; THEY APPROACH EACH OTHER,
AND THE NIGHTINGALE IS SHUT UP IN A CAGE

He who sets out to adorn his countenance
Makes plainer the expression of his face,
And thus it fell that when the Nightingale
Felt his breast severed by the thorn's assault,
Far wandering from the glade of Gulistan,
He traversed many a field and meadow plain.
And as he thus for consolation sought,
He saw a poor man in a quiet nook,
Who sat in weakness and in misery,
His figure bowed in deep despondency.
He seemed down-trodden, blue, and broken-limbed,
As is the life of those whom love has crowned.
He sat in weeds of sorrow on the plain,
For he was clad in robes of mourning blue,
His head sank low upon the mossy sod,
As if his mind wandered beyond the world.
He breathed the fragrant love breath of the grove,

His cup was filled with wine of suffering.
He had a tongue which never uttered sound,
'Twas oft thrust out from very weariness.
And since he filled his vials with his tears,
They called him in the garden violet.
The wounded Nightingale accosted him,
Beholding one all destitute of strength,
But he was overcome with hopeless love,
His frame convulsed with suffering and dismay.
Here Bulbul found a comrade in distress,
And with a question tried to hearten him,
And said: " My friend, what has befallen thee?
How is it love has dealt so hard with thee?
I see, thou art a worthy slave of love,
From which thou art so weak and overwrought.
What is it in thy mind which makes thee sigh?
Pilgrim, why wearest thou this mourning blue?
Is it that thy beloved has done thee wrong?
Or has a rival stepped into thy place?
For grief has bent thee double by its load,
And all thy soul is out tune through grief.
Who is it that has flung thee to the dust?
Who is it gave thee to be rapine's sport?
The feet of men have trod thee to the ground,
As a poor weakling in the gay parterre.
Was it the loved one pierced thee to the soul?
Or is it that a rival tortures thee?
Say, wretched one, what ails thee, for thy pain,
Binds thee at once in kinship with my heart."
He noticed how the violet, weak in speech,
With stammering tongue at length replied to him,
" I, too, am wounded by the darts of love,
And thus my case is witness to thy wit,
'Tis love that bows my bosom to the dust,
'Tis grief that thus has flung me to the earth.
For oh, my soul has taken the fire of love,
I burn for satisfaction and relief.
The breath which from my lips forever comes
Has tinged my raiment with this mournful blue,
And longing for the Rose has done to death.

Absence from her has thus afflicted me;
'Tis love that makes me grovel in the dust.
And in this guise I traverse all the world.
I am tormented by the pangs of love,
And finally the dust becomes my home.
Love as I may the beauty of the Rose,
Alas, that beauty I may ne'er enjoy.
For she is ignorant of my distress,
And I may never paint it to her heart.
And no man knows the anguish of my mind.
I have no friend familiar on this plain,
And now I am so wan and courageless,
I cannot even speak of my distress."
Now when the Nightingale this poor man saw,
He felt compassion for his misery,
And each one to the other freely spoke
Of all their woes, and many things besides.
Then suddenly the royal spy approached,
With darkling eyes and cunning looks askew,
And while these two together converse held,
And mourned over the ardor of their love,
The cunning snare was spread above the bird,
And corn was scattered for the prey's decoy.
The Nightingale was seized with cruel hand,
And in a moment into durance cast.
And for the pain and anguish of the wretch
A cage was brought with many an iron bar,
And then he was imprisoned in the cage.
The cage must be his dungeon evermore,
And now the Nightingale at last was caught,
And banished evermore from peace and joy.
Like a poor anxious prisoner was he now,
For what more like a prison than a cage?
And night and day within that cage he wept,
O'erwrought by absence and the pang of love.
They brought him in his cage before the shah,
Before the shah he sang his well-a-day.
The Nightingale was sick from suffering sore.
Ah, see, what a deluding world can do!

XXXVIII

King August Appears in the East and Devastates the Earth

O HEART, thy tongue now kindle into fire,
Soften thy disposition with desire.
Build up a burning story out of truth,
And with hot breath go raging through the world.
Oh, let the utterance of the pen stream fire,
And let the world itself go off in fire.
Whoever sets ablaze the narrative
Shall lighten up the circle of the world.
In Eastern lands there sat enthroned in might
A mighty monarch potent and revered.
A sovereign who could set afire the earth,
He was a hero of a fiery heart.
His marrow was with happiness aflame,
And the world sighed beneath his conquering arm,
And he was wont with his prevailing wrath
To lay in devastation all the land.
He blazed in every confine of the earth,
And glowing ardor shone where'er he trod.
Although he was of fervent nature born,
All that he counselled was by wisdom marked.
He touched the mountain with the brew of life,
And gave to all the world her energy.
A king of flame who sat enthroned in light,
His name was that of sun and moon in one;
His happiness was heat on heat increased,
And the world swooned submissive to his sway.
And more and more his fervor he increased,
His rage and heat laid desolate the earth,
The world was kindled like a flame of fire,
His deadly hand threw conflagration round.
The people doffed the garments they had worn,
So much they feared the coming of his rage.
During his reign went no one out of doors,
And all the people kept themselves at home,

Until they wearied of this quietude,
And all were willing to endure his glow,
And all were willing in the shade to be,
Some in the garden, some by city wall.
Meanwhile the world flamed out in cruel plight,
And like a templed altar worshipped him.
The sparks of horror seethed with higher glow,
And the great banners of his power rose higher.
At last he styled him " Emperor of the World,"
His banners flaunted in the firmament,
The hues of heat were painted in the sky.
The dust was in his honor turned to flame,
His blaze subdued the universe in light,
His fury kindled like a furnace coal.
In time he sent his heat out far and wide,
The scent of scorched wild-fowl went o'er the land,
His fury choked the very sigh of love,
And in the watercourse he scorched the stone.
And by the influence of his raging fire
The circling birds were roasted as they flew,
And every grain was parched upon its sod.
The scent of musk, in conflagration quenched,
The world made nothing but a pit of ash,
And nothing green was left upon the plain.
And greater still grew up the tyrant's power,
And the burnt streams were dried within their beds.
And more and more with grisly cruelty,
What time the people lay upon the rack,
The ladder of the heavens was all aglow,
And sent out sparks like to a furnace grate.
And the earth felt his ardor like a scourge,
And melted ashen-colored into dust.
And no one wore a shoe for very heat,
And the brain reeled beneath the o'erpowering blast,
And in the river that reflecteth heaven
The fish and cattle were but shrivelled forms.
In short, the world was made a weary waste,
Fire raged around on every side, and heat,
Brought by the bitter fury of the blast,
Took all the beauty from the realm of man.

XXXIX

KING AUGUST SENDS THE HOT WIND WITH FIRE TO THE
ROSE GARDEN

WHOEVER sets afire this history
Has fed with fuel a refulgent lamp;
For August, sitting on his royal throne,
Is mighty in his exercise of power;
He gathered all the nobles of the land
To heaven, to meet him at the great Divan.
He was by fortune and by greatness warmed,
And through his power and lordship, filled with pride.
And thus he spake among his mighty lords:
" Speed as ye may o'er earth's remotest line,
I now am lord of all the universe;
See in my hand it melt, how weak it is!
The ardor of my fury works in it,
And my heat flies from brow to sweating brow.
And lives there now on earth a single wight
Who has not felt the ardor of my breath?
And is there king of greatness and of might
Who has not felt the flaming of mine eyes?"
They answered: " Sire, the world is all aglow!
'Tis very true thy fury sways the world.
And yet in Rūm there is a little town
Such as the world has never seen before.
'Tis governed by a monarch of its own;
His throne with budding honor is adorned;
The town is called the Garden of the Rose,
The king is named the monarch of the spring.
There the green blade that tranquil lifts its head
Has never felt the fury of thy heat."
Soon as these words the monarch August heard
His bosom with tempestuous heat was filled.
He said: " At once we undertake the task
Of devastating that forgotten realm.
And while its monarch joys with placid heart
Disaster shall rain down upon his head.

And yet 'tis necessary, first of all,
A messenger from me be sent to them,
To testify my grandeur in their sight
And bear the tidings that I send to them.
That when they learn of my design, through fear
Their courage may dissolve like ice in spring.
For he must say that I to conquer come
And captive take the people of the town.
The monarch must be yielded to my hand,
And all must live in terror of my power."
There stands a courier at his behest,
Who, like a flea, now here, now there is found;
Like lightning sudden is he in his flight,
And rapid as the flame, or as the thought.
From his breath, warmed as by a fever's heat,
He had been Samum named and known to all.
And he was with the East Wind closely bound,
His elder brother, as it seemed to be;
The first of them is the delight of Spring,
The second is King August's servant true.
He waits to bear the message of the king,
Who said, " O lightning-speeding messenger,
Now hie thee swift to yonder rose garden,
And to the king who rules there stoutly speak
With thy warm breath and with thy violent speech.
Stir up fierce fire within that little realm,
For from thy mouth does fire like rain descend,
Thy tongue can scatter devastation round.
Take care thou speak not gently to the king,
Take care that not too furiously thou speak.
Say to him: " Thou to ruin doomed, keep still,
For soon my fury burns thee up with fire.
For what permission has been given to thee
To reign in peace amid this rose garden
Without a fear for my o'ermastering might,
Without a thought upon the season's rage?
Wilt thou not listen to the word which tells
Of the resplendent lightning of my rage?
Take to thy mind and in thy brain revolve
How thou mayst save thy country from my drought.

Surrender like a slave thy throne and crown,
And stand outside the threshold of my gate.
Give up thy realm, withdraw thy hand from it,
And thus win peace and pardon for the land.
But if thou art rebellious to my will,
And dost not yield to me thy land and throne,
Be sure of this, that on thy luckless head
Swift ruin shall descend without reprieve."
When Samum took this message from the king
Swift as a storm he hurried on his way,
He blighted every meadow land he crossed,
And found his journey's end in Gulistan.

XL

SAMUM ARRIVES AT THE TOWN OF ROSE GARDEN AND GIVES TO THE MONARCH OF SPRING THE MESSAGE OF FIERCE KING AUGUST

HEADLONG he rushed into the rose garden,
And furiously he set it full afire;
The tulip drew her tongue that burned like fire,
And panted feverish in the rose garden.
The tulip glittered like a spark of fire,
Narcissus, like a lantern, shot her ray,
Then danger threatened the inhabitants,
And the Rose blushed more beauteous still for shame.
The king himself was in the direst need,
And with a glance of fire his voice he raised.
He pondered well what had befallen the state,
And saw the true proportions of the case.
And as he took full knowledge of his plight,
The parching heat consumed him to the heart.
Then full of royal courage bold and high,
He braced his soul and searched for counsel fit
And said: " What conflagration visits us?
Who is this tyrant August, and what deed
Of mine has roused his fury that he seems
So headstrong and so burning in his rage?
The rancor of his flames I will repress,

My sword shall quench his ire as water flame.
He is to me no object of alarm,
Nor twenty thousand furnaces like him,
He shall not venture further on this sod,
My sword shall slay him as heat is slain by stream.
Go, say to him, and bid him be ashamed,
And mitigate this devastating heat,
And draw away his flames from out the land,
And cease this wild campaign about our walls,
Or he himself in his own flames shall soon
Be brought to ashes by command of mine."
With such an answer Samum made return
Unto the monarch of the summer time;
He gave him tidings from the Shah of Spring,
Speaking the answer faithful word for word,
And August, when the message he had heard,
Burst out into a rage of frenzied heat.
And storming, he at once gave his command,
"Let all my kingdom gather under arms,
And hot and fast be preparation made.
The rose garden in ruin must be laid."

XLI

KING AUGUST SENDS HIS SON AS FIELD MARSHAL TO THE
CITY OF ROSE GARDEN, AND THE KING OF SPRING,
UNABLE TO OPPOSE HIM, RETIRES TO THE HEIGHTS

THERE was a messenger by nature high,
From head to foot he shone with dazzling light.
His nature was illumination's soul,
His traffic was the ministry of fire,
He scattered light throughout the universe,
And to the zenith reared his lofty brow.
'Twas fire that wrought the jewelry of light,
His name was nothing but the morning sun.
As lord and as field marshal forth he went
And spurred his courser into Gulistan.
King Spring was startled by the news he heard,

That thus his foe had hither made his way.
He gathered all his nobles for advice,
And stirred up all his force for feats of arms.
He roused them all for war, the residents
Of rose garden he summoned to the strife.
The lily drew her broadsword from the sheath,
The thorns in hand their pricking arrows held.
Even the cypress now prepared for war,
Stood ready with her needles like a lance.
The tulips spread their petals like a bow,
And even the dew prepared its pebble-stones.
The violets bent them to a hostile bow,
The daisies shot their arrows into air,
The stream put on its glittering coat of mail,
And stood enclothed in panoply of steel.
Like janizaries all the plants around,
Held in their hand their pikes and partisans.
And every bud a threatening bludgeon bore,
And put themselves as shields before the Rose.
They stood in ordered ranks as warriors ranged
For war and conflict in the cause of right.
Now when the sun into rose garden came
A fiery volley straightway he discharged,
And with his heat began to devastate,
Like to some torch-bearer of Eastern kings.
And lo! the dwellers in the rose garden
Dwindled, consumed like tapers in a mosque.
The lily wilted like a sinking flame,
And quickly dropped the broadsword from her hand.
The crimson tulips burnt to dusky black,
And dropped their blazoned targes from their hand.
In a rude mass the verdant bowers collapsed,
And the whole city into ashes turned.
Who can withstand the ravages of the fire?
Who can wage war against its deadly line?
When to Shah Spring this news at last was brought
His splendor and his power faded away.
Although he struggled to maintain the strife,
He saw that he was fated to defeat,
And straightway he betook himself to flight,

Forsook the field of battle for retreat.
Retreat is cowardly, yet there are times
When stoutest valor counsels a retreat.
When stronger foes o'ermaster those who fight
Retreat is better than to rashly stand.
Such was the thought that swayed the monarch Spring,
And so he took the Rose and fled with her.
He mounted quickly to an alpine crag,
Which bordered on a chain of savage hills,
And all his followers he took with him,
And all the mountain side was peopled o'er,
And so he rested on the towering peak,
And lived henceforth in safety and in peace.
And from that alp there sloped a verdant plain
Where happiness and fruitfulness abode.

XLII

THE MONARCH SPRING FLEES ALSO FROM THE PEAK OF
THE MOUNTAIN AND DISAPPEARS, AND THE MONARCH
AUGUST, IN HIS FURY, BURNS UP THE CITY OF ROSE
GARDEN

MEANWHILE the sun, field marshal of the fray,
Had to surrender brought the rose garden.
Then comes the monarch August with great joy,
To take his seat on the vacated throne.
The garden dwellers mourned in anxious care,
For still the flame of fury burnt its way,
And all the noblest houses were consumed,
For the fierce glow of fire had drunk their blood.
Its fury hastily the tulips parched,
And burnt to blindness the narcissus' eyes,
The Rose parterre is wrapt in dazzling flame,
And fire amid the thickets reigns supreme.
And soon as he had blasted every bower,
He sallied forth to find the monarch Spring.
And said to each, " Where is the monarch Spring?
And whither has retired the Princess Rose? "

They told him they had fled to mountain heights,
Where cool fresh alps looked down upon the scene.
And when the King of Summer learnt of this,
He sent his army in pursuit of him,
He said: "Despatch and lay the monster waste,
Let the fire burn it like a living heart.
Seize and bring hither monarch Spring to me,
And drag the Rose into the mire for me."
As soon as he this firman had pronounced,
The sun his way directed to the alps.
And with his army devastation wrought,
As if he would the world in ruin lay,
And when the monarch Spring appeared in sight,
The tyrant would him fain assassinate.
In a short time he held the king at bay,
Seized on the Rose, and straight forsook the land.
Where'er he went was nothing left behind.
Nothing appeared where once his path had been.
No trace was left of monarch Spring's domain,
The Rose was nowhere seen upon the mead.
Both from the mountain side had disappeared,
And no one knew to what point they had fled.
The sun triumphant had a victory
Complete o'er every remnant of the foe.
He said, " The monarch Spring is banished quite,
And not a foot-track can be found of him,
And no one seems to know where he is gone,
And where to seek the glory of the Rose."
And when the monarch August pondered this,
No longer was a care left in his breast,
And in one day he made the rose garden
Naught other but a revel place of fire.
And yet he blent advantages with waste,
Pouring a thousand graces on the spot.
What was unripe he mellowed and made sweet,
To what was crude maturity he brought.
Into the landscape sent tranquillity,
And mingled a bland sweetness with his rage.
At last he quite forsook his camping ground,
And made his homeward journey to the East.

He glided lightly forth on ether's wing,
And reached at last his station permanent.
And as he left the placid meadow land,
He heard the news of more important things.

XLIII

AUTUMN COMES FROM THE NORTH WITH THE INTENTION OF ADMINISTERING THE CITY OF ROSE GARDEN

THERE was a king, distributor of gold,
Well skilled the world to deck in brilliant hues,
Upon the world he shed magnificence,
A glorious king munificent of gold.
High in the North his palace home was set,
There ever throned in clemency he sat.
This king was of a disposition cold,
And moderation was his ruling trait.
His sole employment was to scatter gold,
To give mankind the pleasure of its glow.
In other excellencies he was rich,
But there was none that scattered gold like him.
He was a painter, too, of rarest skill,
Unique in art and generosity.
Before the glory of his varied tints
Pale all the masterpieces of the world.
He tints the leafy curtain of the earth,
And Mani's self might wonder at the work.
He is a painter great, of faultless touch,
A colorist of an unerring skill,
He gives a soul to every quivering leaf,
Until it shows a hundred tints of fire.
He stamps it with the lustre of the gold,
Until its very shadow is aflame.
He colors with the potency of skill
With haze of rose and saffron every copse.
The master of a double art is he,
And famous for his skill in either part,
And every artist to whom he is known

Him by none other name but Autumn calls.
In might and wisdom he is affluent,
And by his grace and kindness ever warm,
And through his reign the world was kept at peace,
Because he gave such freedom to the world.
He showered his gifts on every land and clime,
A paragon of generosity,
And through his gifts, at last reduced to earth,
He leaves at least the hungry satisfied.
Through him of little worth was reckoned gold,
He scattered it around like dust and soil.
Though he was famous for his graciousness,
Well did he know to injure by his might.
When he was angry all his breath was frost,
And those who saw him with affright grew pale.
The world its face of summer loveliness
Was changed to other colors at his touch,
For fear of him the rose garden grew faint,
And sallowed into tints of mellow gold.
He was a wonder worker of his kind,
Pity in him went hand in hand with rage.
Cold was he by his nature, half of ice
And half of water was his intellect.
Yet ofttimes did he blaze with glance of heat,
The blessing that he brought outweighed the bane,
And when he gently spoke with anyone
His countenance was lit with radiant warmth.
Yet toward the end he turned to bitter cold,
And kept that bearing to the very end.
Shah August once in regal state assumed
His seat among the nobles in Divan.
He gathered round him all his ministers
To greet his emirs and his noblemen,
When suddenly there came to him the news
That all the garden's realm in ruin lay.
That banished was the monarch of the mead,
And the bower's beauty all was devastate.
And when the monarch August heard the news
The tidings made him quiver like a leaf.
Full of impatience and anxiety

He hastened to explore the garden glade.
Although he well believed the tidings true,
He wished to have authentic evidence,
And that this evidence he might attain,
A spy must needs be on the errand sent.

XLIV

King Autumn Sends a Reconnoitring Party to the City of Rose Garden, and in a Moment Conquers It, and Paints It in His Own Livery

A RIGHT swift messenger he had despatched,
Like dust upon the wind the herald sped.
His nature was of heat and frost combined,
The Persians called him Scatterer of the Leaves;
And when this title was accorded not,
They called him Plucker of the Summer Leaves.
The monarch August thus accosted him:
" Now hear my words aright, thou speedy one,
Beget thee at this instant to that bower,
And bring me news of all that thou shalt see,
And as thou flittest like a spirit free,
Show thyself merciful to Gulistan.
Let moderation all thy conduct rule,
And gain the hearts of all the country side.
Show not thyself a sudden blast of frost,
But first appear a warm and sultry air;
Begin to scatter round the kindly gold,
And happiness through power and honor bring.
As thyself thou art in color rich,
Scatter thy tints o'er every leaf and blade."
As the leaf-plucker heard the monarch's speech
In silence he departed on his way.
Quickly arrived he at the rose garden,
Fulfilling the commission of his king.
He scattered light and beauty as he went,
And everything he overlaid with gold.
And yet his bearing was not harsh or strict,

And he brought blessing whereso'er he went.
He mingled in the middle of the flowers,
With kindly tenderness he played with them,
He made inquiry, as he well was fit,
With his impetuous pertinacity.
And the parterres with many a hue were stained.
Needless his operations to recount.
When he the plight of the rose garden saw,
Straight to the King he made a swift return.
Telling to him of all that had befallen
Of good and bad unto the rose garden.
The king at once commanded that in arms
His cavalry should charge the garden realm.
He throned himself as monarch in the glade,
And all the dwellers there were captive made.
And as his wont, to happy make the world,
He scattered wide his gold on every head.
And everyone at once grew rich in life,
And everyone a golden caftan wore.
His hand was full of graciousness and gift,
Wherewith he strewed the land on every side.
He gave them such a mess of gold for prize
That head to foot they glimmered with the ore.
And thereupon the master of the realm
His manner altered in a high degree.
For where his voice was gracious and benign,
He now displayed his fury and his hate.
And all the garden people, white with fear,
Fell to the earth o'ermastered by alarm,
And as he was at first both sweet and kind,
So now he ravaged with the wildest rage.
He flung the dwellers of the garden out,
The garden naked lay in horror vast.
He threw the floral decorations low,
The leaves and branches scattered o'er the sod.
And as he devastated all day long,
And at the last there followed placid calm.
And thus while nature's course its way pursues,
Quiet and peace result from violence.

XLV

KING WINTER APPEARS IN THE EAST AND BLOWS HIS COLD BLASTS OVER THE EARTH

THE messenger upon his errand sped,
With chilling words his message to convey.
" A king," he said, " was throned in the far West
Whose breath was cold, whose very glance was frost.
Chill was his breath and chill his aspect drear,
His heart and every action cruelty.
To moderation he was deadly foe,
And plagued the people with his blasting frost.
He was a sovereign who prevailed by cold,
King of the world who men as Winter knew.
Soon as his voice was heard amid the land
The people shuddered at his fierce attack;
His chilling breath could quench the heat of hell,
For he was colder than the touch of ice,
And as his power could cool the fire of hell,
His rage could change an Eden into hell.
For when his breath was fiercest, like a fire,
He burnt and made men feel the pain of hell.
His wild, inconstant, and unerring rage,
In ruin laid the elemental world.
When once his lance was on the people shot
'Twas like a poker stirring up the fire,
And when a householder his face discerned,
He swiftly turned him back into the house,
And while his fury was without restraint,
He drove the people to the ingle fire.
And so he waxed in furiousness of frost
That the world lit its fires and sat by them.
The streets were blocked by his invading might,
And in the houses piles of fuel blazed.
The people in the mosques assembled thick,
For refuge in the blaze of altar fires.
To save herself from his invading power
The rose garden became a blazing hearth,

'And yet he did not spare his breath of frost,
But laid his hand on Autumn's kindly glow.
And when that monarch showed himself on earth
He ran him neck to neck for victory,
And like a flood his fury ran apace,
And everything was stiffened in his way.
The water curdled into solid ground,
And the world's eye was filled with crystal tears,
And each one went about with covered head.
The sun in heaven concealed himself for fear.
The poor man and the rich alike were forced
To warm themselves in skins and cloaks of felt.
And each one of the city elegants
Wound round his head a costly robe of fur.
In short, the Winter reigns, a king supreme,
Throughout the period of the dwindling days,
And swift as water hurried his command,
And like the wind o'er every country swept.
While he himself in sombre dignity
Scattered his silver frost on every side,
His silver with such lavish hands he spread
That house and heather shone with silvery gleams.

XLVI

KING WINTER DEVASTATES THE ROSE GARDEN IN A SNOWSTORM

AND then he gave command unto his hosts.
" Make ready," said he, " for a long campaign.
Let all our army speed to rose garden
And fall upon it with the force of fire."
Upon the general a command was laid
To overthrow the palace of the Rose.
He stood at Winter's beckoning, a slave,
A minion, who attended his command.
He was himself of Winter's temperament,
And in the world he bore the name of snow.
White was he as the crystal camphor is,

And he was as the crystal camphor cold,
And he was soft as cotton to the touch,
But chilly as the hardest cake of ice.
He was the winter's steadiest adjutant,
And he was sent to ravage Gulistan.
And straight he set himself upon the way
To wage his warfare upon the rose garden.
And suddenly as is the hand of fate
The snow came down amain with fleecy cloud,
And in one night within the rose garden
Triumphant reigned in valley and in field.
High was it piled above each arching roof,
And over all the whitening cloak was spread.
It threatened men and horses to ingulf,
And like a camphor shower enshrouded all.
When Gulistan this sad disaster saw
A reign of terror rose in its domain.
The snow was seen to dance on every roof,
And glitter down like swords and lances bright.
And as the snow covered the woodland limbs
The winter on the garden settled down,
And all his army in their tents encamped,
And the whole city at their mercy lay.
And Autumn, when of this he was aware,
Shuddered and shook like aspen foliage.
Though he would fain have entered on a fight,
He saw 'twas vain to hope for victory.
At last, quite conquered, in retreat he fled
And sought his former dwelling and his seat.
But Winter still his domination claimed,
And sat enthroned as king in Gulistan.
He gave command, " Let no one from this time
Of bower and garden pleasance question make."
And while he stayed there all the rose garden
Should to a heap of ashes be reduced,
And he who would be rash enough to dare
This edict to decry and disobey,
He who should violate this strict command,
With anger should be straightly visited.
So everyone about that place was sad,

And all the place was bound in bitter frost.
And everyone who but held out his hand
Was stripped and blighted like a withered bough,
And by the direful tyranny of cold
The happiness of all the folk was changed.
And as this destiny befell the glade
Each creature pressed impetuous round the fire.
Gray hairs and hair still glossy bright with youth
Pressed as to the high altar round the fire.
Early and late the fire burned round the hearth,
The fuel was as precious as the flame,
And to give heat unto a single hearth
Was worth the value of an aloe flower,
And those who sold the fuel were in glee,
And the wood market was a kingly realm,
And he who bore with him a bag of gold
Was poorer than the man who owned a wood.
In short, the tyrant cold was lord o'er all,
And each man found his house a prison cell.
For Winter's mighty tyrant reigned o'er all,
And ravaged freely over all the wood.
He scattered silver with a lavish hand,
And all the world in silver frost was sunk.
The cedars donned a silver coronet,
And all the garden wore a silver braid.
The very streams in silver mail were clad,
And clumps of silvery ice adorned their banks.
Thus Winter made his campaign for a time
Within the precincts of the rose garden.
But listen how it happened at the last
That he retired and left the garden free.

XLVII

THE MONARCH SPRING RETIRES TO THE SOUTH TO THE KING
OF THE EQUINOX, FROM WHOM HE ASKS HELP, AND
WHO IMMEDIATELY ASSURES IT TO HIM, AND HE RE-
TURNS THEREWITH TO THE CITY OF ROSE GARDEN

O NIGHTINGALE, whose voice is ever loud,
And ever sounds within the entrance hall,
Of what avail has been thy clamorous lay,
For has the hour of thy fruition come?
Within the cage thou must thy sojourn make,
Who once couldst walk amid the rose garden.
Surely thou hast enough of suffering spread,
And now must still in disappointment pine.
Thy flight has brought thee but to contumely,
Now to fruition spread thy eager wings.
For when misfortune gains its highest point,
Relief is given to the suffering one.
And all thy lamentations, what are they
Unto the Rose who laughs amid thy woe?
He who has drunk his full from legend's cup
Sings thus, deep, low in dregs of misery.
And when the king who burns the world with fire,
And has the happy August for his name,
Conquered the city of the rose garden,
And subjugated it and held it fast
And vanquished all the treasures of the Spring,
To leave his palace and his court behind,
The monarch Spring, forsaking his estate,
Fled to the safest city of the South.
Many a day with toil and pain he rode,
And came at last into a distant land,
In the dominion of a mighty czar,
Whose brows were crowned with buds of happiness.
He was a monarch of astounding might,
Full of munificence and mightiness.
His noble bearing was with mildness formed.
Gentle his mind, friendly, and delicate.

For he was born beneath auspicious stars,
Of those high stars that herald in the day.
A lord of light was he, exalted high
From his nobility and mighty fame;
His happiness the world flooded with light,
His name was called the Harbinger of Spring.
Well was the Spring acquainted with this shah,
Who was direct descendant of his line.
And as King Spring these tidings spread abroad,
The Harbinger of Spring the message took,
And went to meet the Spring on his approach,
Giving him honor high in every way.
The monarch who 'mid gentle breezes moved,
Gave many honors to the prince of Spring,
And as he came, unto the throne drew near,
He took him by his side upon the throne.
And for one day was feast and welcome held
In honor and in glad festivity.
And lo! among the guests the question rose
What is the true condition of affairs?
Then spake the monarch, asking of the Spring,
Why he had fled away from Gulistan.
" How art thou come," he said, " and whither bound?
What has directed your affection here,
To leave the garden's blest tranquillity,
And o'er the routes of travel toil thy way? "
So monarch Spring narrated to him all
That had befallen the town of rose garden,
And how that king who man had August named
With violence had overrun the land,
How he had wasted it with furious flame,
And all the bowers of roses turned to ash;
How Autumn had the spot to ruin brought,
And how black Winter devastated it.
And all that happened in the rose garden
He told in detail to the mighty shah.
And when the king the dismal tidings learnt,
His soul within him was to fury turned,
And soon as monarch Spring had related all
The Harbinger of Summer cried aloud:

"Lord of the world, let naught confuse thy soul,
Away with sorrow from thy anxious breast;
No longer shall thy patient mind be tried,
For there is hope again for Gulistan.
And if the Lord of heaven good fortune give,
Thou shalt again unto thy realm return,
And throned in power once more in rose garden
Shall trample every foeman in the dust."
And when the monarch Spring this comfort heard
He seconded the promise with a wish,
And said: "O king, thou art a constant friend,
And never may misfortune cross thy path.
Mayst thou live long in honor and renown,
And thy felicity be girt with power,
Soon as I heard that lofty word of thine
Into my soul tranquillity returned.
Though the campaign has devastated all,
It has not taken from me all my hopes."
The Harbinger of Spring, when this he heard,
In silence placed his hand upon his brow,
And hurriedly his preparations made
For a campaign toward the garden bower.
So that the shah elected to this place
Might in the bower of roses pitch his tent.

XLVIII

THE HARBINGER OF SPRING GAINS POSSESSION OF THE CITY
OF ROSE GARDEN, VANQUISHES KING WINTER, AND
MAKES THE MONARCH OF THE SPRING TRIUMPHANT

WHEN o'er the land the breath of morning came,
The world was filled with blissful radiancy.
The news of fresh arrivals filled the glade,
And the trees ranged themselves in serried ranks.
And everything that in the garden grew
Was seared and mildewed by the past distress,
And yet anew life's waters woke again,
And all was tinged with Spring's perennial green,

Though all in death had lain for many a day,
Now living once again they raised their hand,
And everything with ardent passion throbbed.
And the East Wind came by with soft approach,
And benediction followed on his course.
And all the flowers their faces showed again,
And over all the light of summer shone.
The cypresses wore garments of delight,
And danced in many a ring along the mead
And each narcissus started from its sleep.
The tulips raised again their shining brows,
And as war's cruel visage disappeared
The land again was peopled as of yore.
And when King Winter in the sunlight saw
The people of the land come back again,
And that the meadows which he had o'errun
Were finally relinquished to the foe,
He was o'ercome with grief and shame and ire,
And heated by the sense of his defeat.
The snow, o'ercome by advent of the Spring,
In utter shame betook itself to earth.
In sooth, already had it drabbled o'er
The rose garden with her enkindled wrath,
For snow now felt itself o'ermastered, weak;
His host was overcome at every point.
And as the snow dissolved into the ground,
A flood of tears was spread on every field.
The Winter could no longer stand his ground,
And rapidly he started in retreat.
He turned him back again toward the West,
And gave up occupancy of the land.
And on the land the light of justice shone
And truth prevailed and error was abashed.
And as Spring's herald occupied the land,
King Spring himself returned to claim his own
He took his seat once more upon his throne,
And then his herald vanished from the scene.

XLIX

THE MONARCH SPRING MOUNTS UPON HIS THRONE AND
MAKES HIS RESIDENCE IN THE CITY OF THE ROSE GARDEN

As monarch Spring now on his radiant throne
Flourished, as in the glorious days of yore,
He opened there the treasures of his might,
And in the dust he scattered radiant pearls;
He lavished honors on each denizen,
And all were clad in mantles of the green,
And Gulistan is once again restored;
And grove and garden open wide their hearts,
And light is shining in narcissus' eyes,
And joy is in the heart of all the world;
The tulips don once more their ruby crowns;
The glade of Gulistan is filled with flowers;
The cypress once again his office takes,
And stands as porter at the garden gate.
And all the lilies drew their swords again,
And every thorn whetted its arrow point,
The sandbach opened out his gleaming rolls
In harmony with nature's odorous life.
The tapestry of vegetation, new
With satin green, the field and fallow clothed.
And all the people of the world repaired
Into the garden as a paradise.
The world from happiness an Eden grew,
And vernal freshness sparkled in the Spring.
The Rose ascended to her throne again,
The hyacinth her locks of purple wore,
The messenger East Wind within the grove
Awoke to life from out his skeleton;
And every stream with ardent passion ran,
And every flood with towering head advanced;
The rose garden again its beauty takes,
And peace and quiet reign on every side.
And as the Rose her lofty throne ascends,
In ranks the nobles at her bidding come;

The dew her favorite beverage provides;
The tulips in her service goblets bring,
And each man drinks according to desire;
And honor and good wishes follow wine.
And all the time does festive gladness reign,
By day and night the joyous feast goes on.

L

The Fair Rose Sends the East Wind to Cheer the Mourning Nightingale

AND once upon this festal holiday
The Rose bethought her of the Nightingale,
And said: " Where is that miserable fool
Who was inebriate with wine and love?
How fares it with the man of sighs and tears?
How can he live dissociate from our grove?
Shall we no longer hear that lute of his?
What is it that has checked his thrilling lay?
And has his heart been snatched away by pain?
And was he haply driven from grief to dust?
And has the flame of absence burnt him up?
And is he slain by moody glance of mine?
Is it the thorn has laid him suffering low,
And him enlisted 'mid my deadliest foes?"
They said to her, with salutation kind:
" O Rose, the fairest paragon of charms,
The wretch that was impaled upon the thorn
Has since been prisoner made within a cage.
By night and day behind the cage's bar
He sings aloud his melody of woe.
Still he laments, and all his dolorous song
Pierces the heart of hearers to the quick;
And in the dreary prison-house enthralled
Him no refreshment of delight consoles."
And when the tender Rose these tidings heard,
She breathed a sigh over the beggar's lot.
" And shall the prisoner, detained in gyves,

Never attain felicity again?"
And full of pity, as his rescuer,
She called for the East Wind, her messenger,
And said: "East Wind, who cheerest every soul,
Now let thy breath upon that beggar blow.
Find him, and greet him wheresoe'er he be,
And do him honor every way thou canst.
And say to him, 'O heart with suffering full,
That without consolation feelest pain,
How has the pang of absence slain thy soul?
What is the blow that grief has dealt to thee?
Thou art within this narrow cage confined,
And overcome with pain and grief and fear.
The dagger of thy grief has pierced thy heart;
The agony of absence wastes thy breast;
Long hast thou borne the languor absence brings;
'Tis time that thou should'st know fruition's bliss.
Though absence rages o'er thee like a storm,
Thou still art worthy of the joy of love.'
Go, my East Wind, and with such words as these,
Seek to console him with the news of bliss.
Absence no more shall waste his mind away,
Console him, then, and bring back heart to him."
The messenger East Wind, when this he heard,
Answered "Long live the Queen," and forth he went.
He journeyed wide, and everywhere he sought
To find where dwelt the mournful nightingale.

LI

THE PINING NIGHTINGALE LIES IN AFFLICTION IN THE CAGE
AND TURNS HIMSELF TO GOD. THE KINDLY EAST WIND
ARRIVES AND GIVES HIM INFORMATION AS TO THE CON-
DITION OF AFFAIRS

AND Bulbul in the distance suffered pain,
In the hard strait of absence from his love;
And in the cage he sang his dolorous lay,
Renouncing every hope of happiness.

And in the cage he stood, lamenting loud,
And mourning was his orison of morn;
For every morning did he pray to God,
To send him help in his disastrous plight,
And said: " O God! I languish in the dust,
A prey to anguish in this narrow cage;
The halter of estrangement binds my neck;
Estrangement from my love fetters me here.
My soul within my sickening self confined
Is like a wretched bird within a cage.
Power and unrighteousness have dashed me down
Into one narrow corner of the world.
O God! Why does not life escape this cage
And find its habitation in the stars?
Sometimes thou art benign to mortal prayer,
Oh, set me free from this accursed cage!
I never cease to utter my lament,
For I am slain by separation's pain;
And no one listens to my tale of woe,
When I lament upon my absent love.
And there is no one brings me, in my love,
The tidings that I crave of my beloved.
O that the Queen would some compassion show,
And smile in recognition on her slave!
O Lord, I flee to thee to gain thy help,
And upon thee my firm foundation place;
Therefore I melt thy Spirit with my sighs;
Thou canst not fail at my petition's plea.
O God, my God, by all thy radiant light,
Give succor to me, leave me not forlorn!
Thou who the Author art of things that are,
Open to me the door of my release."
As thus the wretched bird his song pursued,
The deity the suffering suppliant heard;
For when a tortured soul appeals to God
God ever listens to his loud complaint.
And all the time the Nightingale was heard,
As is each soul that prays with earnestness.
The sufferings that round that prisoner rose
Were almost now unto their limit brought;

For the East Wind, that cheers the souls of men,
Arrived and saw the Nightingale encaged,
And came and said, " My greeting to your Grace,"
And bowed his forehead to the very dust.
He said: " How fares it with thee, prisoner?
How is it thou art prisoned thus by pain?
And what transgression art thou guilty of,
That thou art thus imprisoned in a cage?
Who is it found thee guilty of a crime,
That to confinement thou hast been consigned?
Who is it that hath slandered thee abroad,
And set thee thus behind the prison bar,
When thou in freedom findest such delight,
Who is it that has tortured thus thy heart?
How is it thou art thus a prisoner found,
Tormented with the anguish of thy heart?
Come back again to glades of Gulistan,
And let us hear thee speak thy heart's desire."

LII

THE CAPTIVE NIGHTINGALE ANSWERS THE KIND-HEARTED EAST WIND, WHO BRINGS TO THE PINING LOVER GREETING FROM THE RADIANT ROSE

SOON as the Nightingale this message heard
He was in ardent passion overwhelmed.
He cried aloud with sighs and deep lament;
" Hear me; I will my woe relate to thee.
I, a poor man, for lovingness atone,
And all the guilt is in the jailer found.
Love is the only guilt that I avow,
This is the cause of all my sorrows here.
While love has thus enchained my inmost life,
My song alone the note of freedom sounds."
And the East Wind responded to this speech.
" Heroic sufferer," he replied to him,
" Torment thyself no more, the course of love
'At last is tending to the goal desired;

Long hast thou borne this dire adversity,
The hour of happiness at last draws near.
The queenly Rose her greeting sends to thee,
And makes the message through this herald known;
Thy long-continued passion finds its end,
'Tis time the volume of thy pain be closed.
Soon shalt thou from thy prison-house be freed.
Lament no more, thy succor is at hand."
Then the East Wind the pleasant message gave,
With which the Rose had sent him on his way;
And when the bird received that sweet despatch,
He fell to earth, quite overcome with joy.
And said: " Oh, let me know the news she sends,
For it has reached me in a happy hour;
The hour in which I fell to earth for grief,
There comes to me the news of happiness."
And with a thankful heart he thanked the Lord;
And to the East Wind every blessing wished,
And on his backward way the East Wind went,
And songs of thankfulness the bird began.
And when the East Wind reached the happy Rose
He said: " O Light that glorifiest the world,
The Nightingale is prisoner in a cage;
The cage is like a dungeon to the bird;
And he is overwrought with love for thee;
And languishes amid the pangs of love.
His strains betray the languor of his heart,
Oft as he breathes them on the listening wind.
And ofttimes he reflects, that all his life,
Is now surrendered to a narrow cage;
And soon his spirit will surrendered be,
Unless the anguish of his song be stilled.
And tho' full many a sufferer I have seen,
Saw I none ever in such languishment."

LIII

WHILE THE NIGHTINGALE LIES A PRISONER SUFFERING IN HIS CAGE, THE ROSE COMES TO PAY HIM A SICK VISIT, AND TO LEARN OF HIS HEALTH

AND when the Rose these tidings had received
She said: "Alas! him genius has endowed,
Poor, wretched one, with melody of pain!
Long has he lived devoted to my love,
And many pains and anguish has he borne
Because he cannot look upon my face.
Yet since this mendicant is so forlorn,
And so overwrought by his melodious pain,
'Tis time that I his disposition learn,
And pay a visit to the lonely one.
'Tis duty bids us go and cheer the sick;
And my great duty now concerns this bird.
Come, thou East Wind, that cheerest earthly hearts,
Point me the way unto his dwelling-place.
'Tis thine to bring the wandering outcast joy,
And free him from the barriers of the cage."
Approvingly the Wind of East replied:
"Thou, who, like gold, has stood the test of time,
Long mayst thou all the bliss of life enjoy,
And in both worlds mayst thou find happiness.
Now it is time that thou shouldst yonder wretch
Console in pity ere he breathe his last."
The graceful Rose straightway her journey took,
And to the Nightingale her course she bent.
And while the Nightingale his theme pursued,
And still in disappointed ardor pined,
His heart swelled high with tidings of delight,
When all was told him of the Rose's word.
With full dependence on the grace of God,
He decked himself in radiant array,
And he bethought himself that he would be
Like sunlight shining in the motes of earth;
So should his face the happy sunlight show,

When 'mid the stars the day god shines on high,
And day has reached the zenith of the noon,
And the orbed moon with its full radiance shines.
And now the Rose to visit him appeared,
And asked him the condition of his life.
She saw him quite o'ermastered and undone,
And all his strength by adverse fortune broken.
And when she saw him, she astonished stood,
And through astonishment was motionless.
Soon as the Nightingale set eyes on her,
He recommenced his melancholy song,
And fainting, fell through passion to the ground,
And motionless he lay from wounds of pain.
He closed his eyes and to the dust he pressed
His cheeks, by tears of absence long grown pale;
While ardent passion through his bosom flamed.
Like to a suppliant he lay grovelling there,
And said: " O God, what dream is this I see?
Am I transported into fancy's realm,
So that the sun of happiness shines out,
And I behold the lustre of the moon?
That happiness at last descends to me;
And that the moon her face through tempests shows;
That my disasters have an end at last;
That exile in reunion comes to end;
That healing falls upon the wounds of pain;
And that my heart the balm of mercy meets? "
While thus the bird in languishment reclined,
The Rose regarded him with tenderness;
And there was naught for him but kindly thought;
In gentle pity opened out her soul.
And sweetly did she question how he fared,
And how it went with his calamities,
And pity her majestic heart enthralled,
While he, she saw, with ardent passion glowed.
And while the Rose her jewels scattered round,
The Nightingale gave utterance to his soul.
The bird sang loud, the flower lent listening ear,
And soft caresses thus were interchanged;
And many things were said on either side,

And when their mutual greetings closed at last,
And the Rose started on her journey home,
The Nightingale broke out in strains of song.
And when the well-beloved had flown away,
The amorous bird cried after her in vain;
And once again began his loving lay,
Reiterating echoes of his pain.
All his great passion had come back to him,
That momentary bliss was but a dream.
He said, in wanderings of wonder lost,
"Whither has fled this union sweet of bliss?
Oh, what a wondrous incident is this!
Hard to believe has this occurrence been;
And since the world is unsubstantial show,
How is it that to me true suffering comes?
Where is distress, and where is happiness?
Where is compassion, what is trustworthy?
And this fair Rose who stood before my cage,
Where are the sweet caresses of my friend?
Shall happiness return to me through her?
Or was my hope nothing but fantasy—
The fantasy of overwrought desire—
That it so quickly fades upon my sight?"
And in this plight the wretched singer gave,
From throbbing throat, his call for pity's aid.

LIV

THE LOVELY ROSE SENDS THE CHEERFUL EAST WIND TO THE
MONARCH OF SPRING ASKING HIM TO FREE THE NIGHT-
INGALE

Ah, lovely Rose, she has a heart of gold,
And much she mourns for the lorn Nightingale;
And said: "East Wind, my herald messenger,
Blow thou my message o'er the world's domain.
I wish thee to become my instrument,
Through which release and help my bird shall ease.
Ah! that the Bulbul with the open heart,
No more might suffer in the deadly cage!

Now show thy pity for that wretched soul,
And gain him freedom from the iron bars.
Betake thee to the monarch of the world;
And speak to him in many a pleading word;
And then occasion will be granted thee
The Bulbul's dreary tale to tell to him.
And tell him how the wretch in prison pines,
O'erwhelmed in suffering and misery;
The king will have compassion on his lot,
And show his favor to the destitute.
He will be just and kindly to the bird
And willingly release him from the cage."
The East Wind ran on hearing this command,
And quickly to the monarch took his way.
Upon the palace threshold laid him down,
And in the dust his countenance he set.
His wishes and his prayer expressed to him,
In answer to the royal questioning.
And many tidings told of this and that,
Till to the end of all his news he came.
Of many things he spoke in many ways
And information gave of this and that.
And then it happened that he came at last
To tell the story of the Nightingale,
And said, " O thou, the high illustrious one,
A king endowed with each attractive gift,
How is it possible that in thy day
The cry of guiltless suffering should arise?
That the poor prisoner in a cage should pine?
And that the mighty should oppress the weak?
That night and day the weak should utter woe,
And without guilt endure the stroke of pain?
That he should lie in fetters and in gyves—
He whose sweet voice is ever eloquent?
And is it well that king so just as thou
Should trample on so innocent a wretch?
That he within the cage should cry for help,
Through such a tedious period of distress?
That he, by night and day, should make lament
And no one listen to his dolorous song?"

When this the lofty monarch of the world
Had heard, he said: " And lives that beggar still?
And is he still imprisoned in the cage,
Caught in the meshes of his pain and woe?
Now must his sad imprisonment have end.
Fetch him and let me look upon his face."
Soon as the firman of the Shah went forth,
The tidings of it reached the Nightingale.
For one among the courtiers hurried forth,
To bring the hapless one to happiness.
And from the cage he was at once released
And brought into the presence of the king.
And soon as the celestial monarch's eye
Beheld the plight and misery of the wretch,
And saw how vile and weak he did appear,
And how he was reduced to skin and bone,
And all forespent by separation's pang,
And dwindled like the crescent of the moon,
He questioned him of each particular,
And of his public conduct in the past.
The Bulbul called down blessings on his head,
And in the dust he bowed before his face;
Then he ran on in ardent passion's tone,
As a gazelle in his swift circle turns;
From his sweet lips he warbled to the Shah
The whole expression of his gifted heart.
And as his ardent trills and mournful notes
Filled with astonishment the royal mind,
He owned him, in the usage of his art,
A singer perfect of consummate skill.
And as the monarch listened to his strain,
He felt the tide of pleasure flood his heart,
And said: " Oh, what an artist do I hear!
Well fit to fill my bosom with delight.
It is injustice to this wretched man
To put him pitiless in prison cell,
Because forsooth within the rose garden
He sets himself as friend beside the Rose.
For since this beggar is a very seer,
I think he is companion for a king.

Now let the Nightingale attend the Rose,
And let him stay with her where'er she bide.
She has no slave so faithful to her heart,
So let him speak with her where'er she be."
And instantly the monarch gave command
Within the rose garden to bring the bird,
That he might medicine and healing bring
To all the suffering of the pining Rose.
The Nightingale bowed low upon the ground,
With songs of benediction did he praise
The king, and beamed with longing and desire,
And came at length unto the rose garden.

LV

The Gracious East Wind Brings News to the Rose of the Nightingale's Release

He met the cypress and with honor hailed,
And courteous salutation yielded him.
Who asked the Bulbul whither he was bound,
And who had given peace to his desire;
And he related to him every jot,
How he had been released from bitter pain.
The cypress wore a look of wonderment,
Hither and thither did he toss his head,
And said to him: "At last, my treasured bird,
Upon my summit shall thy home be made."
So there the cypress and the Nightingale,
Henceforth consorted in a friendship true.
But the East Wind had fluttered to the Rose,
Swift as the arrow from the bowstring shot,
And in a voice of joy his message said:
"O Rose, rejoice! for good the news I bring;
The Shah at liberty has Bulbul set,
And given happiness to the forlorn,"
And then he told her all that had befallen;
As everything he had been witness to.
The day was warm and the Rose laughed aloud,
And rocked herself with pleasure 'mid the leaves.

In haste she put her crimson mantle on,
And gave her garment, grateful, to the Wind.
Into his hand she placed a ruby gem,
And breathed upon him all her gracious scent.
And gold was strewn about the rose garden,
And all the folk for dust walked over gold.
And the Rose bloomed in all her stateliest pomp,
And laughed with joy in her enkindling heart.

LVI

DESCRIPTION OF THE MORNING FEAST GIVEN BY THE LOVELY ROSE, TO WHICH SHE ASKS THE NIGHTINGALE, AND ENJOYS HERSELF WITH HIM IN ARDENT PASSION AND KINDNESS AND PURE LOVE

UPON a certain morning, when the day
O'er all the world lay like an open rose,
When day was bright with sweet fruition's bliss,
And the world's face was like a rose fountain,
When the world opened like a petaled rose,
And folk like nightingales sang out for joy,
Then was it that the Rose, in Gulistan,
Adorned herself with caftan of pure gold.
Red was she both without, and red within,
And red the turban high that crowned her brow.
She decked herself with gladness and with joy,
And o'er her shoulders flung a mantle green.
And to atone for all past suffering
She sends out invitations to a feast,
That she may cheer with brightness troubled hearts,
And fill their goblets with the wine of joy.
She gave the tulips word of her design,
And bade them crown with wine the gleaming cup.
She told the dew to pour its sparkling wine
Into the chalice of each opening flower.
She bade narcissus with his beaker full,
To show himself that day a roysterer,
And that the cypress should before the gate
Stand seneschal, awaiting her command.

She saw the meadow carpeted with green,
And all new garmented the world of flowers.
The stately lily dropped her gleaming sword,
And stood with peaceful mien beside her hearth.
The hyacinth forsook his plots of ill,
And thought upon his rightful services.
And as the Rose this firman sent abroad,
All Gulistan was decked for holiday.
And to the garden feast they hurried fast,
Bent on the recreation of their hearts.
The Rose herself, with happy mien, assumed
The place of honor in the rose garden,
And all the other nobles sat around,
In ranks and orders at the garden feast;
And the bright cup went round from lip to lip;
And each to other pledged the beady wine.
In cup of virgin gold, a foaming draught
The Rose with loving laughter drank to all.
And twice again the ruddy wine she quaffed,
With heart and eye fixed on the Nightingale.
She saw that from the circle of her court,
The bird, all solitary, sat aloof.
And then her veil she lifted from her face,
That she, against her wont, might plain be seen;
And said: " The time for sorrow has gone by,
Now let each sufferer plead his cause to us.
Then wherefore should the Bulbul sit apart,
Rather than gladden with his lays our feast?
For now in separation's deadly night,
Well has he earned the glory of the dawn.
" Go," to the East Wind said she, " bring to me
That mourning minstrel for this festal hour."
The East Wind, nourisher of all that lives,
Well knew the goodness of the princess' heart;
And thus he spoke unto the Nightingale:
" O sorrow singer, let thy lot be bliss.
The Rose, who greets thee now with kindliness,
Invites thee to her festal gathering;
O Bulbul, now distress thyself no more,
For thou hast reached the goal of thy desire."

And as these words the pining Bulbul heard,
He turned himself to God with thankful heart.
At last he came, with many a tender thought,
Unto the festival the Rose ordained.
The Rose all honor did him in her power;
And took him to herself to cherish him.
And said, " Ah, sad one, what has pained thee now?
Thou art for all thy absence now consoled.
And now it is ordained by happy fate,
That I should give to thee a little pledge.
My flight has put thy song quite out of tune,
And turned aside the music of thy song.
Now let thyself no longer rove away,
For thou canst rightly linger here a while;
For all the sickness I have caused to thee,
A thousand faithful pledges be returned.
It is the custom of the beauteous one,
That she should crown affliction with her trust."
As to the Nightingale these gracious words
Were in caressing accents thus addressed,
He charged himself with fault a thousand times,
And mute he stood, and weak and tottering.
He said: " The word that falls from thee is good,
And trust that follows after suffering
Is good, and what thou doest is well done.
For above all a loving sweetheart stands;
And I have shed my blood for love of thee,
And shouldst thou slay me I would not complain.
For thee, the breath of life within me heaves,
E'en separation as delight I hail."
'Twas thus the Rose and Nightingale beguiled
The time in conversation amorous.
Then they began to quaff the ruddy wine;
And many a goblet sparkled to the brim.
Draughts of the rosy-tinted wine they took,
And in the feast the pastoral pipes were heard,
And Bulbul his clear notes with ardor poured.
They rang through all the ranks of Gulistan,
Like some sweet lute they floated on the air,
And oft in loudest trills they burst like flame.

His look was fixed upon the lustrous Rose,
In ardent longing soft as a caress.
Now his love burst in flame like aloe flowers;
And in his glowing song he uttered sighs.
Although made happy by his keen delight,
He still in sighs the longed-for kisses craved.
With golden draughts the goblet oft was filled,
But kisses were the sugar in the cup.
For while the bird began to sip the wine,
He stole a kiss from the fair Rose's lips;
Warmer and warmer with the feast he grew,
With hearts quite melted went they arm in arm,
And as the liquor mounted to his brain
The banqueter lay senseless on the ground.
And the glass circled round amid the feast,
Till heaven its circuit had to evening brought.

LVII

THE DESCRIPTION OF THE NIGHT AND THE NIGHT-LONG REVEL AMID THE SOUND OF TRUMPETS AND CASTANETS

AND when the day dissolved the company,
The feast renewed itself through all the night.
Soon as in heaven the constellations bright,
Assembled round the moon, their empress queen.
The stars that fluttering like butterflies,
Were gathered in the palace of the moon,
So gathered nobles in the rose garden,
With friendship and with pledging of the wine.
And now the Rose was filled with wild desire,
The Nightingale his loveliest chanson poured.
And the narcissus lit his golden lamps,
And brightened all the spaces of the grove,
And the glass circled 'mid the merry throng,
And lute and castanet their music made.
The flutes with their shrill notes began to sound,
Commingled with the tinkling tambourine.
And round in rank on rank the flowers were ranged.
Buds blew the horn, and roses beat the drum,

The very violets in the music joined.
While all the larch-trees rustled in accord.
Narcissus beat the drum with thundering note,
Through the whole rout the pattering tomtom rang,
The lilies took the hautboys in their hands,
The tulips blew their bagpipes, and each played
On every side the instrument he chose,
And so the merry concert filled the groves.
The cypress led the dance at his own will,
His step kept time to the musician's note,
And the East Wind sighed softly over all,
Amid the clangor of the flute and horn.
And so the revel sounded deep and high
As flutes, or dying harmonies ordained,
And clamor filled with shouts the rose garden,
And all the city rang to beat of drum.
And drowsy fumes of wine made tottering feet,
The red from many a lip was kissed away.
The Nightingale is drunk for happiness,
Sunk in the melody of his desire.
He thinks upon the lips of her he loves,
And ceases not to sip the ruddy wine,
And the Rose blushes as she pledges him,
And all his keen desire she turns to bliss.
And tender protestations there are heard,
And happy pledges are between them made,
And love from both sides breathes its scented breath,
And the sweet pang of passion fills that hour,
And not a cloud was in the placid sky.
The lover stood possessed of his beloved,
And ever higher mantled pleasure's tide,
Till all the consciousness of life was lost.
The Rose and Nightingale together there,
In undisturbed communion abode.
And many a word of tenderness they spoke,
Threading in speech the mazes of their love,
Propitious was the opportunity.
They were united ne'er to be divorced.
The lover and the object of his love
Were rendered one in passion's glowing hour.

The dance of love went on till morning light,
The feast of passion lasted till the dawn.
No sleep their eyelids closed, and till the morn
They ceased not quaffing of the ruby wine.

LVIII

The Happiness of the Rose and Nightingale Does Not Continue

And in this wise for many and many a day,
The Rose and Nightingale held festival,
Until the furious cruelty of fate
Turned all their love to abject misery.
The Rose became the prey of every wind,
The Nightingale fell headlong in the dust,
The course of fate ordained for them to drink
The cup of desolation to the dregs.
Those upon whom companion's smile is turned,
Are never infinitely destitute,
And this too treacherous world betrays us all,
With craft and the sharp edge of trickery.
And when the dish gives honey to our lips,
A deadly poison lurks within the bowl.
And if we trust one moment to a cup
It kills us till the blood in torrents flows.
When did two days award an equal calm
But that distress did not the next ensue?
When was it that the highest bliss was given,
But that at last there followed misery?
The treasure is a snake, the gold but dross,
Their grace a fading leaf, their balm is blight,
And pain is but the sequel of delight,
Their life to nothing but a vapor turns.
Darius, Alexander, where are they,
Who once were conquerors of every land?
For both of them at last exchanged for grief,
For grief of death, the glory of their life.
Where is the sovereign Solomon, whose throne
From peak to peak of Caucasus was set,

He whose high throne was sport to every wind,
To waft it as it wished to every pole?
At last the wind bore off the lofty throne,
And Solomon to-day is but a name.
Where is Schamshid, through whose profound design
The world was moulded into living form?
But even his genius vanished in the wind,
And suddenly he mouldered into dust.
Where now is he, the Lord of all the world,
The lord of lords, illustrious Feridun?
He also to the spoiler yields his power,
Flung to the ground to mingle with the dust.
Still in this house there lingers only one,
The everlasting, everliving God.
This world has but two portals, which indeed
Are separated from each other far,
For by one door man enters to the house,
And by the other he an exit makes.
Who in this house forever gladly stays,
From which the very Prophet took his flight?
And since he never lingered in this house,
How canst thou think eternal there thy lot?
What is the world, O Fasli, but an inn
Where caravans halt only for night?
Put not thy trust, then, in its permanence,
For ambush ever lies in wait for it.
Distrust it, then, for it can ne'er endure,
Despise it, for it has no help for thee.

LIX

DECLARATION OF THE HIDDEN MEANING WHICH FOR THE MYSTIC LIES IN THIS TRUE HISTORY AND MOURNFUL NARRATIVE

THOU who hast on these pages fixed thine eyes,
If there is any knowledge in thy mind,
Look not on these events as idle tales,
For in the words a meaning there abides.

And what from idle tales can come of good,
Unless some meaning there be hid in them?
Some doctrine from a fable often comes,
So idle tales are often profitless.
And hence the hidden sense of history
Declares the sequel both to me and thee.
For now when to an end the story comes,
Thou needs must learn the lesson of the tale.
The Shah, the radiant monarch of the Spring,
Is intellect that bides for evermore.
The Rose, which is the daughter of the Shah,
Is genius, offspring of the intellect.
The city which is named the rose garden
Is life when spent on beds of luxury.
The Nightingale upon the rose parterre
The human heart, which after genius longs.
The heart by genius is perfected,
And therefore is of genius amorous.
The East Wind is the breath of suffering,
Which ever blows between the heart and soul,
And the clear vision which in life abides
Is the narcissus in the rose parterre.
The tulip, in a circle bends its cup,—
'Tis friendship with its tender-heartedness.
The cypress, I would fain expound to you,
Is the free symbol of integrity.
The rivulet is purity of soul,
Wherein the well-beloved is mirrored clear.
And in the dew which serves the flowers for wine
Is seen the shining tenderness of God.
What is the lily else but bravery?
The violet is loveliness of heart,
The hyacinth is bitter jealousy,
The thorn is anger which estranges all.
And that which Summer I and Winter call,
Must also have a double sense to thee.
For one brings many blessings to thy life,
The other desolates this world of ours;
And on the character of each of these
All of the year's vicissitudes depend.

The one is strong as anger in its day,
And with it carries off the strength of man;
For man when fiery ardor rules the sky
Finds all his life with flames of heat consumed.
And this is August burning like a brand,
Which desolates the city of the soul.
Thus will be clear to thee how any fire
Destroys the happiness of monarch Spring.
So soon as suffering seizes on the life
It overcomes the soul and intellect.
For intellect its office fails to fill,
So anger has with all things laid it waste.
The other source of strength is love of kind,
Which always brings a blessing in its train.
Its action is to deepen graciousness,
And give new color to the sense of life.
And so I name it Autumn: well is known
Its character as separate and distinct—
Since rage and passion then are satisfied,
And life into a mellow twilight comes.
While all the time nature in calm decay
Is like the chill of man's declining day.
And thus the king of winter seems at last
The human life and spirit to usurp.
The king who does the rose garden restore
Is but the light and health that clears man's soul.
Anger and passion both give way to him,
And God's own light at last pours blessing down.
This king brings help to heart and intellect,
And takes possession of the whole domain.
He frees the spirit from the charge of sense,
And widens out the prospect of the soul;
Then heart and spirit in a kiss unite,
The bridal of the Rose and Nightingale.

LX

The Close of the Book

Thank God, these pages, numbered to the full,
Are pleasant as the petals of a Rose;
Where genius is as the Nightingale,
And plucks them ardently from off the flower.
'Tis genius blent the sweets of Gulistan,
Tinting narcissus' cheeks with fresher hue.
Each verse is like a gayly-painted rose,
And Bulbul is the guardian of the grove.
The letters like to cedars stand in line,
The lines run o'er the page like rivulets.
The words like rank and file their order take,
The sense is as the diamond in the mine.
And thus the poet has prepared for you
A feast of tenderness, a dainty feast,
A bosom book of the sublimest lore,
Which all the world will welcome with delight.
The book towers up like some tall monument,
And every verse of it is Eden's door.
And I have put a meaning under it,
Which is the Gulistan of its fair words.
It sprang from out the well of my pure wit,
My genius is enthroned on its renown,
'Tis I who clothed the legend in these words,
The language and the meaning both are mine,
And in this legend there is naught of guile,
My taper's light no *ignis fatuus*,
And he who sees the symbol will esteem,
The book from title-page to colophon.
I borrowed no man's phrases and I trod
No path that had been trodden hitherto.
Forth from the portal of my intellect
There streamed the words of evil and of good.
And many a lovely lay have I composed
From the sad music of the Nightingale.
So that this book, so fascinating fair,

Will by the fair ever be beloved.
I hope that God the volume will protect,
And keep it safe from misadventures twain.
First from a critic ignorant and dull,
Who like a mule the poet tramples down,
A critic without intellect and sense,
Who cannot see the meaning of the words,
But twists the sense of every graceful line,
And does not hear the music in the verse.
One point he dwells on, to another blind,
And mixes up the poetry and prose.
Presumes himself to boast poetic fire,
And to set right a hundred lines of mine.
Then from the writer who, like one bewitched,
Does naught but blot each blemish in the book.
He scores the book with blots as with a cloak,
And all its beauties in concealment keeps.
He sticks his mark where is no need of it,
And blunders every time he would correct:
His criticism should be criticised,
And his misuse of language makes me smile,
Even misspelling he is guilty of.
His very letters does he scarcely know,
His very pen itself cannot run straight,
His knotted fingers scarce can hold the pen.
Now, Fasli, comes at length thy poem's end.
Thank God for all the beauty of thy lays.
Leave poetry and turn thy mind to God,
And thank him thou hast reached the colophon.
Thy book is one of happiness and bliss,
In lovers' bosoms it will oft be borne.
And now the numbered verses thus conclude
The story of the Rose and Nightingale.

HISTORY OF THE FORTY VEZIRS

HISTORY OF THE FORTY VEZIRS

INTRODUCTION

I T is related that the wife of a great king unjustly accused his son, by another mother, of an act of treachery against his father; and that that king was wroth, and for forty mornings caused his son to be led forth to be slain; and that that king had many vezirs, all of whom were peerless in the sea of understanding, and in thoughtfulness and sagacity, and full of plans and devices; and that when the king each morning caused his son to be led forth for execution, these vezirs gave the king counsel, and each morning a vezir, telling a story, calmed the king's heart and turned away his wrath, and saved the prince from his hand; and again, that each night that crafty lady, letting not the king rest, ever incited him to the slaughter of the prince, and with enticing and beguiling words, repeated each night a story to the king, and made his understanding forsake him; and that through the words of that crafty lady, every morning for forty days he caused his son to be led into his presence to be slain; and that the vezirs by telling a story delivered him. After forty days the innocence of the prince was manifested and the falsehood and calumny of the crafty lady disclosed; and she received her due, and the prince was greatly loved and esteemed before his father when the truth of his affair was known. The adventures of the king, and the lady and the prince, and his governor and the vezirs, and what befell between them, will be related; and sixteen of the stories told by the vezirs in the forty days, and by the lady in the forty nights will be set forth and narrated. " With God is grace: how excellent a friend is he ! "

They tell in history books, that there was in Persia a great
king, whose name was Khānqīn, and in the grasp of whose
possession were the Seven Climes. As he was gracious and
able and sagacious, kingliness and the bases of empire were
present in him. God most high had give him a fair son, by
whose beauty the people of the world were bewildered. Who-
soever looked upon his loveliness would say, " Is it magic,
this? " [1] and he who beheld his tall figure would exclaim,
" This is no mortal! " [2]   Fair was his beauty and charming was
his self, and desired of lovers. Moreover, his were accomplishments and perfections; he had no rival in the reading of
science, or in penmanship, or in archery, or in horsemanship;
and his fair character was talked of and celebrated among
high and low. The king, too, whenever he saw him, experienced a hundred thousand pleasures, and looked upon him
as the source of his life. The mother of this youth was
of the lovely ones of China.[3]   One day she fell ill, and at
length, no remedy availing, she was received into Mercy.
Thereupon, after some time had passed, his father married the daughter of a great king and brought her to his
palace.

After a while this lady fell in love with the prince. For a
long time she hid her love in her heart, and, saying in herself,
" He is my step-son, what help for it! " she disclosed it not.
But when, day after day, she looked upon his beauty, she was
no longer able to bear with patience the fire of love, and, bringing into the field the wallet of craft, she was busy night and
day with stratagems. Now the king had given the prince
to a governor to be taught the sciences of astronomy and
astrology, and the boy was night and day occupied acquiring
them. One day the governor looked at the youth's horoscope,
and perceived there was a space of forty days in most sinister
aspect. Did he say a word about this, he would be pointing
out a great calamity; so he was exceeding grieved, and his
heart was contracted. But he said to the prince, " I have this
day looked at thy horoscope and seen a most sinister aspect;
such is it, my life,[4] that thou must obey the command and

---

[1] Koran, lii. 15.
[2] Ib. xii. 31.
[3] Not necessarily a Chinese woman,
simply a beauty; China and Chinese

Tartary being regarded as pre-eminent
for the beauty of their women.
[4] A term of endearment.

decree of God most high, and observe my injunction, else thou shalt die."

The prince heard these words of his governor and his color changed, and he said to his teacher, "Order what thou wilt: command is thine." Quoth the teacher, "O son, the way of averting this calamity is thus stated in the book: for the space of forty days thou shalt not speak one word though a naked sword be above thy head." Then he bade the prince bear in mind certain of the holy names and blessed litanies, and sent him to his father. The governor thereupon hid in a vault and concealed himself.[5] When the prince came to his father, the latter said to him, "My son, what hast thou read and written this day?" but the prince gave no answer to his father. Again quoth the king, "O my life, what does thy master?" again he gave no answer. Again his father said, "O life of my life, what has befallen thee? Why dost thou not speak?" Again he gave no answer. Then said the king to his son's guardian, "The boy is sad to-day, take him to his mother, maybe that his heart will expand." Then the guardian took the youth to the lady and said, "Lady, this youth is sad, he has not uttered one syllable to his father this day, therefore has he sent him to thee, that peradventure he may speak beside his mother." The lady was glad and said, "Clear the house, go, be off; that I may learn somewhat of the prince, and banish his sadness and grief."

When she was alone with the youth the lady threw her arm round his neck, and said, "O my life, ah, my lord, what has befallen thee that thy heart is thus sad, and that thou art disconsolate and mournful? Whatever thy father possesses is in my hand; if thou wilt make thy heart one with mine, and act according to my words, I will turn away thy sadness." To her too the prince gave no answer. Again said the lady, "Thou art a grown-up youth, I too am a young lady; thy father is a decrepit old man, with neither thought nor discernment; if thou wilt assure me, and swear to me, and accept me as thy legal wife, I will make shift to kill thy father and make thee king in his stead. First, I swear by God, and for God, and in God, that I speak these words from the bottom of my heart

---

[5] Probably he was afraid lest the king should put him to death for giving such bad news.

and from my very soul, and that I will not falsify these words; do thou likewise assure me, and swear to me that I may act accordingly." The prince answered not a word.

Quoth the lady, "O dearer than my life, should thou ask how I will kill thy father; lo, in the treasury are many kinds of poisons, of one of which if a person eat, he turns ill and after three months dies. The people will not know the cause of his death, and will not suspect that he has eaten poison. They will say he but took ill, and will doubtless make thee king. Should thou say I am thy step-mother and wonder how thou art to marry me, the way is this: send me off to my own country, and while yet on the road, send someone after me who shall come in the guise of a robber and pounce upon us by night and seize me; so it will be said that robbers have seized me. Then buy me as a slave girl from that man, and make me thy wife; so none will know." But the prince answered her not at all, and spake not. Then the lady grew desperate at his not speaking, and her patience was exhausted, and she said, "O my soul, O my gliding angel, why wilt thou not speak to me?" And she put her arm round his neck and drew him to her and made to kiss him. And the prince was wroth, and he smote the lady's mouth with the back of his hand, so that her mouth filled with blood.

When she saw this conduct the fire of anger blazed up in the hearth of her breast, and the sparks from the fumes of her pride gained her heart, and she cried, "Out on thee! fool! boy! I sought to raise thee to the throne and make thee king, and thou didst strike me thus; now will I speak to thy father that he shall hew thee in pieces, small even as thine ear." And she dishevelled her hair and smeared the four sides of her robe with the blood of her mouth and sat down, sad and tearful, feeble and wailing. Then the youth went to his private apartments. After a time the king came to the harem, thinking to inquire of the lady concerning the affair of the prince, and he saw her seated besmeared with red blood. And the king marvelled at this sight, and said to the lady, "What is this matter? explain to me." She said, "O king, that degenerate son of thine! God forbid that he be son of thine!" "What is the matter?" said the king.

The lady replied, "I saw that degenerate youth that he was

sad, and I cleared the palace that I might banish his sadness, and I said to him, ' My son, why art thou sad?' Then he stretched forth his hand and made to do me wrong, but I prevented him. Then he said to me, ' Why dost thou flee me? if thou wilt be my mistress and make thy heart one with mine, and assure me thereof, it is my intention to kill my father and make thee my wife; and the riches, and the country, and the throne, and the kingdom will be ours.' But I consented not, and he desired to kill me that I might not make known this matter to the king. And I cried out for the saving of my life, and he left me in this plight and went away. Now, O king, know of a surety that he purposes evil against thee, and see to the saving of thine own life, else crown and throne will go from thy hands; so ere he kill thee do thou kill him that thou be secure from his wickedness." When the king heard these words from the lady he was wroth, and that night sleep came not to his eyes.

In the early morning he went forth and sat upon his throne, and caused the prince to be brought before him, that he might order the executioner to smite off his head. The courtiers who were beside him got the executioner to delay, and at once sent word to the vezirs. As soon as they knew what was happening, the vezirs came with all speed to the presence of the king, and said, " O king, how has the prince this day thus merited the anger of the king?"

The king related to the vezirs the events that had taken place, whereupon the grand vezir said, " Slay not thy son, trusting on the woman's word; do not a deed beyond the ordinance of God and the law of the Messenger:[6] and there is no permission in the law for one to act on a woman's word. If there were witnesses that the prince had done this thing to the lady, then were command the king's; but spill not blood unjustly, that afterward thou suffer not regret and remorse. They have said that whatsoever oppression there be in a country it is incumbent on him who is king to banish it; where then were room for kings to do deeds beyond the law and spill blood unjustly? If they be negligent in the matter of banishing oppression, God most high will visit and afflict them with four sorts of troubles: firstly, he will make their life short;

[6] The Prophet Mahomet.

secondly, he will let the enemy prevail against them; thirdly, he will give the enemy aid and victory; and fourthly, on the resurrection day he will be wroth with them and consign them to the torment of hell.

" He then is wise who will not for a five-days' life lose the hereafter, and is not needless. And, moreover, the holy Messenger (peace on him!) when going to perform the ablution would first of all perform it with sand; the companions asked, ' O Apostle of God, is it lawful to perform the sand ablution when there is water? ' The most noble beloved of God replied, ' I fear lest death let me not reach the water.' Now, O king, be not presumptuous through worldly fortune and kingship, and consent not to a deed contrary to the law, and ruin not thy hereafter, trusting in the woman's word. For by reason of the craft of woman has many a head been cut off; and the blessed Messenger hath said, ' Whatsoever misfortunes befall my people will befall them through women.' And wise is he who looks at the beginning and end of an affair, like that king who took counsel with his sons and his vezirs and the elders of the country, and was prospered alike in the world and the hereafter. And that story is a fair story; if the king grant leave I will relate it." The king said, " Tell on." Quoth the vezir :

TRIAL OF THE THREE SONS

" There was of old time in the palace of the world a great king, such that the world was under his rule. He had lived enjoying sovereignty for a hundred and twenty years in the palace of the world, and was grown old and knew that in the near future he would be given to drink of the potion of death. And the king had three moon-faced [7] sons and likewise three able and skilful vezirs. One day quoth the king to his vezirs, ' The end of this my life draws nigh; the natural life of man is a hundred and twenty years, after that not an old man remains. Now I have reached that state and the affair is thus, I wish to appoint one of my sons to my place, and, leaning my back against the wall of abdication, take rest. Which of my sons do ye deem worthy of the throne? ' The vezirs said,

[7] I. e., beautiful.

'O king, long be thy life; a person's good and bad are not known till he have been proved; for two things are the touchstone of a man; the first is wine, the second, office; in these two things is a person's manfulness apparent and manifest. This were best, for nine days let these thy three sons enjoy the throne and sovereignty, and with this touchstone let the king prove them; whatever be the character of each of them, it will appear; for the rest, let the king order accordingly.'

" When the king heard these words from the vezirs they seemed right good to his heart, and he commanded that each son should sit for three days on the throne and exercise sovereignty, and declared that he would allow whatever they should annul or appoint, and whatever they should grant from the treasury, and whatever justice or oppression they might show, and that no one should say aught. Then the eldest son of the king sat upon the throne and directed the government, and he practised justice and equity on such wise as cannot be described. He loved the doctors and turned from the foolish, and gave the high offices to the learned, and withdrew from listening to things forbidden and what was vain, and strove much in well-doing.

" Then the king, to prove the judgment of his son, sent him three persons from prison, one was a murderer, and one a thief, and one an adulterer; and with them he sent the complainants. When they came before the prince the complainants stated their case and the witnesses bore witness that these three persons were indeed guilty, and that these words were no calumny against them, but true. When the prince knew how the case was, he said, ' On a man's coming into the world he is the blood of his father's and mother's hearts; and, after bearing these many troubles and afflictions, a man in forty years becomes mature; so it is not well to slay him in a minute, as God most high will in the hereafter surely punish him in hell.' And he made them vow that henceforward they would do no such deeds, and set all three at liberty. And for the whole three days he ruled with justice.

" On the fourth day the turn came to the middle son, and he likewise sat upon the throne and directed the government. He abased the learned and promoted the foolish; and adopted as habit wine and music, and as profession avarice and meanness. Brief, he was the opposite of his elder brother. According to the custom, they sent to him too three criminals. When the prince heard how the case was he said, ' Men like these are the thorns of the country; ' and he ordered that the three of them perished. When he too had ruled for three days, the turn came to the youngest prince, and he likewise sat upon the throne and directed the government. He gave to the doctors the post suitable to the doctors, and to the learned the high offices, and to the strong and impetuous young heroes, military fiefs, and to the champions, feudal domains; and he registered their pay. He honored each of them according to his position, and abased the unmannerly. Brief, he put each one in his proper place, like a string of pearls; and he left not his gate unlocked lest the foe should triumph over him.

" The king again sent three culprits from the prison that he might try his judgment. When they were present the servants informed him, and he said, ' Bring them one by one.' Then when the witnesses had borne witness that the man had indeed committed murder, the prince said, ' Murder is of two kinds, the one intentional, the other accidental; and the intentional is also of two kinds, the first when a person strikes another with an iron instrument and kills him, him it is needful to put to death in retaliation; and they have written in the Book of Dues that if one person strike another with a stick and kill him, or if he throw him into a fire, then the fine for blood and the expiation alike become necessary. And the other too is accidental, when the expiation is incumbent, and he is culpable, but the fine for blood does not become necessary. And that is accidental when a person shoots an arrow at a deer, and it glances and hits a man and kills him; as God most high hath said, " Then whoso killeth a believer by mischance, then (the expiation is) the freeing of a believer from bondage . . . but if he find not (the means of doing so), then a fast for two consecutive months." ' [8]

" Then the prince asked and learned that he had murdered intentionally; so they executed him. After that they brought the thief; and the prince said, ' If anyone, sane and of age, steal ten minted dirhems of silver, his hand must be cut off, as also if he steal one dīnār of gold, even as saith the Apostle

[8] Koran, iv. 94.

'(peace on him!), " No cutting save for a dīnār or ten dirhems."
When one thus commits theft his right hand must be cut off
at the wrist; if he commit theft again, his left hand must be
cut off; if he commit it a third time, his right foot must be
cut off; and if he commit it yet again, he must be put in prison
till he repent.' Then the prince caused the man to receive the
due of his crime. After that they brought him who had committed adultery, his case also they exposed, and they gave
him the due of his sin conformably to the law.

" The nine days were completed, and the king assembled his
vezirs and said, ' Lo, ye have seen the rule of my three sons,
which of them is worthy the throne?' Quoth the first vezir,
' O king, thy eldest son is worthy.' Quoth the second vezir,
' Thy middle son is worthy.' Quoth the third vezir, ' Thy
youngest son is worthy.' When the king heard these words
of the vezirs his doubts were not removed; and he said, ' O
vezirs, the words of the three of ye are contrary each to other.'
And forthwith he commanded the people of the country that on
the morrow they should all come out to the plain. The next
day the whole of the folk were assembled on the plain; then
the king rose on his feet and said, ' O people, do not to-morrow
on the resurrection day seize hold of my collar and say, " Thou
hast oppressed us," and so wrest from me my meritorious acts
and render me confounded and ashamed. Now be ye kind and
look not at my kingship and know that before God most high
there is none meaner or more abject than myself.' And he
wept full bitterly. And the rich and poor assembled there
wept all of them together.

" Then turning again, the king said, ' O friends, lo, my time
is at hand; do ye absolve me for the hereafter. I have three
sons, whichever of them ye wish, him will I seat upon the
throne. If he be just, ye will enjoy rest and bless me, and I
shall be at rest in the place where I lie; but if he be cruel, ye
will not have rest neither shall I have rest.' The people said,
' May the king's life endure full many a year! may God most
high be well pleased with our king! We are well pleased with
our king; whatever we may have against our king, let him
be absolved. We are pleased with whichever son he see worthy
the throne; but since the king has given the choice into our
hands, let him seat his youngest son upon the throne. He

is wise as well as learned and skilled in the affairs of the world; if the king see fit, the wise is worthy the seat of honor, as this has come down in the traditions, " A wise youth taketh precedence of a foolish elder." For the rest, the king knows.'

" Then the king went to the palace and ordered that they adorned the throne, and the grandees of the state came, and all were present. Then he took his youngest son by the hand and made to seat him on the throne, when his brothers came forward and said, ' O father, all the folk say that he is accomplished and wise and that he knows well the law and the government; now we have some questions to ask of him, which if he answer, we also will contentedly resign to him the throne and stand in his presence with folded hands; [9] but if not, the crown and throne indeed become him not.'

" The king said to his youngest son, ' What sayest thou?' He replied, ' Whatsoever their questions be, let them ask them.' They said, ' What is meant by Sultan?' He answered, ' By Sultan is meant one who has certificate and warrant, that we obey the command and ordinance of God most high: the Sultan is the shadow of God on the earth.' And they asked, ' To whom is it worthy to be king by birth?' He answered, ' First the king's lineage must be manifest, then his descent must be perfect, then he must observe the habits of the just monarchs. They said, ' Who is just?' He answered, ' The just is he who transgresses not the law.' They said, ' Who is unjust?' He replied, ' He who rather than obey the law, brings in innovations of his own, so that it may be easy to amass wealth with oppression.' They said, ' What manner of persons should kings appoint vezirs?'

" He answered, ' They should appoint those persons in whom are two characteristics, the first of which is that they be endowed with prudence and resource, and the second that they be wise and accomplished; for learning in a man is a second understanding.' They said, ' How many sorts of people are needful to kings?' He answered, ' Four kinds of people; the first, skilful vezirs; the second, valiant warriors; the third, an accomplished scribe who is perfect in Arabic and Persian and the science of writing; and the fourth, a clever physician who

[9] As servants do.

is most able in the science of philosophy.' They said, ' How many different things ought always to be in the thoughts of a king?' He answered, ' Four different things; the first, to do justice to the people; the second, to use aright the money that is in the treasury; the third, to distribute offices properly; and the fourth, to be not negligent concerning enemies.' They said, ' How many different traits should the king adopt as his wont?' He answered, ' Four; the first is a smiling face; the second, a sweet speech; the third, generosity; and the fourth, mercy to the poor.' They said, ' How many kinds of courtiers are needful to the king?' He answered, ' Four classes are requisite; first, the wise; second, the learned; third, the valiant champions; and fourth, musicians: from the wise he will learn the law, from the learned he will acquire the sciences, from the valiant champions he will acquire chivalry, and by the musicians will his heart be expanded.'

" They said, ' Of which class should the king consider himself one?' He answered, ' Let him consider himself of the great sheykhs who have reached God, for it will cause him to be just.' Then he turned to his brothers and said, ' O my brothers, ye have put these many questions to me and I have answered the whole of them to the best of my power: I too have a question.' So they said to him, ' Ask on.' Quoth he, ' What do the kings of the world resemble, and what do their agents resemble, and what do the people resemble, and what do the king's enemies resemble, and what do the sheykhs resemble?' Then they both bent their heads and pondered. After a time the prince again said, ' This is no time for pondering; lo, there the question; lo, there the throne.' Quoth they, ' We are unequal to this question.' Then the king took his youngest son by the hand and seated him on the throne and said, ' O son, may God ever aid thee and may thy foes be overthrown!' Then all the nobles of the state and the people came and said, ' May the throne be blessed!' And they made him king over them.

" Then the king said, ' O son, do thou answer the question thou puttest to thy brethren, that we may hear.' Quoth the prince, ' O my father, this world resembles a pasture, and these people resemble the sheep that wander in that pasture, and the king resembles their shepherd, and the owner of the sheep is God most high, and the nobles resemble that shepherd's dogs, and the enemy resembles the wolf, and the sheykhs and the wise resemble the guardians appointed by God most high over the shepherd, who forbid the shepherd by the order of God most high whenever he would do evil to the sheep. O father, in very truth I am a feeble shepherd, I see the sheep, and I perceive that even while we say, " Let not them come and hurt the sheep," we become ourselves partners with the wolf. Should the Owner of the sheep ask us about his lambs, woe, woe to us!' And he wept full bitterly. The princes acknowledged the sovereignty of their younger brother.

" Then the King took up a handful of dust and put it on his eye and said, 'O eye, how long a time is it I have been king, and how great wealth have I amassed and brought before thee by this much oppression and justice, and thou wast never satisfied! And with how many beauties have I made merry and enjoyed the best of what they had till thou hast lost all pleasure in taking it! And how many delicacies have I eaten and how many sherbets have I drunk, and thou art not content! Why then didst thou not look to these affairs and see not? True is it what they say, " Naught fills the eye save a handful of dust." Woe, woe, to us!' And he wept. And all the nobles assembled there were moved to pity and they wept together. Then the king arose and went to his oratory and gave himself up to devotion.

" After some time the king laid his head upon the pillow of death and felt that his life had touched its end, and he said, ' Do now before my eyes that which ye should do when I am dead, that I may see it.' Then they laid the king upon his throne in the palace. And they scattered sifted dust below the castle and cut up strips of damask and strewed them with dust. And all the slave girls put on black and dishevelled their hair and scattered dust upon their heads and began to weep together, crying, ' Alas! woe! alas!' so that hearts were rent. Then came the vezirs, who likewise fell to weeping together and exclaiming, ' Shall a king so just as this be found?' After that they ordered that they brought a coffin with great reverence; then the three princes, when they saw the coffin, wept blood in place of tears and cried, ' This is the horse our father rideth now!' And they adorned it with jewels and placed upon it a jewel-set crown and held over it the royal parasol.

"Then four great lords came and took hold of the frame of the coffin and bare it away. And before the coffin went the sheykhs singing chants and hymns. And the devotees held copies of the sacred volume before them; and great nobles and nobles' sons marched in front. Before them were a hundred sweet-voiced dirge singers who wept and cried, 'Ah! woe! alas!' And from one side they scattered gold and silver and jewels on the coffin; and there were some 10,000 horsemen with golden saddles and broken stirrups and snapped bows. And behind these was an array of slave girls, all clad in black, whose wails and cries rose to the heavens.

"When the king saw those things he sighed and ordered that they took him down from the throne; and he turned and said, 'While yet alive I have seen my death.' And he took a handful of earth and threw it on his head and said, 'Earth, though this long sovereignty has been mine, I have done no righteous deed which will endure.' And again, 'O vezirs, I would that ye endow for me.' Thereupon the vezirs wrote what amounted to 10,000 aspres a day; and they founded free kitchens and colleges, and they settled the revenues of certain towns and villages on the free kitchens. When the business of the endowments was finished, they brought the sections of the Koran, and to each section reader they gave five sequins; and to each of the devotees and dervishes they gave 500 sequins.[10] Then they brought the food, and all the plates were of gold or silver; and to all before whom they placed a dish they said, 'Thine be food and plate.' When the banquet too was finished they freed all the male and female slaves; and three days later the king departed for the Abiding Home.

"Now, O king, I have told this story for that the king may, like that sovereign, inquire, and act conformably to the words of the vezirs and the people, and in compliance with the command of the law, that he be not a prey in the world to remorse and in the hereafter to torment." And he kissed the ground and made intercession for the prince. When the king

[10] In the time of Murād II an aspre was worth about 2½d. stg. Turkish sequins were not struck till the time of his successor, Mahomet II, when they were equivalent to about 12s. 6d. Foreign gold coins, especially Venetian, were used previously.

heard of these wondrous events from the vezir, he perceived how the world had no stability and he sighed and sent the youth to the prison and went himself to the chase.

When it was evening he returned and came to the palace, and went in to the lady who rose to greet him, and they sat down. After the repast the lady began to speak about the youth and asked concerning him. Quoth the king, " I have again sent him to the prison." The lady said, " This matter which has happened is no light matter, but thou art negligent and wouldst act upon everyone's word; and they have said that the negligent person is not exempt from one of three conditions; either he is a fool, or he is ignorant, or fortune has turned its face from him. O king, the negligent does no perfect deed; be not negligent, for to be negligent in this affair is madness. O king, this thy story resembles that of another king, upon whom five times fell the enemy by reason of his negligence; but mayhap my king has not heard that story." The king said, " Tell on, let us hear." Quoth the lady:

STRATAGEM GREATER THAN STRENGTH

" There was of old time a king, and he had an enemy greater than himself. One day that hostile king assembled a mighty host and came against that weak king. The latter, having no other resource, assembled all his army and went forth to meet him. Although he much besought that strong king and said, ' War is not a good thing, come, consent not to this calamity, make not thyself guilty of the blood of so many Moslems;' and mentioned how the holy Apostle hath said, ' If two Moslems fight against each other with swords or other implements of war, and one kill the other, both the killer and the killed shall enter hell;' and made many and many an excuse, it was in vain.

" When the king saw that all his entreaty was of no avail with the enemy, he perceived that it was necessary to find some plan to avert this evil. Now the king had three skilful vezirs, these he summoned to give counsel. He said, ' O my vezirs, what is your advice in this matter?' The chief vezir came forward and said, ' My king, in the present circumstances the military might of our enemy is great; most assuredly are we unable to oppose him. Now the best way were this, that we put off the battle and return to our country; he will certainly come after us, but we will enter into a strong castle and rest there till that time when fortune will surely turn toward us likewise; thus are the affairs of the world, now gladness, now woe.' He likewise asked the second vezir, ' What is thy advice, let us see?' So he said, ' O my king, all that the first vezir has said is wise; but it is never allowable to show weakness before the enemy, for inasmuch as thou displayest weakness will he become strong; so if now thou shun battle and flee, thou wilt be giving him opportunity. Wise is he who, although the enemy appear overwhelming, fears not death and gives the foe no answer but the sword.'

"Then, said the king to the third vezir, ' What is thine advice in this matter?' The vezir answered, ' O king, manliness is of ten parts, nine of which are stratagem and one of which is strength; and by stratagem is the affair of enemies ever finished, for they have said that the affair which one stratagem finishes 100,000 soldiers cannot finish. If the king will be guided by this humble one, to-night of a sudden we will attack the enemy and fall upon his camp, and, if it please God most high, we will cut off the heads of many of them.' The king approved this stratagem of the vezir, so when it was midnight and the enemy was negligent they fell upon his camp from every side, and slaughtered the foes till morning, and their king fled to his own country.

"So was this weak king victorious, and he returned to his own land. But that fugitive king went to his country and assembled an army, and again marched against this king. Then the weak king, having no other resource, went forth to meet him, and they pitched opposite each other.

"The weak king said to his vezirs, ' What is your advice this time, let us see?' Then quoth the third vezir, ' O king, we shall again finish our affair by stratagem.' Said the king, ' What stratagem shall we use? they will be very watchful this night.' The vezir replied, ' Stratagem is not one; let them keep watch till morning, we shall this time employ another stratagem.' Quoth the king, ' Speak on, let us see.' The vezir said, ' We will hide in ambush 2,000 strong impetuous youths; and as soon as it is morning we will go out against the enemy

and fight a little, then we will appear to flee, and they shall follow after, thinking to fall upon us; and when the foremost of
the host reaches us we will turn and fight with them and cut
them down. Thereupon our soldiers who are in ambush will
rush into the field and take the hostile army in the centre; and,
if it please God most high, we will strike hard with our swords
and seize their leaders, and take their flags, and tear in pieces
their ensigns; and in this way will we overcome the foe.' The
king liked this plan of the vezir, and by this stratagem they
sabred the foe and were again victorious. And the king returned smiling to his country.

" The other strong king in the greatness of his wrath cried
out, ' What means this that thus weak a king routs my army
and puts me to flight on this wise! God most high gives victory to whom he will!' Then he assembled an army of which
he, himself, knew not the number, and went against that poor
weak king. They gave the king word, and he, having no other
resource, went forth again, and they pitched opposite each
other. Again the weak king questioned his vezirs. Then the
the third vezir said, ' O my king, our affair is finished by
stratagem.' Quoth the king, ' What stratagem shall we employ?' The vezir said, ' O king, let us send an adroit headsman, who will go and by some stratagem kill him; and when
the head goes the foot is not steady.'

" The king approved the vezir's words, and sent a headsman
with a dagger, who went and somehow made shift to smite
that strong king that he well-nigh slew him, and then took
flight. But while he was fleeing they caught him and hewed
him in pieces. When they saw their king that he had reached
the bounds of death, they said, ' There is no fighting in such
plight;' and they fled, bearing their king. They came to their
country and appointed a physician, and after some days the
wound got better. And that king again assembled a host
and came against the poor weak king. The latter, having no
other resource, went forth to meet him and again sought counsel of his vezirs. The third vezir said, ' O my king, our affair
is finished by stratagem.' The king asked, ' What stratagem
wilt thou employ this time?' The vezir said, ' This time let us
send an ambassador and offer some money and some slave
girls and say, " We submit to thee." And we will give poison

to one of the slave girls we send, and tell her to give it to the king to eat when she finds an opportunity; and in this way will we gain the victory over him.'

"The king deemed the vezir's words good, and by that stratagem they poisoned that king. And this king mounted and attacked his army, and, as when the head goes the foot is not steady, it was beaten. They took their king, and, after a thousand stratagems, conveyed him to a castle and tended him, and at length he recovered. Again he assembled an army, and again they went against that weak king. So the latter, having no other resource, again went forth to meet him. He summoned his vezirs and asked advice. Again the third vezir said, 'O king, our affair is finished by stratagem.' Quoth the king, 'Give advice.' The vezir said, 'O king, this time he comes with great caution, and has posted men on the roads and at the stations who seize on everyone who passes. If the king deem good, we will write a letter and address it to his vezirs and great nobles, and it shall be on this wise:

"'"After greeting: Be it not concealed that your letter has come and all that you say is understood. Long life and health to you! We indeed hoped it from you. Now let me see you. Display manliness and valor. Seize him on the road and bring him to me, and that country shall be yours; such and such a place to so and so, and such and such a district to so and so." Then we will seal it, and split a staff and put it therein, and give it to a man and send him to them. They will find the staff and take it to the king, who will undoubtedly read it, and look upon those vezirs and nobles as traitors, and murmurings will arise among them and they will split into parties. And by this stratagem we will again find relief.'

"The king did so. And in that way they brought the letter to that king, and as soon as he had read it, fear for his life fell upon him. Then he turned back and went to his country and seized those vezirs and nobles and slew them. At length all the nobles turned from him and wrote a letter and sent it to this king, and it was thus: 'For the love of God come against this tyrant, and we will aid thee.' When the king had read the letter he assembled an army and went to that country, and on the battle day all the nobles came and submitted to him, and they seized the other king and surrendered him. So he took that country through stratagem; and because that strong king was negligent he lost his country and his head, for they slew him.

"Now, O king, I have told this story for that my king may know and not be negligent, and lose not life and kingdom through the stratagem of that unworthy youth." When the king heard this story from the lady he was wroth, and said, "To-morrow will I slay him."

When it was morning and the sun showed his face from behind the castle of Qāf,[1] and illumined the world with light, the king came and sat upon his throne, and commanded the executioner that he bring the youth and he gave the word, "Smite off his head." Then the fourth vezir came forward and said, " O my king, it is not seemly in kings to hasten in all things with precipitancy; above all the spilling of blood unjustly is deemed by the wise most blameworthy and hateful. They have declared that the trials of a king are four: one is haste; another, trusting to wrong; another, considering not the end of matters; and another, negligence. Haste is that which disappoints those who seek good and profit for themselves; wrong is that which brings about wars and uses armies unjustly and does evil things; considering not the end of matters is that which employs hurry instead of deliberation; and negligence is that which inclines to music, and lust, and taking counsel of women. And they have said, ' Let one take counsel of a woman and do the opposite of what she says;' even as spake the holy Apostle (peace on him!) ' Consult them and do clear contrary.' [2]

" In compliance with this tradition the king must not obey the woman's word; and through the words of women have many men suffered remorse and fallen under the wrath of God. And the story of Balaam, the son of Beor,[3] is a strange story; if the king grant leave, I will relate it." The king said, "Tell on, let us hear." Quoth the vezir:

---

[1] Qāf is the name of a fabled mountain chain, formerly supposed to encircle the world; " the castle " is simply a metaphor for the mountain peaks.

[2] This famous speech is usually attributed to 'Omar, the second caliph.
[3] Bal'am-bin-Bā'ūr.

THE WILES OF WOMAN

"One day Moses (peace on him!) went against a tribe, and they were of the people of 'Ad, and they called their chief Og, the son of Anak.[4] One day Moses (peace on him!) by command of God summoned these to the faith, and resolved to fight and war with them if they were not obedient. So Moses (peace on him!) assembled four hundred and four-score thousand men and proceeded against the 'Adīs. When they were come near the 'Adīs, he sent twelve men as ambassadors to that tribe. Now Og had gone out to look about, and he saw the twelve men coming, so he put the whole of them into his sack and slung it over his shoulder and turned back and went away. He brought them to his tribe the 'Adīs and said, ' See the host of the Messenger Moses which is come seeking to make war with us; ' and he held the mouth of the sack downward and the twelve men rolled out.

"And that tribe saw them that they were small of stature, for their own stature was twice that of these. And they all made mock of them and laughed at them; but they killed them not, but sent them back. They returned and told these things to Saint Moses, and fear fell upon all the host. Then Saint Moses (peace on him!) took his rod in his hand and went against that tribe of 'Ad. Og the son of Anak saw that Moses (peace on him!) was himself coming, and straightway he went and pulled up a rock like a mountain and put it on his head, and went that he might cast it upon the host of Moses (peace on him!). But God most high commanded an angel that he went in the likeness of a bird and smote that rock with his beak and clave it, and thereupon it passed like a circle of cursers down before the face of Og. And straightway Saint Moses came up, and his stature grew to forty cubits, and his rod to forty cubits, and he leaped up forty cubits, and smote Og on the heel with his rod; and God most high slew Og.

"Then Saint Moses (peace on him!) returned to his people and gave them tidings of Og being slain; and they were all glad. Then Saint Moses passed thence and made for the country of Sheykh Balaam, the son of Beor. When he was

---

[4] 'Uj-bin-'Unuq. He is said, in the Talmud, to have been a monstrous giant. The 'Adīs, we are told, were from sixty to one hundred cubits high. Compare Numbers xiii. 33.

come nigh, they brought word to the sheykh that Saint Moses was coming against him with many warriors. Whereupon the sheykh's disciples said, ' O sheykh, if that host come into our land, it will lay waste all our land; thou must find some help for this.' Then were they silent. The sheykh said, ' What should we do?' They answered, ' Curse him.' The sheykh said, ' He is a Messenger; I cannot curse him.' And howsoever much they urged the sheykh, it was in vain. Now the sheykh had a cunning brawling wife; her they besought, saying, ' Speak to the sheykh, and we will give thee much money.' The woman answered, ' I will manage it.' When the sheykh came to his house he desired to take counsel of his wife; she said, ' Curse him.' The sheykh replied, ' He is a Messenger; how can I curse him?'

" The woman persisted so that the sheykh was constrained to lift up his hands and curse him. His curse was heard; and Saint Moses, who was fourteen leagues distant, remained for forty years in the wilderness; even as God most high saith in his Word, ' For forty years shall they wander about in the earth.' [5] Then Saint Moses knew that there was some reason for this, and he prayed and humbled himself before God most high, and said, ' My God, send him who is the cause of our thus wandering, from the world to the hereafter without the faith.' His prayer was accepted at the court of God, and that sheykh went from the world to the hereafter without the faith by reason of a woman; even as God most high hath said, ' And his likeness was as the likeness of a dog.' [6]

" Now, O King, I have told this story for that these many men have been cast forth from the court of God for following the words of women. Then is it incumbent on the king that he judge accordingly, so that he become not a prey to remorse; for too late repentance profits not. Beware and beware, slay not the prince on the woman's word." And he kissed the ground and made intercession for the prince for that day. When the king heard this story from the vezir, he sent the prince to the prison and went himself to the chase.

When it was evening the king came to the palace, and the lady rose to greet him, and they sat down. After the repast

⁵ Koran, v. 29.   ⁶ Koran, vii. 175.

the lady again began to speak about the youth, and the king said, " This day too my vezirs would not let me be, so I have sent him to the prison." Quoth the lady, " I know all the plot of those vezirs, day by day each of them plans some trick or wile; they purpose to discredit me with thee, so they say that women are lacking in understanding, and that by reason thereof they are plotters and liars. These words of theirs are false, do not assail the truth; for these see me, that my trust in my king is strong. Yet I am aware of their case and their hurtful deeds; and for that I would defend my king from their craft and malice, are they enemies to me. An thou desire, my king, I shall say no more; and they may do whatsoever they will. But all these are of single tongue and single aim, and I fear they will bring some calamity upon thee and some evil upon me; and afterward thou shalt repent, but it will avail not.

" My king, thou hast assembled some men of low birth and made them vezirs and confided all thy affairs to them, and thou thinkest them honest; Heaven forefend they should be honest when some of them are the sons of cooks, and some of bakers, and some of butchers; it is even as when Khizr [7] (peace on him!) showed another king the origin of his vezirs, but mayhap my king has not heard that story." The king said, " Tell on, let us hear." Quoth the lady:

THE SEARCH FOR KHIZR

" There was in the palace of the world a king who was very desirous of seeing Khizr (peace on him!); and he would ever say, ' If there be anyone who will show me Khizr, I will give him whatsoever he may wish.' Now there was at that time a man poor of estate; and from the greatness of his poverty he said in himself, ' Let me go and bespeak the king that if he provide for me during three years I will show him Khizr; by three years either I shall be dead or the king will be dead, or he will forgive me my fault, or I shall on somewise win to escape: and in this way shall I make merry for a time.' So he went to the king and spake those words to

[7] A mysterious being, of the number of the prophets, who appears to and aids Moslems in distress; he is frequently mentioned in Mahometan fiction, where he plays a part similar to that of Elijah in the Talmud.

him, The king said, 'An thou show him not then, I will kill
thee;' and that poor man consented.

"Then the king let give him much wealth and money, and
the poor man took that wealth and money and went to his
house. Three years he spent in merriment and delight, and
he rested at ease till the term was accomplished. At the end
of the time he fled and hid himself in a trackless place, and
he began to quake for fear. Of a sudden he saw a personage
with white raiment and shining face who saluted him. The
poor man returned the salutation, and the radiant being asked,
'Why art thou thus sad?' but he gave no answer. Again the
radiant being asked him and sware to him, saying, 'Do indeed
tell to me thy plight that I may find thee some remedy.' So
that hapless one narrated his story from its beginning to its
end; and the radiant being said, 'Come, I will go with thee
to the king and I will answer for thee;' so they arose.

"Now the king wanted that hapless one; and, while they
were going, some of the king's officers who were seeking met
them, and they straightway seized the poor man and brought
him to the king. Quoth the king, 'Lo, the three years are
accomplished; come now show me Khizr.' That poor man
said, 'My king, grace and bounty are the work of kings; forgive my sin.' Quoth the king, 'I made a pact; till I have
killed thee I shall not have fulfilled it!' And he looked to his
chief vezir and said, 'How should this be done?' Quoth the
vezir, 'This man should be hewn in many pieces, and these
hung up on butcher's hooks, that others may see and lie not
before the king.' Said that radiant being, 'True spake the
vezir; all things return to their origin.' Then the king looked
to the second vezir and said, 'What sayest thou?' He replied,
'This man should be boiled in a caldron.' Said that radiant
being, 'True spake the vezir; all things return to their origin.'
The king looked to the third vezir and said, 'What sayest
thou?' The vezir replied, 'This man should be hewn in small
pieces and baked in an oven.' Again said that elder, 'True
spake the vezir; all things return to their origin.'

"Then quoth the king to the fourth vezir, 'Let us see, what
sayest thou?' The vezir replied, 'O king, the wealth thou
gavest this poor creature was for the love of Khizr (peace
on him!). He, thinking to find him, accepted it; now that

he has not found him he seeks pardon; this were befitting, that thou set free this poor creature for the love of Khizr.' Said that elder, ' True spake the vezir; all things return to their origin.' Then the king said to the elder, ' O elder, all my vezirs have said different things, contrary the one to the other, and thou hast said concerning each of them, " True spake the vezir; all things return to their origin.' What is the reason thereof?' That elder replied, ' O king, thy first vezir is a butcher's son, therefore did he draw to his origin; thy second vezir is a cook's son, he likewise proposed a punishment as became his origin; thy third vezir is a baker's son, he likewise proposed a punishment as became his origin; but thy fourth vezir is of gentle birth, compassion therefore becomes his origin; so he had compassion on that hapless one and sought to do good and counselled liberation. O king, all things draw to their origin.' [8]

" And he gave the king much counsel and at last said, ' Lo, I am Khizr!' and vanished. Then the king went forth from his palace, but could see no sign or trace of that radiant elder; and he said, ' I much longed to see Khizr (peace on him!); praise be to God, I have attained thereto, and he has told me the origin of my vezirs.' And he commanded that they gave that poor man much wealth.

" Now, O king, I have told this story for that thou mayst know that thy vezirs are of low origin, and that fidelity will not proceed from them. In this matter too their words tally with their origin; lose not the opportunity, for to spare an enemy is great folly." The king heard this story from the lady, and said, " To-morrow will I roll up the scroll of his life."

When it was morning and the world, like to him who had won to Khizr, was illumined with light, the king sat upon his throne and commanded the executioner that he bring the youth, and he gave the word, " Smite off his head." Thereupon the fifth vezir came forward and said, " O king of the world, slay not the prince thus hastily, and cast not to the winds the counsels of these many vezirs; for as they take pearls from the sea and string them, so do these string their

---

[8] Compare Boethius thus translated by Chaucer: All thynges seken ayen to hir propre course, and all thynges re- joysen on hir retourninge agayne to hir nature.

words; they are speakers such that Mercury in the sky could not match their suggestions. O king, the reason of that which thy vezirs have said to thee is this, that the Apostle (peace on him!) hath said that whoso seeth his king do an act contrary to the law, and hindereth him not therefrom, hath departed from the Canon. Now, O king, deem not the words of thy vezirs mistaken; it is even as they have said, 'Let him who would see Khizr in the flesh, look upon a wise, accomplished and learned vezir.' And again, 'If one seek to do a righteous deed, let him arrange the affair of some poor creature with a king.' Mayhap the king has not heard the story of Khizr and a vezir." The king said, "Tell on, let us hear." Quoth the vezir:

THE VEZIR AND KHIZR

"There was, of old time, a king who had an experienced vezir; and Khizr (peace on him!) would ever come to that vezir. One day the vezir looked upon the affairs of the world, how they abode not with anyone; and he withdrew from the vezirship, and chose the corner of retirement, and gave himself up to worship. A long time passed, and Khizr (peace on him!) never once came to him. The vezir marvelled and said, 'Why does not Khizr (peace on him!) come to me? Now ought he to come every day.' Then he said, 'There must indeed be some reason for this.' Thereupon he saw that Khizr had appeared, and he said, 'O Khizr, while I was vezir thou didst ever come to me, is it for that I have withdrawn from the world that thou comest not now?' Khizr (peace on him!) replied, 'O vezir, outwardly thou didst perform the duties of vezir, inwardly I did; therefore was there a bond between us; now thou hast withdrawn therefrom, and that bond is gone from between us, so I come not to thee.' When the vezir heard these words from Khizr, he went and asked back the vezirship, and he received it, and Khizr (peace on him!) came to him as before and ceased not.

"O king, I have told this story for that the king may hearken to the vezir's words and follow them, and pass his life in happiness. Beware, O king, be not overhasty in this affair, that afterward thou suffer not remorse." When the king heard this story from the vezir, he sent the prince to the prison and went himself to the chase, and that day he took much game.

In the evening he came to the palace, and the lady rose to greet him, and they sat down. After the repast the lady asked about the youth; the king said, " This day again such an one of my vezirs made intercession for him, and I sent him to the prison." Quoth the lady, " O my king, how good were it, could he be reformed by such conduct; but this youth is incapable of reform; for he resembles that snake which first stings his mother as she bears him and kills her, and then stings his father and kills him. God most high will take vengeance on him; and his eyes will be blinded as though he had looked upon an emerald.[9] If a drop of an April shower fall upon a snake it becomes poison, but if it fall into an oyster it becomes a pearl; [10] and if the Koran, great of glory, fall upon a believer's heart, it is faith and knowledge. And it is notorious that whoever nurses a snake falls at last a prey to its poison. A certain man formed a friendship with a snake and used every day to bring it a portion of food. He went to the snake's hole and laid it there, and the snake would put its head out of its hole and eat that food, and when it was satisfied it would frolic about, and that man would play with it. One day he came and saw that the snake was out of its place and quite stiff from cold; ' O poor thing,' he said, and took and put it in his bosom. When the snake got warm it at once raised its head and stung that unhappy man, and killed him, and fled and entered its hole. And thus have they said, that if one foster a swine, that brute will not leave off till in the end it hurt him. It is even as the story of that sherbet-seller and the Moor." Said the king, " Tell on, let us hear." Quoth the lady:

The Sherbet-seller and the Moor

" There was of old time in a great city a sherbet-seller, and he had a son, a loveling of the age, who was so fair that he seemed a second Joseph; [1] and he used to sell sherbet in the shop. The folk would come to gaze upon this youth's beauty,

---

[9] The emerald was supposed to have the effect of blinding snakes when they looked upon it.

[10] There is an Eastern myth to that effect.

[1] Joseph is the type of youthful beauty.

and they would give a sequin for each cup of sherbet, and drain it; and whenever they drank a cup they would say it was the water of life. Now one day a swarthy Moor came to that country; and as soon as he saw the youth, the hapless Moor's power of speech left him, and he could not stir one step from where he stood, but leaned against the opposite wall bewildered. After a time he recovered his understanding, and, rising and falling like one drunk, he came up as best he could to the youth, and gave a sequin and drank a cup of sherbet, and went away. For a time he came every day and drank cups of sherbet at a sequin each, and looked on the beauty of the youth.

"One day the youth told this thing to his father, and his father perceived that the Moor was ravished with the boy, and said, 'O my son, bring that Moor to the house to-morrow, and let us see what manner of man he is.' The next day when the Moor came to the youth, he invited him to his house, and took him and went to his father. After they had eaten, the father of the boy asked of the Moor's case and dwelling. The Moor saw what his intention was, and answered, 'I have no dwelling, I am a stranger.' The boy's father said, 'Thou art a stranger; we will give thee a dwelling, stay with us.' The Moor was glad and counted it a boon to his soul; even as they have said, 'The loved one's ward is paradise.' So they showed the Moor a dwelling. He abode for some days, and gradually his love for the boy increased; and one day he showed him a precious stone, and said, 'An thou let me take one kiss of thee, I will give thee this stone.' With a thousand graces the boy consented, and the Moor gave him the stone and kissed him, and said, 'My life, my master, I love thee from heart and soul, flee me not; I know a talisman which will open before thee; if thou wilt come with me I will open it, and give thee so much gold that thou shalt never again know poverty.'

"The youth told this thing to his father, and his father gave him leave; so the Moor took him, and they went without the city; and he brought him to a ruin. Now there was a well there, full to the mouth with water; and the Moor wrote on a piece of paper and laid it on the well, and thereupon all the water vanished from the well. The Moor and the boy descended to the bottom of the well, and saw a locked door. The Moor wrote a charm and fastened it on the lock, and it opened forthwith. They went in and saw a negro holding in one hand a great stone to throw upon anyone who entered. The Moor repeated a charm and blew upon the negro, and the negro laid the stone that was in his hand upon the ground, and let them pass. They went on and saw a dome of crystal, and at the door of the domed building were two dragons, who stood facing one the other with open mouths like caverns. When they came near, these flew at them, but the Moor repeated a charm and blew on them, and they vanished.

" Then the door of the domed building opened and they went in, and they saw that in one corner thereof was gold, in another corner silver, in another corner all manner of jewels, and in another corner was raised a throne upon black earth, and on that throne was a coffin, and in that coffin lay a renowned man dead. Upon his breast was a gold tablet, and on that tablet was written: ' I was a king, and I ruled the whole earth, and whithersoever I went in this world I conquered. I had many many champions and great wealth and treasure. Some little of the wealth I owned I gathered here. Me too death spared not; but made me even as though I had not come into the world. Now, O thou who seest me in this plight, take warning by me, and remember my soul in prayer, and be not presumptuous through the wealth of this world for a few days' life.' And that was all. Then the Moor and the youth took as much as they desired of the gold and silver and precious stones and black earth, which was the philosopher's stone, and went out. The Moor repeated a charm and blew upon the well, and it was again all full of water; and he went back with the boy to their house, and they gave themselves up to mirth and merriment. Day and night they ceased not therefrom an instant.

" One day the boy asked the Moor to teach him the charms he had repeated in the talisman. The Moor consented, and instructed him for many days and taught him. One day, of a sudden, the boy said to his father, ' O father, I have learned the whole of the charms for the talisman, so we have no longer any need of the Moor; let us poison him.' But his father consented not, and said, ' Let us turn him away; let him go elsewhither.' Quoth the youth, ' The turning away of him would not do; he is a great master, he might do us an injury, so let us poison him ere he play us some trick; and I will take as much gold and silver as is needful from that buried treasure.' The Moor heard him and knew that fairness purposed foulness, and he straightway disappeared from there.

" Now, O king, I have told this story for that the king may know that no good has ever happened to anyone from youths. Yea, O king, be not negligent, kill the youth, else the affair will end in evil." When the king heard this story from the lady he was wroth and said, " On the morrow will I slay him."

When it was morning the king sat upon his throne and caused the youth to be brought, and commanded the executioner, " Smite off his head." The sixth vezir came forward and said, " O king of the world, beware, act not on anyone's word till the crime be proved against the prince; for the resurrection is at hand, and lying and cunning and craft abound. The wise man is he who turns off sin and evil that he may not afterward begin to bite upon the finger with regret and remorse and be repentant, and who takes the woful by the hand and gives happiness to the unhappy, and who repulses not him who comes to his door, but sees his needs and provides for him, and who never lets himself be deceived by a woman's word; for these laugh in one's face. Mayhap my king has not heard the story of the tailor youth and the woman." The king said, " Tell on, let us hear." Quoth the vezir:

The Tailor and the Woman

" Thus relate they: In the time of Saint Jesus (peace on him!) there was a tailor youth who had a fair wife, and they greatly loved one another. One day they made a pact that if the woman died first, her husband should take no other wife, but throw his arms round her tombstone, and weep till morning; and if the youth died first, the woman should do likewise. By the decree of God the woman died. After the tailor had wept and lamented he buried her, and fulfilled his pact, and threw his arms round his wife's tombstone and wept. And he constantly kept watch over the grave. One day Jesus (peace on him!) when passing by that place, saw a youth weeping and embracing a tombstone, and he went up to him and asked why he wept. The youth related all.

"Then Jesus (peace on him!) prayed, and the woman became alive, and came forth from the grave in her shroud. And Jesus (peace on him!) proceeded on his way. The youth said, 'One cannot go thus in a shroud; wait thou here a moment till I go and fetch clothes from the house; then thou shalt put on these clothes, and we will go together.' And he went quickly to the house, leaving the woman there. Suddenly the son of the king of that country passed that spot, and saw a fair woman sitting wrapped in a shroud. As soon as the prince saw that woman he fell in love with her from heart and soul, and he said to her, 'Who art thou?' She answered, 'I am a stranger; a robber has stripped me.' Thereupon the prince ordered his servants to take the woman to the palace, and clothe her in clean garments.

"When the youth returned with the clothes he found not the woman there, and he cried and asked of the passers-by. No one had seen her. The poor man, asking and asking, met the prince's servants. These asked the tailor why he wept. He replied, 'For a time my wife was dead; but now, praise be to God, she is become alive through the prayer of the messenger Jesus; I went to fetch her clothes, but she has disappeared: therefore do I weep.' They answered, 'The prince sent that lady to the palace this day.' Thereupon the tailor went before the prince and complained, saying, 'The woman thou hast taken is my wife.' The prince asked the lady, she denied and said, 'This is the robber who stripped me of my clothes and made off; praise be to God, if thou kill him now, thou shalt gain great reward.' The prince commanded that they bound both the tailor's hands behind his back. Although the poor tailor cried aloud, it was no avail; they put a rope round his neck and led him to the gallows.

"Then they perceived Saint Jesus on the road, and they waited. When he came near he asked of their case, and they told him. Then he bade them stop and went himself to the prince; they called the woman, and he said, 'This woman is the wife of yonder youth; I prayed and she became alive.' When the woman saw the messenger she was unable to deny, but spake the truth. Jesus (peace on him!) prayed again, and that woman died; and the youth was rescued from the abyss whereinto he had fallen, and he repented of his having wept so long a time.

"Now, O king, I have told this story for that thou mayst know that the inclinations of women are ever to works of evil, craft, and wickedness." And he kissed the ground and made intercession for the prince's life. When the king heard this story from the vezir he sent the prince to the prison, and went himself to the chase.

In the evening he returned from the chase and came to the palace, and the lady rose to greet him, and they sat down. After the repast the lady fell to speaking about the youth. The king said, "To-day such an one of my vezirs made intercession for him, so I have again sent him to the prison." Quoth the lady, "O king, thou dost not believe my words; but at length, in the near future, some hurt will befall thee from the youth; for this night I saw a vision, which it is, as it were, a duty on me to tell my king, and incumbent on thee to hear." Said the king, "Tell on, let us hear." The lady said, "This night thou wast holding in thy hand a golden ball, and that ball was adorned and set round with rubies and jewels, and its brilliancy lit up the world; and thou wast playing, throwing up the ball and catching it in thy hand. And this youth was sitting by thy side watching, and ever and anon he asked for the ball, but thou gavest him it not.

"Of a sudden, while thou wast heedless, he snatched the ball, and for that thou hadst not given it him when he had asked was he angry, and he struck the ball upon a stone, so that it was shattered in pieces. And I was grieved, and I went and picked up the fragments of the ball, and gave them into thy hand, and thou didst look upon those fragments and didst marvel, and with that I awoke." Quoth the king, "What may the interpretation of this vision be?" The lady said, "I interpreted this dream: that ball is thy kingdom; and this youth's snatching it from thy hand is this, that this youth came to me and said, 'I wish to kill my father and sit upon the throne, and I desire to make thee my wife; and all the men of the kingdom have turned to me, and now the kingdom is wholly mine, do thou likewise submit to me?' Had I submitted to him, ere now he had killed thee and accomplished his affair. Ah! the fortune and auspiciousness of my king averted it. And his striking the ball upon the stone is this, that if he had become king after thee, he would have utterly ruined the kingdom. And my going and picking up the fragments and giving them to the king is this, that for that I obeyed not the youth, but came and told the king, he seized him, and the kingdom remained in his hand. But had not I done so, know of a surety that ere now the kingdom would have passed from thy hand; yea, thy life, too, would have gone. That is the interpretation of the dream. O king, the story of this degenerate youth resembles that of a certain king's son; mayhap my king has not heard it." The king said, " Tell on, let us hear." Quoth the lady:

STORY OF THE ADOPTED SON

" In the palace of the world there was a king in whose country was a robber, such that none could escape from his hands. And in that king's country was a great khoja. That khoja and his wife were travelling with some money, when of a sudden, while they were on the road they met that robber. He forthwith stripped them and made them naked and took them captives. He put their clothes in the cave which he had chosen for his dwelling, and bound both the khoja's hands behind his back and laid him in a corner; and then he gave himself up to mirth and merriment with the woman. After seven or eight months the robber released the khoja and his wife. So these went forth from the cave, and saying, ' There is nor strength nor power save in God, the high, the mighty,' they set their faces in a certain direction, and fared on till one day they entered a city. And they took a dwelling in that city and settled there.

" When the woman's time was come she gave birth to a boy; but as they knew that the boy was the robber's, they would not accept him, and they laid him at the door of the mosque. The king of that country happened to pass by and asked concerning him, and the people who were present answered that his parents had no means of bringing him up and so had left him there. Now the king had no son, and he took pity on this child and adopted him and made him his son, and said, 'If God give him life and he die not, he shall sit on the throne after me and be king.' So they took the boy and brought him to the palace, and appointed him a nurse, and made him clothes of all manner of stuffs. Day by day he grew, and when he had reached his seventh year he was a moon-faced boy, such that he who looked upon his countenance desired to look thereon again.

"And the king appointed a teacher and a governor for the boy, and he learned science and good conduct. When he had reached his twelfth year he had acquired sciences and accomplishments. After that, they instructed him in horsemanship; that too he acquired in a few days. And every day he would go into the square and take a ball and play; and all the world marvelled at his beauty and dexterity, and the king felt delight as often as he looked upon him. Now the king had also a daughter peerless in beauty. In the course of a few years this girl grew up and reached the age of puberty, and the boy fell in love with her. He would brood over this, saying, 'Alas! would she were not my sister, that I might marry her.' Now the boy was a valiant youth, such that the king's emirs and vezirs applauded his valor; and he overcame the king's enemies who were round about, and made them subject to his father; and no one could stand before his sword. The king had betrothed his daughter to another king's son, and when the time was come they wished to take the girl from the king.

"And the king commanded that they should make ready; and thereupon the youth, to make clear what was in his heart, asked a legist this question, 'If a person have a garden and the fruit of that garden ripen, should that person eat it or another?' The legist replied, 'It were better that person should eat it than another.' Now the prince had a learned companion, and that companion knew the prince's desire; for science is of three kinds: one the science of the faith, another the science of physiognomy, and another the science of the body; but unless there be the science of physiognomy, other science avails not. Straightway that companion said, 'O prince, if there be in that garden you ask of, a fruit forbidden by God most high, it were better that the owner eat it not; but if God most high have not forbidden it, then is it lawful for that person to eat it.' Quoth the prince, 'Thou knowest not as much as a legist; yon man is a legist; I look to his decision.' And he arose and went to his sister's palace, and that hour he took his sister and went forth the city, and made for another city.

"Then the slave girls with great crying informed the king, and thereupon the king's senses forsook him, and he commanded, ' Let the soldiers forthwith mount their horses and pursue the youth and seize him.' Straightway the soldiers mounted and went after the youth; and the king said, ' From the low born fidelity comes not;' and he repented him of his having taken him to son. The king and the soldiers appeared behind the youth, and the latter sprang into a hiding-place. And while the king and the soldiers were passing he slew the king from that hiding-place; and when the soldiers saw that the king was slain they each one fled in a different direction, and were scattered in confusion. And the youth took the girl and went to a city and took a house therein, and made her his wife; and he adopted the whole of what had been his father's business, and turned robber.

"Now, O king, I have told this story, for that thou mayst know that the desire of this degenerate youth is to kill his father as that low-born one slew his; the rest the king knows." When the king heard this strange thing from the lady, he said, "On the morrow will I slay him."

When it was morning the king went and sat upon his throne, and he caused the youth to be brought and commanded the executioner, "Smite off his head." Whereupon the seventh vezir came forward and said, "O king of the world, first look to the end of every business thou undertakest and then act accordingly; for on the day of battle it is needful, first to think of the way of retreat and then to set to, so that when it is ' or fate or state,' one may save his life. They have said, ' On the day of strife be not far from the nobles: in the chase and the palace go not near them;' and ' He is profitable in the councils of a king, who in the day of security looks to the matters of war and the provision of weapons, and stints not money to the troops that these on the day of battle may be lavish with their lives in the king's cause.' It is incumbent on the king that he kill those who flee when they see the enemy (and after that the foes); for they resemble those who give up a stronghold to the adversary. And they have said that a good scribe and a man who knows the science of the sword are very needful for a king; for with the pen is wealth collected, and with the sword are countries taken. Mayhap the king has not heard the story of a certain king and a vezir." The king said, " Tell on, let us hear." Quoth the vezir:

THE KING AND THE VEZIR

" There was in the palace of the world a king and he had two vezirs, one of whom was wise and learned and one of whom was foolish and ignorant. On the king's taking counsel of them concerning the management of the affairs of the state, the ignorant vezir said, ' O king, expend not money, give not money to the soldiers and warriors, or if thou give, give little; and let him who will stay, stay; and let him who will not stay, go. When thou hast money on the battle day, many will be soldiers to thee: where the honey is, there surely come the flies.' His words seemed good to the king, who one day said to the learned vezir, ' Get me a few men who will be content with little pay.' On the vezir's replying, ' Men without pay are not to be had,' the king said, ' I shall have money when anything befalls, and shall find many men.' Quoth the vezir, ' So be it, I shall find men for the king who will take no pay and stir not day or night from his gate.' The king was glad and said, ' Get them, let us see.'

" The vezir went and found a painter and brought him, and he painted a large room in the palace so that the four walls of that room were covered with pictured figures of men, and he decked all the figures with arms and implements of war, he depicted a mounted and armed host standing rank on rank. When it was completed the vezir called the king, and the king arose and went with him to that wall of pictures, and he showed the king the whole of them. The king looked and said, ' What are these pictures? why hast thou ranged these here rank on rank?' The vezir replied, ' O king, thou desiredst of me men without pay; lo, these youths want no pay; so they will serve the king.' The king said, ' There is no life in these; how can they serve?' The vezir answered, ' O king, if lifeless pictures will not serve, no more will payless soldiers serve. Fief and pay are as the life of the soldier; when thou givest not a man his fief or pay, it is as though thou tookest away his life; judge if a lifeless man could serve.'

"Again, 'O king, if a paid army be not needful for thee, these will suffice; but living men require to eat and drink. If they get no pay they will not sacrifice their lives in the cause of the king or face the enemy; but they will hate the king and turn from him and evil will befall the king; but if the king be bountiful they will obey. Thus a noble had a young steward who used to serve him. One day the noble asked the youth his name. He replied, "God on thee, my name is Wittol." Said the noble, "Can anyone be so called?" The youth answered, "Anyhow it is my nickname, never mind." So they used to call that youth Wittol so long as he was at that noble's gate. One day he went from that noble's gate to another's. One day that noble in whose service he had been happened to meet him, when he cried out, "Ho, Wittol, how art thou?" The youth replied, "O noble, say not so again, or thou shalt see." The noble said, "My life, thou didst tell me Wittol was thy name; why art thou now angered?" The youth answered, "Then did I serve thee, and thou bestowedst on me worlds of bounties, so though thou calledst me Wittol, it offended me not; but now I never get a favor from this man that he should call me so."

"'Quoth the noble, "He who called thee so just now was I, not he; yet thou wast angered with me." The youth replied, "God forbid I should be angered with thee; but if to-morrow the other were to hear that word from thee, he too would wish to use it; now was I angered lest he should call me so."' Then that vezir laid a dish of honey before the king; as it was night no flies came to it. And the vezir said, 'They say that where there is honey, thither will the flies surely flock; lo, here is honey, where are the flies?' Quoth the king, 'It is night, therefore they come not.' The vezir said, 'My king, it is necessary to give soldiers money at the proper time; for bringing out money on the battle day is like bringing out honey at night.' When the king heard these words from the vezir he was ashamed; but he greatly applauded the vezir, and thenceforth did whatsoever he advised.

"Now, O king, I have told this story for that thou mayst

know that attendants and servants are needful for kings, and that masters of device and resource are requisite. Kings should take counsel of their vezirs in such matters that no defect may mar their fortune in the world or the hereafter. Now the prince is thy support and asylum, and all the folk, high and low, ask why he is fettered with the bonds of woe and a prisoner of the dungeon. And slaying the prince were like slaying the vezirs and all the world. Who would sit on the throne after thee that should know our circumstances? All the grandees of the empire and lords of the state and noble seyyids would be cast down, and scattered to the winds and ruined. This woman is a woman lacking in religion and understanding; to give ear to and thus countenance those who are so lacking is not worthy our king." And he kissed the ground and begged for the prince. So the king sent him to the prison.

Having returned from the chase, the king went to the palace, and the lady rose to greet him, and they passed on and sat down. After the repast the lady again asked for news of the youth. The king answered, "To-day too I have sent him to the prison." The lady said, "Thou art a wise and just king; we will talk together this night and see whether or no by principle, by the law, and by custom, thou dost sin in thus vexing my heart. O king, there are many rights between husband and wife. And they have said that it is better to give a woman a handful of words than a skirtful of money. Mayhap the king has not heard the story of the sparrow and his mate." The king said, "Relate it, let us hear." Quoth the lady:

THE SPARROW AND HIS MATE

"There was in the blessed service of Saint Solomon (peace on him!) a little sparrow whose many tricks and gambols were ever pleasing to Saint Solomon. One day Saint Solomon saw not the sparrow by him, and he commanded the sīmurgh [2] bird to go fetch the sparrow wherever he might find him. For a long time the sparrow had not gone to his mate, and his mate had upbraided him, saying, 'For this long time thou

---

[2] A fabulous bird of great size. Solomon, it should be said, according to the Talmudic and Koranic legends, was acquainted with the language of beasts and birds, with whom he used often to converse.

hast left me and been with Solomon; dost thou love him
more than me, or dost thou fear him? tell me.' The sparrow answered, 'By God, I would not give thee for the world:
I am come but once to earth and shall not come again; I go
to Solomon for diversion, I have no dread of him.' While
he was talking with many such vaunts and boasts, the sīmurgh
arrived in haste and heard the sparrow bragging and said
harshly, 'Up, let us off; Saint Solomon wants thee.' Then
the sparrow, being beside his mate, plucked up courage and
replied, 'Off, begone, I will not go.' The sīmurgh said, 'I
will indeed take thee.' The sparrow answered, 'Off with thee,
get thee hence, or I will seize thee and rend thee in twain.'
Quoth the sīmurgh, 'Until I take thee with me I will not
budge from here.'

"Yet the sparrow heeded not, and the sīmurgh waited
a while, but the sparrow would not go. Again said the sīmurgh
to the sparrow, 'O my life, give me an answer.' Quoth the
sparrow, 'I tell thee begone from here; if thou speak again,
my heart will bid me do somewhat else; but no, I will not slay
thee. Off, begone, or I will do thee some hurt, and then go
to Solomon's palace and smite it with my foot, and overturn
it from its foundations and pull it down about his head; now
then, away fool, off, begone the road thou camest. Thou chat-
terest here and sayest not, "This is the sparrow's harem; he
is ill."' And he gave the sīmurgh a kick such that the latter
knew not where it touched him, but he flew thence and reported the sparrow's words to Saint Solomon. Solomon said,
'When the sparrow spake these words where was he?' 'His
mate was there,' answered the sīmurgh. Then quoth Solomon
(peace on him!), 'There is no harm in one thus boasting and
bragging in his own house before his wife. Though every
stone of this my palace was raised by the toil of these many
demons, still wonder not at his saying when beside his wife
that he could shatter it with one foot.' And this was pleasing
to Solomon (peace on him!), and when the sparrow came he
made him of his boon companions.

"O king, I have told this story for that thou mayst know
that one should thus love his wife and vex not her little heart,
so that his wife may have naught against him. And God
most high has given thee understanding; weigh my words in

the balance of understanding, and try them on the touchstone of the heart; if they stand not the test, I shall speak no more. I tell thee that this youth has stretched forth his hand to me and has been treacherous, and has moreover purposed against thy life; can there be greater crimes than these? O king, beware, be not negligent in this matter; for there is fear and danger for thy life and kingdom." When the king heard these beguiling words of the lady he said, "On the morrow will I make an end of his affair."

When it was morning the king sat upon his throne and commanded the executioner that he bring the youth, and he said, "Smite off his head." Whereupon the eighth vezir came forward and said, "O king of the world, slay not the prince on the woman's word. One should be forgiving; above all, as no man is exempt from sin; for they have said that humanity is composed of forgetfulness. A man falls sometimes through the intrigues of an enemy and sometimes through the maleficence of the cruel sphere; or else he attains prosperity and falls into adversity. Mayhap the king has not heard the story of a certain vezir." The king said, "Tell on, let us hear." Quoth the vezir:

THE CRAFTY VEZIR

"Of old time there was a king, and he had an experienced and learned vezir. One day the latter went to the bath, and while he was sitting beside the basin, his ring fell from his finger into the water; and it sank not in the water, but floated on the surface. Whenever the vezir saw this he sent men to his house and treasury, saying, ' Go quickly, and hide in a certain place whatsoever I have in the treasury of gold and silver or rubies and jewels; for now is the king about to seize me.' Then they went and acted according to his order. And as the vezir was coming out from the bath, men from the king arrived and seized him; and they put him in prison and took possession of whatever he had in his house and treasury.

"One day, after the vezir had been imprisoned for a certain time, his heart longed for a conserve of pomegranate pips, and he ordered the jailer, saying, ' Make me ready a conserve and bring it, for my heart doth greatly desire it.' Now the king had forbidden that dish, and the jailer was afraid and made it not. And the vezir's desire increased and he begged it of all who came to him, but no one made it and brought it through fear of the king. Brief, the vezir lay for a year in prison and longed for that dish, but no one found means to bring him it. One day the jailer made shift to cook that dish and bring it to the vezir. As soon as the vezir saw it he was glad; and they put it before him, but ere he had stretched out his hand to it, two mice, that were struggling with each other above, fell into the dish, and the food became unclean.

"Thereupon the vezir said, 'It is good;' and he arose and commanded his servants, saying, 'Go, furnish the mansion, put that wealth you hid back into its proper place; my king is about to take me from prison and make me vezir.' Then his retainers went and did as he had commanded. Hereupon came a man from the king who took the vezir from the prison and brought him before the king. Then said the king to comfort the vezir's heart, 'I put thee in prison seemingly to afflict thee; but really that thou mightest know, from experiencing imprisonment, speedily to intercede for the men whom I cast into jail.' Quoth the vezir, 'Nearness to a sultan is a burning fire: whatsoever conduct be observed toward me by the king is pleasant teaching.' The king was pleased and commanded that they bring a robe of honor, and he put it on him and made him again vezir.

"Then when the vezir was come to his mansion his retainers and others asked him, saying, 'Whence knewest thou of the king's being about to imprison thee and seize thy wealth, and whence knewest thou of his being about to take thee out and make thee vezir?' The vezir replied, 'While in the bath my ring fell into the water and sank not, so I knew that my fortune had reached its perfection, and that what follows every perfection is declension, therefore did I so command; and for a whole year, while I was in prison, I longed for a dish of pomegranate pips, at length I got it, and mice polluted it so that I could not eat it, so I knew that my misfortune was complete and that my former estate was returned. And I was glad.'

"Now, O king, I have told this story for that the king may likewise know that every perfection has its declension. Until now the prince and the vezirs were safe and esteemed before the king. Now he knows not in what malefic sign our stars may be imprisoned. A woman has rendered us despicable before the king and has bound him about with craft and wiles, so that these many learned and sagacious vezirs are impotent against her incitements; even as it is clear that when a fool throws a stone down a well a wise man is powerless to get it up again. O king, haste not in this affair; too late repentance profits not; for the prince is like a young bird that can neither fly nor flee, grant him a few days' respite, haply this difficulty may be solved; and there is a reason for his not speaking. He is ever as a prisoner in thy hand; afterward, if thou will, kill him; if thou will, free him." And he kissed the ground and begged for the prince. When the king heard this story from the vezir the fire that was in his heart was increased ten-fold and the tears poured from his eyes; and he sent the prince to the prison and mounted for the chase with his own cares.

When the king returned he entered the palace, and the lady rose to greet him, and they sat down. After the repast the lady asked for news of the youth. The king said, " To-day too such an one of my vezirs made intercession for him, and I sent him to the prison." Quoth the lady, " O king, I have given thee this much counsel, and it has produced no effect upon thee. It is as though a physician treated a sick man, and the treatment was without result, and that physician was powerless and attempted no other treatment, but left off; for if he treated that sick man again, he would kill him. Now, I too am powerless to speak to thee. I should say, ' I will speak no more nor waste my breath in vain;' still my heart pities thee, for the king's realm and life will be destroyed. My head, too, will fall; for that I am in the same peril with the king do I speak. It is even as once when they cut off a person's hand and he uttered no sound; afterward he saw someone whose hand had been cut off, and he wailed aloud and wept. Those who were present wondered and asked, saying, ' O man, when thy hand was cut off thou didst not weep; why weepest thou now?' That person answered, ' By God, then, when they cut off my hand, I saw that there was not among you one who had met the like, and I said in myself that if I wept each of you would speak ill of me, for ye knew not the pain of it; now that I have found a companion in my plight do I weep, for he knows the anguish I have suffered.' Now, O king, thy head and my head are like to fall; if the king know not my plight, who should know it? Mayhap my king has not heard the story of the three princes and the cadi." The king said, " Tell on, let us hear." Quoth the lady:

THE THREE PRINCES AND THE CADI

" In the palace of the world there was a king and he had three sons. One day this king laid his head on the pillow of death and called those sons to his side, and spake privately with them. He said, ' In such and such a corner of the palace I have hidden a vase full of pearls and jewels and diverse gems; when I am dead do ye wash me well and bury me, then go and take that vase from its place and divide its contents.' The king lay for three days, and on the fourth day he drained the wine of death and set forth for the abiding home. When the princes had buried their father according to his injunctions, they came together and went and beheld that in the place of those jewels the winds blew. Now the princes began to dispute, and they said, ' Our father told this to us three in private, this trick has been played by one of us.' And the three of them went to the cadi, and told their complaint. The cadi listened and then said to them, ' Come, I will tell you a story, and after that I will settle your dispute.

" ' Once, in a certain city, a youth and a girl loved each other, and that girl was betrothed to another youth. When the lover was alone with that girl he said, " O my life, now thou comest to me and I am happy with thee; to-morrow when thou art the bride of thy betrothed, how will be my plight? " The girl said, " My master, do not grieve; that night when I am bride, until I have come to thee and seen thee, I will not give the bridegroom his desire." And they made a pact to that end. Brief, when the bridal night arrived, the girl and the youth went apart; and when all the people were dispersed and the place was clear of others, the girl told the bridegroom of the pact between her and the stricken lover, and besought leave to fulfil it. Whenever the bridegroom heard these words from the bride he said, " Go, fulfil thy plight and come again in safety." So the bride went forth, but while on the road she met a robber. The robber looked at her attentively, and saw that she was a beautiful girl like the moon of fourteen nights; never in his life had he seen such a girl, and upon her was endless gold, and she was covered with diverse jewels such as cannot be described. Thereupon the bridle of choice slipped from the robber's hands; and as the hungry wolf springs upon the sheep, so did the robber spring upon that girl. Straightway the girl began to sigh, and the robber felt pity and questioned her.

" ' So the bride related to the robber her story from its beginning to its end, whereupon the robber exclaimed, " That is no common generosity! nor shall I do any hurt or evil thing to her." Then said he to the girl, " Come, I will take thee to thy lover." And he took her and led to her lover's door and said, " Now go in and be with thy lover." Then the girl knocked at the door, and that youth, who lay sighing, heard the knocking and went with haste and said, " Who is that? " The girl answered, " Open the door; lo, I have kept my plight, nor have I broken it, I am come to thee." The youth opened the door and came to the girl and said, " O my life, my mistress, welcome, and fair welcome! how hast thou done it? " She replied, " The folk assembled and gave me to the bridegroom, then all dispersed and each went his way. And I explained my case to the bridegroom and he gave me leave. While on the road I met a robber, and that robber wished to stretch forth his hand to me, but I wept and told him of my plight with thee, and he had pity and brought me to the door and left me, and has gone away."

" ' When the youth heard these things from the girl he said, " Since the bridegroom is thus generous, and has given thee leave to fulfil thy plight with me, and sent thee to me, there were no generosity in me did I stretch forth my hand to thee and deal treacherously; from this day be thou my sister; go, return to thy husband." And he sent her off. When the girl went out she saw that robber standing by the door; and he walked in front of her, and conducted her to the bridegroom's door. And the girl went in, and the robber departed to his own affairs. While the bridegroom was marvelling the bride entered, and the bridegroom leaped up and took the bride's

hands in his, and they sat upon the bed. And the bridegroom turned and asked her news of the bride; and she told
all her adventures from their beginning to their end.' Then
quoth the cadi, ' O my sons, which of those showed manliness
and generosity in this matter?' The eldest youth said, ' The
bridegroom, who, while she was his lawful bride, and when
he had spent thus much upon her, gave the girl leave. What
excellent generosity did he display!' The middle youth said,
' The generosity was that lover's, who, while there was so
much love between them, had patience and sent her back.
What excellent generosity: can there be greater than this!'
Then asked he of the youngest boy, ' O you, what say you!'
Quoth he, ' O ye, what say ye? when one hunting in the
night met thus fair a beauty, a torment of the world, a fresh
rose; above all, laden with these many jewels, and yet coveted her not but took her to her place. What excellent patience,
what excellent generosity!' When the cadi heard these words
of the youngest boy he said, ' O prince, the jewels are with
thee; for the lover praised the lover; and the trustful, the trustful; and the robber, the robber.' The prince was unable to
deny it, and he took the jewels from his breast and laid them
before the cadi.

"Now, O king, I have told this story for that thou mayst
know that in that I am true I would aid my king; and that
the vezirs, in that they are traitors, would aid the traitor prince.
And they are forty men, each one of them a wonder of the
world, while as for me, I am but one and a woman, lacking in
understanding: the rest the king knows." When the king
heard these enticing and beguiling words of the lady he said,
" Grieve not, to-morrow will I kill him."

When it was morning the king sat upon his throne and thus
commanded the executioner, " Smite off the head of that traitor
youth." Whereupon the ninth vezir came forward and said,
" O king of the world, beware, slay not thy son on the woman's
word, and be not heedless of the import of this verse which
God most high hath spoken in his Word: ' And the stiflers
of wrath, and the pardoners of men; and God loveth the beneficent:'[8] that is they are his peculiar servants. And the
holy Apostle (peace on him!) hath said, ' Whoso bridleth his

---

[8] **Koran, iii. 128.**

anger, he having power to avenge—God will call him on the resurrection day over the heads of the creatures that he may give him to choose from the houris which he pleaseth:' that is he shall surely enter Paradise. Let one pardon him who has wronged him and forgive his servants their misdeeds, that God most high may pardon him and be beneficent to him; even as saith the Apostle (peace on him!) 'The proclaimer shall proclaim on the resurrection day:—Where are they whose reward is (incumbent) upon God; none shall rise save him who hath forgiven.' Mayhap the king has not heard the story of Hārūn-er-Reshīd [4] and the slave girl." The king said, " Tell on, let us hear." Quoth the vezir:

The Caliph and the Slave Girl

" Once the Caliph Hārūn-er-Reshīd sat upon his throne of estate; and the people of the city of Bagdad were late in coming to salute him. Therefore was the caliph exceeding wroth, and he thus commanded the chamberlains, 'Whoso comes now do ye turn off and cast into prison.' And they seized and cast into prison all of the grandees of the city who came. For three days the caliph went not out, neither spake with anyone; but sat full of fury: who could have dared to address a word to him?

" While in this state he desired to eat, and he ordered one of the slave girls to bring food. She brought it before him, but while laying down the dish, she was careless and spilt some part of it over the caliph. Forthwith the caliph rose in wrath and was about to hew the girl in pieces, when she said, 'O caliph, God most high saith in his glorious Word, " And the stiflers of wrath." ' [5] Straightway the caliph's wrath was calmed. Again saith the slave girl, ' " And the pardoners of men." ' [5] Quoth the caliph, 'I have forgiven the crimes of all the criminals who may be in prison.' Again said the slave girl, ' " And God loveth the beneficent." ' [5] Quoth the caliph, 'God be witness that I have with my own wealth freed thee and as many unfreed male and female slaves as I have, and that this day I have for the love of God given the half of all my wealth to the poor in alms.' After that he let

---

[4] The celebrated Caliph of Bagdad, and hero of so many of the stories in the " Thousand and One Nights."
[5] Koran, iii. 128.

bring into his presence all the prisoners who were in the jail and begged absolution of them; and as he had attained to the import of that noble verse, he put on each of them a robe of honor, and devoted himself to justice and equity. And now whoso mentions him doth add, ' The mercy of God on him!' [6]

" O king, I have told this story for that I have seen this day that thy wrath was great. I would that thou pardon the prince and grant him his life and so do a meritorious deed; and in this matter, beyond doubt and beyond uncertainty, thou shalt become deserving of the mercy and paradise of God most high." And he kissed the ground and begged for the prince. When the king heard this story from the vezir he sent the youth to the prison and mounted for the chase.

That day he found no game and returned in wrath to the palace. Again the lady rose to greet him and they sat down. After the repast the lady began to speak of the youth. The king said, " Look, my mistress, now all is over, and my prince is still upon thy tongue; to-day too one of my vezirs begged for him and I sent him to the prison." The lady saw that the king was vexed and said, " My king, be kind, be not vexed with me; for I know that soon no good will befall thee from that youth, for he is very covetous of wealth and kingship, and the covetous is ever balked. I saw him without understanding and without discretion; he knows neither his words nor himself; he is even as the sons of that king who took the metaphorical words of their father as literal, and at length lost what wealth was in their hands. Mayhap my king has not heard that story." The king said, " Tell on, let us hear." Quoth the lady:

THE FOOLISH PRINCES

" There was in the palace of the world a great king, and he had three sons. One day that king laid his head upon the pillow of death and called his sons before him and said, ' O my sons, my life has reached its end; I have counsel to give you, which when I am dead do ye observe.' His sons replied, ' On our heads be it; speak, father.' To his eldest son he said,

---

[6] D'Herbelot relates the same story in his " Bibliothèque Orientale," but substitutes Hasan son of 'Ali, the Prophet's son-in-law, for Harun-er-Reshid.

' Build thou a house in every city.' And to his middle son,
' Marry thou every night.' And to his youngest son, ' Whenever thou eatest, eat honey and butter.' The king lived not
long after giving these injunctions, but died. The eldest son
fell to building a house in every city; the middle son married
a wife every night, and on the morrow gave her her dower and
sent her to her father's house; and the youngest son, whenever
he ate, mixed honey and butter and ate it. A long time passed
on this wise; we may say that though the middle and the
youngest sons spent money, they at least had pleasure for it;
but that bewildered and senseless eldest son spent this much
money, and if the buildings he raised were fit for habitation,
still they pointed to folly.

"One day a wise man asked them, ' Why do ye thus?' The
princes answered, ' By God, our father thus enjoined us.' The
wise man said, ' Your father's injunctions were not thus, but
ye have not understood his riddles. And there is a tale suitable
to this your plight, I will tell it you; afterward I will teach you
your father's riddles.' The princes said, ' Pray do so.' Quoth
the wise man, ' Once there was a king who always exacted
tribute from the infidels. One day those infidels assembled
their monks and said, " Let us find some trick which the king
will be unable to understand, that thereby we may escape from
this tribute: now do ye each think of some plan." Thereupon
they dispersed and went away. After a time a monk came to
the infidel who was their chief and said, " I shall go to them
and put to them a question, and if they can answer it we will
give them tribute."

" ' So the unbelieving king gave that monk a little money and
sent him. One day he entered the realms of Islam, and the
event was reported to the king, who said, " Our learned men
of the faith will surely answer an infidel without the faith;
let him come." They brought him into the presence of the
king; and the king straightway assembled his doctors and
pious men and grandees. Then the king said, " O monk, now
what is thy question; speak, let us see?" The monk first
opened the five fingers of his hand and held the palm opposite
the folk, then he let the five fingers droop downward, and said,
" What means that? know ye?" And all the doctors were
silent and began to ponder, and they reflected, saying, " What

riddles can these riddles be? There is no such thing in the Commentaries or the Traditions."

" ' Now there was there a learned wanderer, and forthwith he came forward and asked leave of the king that he might answer. The king gladly gave leave; then that wanderer came forward and said to the monk, " What is thy question? what need for the doctors? poor I can answer." Then the monk came forward and opened his hand and held it so before the dervish; straightway the dervish closed his fist and held it opposite the monk. Then the monk let his five fingers droop downward; the dervish opened his fist and held his five fingers upward.

" ' When the monk saw these signs of the dervish, he said, " That is the answer," and gave up the money he had brought. But the king knew not what these riddles meant, and he took the dervish apart and asked him. The dervish replied, " When he opened his fingers and held his hand so to me, it meant ' now I strike thee so on the face;' so I showed him my fist, which meant, ' I strike thy throat with my fist;' he turned and let his fingers droop downward, which meant, ' thou dost so, then I strike lower and seize thy throat with my hand;' and my raising my fingers upward meant, ' if thou seekest to seize my throat, I too shall grasp thy throat from underneath;' so we fought with one another by signs." Then the king called the monk and said, " Thou madest signs with the dervish, but what meant those signs?" The monk replied, " I held my five fingers opposite him, that meant, ' the five times ye do worship, is it right?' The dervish presented his fist, which meant, ' it is right.' Then I held my fingers downward, which meant, ' why does the rain come down from heaven?' The dervish held his fingers upward, which meant, ' the rain falls down from heaven that the grass may spring up from the earth.' Now such are the answers to those questions in our books." Then he returned to his country.

" ' And the king knew that the dervish had not understood the monk's riddles; but the king was well pleased for that he had done what was suitable; and he bestowed on the dervish a portion of the money which the monk had left. O princes, ye have not understood your father's riddles and ye have wasted your wealth in vain.' The princes said, ' What meant our father's riddles?' He replied, 'Firstly, when he said, "Build thou a house in every city," he meant, "gain thou a friend in every city, so that when thou goest to a city the house of the friend thou hast gained may be thine." Secondly, when he said, "Embrace thou a virgin whenever thou embracest," he meant, "be moderate in thy pleasures that thou mayst enjoy them the more." Thirdly, when he said, "Whenever thou eatest, eat honey and butter," he meant, "never when thou eatest, eat to repletion; but eat so that if it be but dry bread thou eatest, it will be to thee as honey and butter."' When the princes heard the words of the wise dervish they knew that their father's signs to them were so, and not that which they had done; and they left off doing those things.

"Now, O king, I have told this story for that with youths is no discretion, but in them ignorance and heedlessness abound. Though thou through understanding have compassion on him, yet will he have none on thee; it will be even as when one day Saint Bāyezīd of Bestām [7] saw a mangy dog, and through pity took it and laid it in a place and tended it many days till it became well, whereon it bit his foot. Bāyezīd said, 'O dog, this is the return for the kindness I did thee—that thou bitest me.' God most high gave speech to that dog, and it said, 'O Bāyezīd, is not the proverb well known, "A man acts as a man; a dog, as a dog"?' Methinks, O king, that in that youth must be an evil vein: for if kindness be to kindness, never so long as he lived could that unworthy one have cast on me an envious glance; above all, never could he have sought to slay my king, his father, the source of his being. I, where am I? Take warning." And she incited the king with very many evil words, so that he was afraid and said, "Grieve not, to-morrow will I slay him." And that night was grievous to the king.

Scarce was it morning and had the sun shown forth the riddle of the whiteness of dawn, like as that dervish showed to the king's sons the riddles of their father, and illumined the world with light, ere the king sat upon his throne and caused the youth to be brought and ordered the executioner, "Smite off his head." Then the tenth vezir came forward and said, "O king of the world, every king desires that whithersoever

---

[7] Bāyezīd of Bestam was a famous saint who, according to Ibn-Khallikān, died in 261 or 264 (A.D. 875 or 878).

he go he may triumph and conquer; and that the earth be subject to his hand; and that whoso comes to his gate hoping, may find that which he seeks; and that the heart of none be vexed. When in the country of a king despairing hearts are many, that host of despairing hearts gathers together and utterly destroys another gay host. Thus it becomes the greatness and glory of kings, that when they see a beast under a heavy load they have compassion on that beast; even as it was when an ass came, dragging itself along, to the chain of the justice of Nūshīrvān the Just.[8]

" Straightway the king caused it to be brought into his presence, and he saw it to be a lean and worn black ass, whose back was broken with bearing loads. When the king saw that animal in such plight his heart bled, and he laid his hand on the beast's face and wept full bitterly and said, " See ye how this poor creature has been oppressed in my kingdom?' And he called for a physician and said to him, ' Go, tend the wounds of this beast, and give it abundance to eat, and wrap round it a good horse-cloth that it be at ease.' Now, it is incumbent on kings that they have compassion on the unhappy and the weak, and pity them, and believe not plotters and liars, nor trust their evil wicked words; and such folk are very many. Mayhap my king has not heard the story of the king's son of Egypt and the crafty woman." The king said, " Relate it, let us hear." Quoth the vezir:

STORY OF THE EGYPTIAN PRINCE

" In the city of Cairo there was a king and he had two sons. One day he reflected on the doings of the cruel sphere and saw how the world was without constancy and remained not to king nor yet to beggar, but trod all under foot. At length he bethought him how it would not endure for himself either; and he took his younger son and made him apprentice to a master tailor, and said, ' After all, a trade is needful for a man; and they have said that the least knowledge of a trade is better than a hundred thousand sequins.' So in a short while the prince became a tailor such that there was not in the city of Cairo one who could ply his scissors and needle. One day

[8] One of the most famous kings of pre-Islamitic Persia, he reigned from A.D. 531 to 579.

the king passed to the abiding home, and his elder son became king. His brother the tailor, fearing for his head, fled and went to the Ka'ba.[9]

" While making the circumambulation,[10] his foot struck against something hard, he looked and saw a girdle and took it up and bound it round his loins, and continued the circumambulation. After a while he saw a khoja who had a stone in either hand and who was beating his breast with these stones and crying, ' Ah woe! alas! I had hidden in that girdle all the wealth I have gained from my youth; whatever Moslem has found it, let him give it me for the love of God and the honor of the Ka'ba, and the half of it shall be lawful for him as his mother's milk.'

" When the prince saw and heard him he knew that that girdle was his, and he said in his heart, ' What has this much wealth and the kingdom of my father done for me? and what should this do for me? I shall not let this poor man weep; I shall give it him.' And he went round and came before the khoja and said, ' O khoja, I have found that girdle of thine; lo, it is round my loins.' The khoja clung fast to the prince, and the prince said, ' What reward wilt thou give me? lo, the girdle is round my loins.' Then the khoja took the prince and brought him to his own tent; and the prince loosed the girdle from his loins and laid it before the khoja, and the khoja took it and clasped it to his heart. Then he brake the seal and poured out what was in it; and the prince saw it to be full of precious stones.

" The khoja divided these stones into three heaps and said, ' O youth, wilt thou take one heap with my good-will, or two without it?' The prince replied, ' Give me one heap with thy good-will.' Then the khoja divided one of those heaps into two and said, ' Which of them wilt thou take with my good-will?' Again the prince made choice of a heap. At length the khoja said, ' Youth, wouldest thou have these remaining jewels, or wouldest thou that we go and that I pray for thee under the Golden Spout?'[1] The prince answered, ' Wealth perishes, but prayers endure; do thou bless me, I have relinquished all these riches.' And they went, and he held up his

---

[9] The Cubical (House), i. e., the Sacred Temple at Mecca.
[10] One of the ceremonies performed by the pilgrims at Mecca.

[1] For a description of it see Captain Burton's " Pilgrimage," vol. iii, p. 164.

hands and said to the prince, ' Say thou, " Amen." ' So the
youth raised up his hands and the khoja began to pray. He
repeated many prayers in himself, and the prince said, ' Amen.'
The khoja drew his hands down his face and said, ' O youth, I
have prayed much for thee; now go, and may thy end be
good.'

" The prince went away; but after a little he thought in
himself, ' If I go now to Cairo my brother will kill me, let
me go along with this khoja to Bagdad.' So he went back to
the khoja and said, ' O khoja, I would go with thee to Bagdad; take me that I may serve thee on the road.' So the
khoja took him; and the prince was in the khoja's service,
and they entered Bagdad and lighted at the khoja's dwelling.
For some days the prince abode there, then he said to the
khoja, ' I may not stay here thus idling; I have a trade, I am
a master tailor, if thou hast any tailor friend, pray take me to
him that he may give me some work to do.'

" Now the khoja had a tailor friend, and he straightway
took the prince and brought him to the shop of that tailor and
commended him to him, and the tailor consented. Then the
prince sat down and his master cut out cloth for a robe and
gave it him; now the prince had checkmated the Cairo tailors,
where then were those of Bagdad? The prince sewed that
robe and returned it, and the master took it and looked at it
and saw that it was a beautiful robe, made so that in all his life
he had not seen the like of it, and he said, ' A thousand times
well-done, youth.' This news spread among the masters, and
they all came to that shop and saw it and admired; and this
prince became very famous in that country. The work in that
master's shop was now increased tenfold, and customers in like
measure. One day that khoja had a quarrel with his wife,
and in the greatness of his heat the words of the triple divorce
passed his lips.

" Then he repented and would have got back his wife, and
his wife also was willing. They sought a legal decision, but
the mufti said, ' It may not be without an intermediary.' [2] The
khoja bethought him whom he could get for intermediary when
the prince came into his mind, and he said in himself, ' That
stranger youth is he; I shall make him intermediary.' So he

[2] Such as is required by the Mahometan law in case of a triple divorce.

married the woman to the prince. When it was evening he took him and put him into a dark house with the lady; but the lady made shift to light a candle, and as soon as she saw the prince she fell in love with him with all her heart. And the prince as soon as he saw her fell in love with her with all his heart. Then these two moons came together, and, after making merry, the lady showed the prince sumptuous stuffs, and countless gold, and precious stones, such as the tale and number of them cannot be written, and she said, ' O my life, all this wealth is mine, it is my inheritance from my mother and my father, and all the wealth too that that khoja has is mine; if thou will not dismiss me to-morrow, but accept me as thy legal wife, all this wealth is thine.'

" The prince consented to this proposal, and the woman said, ' O youth, when the khoja comes to-morrow he will say, " Come, let us go to the cadi; " say thou, " Why should we go to the cadi?" If he say, " Divorce the woman," do thou reply, " By God, it were shame in us to take a wife and then divorce her." And he will be unable to find any answer thereto.' The prince was glad and accepted the lady's advice. When it was morning the khoja came and knocked at the door, and the prince went forth and kissed the khoja's hand. The khoja said, ' Come, let us go to the cadi; ' the prince answered, ' Why should we go to the cadi? ' Quoth the khoja, ' Divorce the woman.' The prince replied, ' By God, it were mighty shame in us to divorce the woman; I will not divorce her.' The khoja exclaimed, ' Ah youth, what word is that? I trusted thee, thinking thee an upright youth, why speakest thou thus? '

" The prince answered, ' Is not this which I have said the commandment of God and the word of the Apostle? ' The khoja looked and saw that there was no help; he wished to go to the cadi, but the folk said to him, ' Khoja, now that woman is his, she is pleased with him and he is pleased with her, they cannot be divorced by force.' The khoja was filled with grief and said, ' He shall not be questioned concerning what he doth; ' [3] and he ceased from trying.

" He fell ill from his rage and became bedridden; then he called the prince and said to him, ' Hast thou any knowledge

[3] Koran, xxi. 23.

of what I prayed for thee under the Golden Spout?' The prince replied, 'I know naught of it.' The khoja said, 'Although I would have prayed otherwise, this came upon my tongue: "My God, apportion to this youth my wealth, my sustenance, and my wife." O youth, would I had not taken from thee yon girdle! O youth, my wife was my existence, now that too is become thine. Now let these sitting here be witnesses that when I am dead all that I possess belongs to thee.' Three days afterward he died; he perished through grief for that scheming woman; and the prince became possessor of his wealth.

"O king, I have told this story for that thou mayst know that fidelity comes not from women, and that their love is not to be trusted. When they cannot help it, they are obedient to their husbands, and, fearing the rod of the law, they wrap their feet in their skirts and sit quiet, otherwise they would ruin the world with craft and trickery. Now, O king, act not on the woman's word." From seven places he performed the salutation due to kings, and begged for the prince's life. The king heard this story from the vezir, and that day, too, he sent his son to the prison, and went himself to the chase.

When it was evening, the king returned from the chase and came to the palace, and the lady rose to greet him, and they sat down. After the repast, the lady brought about an opportunity, and began upon the youth. The king said, " To-day such an one of my vezirs made intercession for him, and I have sent him to the prison." Quoth the lady, " These vezirs are all of them traitors to thee, and they are schemers and plotters. Each of them says words concerning me which if he heard, no true man would bear; a man's wife is equal with his life. All the people marvel at thee, and say thou hast no sense of honor. But these vezirs have bewitched thee. Thy lies, too, are many; every night thou sayest, ' I will kill this youth;' then thou killest him not, and falsifiest thy words. O king, through truth is one acceptable both to God and man. O king, no good will come from a youth like this; it were better such a son did not remain after thee than that he did remain. Mayhap my king has not heard the story of a certain merchant." The king said, " Tell on, let us hear." Quoth the lady:

The Merchant's Bequest

"There was of old time a great merchant, and he had two sons. One day the merchant laid his head on the pillow of death, and he called his sons before him, and brought together some wise persons, and said, ' Moslems, if it please God most high, these boys will live for many years; reckon at the rate of a hundred years from to-day, and allow to each of them a daily grant of a thousand aspres, and whatever the sum may amount to, that sum will I give them, that after me they may stand in need of no one till they die, but pass their lives in ease in this transient world.' Then they reckoned up, and he gave them much money; and a few days afterward he passed to the abiding home.

"The sons buried their father, and then began to waste that money. Their father's friends gave them much advice, but they would not accept it. One of them would enter the shop of a confectioner and buy up all the sweetmeats that were therein, and load porters with them, and take them to the square of the city, and cry out, ' This is spoil!' and the folk would scramble for them, and he would laugh. And his business was ever thus. The other youth would buy wine and meat, and enter a ship with some flattering buffoons, and eat and drink and make merry; and when he was drunk he would mix up gold and silver coins before him, and throw them by handfuls into the sea, and their flashing into the water pleased him, and he would laugh. And his business likewise was ever thus. By reason of these follies, the wealth of both of them came to an end in little time, in such wise that they were penniless, so that they sat by the way and begged.

"At length the merchants, their father's friends, came together, and went to the king and said, ' The sons of such and such a merchant are fallen a prey to a plight like this; if they be not disgraced now, to-morrow will our sons also act like them. Do thou now put them to death, for the love of God, that they may be an example, and that others may not act as they.' Then the king commanded that they bring them both into his presence, and the king said to them, ' O unhappy ones, what plight is this plight in which ye are? Where is the headsman?' And he ordered them to be killed. They said, ' O king, be not wroth at our having fallen into this plight, and kill us not; our father is the cause of our being thus, for he commended us not to God most high, but commended us to money; and the end of the child who is commended to money is thus.' Their words seemed good to the king, and he said, ' By God, had ye not answered thus, I had cleft ye in twain.' And then he bestowed on each of them a village.

"Now, O king, I have related this story for that among youths there is nor shame nor honor, neither is there zeal for friend or foe. Beware and beware, be not negligent, ere the youth kill thee do thou kill him, else thou shalt perish." When the king heard this story from the lady he said, " On the morrow will I kill him."

When it was morning, and the darkness of night, like the wealth of that merchant, was scattered, the king sat upon his throne and commanded the executioner, saying, " Smite off the youth's head." Then the eleventh vezir came forward and said, " O king of the world, hurry not in this affair, and whatsoever thou doest, do according to the command of God and the word of the Apostle; and the holy Apostle hath said that when the resurrection is near, knowledge will vanish and ignorance will increase and the spilling of blood will be oft. O king, leave not the Law, and spill not blood unjustly on thine own account, and pity the innocent; for they have said that whoso taketh a fallen one by the hand to raise him shall be happy; but whoso, having the power, raiseth him not shall himself burn in the fire of regret. Mayhap the king has not heard the story of a certain king and a vezir's son." The king said, " Tell on, let us hear." Quoth the vezir:

THE KING AND THE VEZIR'S SON

"Of old time there was a king, and that king had a sage vezir. God most high had given that vezir a son; and the people of the world were bewildered at the beauty of that boy. And the king loved him so that he could not endure to be a moment without seeing him, and he never parted from him. So his parents yearned for the boy, but what avail? they had needs have patience through fear of the king. One day, the king while drunk entered the palace and saw this boy playing

with another page, and thereupon was he wroth and he commanded the executioner, ' Smite off the head of this degenerate
boy.' And they dragged the boy out. Thereupon word was
sent to the vezir, and he came straightway, and crying, ' My
life! my son!' went up to the headsman and said, ' O headsman, now is the king drunk and senseless and he knows not the
words he says; if thou kill the boy to-night, to-morrow the
king will not spare thee; but will kill thee likewise.' The
headsman said, ' How should we do? he said to me, " Quick,
smite off his head and bring it." '

" The vezir answered, ' Go to the prison and smite off the
head of some man meriting death, and bring it; at this time
the king has not his senses and will believe it.' And he gave
the headsman much gold. The headsman took the sequins and
was glad, and went forthwith to the prison and smote off the
head of a robber and brought it to the king. The king was
pleased and gave the headsman a robe of honor. And the vezir
took the boy and brought him to his own house and hid him
there. When it was morning and the king's senses returned,
he asked for the boy, and they said, ' This night thou didst
command the executioner that he smote off the boy's head.'
As soon as the king heard this he fell senseless and his understanding forsook him. After a while his understanding returned and he sat beating his knees and he fell a-weeping.
Then the vezir, feigning not to know, came before the king and
said, ' O king, what plight is this?' Quoth the king, ' O vezir,
where is that source of my life? where is that spring of my
soul?' The vezir said, ' O king, whom meanest thou?' The
king replied, ' Thy son, who was the joy of my heart.' And he
cried and wept beyond control, and the vezir rent his collar
and wailed and lamented.

" For two months the one business of the king was sighing
and crying; during the nights he would not sleep till dawn
for weeping, and he would say, ' My God, shall I never behold
his face? mayhap I shall behold it at the resurrection. To me
henceforth life is not beseeming.' Mad words like these would
he utter. And he ceased from eating and drinking, and retired from the throne and sought a private house and wept
ever, and it wanted little but he died. When the vezir saw
this, he one day decked out the boy like a flower and took

him and went to the private place where the king dwelt. He left the boy at the door and went in himself and saw that the king had bowed his head in adoration and was praying to God and weeping and thus saying, ' My God, henceforth is life unlawful for me, do thou in thy mercy take my soul;' and he was lamenting, recalling the darling fashions of the boy.

"The vezir heard this wail of the king and said, ' O king, how thou weepest! thou hast forsaken manhood, and art become a by-word in the world.' The king replied, ' Henceforth advice profits me not; lo, begone.' Quoth the vezir, ' O king, if God most high took pity on thee and brought the boy to life, wouldst thou forgive his fault? and what wouldst thou give to him who brought thee news thereof? The king said, ' O would that it could be so! all the wealth that I have in my treasury would I give to him who brought me news thereof, and my kingdom would I give to the boy; and I should be content to look from time to time on the boy's face.' Then the vezir beckoned to the boy and he came in, and went and kissed the king's hand. As soon as the king saw the boy his senses forsook him, and the vezir sprinkled rose-water on the king's face and withdrew. When the king's senses returned he saw the boy beside him and he thought that his soul had gone and returned.

" When it was morning the vezir came before the king, and the king said, ' As thou hast brought the boy to me whole, go, all that is in my treasury is thine.' The vezir answered, ' O king of the world, rather is the wealth which is in my treasury thine; we are both of us the meanest of the king's slaves. May God (glorified and exalted be he!) grant fortune to our king and long life! We too shall live in thy felicity.' The king was glad at the words of the vezir, and bestowed many towns and villages on the son of the vezir, and offered up many sacrifices, and gave away much alms.

" O king, I have told this story for that the king may take profit and not do a deed without reflection, that he be not afterward repentant, like that king, and suffer not bitter regret and remorse. That king suffered so great regret and remorse for a vezir's son, yet this one is the darling of thine own heart. The rest the king knows. Beware, O king, slay not the prince on the woman's word." And he kissed the ground and made intercession for the prince for that day. So the king sent the youth to the prison and went himself to the chase.

When it was evening the king returned from the chase and came to the palace, and the lady rose to greet him, and they sat down. After the repast the lady commenced to speak about the youth. The king said, " To-day too such an one of my vezirs made intercession for him and I sent him to the prison." The lady said, " O king, three things are the signs of folly; the first is to put off to-day's business till to-morrow, the second is to speak words foolishly, and the third is to act upon senseless words. O king, whatsoever thy vezirs say, that thou believest straightway and actest upon. Satan is of a surety entered into these thy vezirs and into thy boy; in whose heart soever he plants the love of office or of wealth, him in the end does he leave without the faith. Mayhap the king has not heard the story of the King and the Weaver." The king said, " Relate it, let us hear." Quoth the lady:

The King and the Weaver

" Of old time there was a great king. One day a man came before him and said, ' My king, I shall weave a turban such that one born in wedlock will see it, while the bastard will see it not.' The king marvelled and ordered that that weaver should weave that turban; and the weaver received an allowance from the king and tarried a long while. One day he folded up this side and that side of a paper and brought it and laid it before the king and said, ' O king, I have woven that turban.' So the king opened the paper and saw that there was nothing; and all the vezirs and nobles who stood there looked on the paper and saw nothing. Then the king said in his heart, ' Dost thou see? I am then a bastard;' and he was sad. And he thought, ' Now, the remedy is this, that I say it is a goodly turban and admire it, else will I be put to shame before the folk.' And he said ' Blessed be God! O master, it is a goodly turban, I like it much.'

" Then that weaver youth said, ' O king, let them bring a cap that I may wind the turban for the king.' They brought a cap, and the weaver youth laid that paper before him and moved his hands as though he wound the turban, and he put it on the king's head. All the nobles who were standing there said, ' Blessed be it! O king, how fair, how beautiful a turban!' and they applauded it much. Then the king rose and went with two vezirs into a private room and said, ' O vezirs, I am then a bastard; I see not the turban.' Quoth the vezirs, ' O king, we too see it not.' At length they knew of a surety that the turban had no existence, and that that weaver had thus played a trick for the sake of money.

" O king, thou too sayest, ' On the morrow will I kill him; I will do this and I will do that;' and yet there is nothing. O king, I had that dream this night, there is no doubt that it is as I have interpreted. O king, if the king's life and throne go, who knows what they will do to hapless me? " And she began to weep. When the king saw the lady thus weeping his heart was pained and he said, " On the morrow I will indeed refuse the words of whichsoever of my vezirs makes intercession for him, and I will indeed kill the youth; for, according to the dream thou hast had, this is no light affair."

When it was morning the king came and sat upon his throne, and he caused the youth to be brought and commanded the executioner, " Smite off his head." Whereupon the thirteenth vezir came forward and sought to make intercession, but the king was wroth and said, " Be silent, speak not." Thereupon the vezir drew a paper from his breast and said, " For God's sake read this paper, then thou wilt know." Then the king looked at the paper and saw that there was written thereon, " O king, yesterday I looked at the astrolabe; for forty days is the prince's ruling star in very evil aspect, such that the prince may even lose his head." Then all the forty vezirs came forward at once and said, " O king, for the love of God and the honor of Muhammed Mustafa, for the forty days have patience and slay not the prince; thereafter it is certain that this affair will be made clear, and when its origin is known must each one receive his due." Then said the vezir, " There is a story suitable to this; if the king grant leave I will tell it." The king said, " Tell on, let us hear." Quoth the vezir:

The Vicissitudes of Life

" There was in the palace of the world a great king and he ruled over the Seven Climes. But he had neither son nor daughter, and he was ever offering sacrifices in the way of God. One day God most high accepted his sacrifice and bestowed on him from his bounty a fair son who was in his time a second Joseph. So the king was glad, and that day he held a high feast, and at that feast he gave robes of honor and money to many men. After that he assembled the astrologers and made them cast the prince's horoscope; and the astrologers looked the one at the other and were bewildered and confounded. Then the king said, ' What see ye that ye stand looking the one at the other ? ' The astrologers replied, ' O king of the world, we have cast the prince's horoscope; and in the astrolabe and the Jāmesb-Nāma they thus rule, that from his thirtieth year to his sixtieth the prince's ruling star is afflicted so that he shall wander in strange lands, with tribulation and pain for his companions: " None . . . knoweth the unseen save God." ' [4] After the king had heard these things from the astrologers, at times his heart would be sad and at times he would plunge into the ocean of deliberation. Saying, ' God knows the end of the boy,' he began to train up the prince. When the latter entered his seventh year he appointed him a teacher, and he passed some years in acquiring reading and writing. When he was become a young man his father got for him a king's daughter; and after a time the prince had two sons. These children, too, in a little time acquired knowledge; and from time to time they would go out a-pleasuring with their father.

" One day the prince's heart desired a sea-voyage, and he commanded that they prepare a ship, and with his children and forty slaves and attendants he entered the ship. For many days they sailed the sea full pleasantly. But there was there a Frankish corsair filled with infidels, and they encountered the prince's ship and straightway flung their grappling-irons, and took captive the prince and his two sons and forty servants, and went off. They took the prince and the forty men and sold them to the cannibal negroes; but the two boys they sold not, but kept by them. The negroes fed up the prince

[4] Koran, xxvii. 66.

and the men with delicate and delicious foods, and every day they took one of them to their king's kitchen and cut his throat, and cooked him at the fire and ate him. When they had eaten the forty men, the prince's turn came, him too they took and brought to the kitchen that they might cut his throat. The prince perceived that plight, and he entreated God in his heart to give him strength, and he burst the fetters that were round his wrists and, striking about with the chains that were in his hands, he slipped through them and rushed out.

"While he was running on, a vast forest appeared before him, he entered it, and although the negroes searched for him they could not find him. Then he came out thence and fared on many stages till one day he came to a great city. The people crying, 'He is an enemy,' rushed upon him. And the prince exclaimed, 'O Lord, what tribulation is this!' and fought with them. Word was brought to their king, and he came and saw that the prince was fighting like a dragon. When the king saw the prince's valor he admired it, and said to his soldiers who were there, 'Let no one attack the stranger.' Then the soldiers dispersed, and the king took the prince and went to the palace. He prepared a suit of clothes, and sent him to the bath, and caused his head to be shaven and made him put on those clothes, and brought him back to the palace. The king said, 'Come, remain by me, I have a daughter, I will give her thee.' The prince consented; so they gave him the king's daughter; and he remained there two years and his lot was right pleasant. One day the prince's wife died; now this was their custom, they had a great deep pit, and if a man died they put his wife with him alive into that pit, and if a woman died they did the same with her husband; and they let down along with them a loaf of bread and a pitcher of water, and covered over the pit with a great stone.

"So they brought the prince and his wife with a loaf of bread and a pitcher of water to that pit, and, saying, 'It is our custom,' lowered both of them into the pit and placed that great stone over them. When the prince saw himself in such case he was bewildered and said, 'My God! what plight is this!' and he prayed to God. And he searched the inside of the pit carefully and saw a fair girl seated there, and he asked her, 'What manner of girl art thou?' She replied, 'I am a

young bride; they have put me into this pit with my husband.'
And the prince examined the pit, and saw it to be all full of
the bodies of men, some of which were decayed and some of
which were writhing in the agonies of death; and dread overcame the prince. Of a sudden, while he was seated, a rustling
sound came from one part of the pit; the prince knew that it
was some beast, and he arose and went with the girl straight
to that place, and he found the passage through which that
beast had come in. They went for a time through that passage, and at length came out on the skirt of a mountain on
the bank of a great river. And they were glad thereat, and
thanked God much.

" And there they found a boat, and they gathered fruit from
that mountain and filled the boat, and they both entered the
boat and went along with the current of the river. That river
grew wider day by day; but it passed underneath a great
mountain. When they came near to the tunnel under that
mountain they could not govern the boat, and the water took
the boat and bore it under the mountain. When the prince
saw this he exclaimed, ' My God! O Lord! what tribulation
is this too! how shall we escape from this!' Helpless they sat
in the boat; now the water dashed the boat against the rocks,
now it made it fly down precipices, and now the mountain
became low and pushed the boat under the water; and they,
never ceasing, emptied the water out of the boat. They knew
not at all whither the boat was going, neither did they know
whether it was night or day. For a long time they were a prey
to that anguish; and scarce a spark of life remained in their
bodies when, at length, after a hundred thousand perils, their
boat came out from under the mountain on to the surface of the
earth.

" They were glad, and they drew their boat to the shore and
got out of it, and took fruits from the trees that were there,
and ate them. While standing there they saw a great white
vaulted building, the dome whereof was of crystal. The prince
and the girl went up to it, and they saw that it was a great
castle, and that the domed building was within the castle, and
on the door of the castle was written, ' O thou who wouldst
open this door, O thou who desirest to overcome this talisman,
bring a five-footed animal and kill it before here, that the bolts

of this talisman may be opened thereby.' The prince marvelled and said, ' Is there in the world a five-footed animal?'
and he wondered. And they sat by the gate of the castle and
lice tormented them, and they began to louse themselves. The
prince killed a louse, and straightway the bolts of the castle
fell, and they knew that the said five-footed animal was the
louse. Then they both entered by a door, and they saw a garden, such that of every tree which is in the world there was
therein; and ripe fruits were hanging there and running
streams were flowing.

"And the prince felt a longing for those fruits and he went
to pluck one of them that he might eat it, when he saw that
those trees were of gold and their fruits of silver and jewels,
and that precious stones were lying at the foot of the trees,
scattered like pebbles in a brook. They passed through and
came to that dome, it was fashioned of crystal, they entered by
a silver door and saw that within that dome was another dome
all of pure gold. It too they entered and saw yet another
dome, all the walls and the top of which were of ruby, built
after the fashion of paradise. They entered it and saw a throne
upon which was a coffin made of jewels, and at the head of the
coffin was a tablet whereon was written: ' O son of Adam,
who comest hither and seest me, know thou that I was a king,
and that all the world was in my hands, and my wealth was
beyond bounds or computation. Men and demons and fairies
and jinn were my warriors; and I lived in the world for a
thousand years, and I never said, " I shall die; " and I made
not any preparation against death. One day, of a sudden, I
fell sick, and I knew of a surety that I was about to die, and
I commanded that this dome was built in three days, and I
made it a sepulchre for myself. And by my head are two
fountains; drink, and pray for me.'

"And the prince saw those two fountains and drank; and
from one of them flowed sugared sherbet and from the other
milk. And they drank of both of them and remained a long
while by that grave, and they nourished themselves on the
milk and drank of the sherbet. At length they found some
vases, and they took of the milk and the sherbet and the jewels
and the gold, and filled their boat with them, and again set
forth on their voyage. After they had gone for a time the wind

drove their boat upon an island, and they went forth from the
boat to look for fruit on the mountain that they might eat.
Of a sudden a body of men came and seized them; and the
prince saw these that they had no heads, their mouths were
in their breasts and their eyes in their shoulders, and their
speech, when they spake together, was as the chirping of birds.
And they took the two and brought them to their king; and
they remained there prisoners a long time.

" At length one day they found an opportunity and escaped,
and again they entered their boat and sailed for a long time
upon the sea. Brief, the prince wandered for thirty years upon
the seas, sometimes happening among nine-headed men, and
sometimes among bird-headed, and sometimes falling among
elephant-headed folk, and sometimes among ox-headed, and
then escaping; and each of them inflicted different torments
on the prince. Still God most high opened a way and he
escaped. And he saw these strange and wondrous creatures,
and he marvelled. At length, through the grace of God (glorified and exalted be he!), the wind drove the prince's ship before
a city, and he saw that the inhabitants of that country were
all men, and he came out. When these saw the prince they
cried, ' He is a spy,' and seized him and bound his arms behind
his back, and tied a rope round his neck, and took him alongside a horse, and said, ' Our lord has put down: when ships
come from the sea and touch at our country, seize their spies
and take them to our king.' And the prince exclaimed, ' What
tribulation is this too! how to go alongside a horse!' And
while he was praying in his heart they reached the city. And
they took the prince in this plight to their king.

" When the king saw the prince he asked, ' What manner of
man art thou?' The prince said, ' Many marvellous things
have befallen me;' and he related his adventures from their
beginning to their end. When the king heard his story he
loosed the prince's bands and took him to his side and clad
him in sumptuous robes of honor. The prince asked for the
jewels that were in his ship. The king bade bring them and
said, ' O prince, I know thy kingdom, and I heard that the
Franks had taken thee; and I know thy father too. Come,
go not away, stay; I have a daughter, I will give her thee, and
we shall live pleasantly together.' The prince replied, ' O king,

when I was born of my mother, my father caused my horoscope to be cast, and the astrologers thus ruled, that my life was afflicted for thirty years; mayhap if I took the king's daughter, some evil might befall the king's daughter by reason of my affliction; I may not consent.' Then the king brought the astrologers and made them cast the prince's horoscope. The astrologers gave good news, saying, 'Glad tidings be to thee, those thirty afflicted years are passed, now his ruling star has entered the sign of good fortune.' The prince was exceeding glad and joyful.

"Thereupon the king commanded that they made ready a festival, and he gave his daughter to the prince, and he greatly honored and reverenced him. After some time the king died, and the prince became king in his stead. One day when he was seated on his throne they said, 'O king, a Frank has come with much merchandise; if the king grant leave, he will bring his merchandise.' The king replied, 'There is leave, let him bring it.' And the Frank brought his merchandise before the king. The king saw his two sons at the Frank's side, then the blood of love boiled, and the affection of paternity yearned for them; and he asked that Frank, 'Are these youths thine?' The Frank answered, 'They are my slaves.' The king said, 'I will buy them.' And he took the youths to a place apart and said, 'Where did this Frank get you?' Then they related their adventures from their beginning to their end; and the king knew of a certainty that they were his own sons, and he pressed them to his heart and kissed each of them on the eyes, and said, 'I am your father.' Then the king arose; and they killed the Frank with a thousand torments.

"O king, I have told this story for that the king may know that haps such as this often befall princes. Their happy fortune passes into the sign of inauspiciousness, and they become a prey to a thousand tribulations and distresses, so that even gold turns into black earth in their hands, and all their friends become enemies to them. Afterward the malefic aspect gives place to prosperity and auspiciousness, then everyone is their friend. O king, this youth's ruling star is likewise afflicted for a few days. Beware, O king, until the days of the malefic aspect be fulfilled, slay not the youth, else afterward thou wilt be repentant, and too late repentance profits not. The rest the king knows." When the king heard this story from the vezir he asked for the youth's governor, but he could not be found. So again he sent the youth to the prison and went himself to the chase.

When it was evening the king returned from the chase and came to the palace, and the lady rose to greet him, and they sat down. After the repast the lady again began to speak about the youth. The king said, " To-day also such an one of my vezirs made intercession for him and I sent him to the prison." And he related to the lady that story which the vezir had told. Then said the lady, " O king, the reason of these vezirs stirring up trouble is that they wish to sow enmity between thee and me. Beware, O king, go not by the words of these, but follow well my words, that thy present state and thy hereafter may be happy. When God most high decrees good between husband and wife he gives mildness and accord. And, moreover, O king, be it good news to thee, a week ago did I conceive by thee; till now I have not told thee, but now I have told thee and do thou believe it true." And the king believed it. Then she continued, " O king, lo, these vezirs say that this youth's star has fallen into a malefic aspect. His star became afflicted what time he made for thy life and thy kingdom and for me. God most high aided us and afflicted his star and brought down his head." And the lady was glad and said, " Thy true son is he that is in my womb; that youth is without doubt base-born. Mayhap the king has not heard the story of him who had no sons." The king said, " Tell on, let us hear." Quoth the lady:

THE KING AND THE SHEYKH

" There was in the palace of the world a great king, and he had neither son nor daughter. And there was in his country a sheykh whose prayers were answered. One day the king, while conversing with the sheykh, said, ' O sheykh, God most high has given me no son; do thou strive in prayer that God most high give me a son.' The sheykh replied, ' Send an offering to the convent that the dervishes may eat, and we shall pray for thee; God most high is a gracious king, he will give thee a son.' Now the king had a golden-ankleted fat ram that was valiant in fight; and he sent that ram to the sheykh's convent with some loads of rice and honey and oil. That night the dervishes ate and were pleased; and the sheykh sent of that meat in an earthen bowl to the king, saying, ' Let him desire a son and eat of the dervishes' portion.' Then the dervishes danced, after which they prayed and besought of God a son for the king. By the divine decree the king's wife conceived that night, and in a short time she brought forth a moon-faced boy.

" The king was delighted, and called the people of the country to the feast; and he took the prince and laid him on the sheykh's skirt, and he bestowed many gifts on the sheykh's convent. One day, some time after that, when the king was conversing with the sheykh, he said, ' O sheykh, what if thou were to pray and beseech of God another son for me?' The sheykh replied, ' The favors of God are many; to pray is ours, to give is his; send then an offering to the dervishes.' Now the king had a favorite plump horse, that sent he forthwith to the convent. The devotees cut its throat and roasted it, and again sent an earthen bowl of it to the king. They ate the rest themselves, and prayed and besought of God a son for the king. By the divine decree the lady again conceived, and in a short time she brought forth a moon-faced boy. And the king was delighted and sent many gifts to the dervishes. Some time afterward the king requested the sheykh to beg of God yet another son. The sheykh said, ' To pray is ours, to give is God's; send again an offering to the devotees.' Now the king had a good mule, that sent he to the convent. The devotees sold that mule and took its price and therewith prepared a confection. And they sent a bowl of that too to the king. After the dance they prayed and besought of God a son for the king.

" Again the king's wife conceived and gave birth to a moon-faced boy. And the king was glad and sent many gifts to the dervishes. When the king's sons grew up, the eldest turned out very valiant; the second proved swift of foot and accomplished and possessed of understanding and sagacity; but the youngest was ill-omened and ill-natured, and oppressed men, and wounded and wasted the hearts of many poor creatures with the sword of his tongue. And the king was sore grieved because of him. One day while conversing with the sheykh he complained of his youngest son and said, ' O sheykh, would that we had not besought of God that youngest boy.' The sheykh replied, ' O king, why art thou grieved? thou art thyself the cause of that youth being thus.' The king asked, ' How am I the cause?' The sheykh answered, ' First thou gavest in the cause of God a ram [5] among beasts, and God most high hath given thee a son of courage among men; then thou gavest in the cause of God a courser of the plain of earth among beasts, and God most high hath given thee a courser of the plain of glory and fortune and understanding and accomplishments among men; and after that thou gavest in the cause of God an ill-omened and base-born brute among beasts, and God hath given thee such an one among men. O king, he who sows barley reaps not wheat.' In the end the king got no rest until he had killed the youth.

" Now, O king, I have told this story for that the king may know that from this ill-omened, base-born one no good will come. They have said that the base-born are of two classes; the one the fruit of adultery, the other the fruit of illicit union. This thy son is without doubt of one of these two sets; lo, thy true-born offspring is about to come into existence." When the king heard these beguiling words of the lady he said, " On the morrow will I kill the youth, be not sad."

When it was morning the king came and sat upon his throne and ordered the executioner that he bring the youth, and he said, " Smite off his head." The fifteenth vezir came forward and said, " O king of the world, it is not seemly to kill the prince in compliance with the woman's word, for the angels that are in heaven are not safe against woman's wiles. Hast thou heard the story of the King's Remorse?" The king said, " Tell on, let us hear." Quoth the vezir:

The King's Remorse

" There was in the palace of the world a famous king and God most high had given him a son. After some time the son became afflicted with a heartburn, and he would ever complain of his heart. The king brought together all the physicians that were to be got, and they treated the boy's ailment;

[5] The ram is a type of courage.

but it was in vain, the physicians were powerless. As often as the boy said, ' Father, my heart,' the king would say, ' Son, my heart aches more than thy heart ; ' and the king was afflicted at his pain. At length the boy died. After the dismay, the king came up by the boy and said, ' Cut him open that I may see what pain was in his heart.' When they had cut open the boy the king saw that a bone had grown on the top of his heart. The king ordered that they took out that bone and then buried the boy ; and the king caused that bone to be made into the handle of a knife.

" One day they placed a water-melon before the king ; the king cut the melon with that knife and ate some of it, and he stuck the knife into the remains of the melon and left it. Then the king caused the chess things to be brought and he began to play ; afterward he went to take up the knife when he saw that the part of the handle which had penetrated into the melon was melted and had vanished. As soon as the king saw this he exclaimed, ' Dost thou see? the cure for my son's sickness was water-melon ; and I knew it not.' And his heart was grieved thereat, and he began to weep, and said, ' Son, it has gone from thy heart and come into my heart ; would that thou hadst not come to earth ! ' And at length that king died of anguish of soul.

" Now, O king, I have told this story for that thou mayst beware and slay not thy child on the woman's word, lest thou too die of anguish of soul." And he kissed the ground and made intercession for the prince. When the king heard this story from the vezir he sent the youth to the prison and went himself to the chase.

When it was evening the king returned from the chase and came to the palace, and the lady rose to greet him, and they passed on and sat down. After the repast the lady began to speak about the youth. The king said, " This day also such an one of my vezirs made intercession for him and I sent him to the prison." The lady said, " O king, this youth is a dragon, until he be killed thou shalt not be safe from his malice ; it is even as it was with a certain king who until he had killed his son could not escape from his pain ; mayhap the king has not heard that story." Then the king said, " Tell on, let us hear." Quoth the lady:

LUQMĀN'S DEVICE

" They have related that a great king was wroth with Luq-mān,[6] and commanded that they lowered him into a pit and closed up the mouth of the pit with a great stone. By Luqmān the sage was a pill, of the bigness of a walnut, which he had made by his science. He ever smelled it, and his hunger was satisfied and his thirst was quenched; and for a long time he remained in that pit. The king who imprisoned him died, and his son became king in his stead. And sickness seized upon this king; and the physicians treated him, but he grew no better, and his trouble increased upon him. They were helpless and said, ' O king, had Luqmān been alive he could have cured thy pain.' Then said the king, ' What manner of man was Luqmān?' They replied, ' Thy father was wroth with him and put him into the pit; by now his bones are rotten. But Luqmān was a man such that God most high hath mentioned him in the noble Koran; such a sage has never come to earth.' The king said, ' If it be so, open the pit, belike he has in some way saved himself.'

" They went and opened that pit and went down and saw him sitting there, and they came and told the king. The king said, ' Quick, go bring him.' They went to pull him out of the pit, when Luqmān said, ' If the king wish me, wrap me in cotton and draw me out; and bring to me a leech every night.' They did so, and after forty days he arose and came before the king, and he saw the king lying without strength. After praising and lauding him, he asked of the king's trouble and felt his pulse, and said, ' O king, thou hast a hard sickness.' Then he asked, ' Has the king a son?' They replied, ' He has.' Luqmān said, ' O king, until the throat of thy son be cut and his blood rubbed on thy body, this thy pain will not leave thee.' The king answered, ' O Luqmān, thou art thyself a great man; I will consent to my own death, but I will not consent to my son's.' Quoth Luqmān, ' O king, I have told thee the cure; the rest thou knowest.' And he arose and went away.

" After some days the king's trouble increased, and he called

[6] A legendary sage. He here pre-tends to kill the boy, that the king may recover through joy on finding his son alive.

Luqmān to his side and said, ' O Luqmān, is there no other remedy?' Luqmān answered, ' O king, there is no cure save the cutting of thy son's throat.' The king's soul came up to his throat through that trouble. Quoth Luqmān, ' O king, when thou art well, sons will not be lacking thee.' Then said the king, ' Now get the boy and cut his throat in a distant place that mine eyes see it not.' Luqmān said, ' There is no good if it be done in another place, it is needful that it be done before thine eyes.' Then they gave the boy into Luqmān's hands. And Luqmān bound the boy's hands and feet, and cunningly tied a bladder filled with blood round the boy's throat, and laid him down before the king. Then he took a diamond knife in his hand and said, ' O king, now look, see how I cut the prince's throat.'

" When the king's two eyes were fixed on the boy, he struck against the boy's throat with the knife and the blood gushed out. When the king saw the blood on the boy's throat he sighed; and when Luqmān saw him he thanked God. And straightway he raised the boy from the ground and kissed his two eyes; and Luqmān said, ' O king, I could find no other way to turn off thy sickness than this trick.' Then the king greatly applauded Luqmān and bestowed upon him much wealth.

" Now, O king, I have told this story for that until the king have killed his son, he too will have no security from trouble." When the king heard this story from the lady he was wroth and said, " To-morrow will I kill him."

When it was morning the king went and sat upon his throne and he caused the youth to be brought and ordered the executioner, " Smite off his head." The sixteenth vezir came forward and said, " O king of the world, it is not beseeming thy glory that thou castest to the waters the words of the vezirs; for men are either good or bad concerning the king, whatsoever they say, the king is informed thereof, and the king is given word of evil or hurt about to be, and all that goes on without is known to the king, that he may make preparation accordingly. It is even as in the tradition, ' Speak to men according to their understanding.' Mayhap my king has not heard the story of the dervish and the king." The king said, " Tell on, let us hear." Quoth the vezir:

The King and the Dervish

" There was in a palace of the world a king and his name
was Aydin (light). One day a dervish came before him and
spake pleasantly with fair discretion; and whatsoever they
asked, he answered the whole of it, and his every word seemed
good to the king. The king said, ' O dervish, go not away,
let us spend this evening together.' The dervish blessed him
and said, ' On head and eye.' Now it was then very cold. So
the king took the dervish, and they went to the palace and sat
down. The king ordered that they laid wood upon the fire-
place and set light to it, whereupon the dervish repeated these
verses—

> ' Take in winter fire from garden-land ;
> Take the goblet from the drunken band ;
> Should there no loveling for cup-bearer be,
> Take from orange-breasted damsel's hand.'

" As these verses seemed right good to the king, he wrote
them in his album; and he said to the dervish, ' Tell some
merry story.' Quoth the dervish, ' O king, once there was a
king, and by him there was a devotee. One day they said to the
king, " Yon devotee is a Rāfizī." [7] The king, to try him, one
day asked that devotee, " O devotee, lovest thou Saint Abu
Bekr the True?" The devotee replied, " Nay." He said,
" Lovest thou Saint 'Omar?" He answered, " Nay." " Then
lovest thou Saint 'Othmān?" He answered, " Nay, nay."
" Then lovest thou Saint 'Alī the Approved?" He answered,
" Nay." Thereupon the king's difficulties from being one became two, and he thought and said in himself, " If this devotee
were a Rāfizī, he would love Saint 'Alī, though he loved not
the other Noble Companions our Lords; if he were a Sunnī,
he would love all of the Four Chosen Friends our Lords."
And he turned and said to the devotee, " Thou lovest none of
the Glorious Companions, whom then lovest thou?"

" ' The devotee replied, " There is at the gate of the bazaar a
loveling of the age; lo, that is whom I love." The king was
pleased with this jest of the devotee and gave him many gifts.'
And that dervish told stories such as this to the king, and he

---

[7] An adherent of the Shī'a sect, which   Bekr, 'Othmān and 'Omar as lawful
acknowledges 'Alī, but rejects Abu-   caliphs.

amused the king with many jests. That night they ate and drank, and when their converse was finished, drowsiness came upon the king, and he would have lain down, but the devotee was at ease and would not rise and go. The slaves thought to say to the devotee, ' Arise and go,' but they feared the king and were silent. The king too wished that the devotee might perceive by his discretion that he should arise; but where was that discretion? The king looked, but it was not.

" Then he called to his servants, ' Strike the fagot that the glow (ishiq) may go out.' The servants understood not and remained still. Thereupon the devotee said, ' Why wait ye? Strike the log that the light (aydin) may spring up.' Now the king's name was Aydin (light) and the devotee's name was Ishiq (glow).[8] The king said, ' I sent thee off with a fagot, that is struck thee with a fagot, but thou didst strike me with a log.' The devotee said, ' My king, thou didst not strike me with a fagot, neither did I strike my king with a log; so do thou rest on the one side of the hearth and I shall rest on the other.' And the king was pleased with these words of the devotee; and they lay down and rested.

" Now, O king, I have told this story for that thou mayst know that a certain freedom is usual with the accomplished. Now there are no learned men equal to these forty vezirs of my king, each one of whom utters these many good sayings and fair words; and indeed the good or bad of these has many a time been tried. And what is incumbent upon my king is this, that he listen not to the words of these inattentively nor cast them to the winds." The king said, " This demand leaves me in bewilderment. Our Lord the Apostle of God hath said concerning women, that they are enemies to you, but that one of them is needful to each of you. And God most high hath said in his glorious Word, ' Your wealth and your children are but a trial.' [9] Now I ask these affairs of this youth and he answers not at all; and so long as he will not speak, will my difficulty remain unsolved. Thus it seems to me that this youth has done this wantonness, and therefore cannot speak."

When the vezir saw this much consideration on the part of

---

[8] So the point of this story turns upon an untranslatable pun.

[9] Koran, viii. 128, and lxiv. 15.

the king he said, " My king, in everything the mysterious
workings of God most high are many; let not my king regard the not speaking of the youth. One day will he speak
indeed; yea, there is also in that noble verse concerning children, ' And God: with him is great reward.' " And he kissed
the ground and made intercession for the prince. And the
king sent the youth to the prison and went himself to the
chase. That day, when they were hunting, a deer rose, and
the hounds pursued it, and all the attendants pushed their
horses after that deer, and the king too pushed on. Each
one went in a different direction, and the king was left alone.
When it was evening there was with him no attendant nor
anyone; the king looked and there was none, and he said,
" There is in this some divine working." And straightway he
disguised himself and pushed on and came to a village and
was guest in a shepherd's house.

On the morrow he rose betimes, and while he was watching
the sheep and lambs, he looked and saw a lamb that had lost
its mother. Seeking about, it went up to a sheep, and that
sheep butted at the lamb, and the lamb fell. It rose again and
went to another sheep; and that sheep likewise butted at the
lamb. The king asked this from the shepherd, " Why do these
sheep butt at that lamb?" The shepherd said, " To-day this
lamb's mother died; these, being not its mother, receive it not."
Then the king sighed in his soul and said in his heart, " May
God most high leave not a servant of his an orphan."

Let us to our story: The attendants returned to the city,
and each one turned his horse's head straight to the palace.
They arrived at the castle, and one of them called out and
learned the circumstance (of the king's absence) from the
watchmen; so they went to look for news of the king. On the
other hand the watchmen informed the grand vezir of the
matter; and straightway the grand vezir commanded that all
of those watchmen were secured in prison,[10] and he himself
walked about the city till morning. He sent a vezir to the
king's attendants, saying, " Go tell the attendants that they
publish not this affair, and do thou go with the whole of them
to seek the king." On her part, the lady looked and the time
passed and the king came not, and she caused the grand vezir

---

[10] To prevent their spreading the report of the king's disappearance.

to be questioned; the vezir sent word to her, " This night there is a great council; our king will not go in."

The vezir questioned the king's attendants; and while they were going to the place where they had left the king, the king himself set out from the village where he was and came to the place where the attendants had dispersed. The attendants saw the king, and brought word to the vezir; so the vezir pushed on his horse and came up to the king. The king said in his heart, " These will have enthroned the prince and sent this vezir to me; now is he coming to give me the sherbet; O how the lady's words were true ! " The vezir saw from the king's countenance that he was thinking thus, and he came up quickly to him, and kissed the ground before the king, and said, " My king, what plight is this plight? Is it beseeming to remain without at such a time? Above all, as the prince has been these many days imprisoned, everyone says that the king's senses have well nigh left him."

Thereupon the king said, " Have ye taken the prince from prison? " The vezir replied, " Nay, my king; the grand vezir secured in prison the watchmen who had learned of my king's remaining out in the evening from the attendants who came to the gate; and he sent me and the attendants to seek my king." The king's mind was somewhat comforted, but his heart would not believe. Then the vezir perceived that the king's heart was not at ease and he said to the king, " My king, thy grand vezir sent me hither in the evening; to learn the events of to-day are my eyes now on the road." And he kissed the ground and was silent. The king said, " If we went on now it were too quick; but let an attendant go and inform the vezir of the affair." They sent on an attendant; and that day, when it was evening, the king came to the palace and found everything in its proper place, and his heart was again at rest concerning his vezir.

After the repast he entered the harem. The lady had rubbed a dye upon her eyes and made them red, and she rose to greet the king as if weeping; and the king passed on and sat in his place. When coffee and sherbets had been drunk she asked of the haps of the night, and the king related the events to her. She said, " O king, the thing thou hast done might be in two ways; the one, of purpose, to distinguish between friend and foe; the other, by chance. In this instance thou hast passed the evening outside by chance, and thy heart is at ease for that thy vezirs have done no unseemly deed. But, my king, beware, trust not these vezirs; for they would make the youth king. Praise be to God! thou art well, but they still watch their opportunity; and this youth has no dread of thee, thou hast brought him up full insolent; that is not good. And they have said that if a person treat thee as a brother, do thou treat him as a master and deem him great. Kings are like fire; if thou be a lion, thou must be on thy guard against the fire, even as lions are on their guard against fire.

" There is a fable suitable to this: The lynxes go along with the lion, but they go not close to him. One day they asked one of them, 'Thou goest along with the lion; why goest thou not near to him?' He replied, 'Firstly, the lion hunts beasts and I eat his leavings; secondly, when an enemy comes against me I go to him and take refuge; as these two things are good for me I go along with him. And the reason of my going not near is this, that his glory is that of a render, one day it might be that he should rend me like the leopard; therefore go I not near him.' Wise is he who acts before kings like the lynx; for nearness to the sultan is a burning fire. Even as the lynx is content with and eats the lion's leavings, must the wise man be content with the king's leavings; else, if he stretch forth his hand to the morsel that is in the king's mouth—the plight of him who stretches forth his hand is notorious. If an enemy appear, it is needful to take refuge with the king; so one must ever be between dread and entreaty, and must measure his words. A word is like an arrow that has left the bow, when once it leaves the mouth it returns not again. Mayhap my king has not heard the story of Sultan Mahmūd [1] and Hasan of Maymand." [2] The king said, "Tell on, let us hear." Quoth the lady:

MAHMŪD AND HASAN

" A word was the cause of Sultan Mahmūd dismissing his vezir Hasan of Maymand, and confiscating all his property and banishing him. So what could Hasan of Maymand do

[1] Sultan Mahmūd, the son of Sebuk-tekin, of Ghazni.
[2] Hasan of Maymand was a minister, not of Sultan Mahmūd, but of that monarch's father. Hasan's son, Ahmed, was Mahmūd's vezir.

but yield consent to misfortune and bear calamity with patience? One day, during his exile, while he was passing along a street, a group of children were playing, one was prince and one was vezir. The prince got angry and wished to banish the vezir and confiscate his property. The child who was vezir said, 'Art thou just or art thou a tyrant?' The prince answered, 'I am just.' Then said the vezir, 'Thou art just; well, when I came to thee I was young, and I have spent my life in thy service and gained my property; now thou confiscatest my property and takest away my office, I now ask back from thee my life that I have spent in thy service; if thou be just, it is right that thou give me my life.' The prince was silent and made that child vezir again.

"Hasan of Maymand liked the child's words, and straightway he went and composed a petition and sent it to Sultan Mahmūd. When the petition arrived they took it and gave it to the king. The king read it, and when he perceived its import, he straightway ordained that he was pardoned and reinstated in his office. So he was dismissed by one word and reinstated by one word.

"O king, I deemed this story suitable in that a master of speech comes not readily to hand; and a master of speech is one who knows the speech that ought to be spoken. For speech is of two kinds; one kind is truth, another kind is folly. A wise man distinguishes between the speech of a sage and the speech of a fool. A sage speaks with understanding, but a fool speaks with trickery. The man who distinguishes not between these is like a beast, for a beast knows only when it is hungry and when it is full. Now this thy degenerate son has made for thy life and thy throne; this is beseeming, that thou give him neither grace nor time. Thou must kill him to-morrow, else he will slay thee." When the king heard this story from the lady he said, "To-morrow will I finish his affair."

When it was morning and the sun shed light (aydin) and, like the words of the king and the dervish, the glow (ishiq) appeared, and the world was illuminated with radiance, the happy-fortuned king passed and sat upon his throne, and he caused the executioner to bring the youth and commanded, "Smite off his head." The eighteenth vezir came forward and said, " O king of the world, two things are indeed incumbent upon kings; the first is to have pity on the folk, and the second is to have mercy in the time of wrath. Long will be the life of the king who is thus, and God most high will protect him from all calamities. It is even as said our lord the Holy Apostle of God, ' Be merciful to those upon the earth that the dwellers in heaven may have mercy upon you.' And the friends of a king who is generous are many, and he triumphs over his enemies, and is of the host of the prophets and the saints. And there is a story of Sultan Mahmūd suitable to this; if the king grant leave, I will relate it." The king said, " Relate, let us hear." Quoth the vezir:

Story of Sultan Mahmūd

" One day while Sultan Mahmūd, the son of Sebuktekīn, was hunting, he got separated from his soldiers, and he saw someone going along in a trackless place. He pushed on and came up to that man and saluted him and said, ' O man, whence art thou and what is thy origin?' The man replied, ' From the kingdom; and my origin my mother knows.' Then the sultan saw that he was wrapped up in black clothes and mounted on a black ass; and the king asked, ' Whither goest thou now?' That man replied, ' I go to Sultan Mahmūd.' The king said, ' What is thy desire of the sultan?' The man answered, ' I want 10,000 aspres of him; I have a debt, perchance he may give it me and I shall be freed from my debt.' The sultan said, ' If he give it not, how wilt thou act?' The man replied, ' If he will not give 10,000, let him give 1,000.' Again the sultan said, ' If he will not give even 1,000, what wilt thou do?' The man replied, ' If he will not give a thousand aspres, let him give a hundred aspres.' The sultan said, ' If he will not give even that, what wilt thou do?' Then the fellow replied, ' If he will not give even a hundred aspres, I shall say, *Bu qara eshegimin durt ayaghi 'avretinin ferjine!* [3] and shall turn and go.' The king wondered at this man's self and words.

" After a little he met his soldiers and went to his palace and sat upon his throne and thus commanded the grand chamber-

---

[3] I have thought it best to leave the uncivil remark of the owner of the black ass in the inimitable simplicity of the original.

lain, 'A man clad in black and mounted on a black ass will come, give him leave to enter.' The next day, early in the morning, that man came, and the grand chamberlain took him and brought him into the king's presence. When he saw the king he knew that it was he whom he had seen yesterday, and straightway he prayed for the king and asked 10,000 aspres. The king said, 'May God give it thee.' The man said, 'Give 1,000 aspres.' Again the king answered, 'May God give it thee.' The man said, 'Let it be a hundred aspres.' Again the king answered, 'May God give it thee.' Then the man said, 'Be thou well; the black ass is tied at the door.' Thereupon a courtier [4] said, 'The king has bestowed nothing on thee; let the black ass be.' The man said, 'If he has not, then it means, *eshegimin durt ayaghi 'avretinin ferjine!* And I shall be off.' But his boldness pleased the king who said, 'This poor man's desire is but to be delivered from distress and find rest, as he got no boon from us he mounts his ass and goes.' And this remained as a proverb, 'The black ass is tied at the door.' However, he bestowed on him somewhat.

"And this story resembles it: A certain khoja was going from Hindustan to Bagdad, and while on the road he thus thought, 'When I enter the city of Bagdad what goods should I buy?' Anyhow he entered Bagdad, and there was there a naked abdal [5] who had plucked out his beard and put it in a piece of paper. He came up to the khoja and said, 'I have heard, O khoja, that thou hast come to buy goods; I have something, buy it.' And he gave the paper into the khoja's hand. The khoja took it and opened it and saw in it the hairs of the beard, and he said, 'What shall I do with this?' The abdal said, 'Take it, and give the money.' The khoja answered, 'I shall not give money for this.' The abdal said, 'Why wilt thou not give money? that is indeed a beard; is it not worth a hundred aspres?' The khoja replied, 'It is not.' The abdal said, 'Let it be ten aspres; is it not worth that?' The khoja answered, 'It is not.' The abdal said, 'Let it be five aspres; is it not worth that?' The khoja said, 'It is not.' Then said the abdal, 'A beard is not worth five aspres; why then dost thou carry one? shave it off and let it go.' The

[4] In Belletête this courtier is said to be Firdausī of Tūs, and he is made to tell Mahmūd the following story of the khoja and the abdal, for which the Sultan rewards him with a purse of gold.
[5] A kind of religious mendicant.

khoja was pleased with this jest of the abdal and gave him a hundred aspres.

" Now, O king, I have told these stories for that the king may know that it is needful for kings to raise the fallen and bestow favors on the poor." And he kissed the ground and made intercession for the prince. When the king heard these stories from the vezir he sent the prince to the prison and went himself to the chase.

When it was evening the king returned from the chase and came to the palace, and the lady rose to greet him, and they sat down. After the repast the lady asked for news about the youth. The king said, " To-day likewise such an one of my vezirs made intercession for him and I sent him to the prison." The lady said, " O king, think not thou this youth would maintain thy place after thee and observe the ordinances of kings. To exercise sovereignty is a hard work. I know that he is no true man; he watches his opportunity, and one day he will slay thee and shed blood, and then they will kill him too. Moreover, family and descent are needful for one; he who is not of family cannot exercise sovereignty. And one's nature must be good. There are men of family and descent who are yet themselves of evil nature; for there is not honey in every bee nor a pearl in every oyster. Then this youth's nature is evil; he has not the qualities of a king; his work would ever be wickedness and he would do wrong to those who do good. It is like the story of a certain merchant's son; mayhap my king has not heard it." The king said, " Tell on, let us hear." Quoth the lady:

Story of the Merchant's Son

" There was of old time a cobbler in the city of Orfa. One day he saw a dervish passing, the seams of whose shoes had given way. The cobbler said, ' Dervish, come, sit down till I sew up the seams of thy shoes and patch the holes.' The dervish answered, ' If thou hast a remedy, apply it to the hole in my heart.' The cobbler gave him his right hand and he came and sat down; and the cobbler gave him food to eat and sewed up the holes in his shoes and said, ' O dervish, I too wish to journey; what counsel dost thou give me?' The dervish answered, ' I have three counsels; see thou keep them:

my first is this, set not out on the journey till thou hast found a good fellow-traveller; for the Apostle of God hath said, " The companion, then the road." My second is this, light not in a waterless place. My third is this, enter great cities when the sun is rising.' Then he went his way. After some days the cobbler found some suitable fellow-travellers and set out. While they were on the road, one day in the afternoon a city appeared before them. The cobbler youth asked, ' What city is this city?' The companions answered, ' It is the city of Aleppo.' The youth said, ' To-day it is near evening; I shall not enter the city to-day.'

" Howsoever the companions urged him, it was no use; so at length they left him and went on. The youth went and lighted on the bank of a stream and remained there that night. Now there were tombs near the youth; and when it was midnight he saw two men coming from the city carrying something which they laid in the graveyard, and then they went away. Then the youth went up to that grave, and, striking a light with a flint and steel, lit a candle; he saw that they had laid there a new coffin, and that from the four sides of that coffin streams of blood were running. The cobbler youth opened the lid of the coffin and looked to see what he might see; there was a body bathed in blood, the garments were of massive gold embroidery and on the finger was a ring in which a stone glittered. The youth coveted the ring and took hold of it that he might pull it off, whereupon the body raised its head and said, ' O youth, fearest thou not God that thou wouldst take my ring?' Then the youth saw that it was a girl like the moon of fourteen nights, a torment of the age, like a lovely rose; and he said, ' What is this plight?' The girl said, ' Now is not the time for questions; if thou be able, relieve me; and afterward I will help thine affairs.'

" Straightway the youth pulled off his outer robe and tore it in pieces and bound up the girl's wounds and laid her in a place. When it was morning he took her on his back and brought her into the city and placed her in a cell in a certain place; and to all who asked of her he said, ' She is my sister; passion came upon me and I brought this plight upon this poor creature, and she innocent.' The youth tended the girl's wounds and in the course of a month or two she became well.

One day she went to the bath, and when she returned she asked the youth for inkhorn, reed, and paper. The youth brought them and placed them before her. The girl wrote a letter and gave it into the youth's hands; and therein was written thus: 'Thou who art Khoja Dibāb, the superintendent of the bazaar, give the bearer of this letter a hundred sequins and send him to me; and disclose nothing to my father of my health or my death; if thou do, thou shalt reflect well upon the issue.' She sealed it and said, 'Go, give this letter to a khoja who sits in such and such a place in the bazaar, and take whatever he gives thee and bring it.'

"The youth took that letter and went to the bazaar and asked, and they showed him to him, and he gave the letter into his hand. When the khoja opened the letter and read it, he kissed it and raised it to his head, and straightway drew forth a purse of gold and gave it to the youth. The youth brought it and laid it before the girl. The girl said, 'Go, take a house, and buy with what is over clothes for thee and me.' The youth went and took a house and bought sumptuous clothes and brought them to the girl. And they arose and went to that house which they had taken. Again she wrote a letter which she gave to the youth who took it to the khoja, who this time gave him two purses which he took to the girl. She said to him, 'Go, my youth, and buy some provisions and furniture for the house.' And the youth went and bought them. Then the girl got another purse of sequins, and she said to the youth, 'Go, buy thyself horses and arms and male slaves and female slaves.' And the youth went and bought them, and he brought them and gave them to the girl, and he said, 'Now tell me what are these matters.' The girl answered, 'Now is not the time, by and bye.'

"Gradually the girl built palaces there and increased the number of her male slaves and female slaves, and whenever she gave the youth a letter he went and got two or three purses of gold from that khoja. One day the girl gave the youth a purse of gold and said, 'In the bazaar is a youth they call Ghazanfer Agha; now go and find him, and ask of him some precious stuff, and he will show it thee, and whatever price he ask for it, give him the double thereof, and take and bring it.' So the youth went and found him, and sat a while and talked with him; and whatever the price of it was he gave the double, and took it; and Ghazanfer Agha marvelled at this. The youth returned and gave it to the girl, and again he asked of these matters, but the girl said that this too was not the time. And she took out a purse of jewels and gave it to the youth and said, ' Take these jewels and go to Ghazanfer Agha and ask him to put a value on them, and take them out and lay them before him, and see what he will say to thee; and when putting the jewels back into the purse present him with three of them.' So she sent him off. The youth said, ' I shall go; but when I come back tell me the things that have befallen thee.' He went and did as the girl had said.

" When Ghazanfer Agha saw these gifts he said to the youth, ' O youth, thou hast made us ashamed; pray be troubled to come once to our house and honor us that we may show our affection.' The youth replied, ' What though it be so; to-morrow I shall go.' And he bade him farewell and he came and told the girl, and the girl said, ' Go to-morrow; but when thou enterest his house look not to this side nor that side, but look straight before thee.' And thus did she warn him. When it was morning the youth arose; and Ghazanfer Agha looked and saw the youth coming and he said, ' Welcome! ' and took him and led him to his house. And the youth looked at nothing, but passed on and sat down; and Ghazanfer Agha treated and entertained that youth with all manner of delicious foods, and then sent him away. And the youth came and told the girl, and she said, ' Go again to-morrow and talk with him, and when thou risest, do thou too invite him; and be not jealous.'

" And the youth reflected and said in his heart. ' This Ghazanfer Agha must be the friend of this girl; anyhow we shall see; whatever God does he does well.' In the morning he went and invited him, and then came to the girl and gave her word and said, ' Tell me and let me hear of the matters of that night.' The girl answered, ' Now is not the time; go and get these things which are needful.' The youth went and got them and brought them and gave her them and said, ' Lo, I have brought them; tell me.' The girl said, ' Now is the guest coming, it cannot be; by and bye I will tell thee.' When Ghazanfer Agha came the youth gave the girl word and she said, ' Go and

meet him, and lead him and bring him here.' The youth said
in his heart, 'This is not without reason; but wait, we shall
see.' And he led him respectfully, and he entered and sat down
with the girl. After that, came foods and they ate and drank
and made merry till the evening. Then the girl sent word and
the youth came in, and she said, 'Take care, be it not that thou
lettest Ghazanfer Agha leave this evening.' And the youth said,
'What is this of thee that thou dost not dismiss him?' The girl
answered, 'I will tell thee afterward.' The youth said in his
heart, 'I shall slay the two of you this night.' And he went
out. When it was night Ghazanfer Agha asked leave to go
away, but the youth would not let him, and Ghazanfer Agha
saw that it was not to be, so he remained; and they brought
out a clean coverlet and mattress and made a bed for him.
And Ghazanfer Agha lay down, and the youth lay down, but
he slept not that he might watch the girl.

"When it was midnight the girl arose and the youth saw her,
but he made no sound, and the girl went up close to Ghazanfer
Agha. The youth, unable to endure it any longer, rose from
his place and said fiercely to the girl, 'What seekest thou
there?' The girl saw that the youth spake angrily and she
took him by the hand and drew him to a place apart and said,
'I am about to slay this Ghazanfer Agha.' The youth said,
'What is the reason of it?' The girl replied, 'The reason of
it is this: I am the daughter of the king of this land, and this
youth was a butcher's apprentice. One day, when going to
the bath, I met this youth selling meat upon the road; as soon
as I saw him I fell in love with him, and the bird, my heart, was
taken, so that I was without rest and could not remain quiet.
I saw there was no help for it, so I got him by force of money,
and sometimes I went to his house, and sometimes I had him
brought in disguise to my palace. One night I went in disguise to his house, and I saw him sitting conversing with a
gipsy, and I got angry and I cursed the two of them. This
youth was wont to use the dagger, and he gave me many
wounds, and thought me dead and put me in a coffin and sent
me with two men who laid me in that tomb thou sawest.
Praise be to God! my time was not yet; thou didst come to
me like Khizr: now, do thou kill him.'

"The youth said, 'I shall kill him. Wilt thou marry me

according to the ordinance of God?' She answered, 'I will not marry thee; but the vezir has a daughter fairer than I, her will I get for thee.' Then the youth smote him and killed him. The girl said, 'In the morning go to my father and give him good news; and go to-night and bring here all the possessions of this youth.' The youth said, 'To-morrow thy father will bring them.' When it was morning the youth went and gave the good news to the king. And the king sent slave-girls who brought the girl to the palace. And her mother was glad when she saw her safe and sound.[6] And they confiscated the property of Ghazanfer Agha and bestowed it on that youth.

"But what would the youth do with the wealth? his desire was the girl. The king's vezirs said, 'My king, it were right if thou give the girl to the youth.' The king answered, 'It is my desire too; for when my daughter disappeared and we sought but could not find her, I made a promise, saying, that to him who brought good news of my daughter I should give her; but the girl does not wish it.' The vezirs said, 'My king, our daughters are thine; make this youth thy client; whichever girl thou pleasest, give her to him.' The king said, 'I shall make a proposal;' and he went and spake with her mother. And the girl's mother went to her and with difficulty persuaded her; and then sent word to the king. That hour they performed the marriage ceremony, and the king made the youth a vezir; and they lived for a long time in joyance and delight.

"O king, I have told this story for that thou mayst know that thy son will not accept counsel, but purposes for thy life. Because that cobbler youth accepted the words of the saints he attained to fortune; and that butcher's apprentice, for that he was a fool, wounded his benefactress, the king's daughter; and if the girl had not killed him, he would have made her disgraced before the world. Do thou then, O king, take profit by the tale; beware, spare not this foolish youth, but kill him; else thou shalt be repentant." When the king heard this story from the lady he said, "To-morrow will I kill him."

When it was morning and the sun had appeared, like as appeared the kindness shown by the king's daughter to the

<hr/>

[6] The original is somewhat more explicit here: Vālidesi qizin muhrini tef-tish eyledi, chun muhrini muhrlu buldi, qizin iki guzinden updi.

butcher's apprentice, and the world was illumined with light, the king passed and sat upon his throne, and he caused the youth to be brought and commanded the executioner, " Smite off his head." The nineteenth vezir came forward and said, " O king, beware, hurry not in this matter, look to the thought of the hereafter and the way of the Law. The Apostle (peace on him!) saith, ' God most high maketh wise in the Truth him to whom he wisheth to do good.' According to this sacred tradition, what is befitting the king is this, that he transgress not the bounds of God. The truth is this, that in this matter the prince is sinless. O king, when can one obtain a son? Slay not thy prince, or grief for thy son will be full hard, and in the end thou shalt be unable to endure it. There is a story suitable to this; if the king grant leave I will relate it." The king said, " Relate it, let us hear." Quoth the vezir:

HASAN OF BASRA

" Hasan of Basra [7] (the mercy of God on him!) was in his first estate a seller of jewels. One day he rose up to trade, and came before a king and transacted business, and then he transacted business with the vezir. The vezir said, ' To-day we go to a pageant at a certain place; wilt thou come with us?' Hasan answered, ' Yea, I shall go.' When the vezir and the king had mounted their steeds, they brought a horse for Hasan likewise, and they all went out of the gate and came to a plain. Hasan saw that in the middle of that plain was a white pavilion, the dome of which reared its head into the air. Then they went up close to that pavilion and all of them alighted. From another side came a procession of people; Hasan of Basra saw that it was a party of doctors and holy men who were carrying their lecterns and copies of the sacred volume. They came and entered that pavilion and recited the Koran with sweet voice; then they came and walked three times round that dome, and then stood at the door and said, ' O prince, what can we? were there release to thy sweet soul by reading of the Koran, we would, all of us, cease not therefrom day or night; but it is the decree of that almighty King; there is no avail for his command save acquiescence and patience.'

[7] Hasan of Basra was a very pious and learned man. He died in 110 (A.D. 728).

"And they went away. After them came white-bearded
elders and devotees reciting chants, and they walked three
times round that dome, and then stood at the door and said,
'O prince, what can we? were there release to thy sweet soul
by chant and prayer, we would, all of us, devote ourselves to
chant and prayer; but what profit? it is the decree of that
almighty King; there is no avail therefor save resignation.'
And they went away. After them came many moon-faced damsels, in the hand of each of whom was a golden dish filled full
of all manner of jewels, and they walked three times round
that dome, and then stood at the door and said, 'O prince, what
can we? were there release to thy sweet soul by the giving of
riches, we would give all these jewels, and we ourselves would
become slaves; but what avail? it is the decree of that almighty King, and he hath no need of such things; there is
no help for his decree save patience.'

"And they went away. After them came an innumerable
army which surrounded that dome, rank on rank, and they said,
'O prince, were there release to thy sweet soul by battle, night
and day would we, all of us, do battle in thy cause; but what
avail? it is the decree of that almighty King; there is no help
therefor but patience and resignation.' And they went away.
After them came the king the father of that prince, and the
vezirs and the nobles, and they walked three times round that
dome, and then stood at the door, and the king said, 'O light of
my eyes, darling of my heart, were there release to thy sweet
soul to be found by science, I had found it by means of the
learned; or were it by gifts and bounties, I had assembled all
my army and made war and attained it; but what avail?
decree is God's. He is in want of naught; there is no help save
patience and acquiescence in his judgment.'

"And he wept full bitterly, and all the nobles and vezirs
wept likewise. When Hasan of Basra saw these things he
asked the vezir, 'What plight is this plight?' The vezir said,
'O Hasan, our king had a son: he was in beauty a second
Joseph; and in writing, reading, chivalry, and all accomplishments he had no rival; and as he was the king's only child he
loved him very much. One day death spared him not, and he
passed to the abiding home. After the wailing and dismay,
as there was no help save patience under the heavenly decree,

they brought him and buried him in this dome. And once every year they come and thus visit the tomb.' When Hasan of Basra heard these words from the vezir and saw these things with his eyes, wealth and riches went forth from his eye and heart; and he abandoned the whole of them and turned dervish and donned the khirqa;[8] and now, when his name is mentioned, they add, 'The mercy of God on him!'

"Now, O king, I have told this story for that the king may know that grief for children is full bitter. As yet thou hast not felt it, and may God most high not show it thee thus through him. O king, slay not the prince, else afterward thou shalt be repentant and shalt sigh and groan until thou die." And he made intercession for the prince for that day. When the king heard this story from the vezir compassion came into his heart, and he sent the youth to the prison and went himself to the chase.

When it was evening the king returned from the chase and came to the palace, and again the lady rose to greet him, and she sat with the king. After the repast the lady asked for news of the youth. The king said, "To-day likewise such an one of my vezirs made intercession for him, and I have sent him again to the prison." The lady said, "O king, why dost thou leave my counsel and act according to thine own understanding? Hast not thou heard these words they have said concerning the heedless: 'Whoso is presumptuous through reason is abased.' And the sages have said that eight things bring disgrace upon a man: the first is going to dine at a place without invitation, the second is interfering between another and his wife, the third is giving ear to everyone's words, the fourth is slighting the king, the fifth is setting one's self above a great man, the sixth is speaking to those who listen not to one's words, the seventh is begging a favor of an avaricious and indifferent person, and the eighth is going to the enemies' gate.

"Now, O king, those vezirs interfere between thee and me. Beware, act not according to their words. They have said that he who acts according to a stranger's word will divorce his wife. Their words are many; and they are forty vezirs, and each one of them for this long time is planning wiles. Mayhap my king has not heard the story of the old gardener and his son." The king said, "Tell on, let us hear." Quoth the lady:

[8] The dervish's cloak.

The Gardener and His Son

"In the by-gone time an old gardener had mounted his son upon an ass and was proceeding to the garden, himself on foot. They met some men who said, 'See this old pederast, how he has mounted the boy upon the ass; and is himself running alongside.' Whenever the old man heard this he made the boy alight and mounted himself. Again they met some other folk, these likewise said, 'Look at this heartless old man, he rides the ass himself and makes the poor child go on foot.' Whenever the old man heard this he took his son up in front of him. Then some people saw them and said, 'See this old pederast, how he has taken the boy up in front of him.' The old man heard this, and he put his son up behind him. Again certain folks saw them and said, 'See this old catamite, how he has taken the boy up behind him.' The old man knew not what to do, so he put his son down and alighted himself and drove the ass before them. The garden was near, and both of them were on foot, and they reached the garden before meeting with any others.

"Now, O king, I have told this story that thou mayst know that no one in the world can escape the tongue of the folk. Each one says a different thing. It is even as when a boil came out on the foot of a certain king who showed it to some-one and said, 'Come, look at this boil; is it ripe or unripe?' He looked and said, 'It is ripe.' Then he showed it to an-other person, and he said, 'It is unripe.' Then the king said, 'We cannot get sure information concerning even one foot.' Do thou too, O king, go by no one's word, lose not the oppor-tunity; no good will come to thee from this youth." When the king heard this story from the lady he said, "To-morrow will I kill him."

When it was morning the king came and sat upon his throne, and he caused the youth to be brought and ordered the exe-cutioner, "Smite off his head." The twentieth vezir came forward and said, "O king of the world, I will speak a good word to thee: all these vezirs who have spoken these many words are well-wishers to thee. The holy Apostle of God hath said, 'Whoso hath believed in God and the last day; when he witnesseth to aught, let him speak with good or let him be silent.' Now, what is best for thee in this thy affair is this, as all thy vezirs say, ' Slay not the prince,' I too say, have patience, else the end of this will be care and sorrow. Mayhap the king has not heard the story of a certain king." The king said, " Tell on, let us hear." Quoth the vezir:

THE DERVISH'S ADVICE

" Of old time there was a great king. One day, when returning from the chase, he saw a dervish sitting by the way, crying, ' I have a piece of advice; to him who will give me 1,000 sequins I will tell it.' When the king heard these words of the dervish he drew in his horse's head and halted, and he said to the dervish, ' What is thy counsel?' The dervish replied, ' Bring the sequins and give me them that I may tell my counsel.' The king ordered that they count 1,000 sequins into the dervish's lap. The dervish said, ' O king, my advice to thee is this, whenever thou art about to do a deed, consider the end of that deed, and then act.' The nobles who were present laughed together at these words and said, ' Anyone knows that.' But the king rewarded that poor man. He was greatly pleased with the words of the dervish and commanded that they wrote them on the palace gate and other places.

" Now that king had an enemy, a great king; and this hostile king was ever watching his opportunity; but he could find no way save this, he said in himself, ' Let me go and promise the king's barber some worldly good and give him a poisoned lancet; some day when the king is sick he can bleed him with that lancet.' So he disguised himself, and went and gave the barber a poisoned lancet and 10,000 sequins. And the barber was covetous and undertook to bleed the king with that lancet what time it should be needful. One day the king was sick, and he sent word to the barber to come and bleed him. Thereupon the barber took that poisoned lancet with him and went. The attendants prepared the basin, and the barber saw written on the rim of the basin, ' Whenever thou art about to perform a deed, think on the end thereof.'

" When the barber saw this he said in himself, ' I am now about to bleed the king with this lancet and doubtless he will perish, then they will not leave me alive, but will inevitably kill me; after I am dead what use will these sequins be to me?' And he took up that lancet and put it in its place and drew out another lancet that he might bleed the king. When he took his arm a second time, the king said, 'Why didst thou not bleed me with the first lancet?' The barber answered, 'O king, there was some dust on its point.' Then the king said, 'I saw it, it is not the treasury lancet; there is some secret here, quick, tell it, else I will slay thee.' When the barber saw this importunity, he related the story from beginning to end and how he had seen the writing on the basin and changed his intention. The king put a robe of honor on the barber and let him keep the sequins which his enemy had given him. And the king said, 'The dervish's counsel is worth not 1,000 sequins but 100,000 sequins.'

"Now, O king, I have told this story for that the king may know that it is as when the dervish said, 'Whatsoever deed thou doest, consider the end thereof, then act.' If thou slay the prince, at last thou shalt be repentant. The rest the king knows." And he made intercession for the prince. When the king heard these words from the vezir he sent the prince to the prison and himself mounted for the chase.

When it was evening the king returned from the chase and came to the palace, and the lady rose to greet him, and they sat down. After the repast the lady again asked for news of the youth. The king said, "To-day such an one of my vezirs made intercession for him and I sent him to the prison." The lady said, "O king, it is related of the Caliph Ma'mūn [9] that he said, 'Four things are hurtful to kings; the first is the nobles being negligent, the second is the ministers being envious, the third is the mean being bold, and the fourth is the vezirs being treacherous.' And the Moorish sages say, 'In nobles there is no friendship, in liars there is no fidelity, in the envious there is no peace, in the indifferent there is no generosity, and in the evil-natured there is no greatness.' O king, these thy vezirs are, like thy traitor son, liars and evil-natured. Thou believest the words of these. The story of thee and this youth altogether resembles the story of those Turkman children." The king said, "Tell that story, let us hear it." Quoth the lady:

[9] El-Ma'mūn, the son of Hārūn-er-Reshīd, was proclaimed caliph in 198 (A.D. 813); he died in 218 (A.D. 833).

THE TURKMAN CHILDREN

" Certain Turkmans from an encampment went one day into a city. When they were returning from the city to the encampment they were an hungered, and when they were come near they ate some bread and onions at a spring-head. The juice of the onions went into the Turkmans' eyes, and the tears came forth from their eyes. Now the children of the Turkmans had gone out to meet them, and they saw that the tears were streaming from their fathers' eyes and they thought that some one of them had died in the city. So without asking and without knowing, they ran back and came to the encampment and said to their mothers, ' One of ours is dead in the city, our fathers are coming weeping.' All the women and children of that encampment came forth to meet them, weeping together. The Turkmans who were coming from the city thought that one of theirs had died in the encampment; so were they without knowledge one of the other, and they raised a weeping and crying together such that it cannot be described.

" At length the elders of the camp stood up in the midst and said, ' May all ye remain whole; the command is God's, there is none other help than patience.' And they questioned them. The Turkmans who were coming from the city asked, ' Who is dead in the encampment?' The others said, ' No one is dead in the encampment; who has died in the city?' Those coming from the city answered, ' No one has died in the city.' They said, ' Then for whom are we wailing and lamenting?' At length they perceived that all this tumult arose from their thus trusting the words of children.

" Now, O king, I have told this story for that the king may know that confusion like to that is brought about by youths. What I know is this, if thou slay not the youth he will slay thee." When the king heard these words from the lady he said, " To-morrow will I kill him."

When it was morning the king came and sat upon his throne, and he caused the youth to be brought and ordered the executioner, " Smite off his head." The twenty-first vezir came forward and said, " O king of the world, yesterday, when reading in a book, I saw that they had written that there was a great king in the land of Hindustan, and in his time there was a work on wisdom, and they laded three camels with it and brought it to him. One day the king said to the sages, ' Abridge this book for me, that I may study it.' Then all the sages of Hind came together and collected the necessary words from that work and made a book. When the king read it he was pleased. And the words that they wrote were these : ' O king, be not presumptuous, being deceived by the world; for the world showeth itself like a fair woman and fondleth men in its bosom; and when they are asleep and heedless, of a sudden it woundeth and slayeth them. Knowing of a surety that it is thus, have care if it offer itself to thee, that thou keep thyself from it, so that thou be prosperous. And expend what thou gainest of wealth in the way of God most high, and guard against iniquity, and show forth thy name through generosity, and abandon avarice.

" ' O king, the light of the world is darkness, and its newness is oldness, and its being is non-being. O king, strive that thou save thyself from it; and incline not to the amassing of unlawful wealth, for it will pass from thy hand and be a woe to thee. Strive to collect wealth lawfully, and expend it on good works, and show thyself just among the folk to the utmost of thy power, that all the people of the world may love thee, and that thou be secured against the punishment of God most high. And guard thy faith for the hereafter. And love not women and tell not them thy secrets. O king, be not deceived by womankind; for in body are they weak, but in guile are they strong.' Now, O king, these counsels are exceeding good counsels, and it behooves the king to keep them; and their saying is true that women are weak in body but strong in guile. Mayhap the king has not heard what befell a certain king with a woman." The king said, " Relate it, let us hear." Quoth the vezir :

A QUEEN'S DECEIT

" There was in the palace of the world a great king, and he had a beautiful wife, such that many a soul dangled in the tresses on her cheek. That lady had a secret affair with a youth, and she used to hide the youth in a chest in the palace. One day that youth said to the lady, ' If the king were aware of this our work, he would slay the two of us.' The lady said, ' Leave that thought, I can do so that I shall hide thee in the

chest and say to the king, " Lo, my lover is lying in this chest; "
and then, when the king is about to kill thee, I shall make him
repentant by one word.' While the youth and the lady were
saying these words, the king came, and the lady straightway
put the youth into the chest and locked it. The king said, ' Why
lockest thou that chest thus hastily? What is in the chest?'
The lady answered, ' By God, it is my lover; I saw thee coming and I put him into the chest and locked it.' Then was the
king wroth, and he bared his sword and thought to slay him
who was in the chest, when the lady said, ' O king, art thou
mad, where is gone thine understanding? Am I mad that I
should advance a strange man to thy couch and then say to
thee, " Lo, he is in the chest?" In truth, I wondered if thou
were sincere in thy trust of me, and I tried thee, and now I
know that thou thinkest evil concerning me.' And she ceased
and sat in a corner.

" Then did the king repent him of what he had done; and
he begged and besought of his wife, saying, ' Forgive me.'
And he gave her many things, and craved pardon for his fault.
When the king had gone out from the harem into the palace the
lady took that youth forth of the chest and said, ' Didst thou
see what a trick I played the king?' And they gave themselves
up to mirth and merriment.

" Now, O king, I have told this story for that the king may
know that guile and trickery such as this abound in women. O
king, beware, slay not the prince on the woman's word, else
afterward thou shalt be repentant, and too late repentance profits not." And he made intercession for the prince for that day.
When the king heard this story from the vezir he sent the
prince to the prison and himself mounted for the chase.

When it was evening the king returned from the chase and
came to the palace, and the lady rose to greet him, and they
sat down. After the repast the lady again began to speak about
the youth. The king said, " To-day too such an one of my
vezirs made intercession for him and I sent him to the prison."
The lady said, " O king, this youth is ignoble. It is even as
when God most high told Noah (peace on him!) of the impurity of his son: said God most high, ' He is not of thy family; verily, it is a work that is not right.' [10] Then it is known

---

[10] Koran, xi. 48.

that if a person follow not the way of his father, and be not endowed with the nature of his father, he cannot be called a lawful son. Therefore, when the wise see a fault in others they hinder and cover it, and if they see that fault in themselves they strive to banish it far from them. There is no help for the ignoble that he should follow the path of the noble. Mayhap the king has not heard the story of a certain abdal and a king." The king said, " Tell on, let us hear." Quoth the lady:

THE ABDAL AND THE KING

" There was of old time a great king, and there was by him an abdal. One day the king mounted for the chase, and the abdal said, ' O king, I am able for soldiering and hunting; give me too horse and gear and bird, that I may go forth with thee to ride about and hunt.' So the king gave the abdal a horse and gear, and gave him a falcon on his wrist, and took him along with him to the chase, and they went off. While they were riding, the king saw a bird go into a bush, and he said to the abdal, ' Go, cast the falcon at the bird.' And the king stood to look on. The abdal went up close to the bush with the falcon, and a man stirred the bush, and the bird came out and flew off. The king said to the abdal, ' The bird is away, throw off the falcon.' And the abdal threw off the falcon from his wrist without slipping the leash, and he swung it round and round his head. The king shouted, ' Out on thee! throw off the falcon!' The abdal said, ' O king, I have thrown it off, what am I to do?' But he left not to swing the falcon round his head. The king shouted, ' Out on thee! let the falcon go!' And the abdal let go the leash; but the falcon's eyes were darkened from its having been turned round, and it could not fly, and fell to the ground. And the king was angry and ill-pleased. Then the abdal said, ' O king, wherefore art thou angry? thou saidest, " Throw off the falcon," and I threw it off; then thou saidest, " Let it go," and I let it go; this falcon knows not how to fly: what fault is mine?' These words of the abdal were pleasant to the king and he fainted from laughing; and he perceived how no good comes from anything ignoble.[1]

[1] The point of this story is lost in the translation. To let fly a falcon at game, is, in Turkish, to swing a falcon; the king says to the abdal, " Swing the fal- con," meaning, let it fly at the bird; but the abdal understands him literally, and swings the falcon round his head.

"Now, O king, I have told this story for that the king may know that no good comes from the ignoble man who follows not the path of his father and mother. Beware, O king, be not negligent in the affair of this youth, or in the end some hurt will befall thee from him; the rest thou knowest." When the king heard this story from the lady he said, "On the morrow will I kill the youth."

When it was morning the king came and sat upon his throne, and he caused the youth to be brought and commanded the executioner, "Smite off his head."

Thus did the king, day after day, order the execution of his innocent son, being temporarily diverted from committing this crime by the stories and wise advice of the forty vezirs, only to be urged again at night to commit the crime by the false accusations of his baffled and revengeful wife.

The story of the fortieth vezir demonstrated how the crafty wife of a tailor played him false and then deceived him with a lying and plausible version of what had happened. After relating this story the fortieth vezir said:

"Now, O king, I have told this story for that the king may know that tricks like to these and all manner of craftiness abound in women. Beware, slay not the prince on the woman's word, or afterward thou shalt be repentant." And he kissed the ground, and made intercession for the prince for that day. And the king granted it, and sent the youth to the prison, and went himself to the chase.

When it was evening the king returned from the chase and came to the palace, and the lady rose to greet him, and they sat down. After the repast the lady asked for news of the youth. The king said, "To-day, too, such an one of my vezirs made intercession for him and I sent him to the prison." The lady said, "O king, be it known that not one of those vezirs is thy friend; God knows what pact they have with the youth. Mayhap the king has not heard what befel between the Sultan of Egypt and his vezirs." The king said, "Tell on, let us hear." Quoth the lady:

THE SULTAN AND HIS TRAITOROUS SON

"There was of old time in the city of Cairo a great sultan, and he had a youthful son. And that youth made a pact with the vezirs, saying, 'If ye make me sultan, I will give you leave to do whatever ye may please.' When they had agreed to this, he sowed enmity between the king and the vezirs and nobles; and each of them rose in revolt in a different quarter, and they took the youth for their chief, and waged war and did battle with the king. The king could not overcome them, and at length they made the youth king. They began to feast with the new king every day, and to accomplish their desires. And the king's father saw that the purpose of the vezirs and the youth was evil, and he called a confidant, and one night they fled in disguise and entered a cave; and for seven days and seven nights the king went not forth from that cave. The new king heard of his father having fled, and he and the vezirs began to seek him and to send out criers, who proclaimed, 'Whoso seizes my father and brings him to me, him will I honor.' And the old king and his courtier went forth from the cave and came to a village, and were guests of an old woman in that village; and that old woman sowed seed. And she bestirred herself to entertain them, and brought them a mat, and they sat down. The king was hungry, and he pulled out a sequin and gave it to the old woman, and said, 'Mother, go, fetch us food that we may eat.' The woman said, 'What will ye do with a sequin's worth of food?' The king replied, 'No harm, fetch it.' And the woman went and brought all manner of delicacies and set them before the king. And they sat down and ate. After the repast they began to talk with the woman; and the woman said, 'What youths be ye?' The king said, 'We are of the servants of the fugitive king; we are seeking our master.' The woman said, 'I fear that ye too are followers of that unworthy youth, and would seize the king and take him.' The king asked, 'Does that unworthy youth seek his father?' The woman replied, 'Does he seek him? What means that? Those traitor vezirs and nobles every day cause criers to proclaim, "To him who seizes and brings that fugitive sultan we will give the lordship of whatever place he may wish; but of him who conceals him, or in whose house he is found, are the head and family gone."'

"When the king heard these words from the woman his soul was troubled, and he said to her, 'And are the nobles also submissive to the youth?' The woman answered, 'He has deposed many nobles, and appointed other nobles; these new nobles are all of them submissive to him.' The king said, 'Is there any of those old nobles whom thou knowest?' The woman replied, 'There is a vezir who was deposed by the fugitive sultan; I go about his house on business—I know him.' As soon as the king heard this he turned and said to his confidant, 'What sayest thou, shall I tell this woman that I am the sultan?' The confidant replied, 'Command is the king's.' The sultan turned and said to the woman, 'O mother, I have a secret; if I tell it thee, canst thou keep it?' The woman said, 'I will give my head, but I will not give your secret.' The king made the woman swear, and then said, 'O mother, dost thou know me who I am?' She answered, 'Nay.' Then the king said, 'Lo, I am the fugitive sultan; be it not that this word escape thy mouth.' When the woman heard this the blood went from her face, and she fell at the king's feet. The king said, 'Hast thou son or daughter?' She replied, 'I have a son.' The king said, 'If God most high seat me on my throne, I will give thy son whatever lordship he please.' The woman bowed down and fell at the king's feet. Then the king said to her, 'Go now to the house of that vezir, and call him to a private place and salute him from me, and say, "The king is now seated in my house and wants thee, be it not that thou flinchest and comest not."'

"When it was evening the woman went to the vezir's house, and took the vezir to a private place, and gave him the king's greeting, and told him all and how that he was sitting in her house. The vezir was glad, and he said, 'Do thou now be off, I too will come now;' and he sent her away. The woman came and told these things to the king. After a little he saw the vezir in the dress of an Arab, and he came and fell at the king's feet and mourned and wept. The king said, 'O vezir, I wronged thee and took thy wealth and deposed thee; ah! the past is past, the gone is gone. Befriend me as much as in thee lies, and if God most high raise me to my throne, I know the honor I will do thee.' The vezir said, 'O king, if thou tookest my wealth, it was thine own wealth; if thou didst depose me, I was thy slave and had done wrong; thou didst well. Now this is the way, that thou follow my words and lay aside kingship till our plan be accomplished; if afterward

thou art wroth with me, then command; now let us work.'
The king said, 'Do what thou wilt; now is not the time for
words.' The vezir said, ' O king, arise and take my lamp in
thine hand, and go on through the desert before thee till thou
comest to my house; if anyone see thee he will think thee
my man and recognize thee not.' The king took the vezir's
lamp in his hand, and they went on and passed through the
bazaars of Cairo, and came to the vezir's house; and the vezir
prepared a private room for the king.

"The king remained there some days, and the vezir secretly
sent word to all the great nobles who had been deposed, and assembled them. And one night he brought them to the king and
reconciled them, and said, ' On the morrow be ye ready and
show zeal each one of you for his estate.' That night they
gathered together all the disbanded soldiers who were there;
and when it was morning they beat the kettledrums on every
side, and ere those traitor nobles and vezirs had arisen they put
many of them to the sword; and they seized the king's son
and all the rest of his vezirs, and brought them before the
king. And the king executed the whole of them, slaying each
of them with a different torment. Thenceforth he sat upon
his throne with tranquillity of heart, and enjoyed happiness and
delight.

"Now, O king, I have told this story for that the king may
know that vezirs are not to be altogether trusted; and be thou
ready, for these vezirs purpose evil against the king, and the
like of this story shall befall thee. I have watched for my
king and told him. And I know of a surety that they have
made a pact if left till the morrow to seat the youth upon the
throne, and to seize thee and to give thee into the youth's
hands. God knows what will happen to ill-fortuned me. Woe
is me!" And she wept full bitterly. When the king heard
this story from the lady, and beheld this plight, he believed
the lady's words, and held them to be true; and fear for his
life fell upon the king. He said: "O lady, weep not; on the
morrow will I seize the whole of the vezirs, and, after I have
put the youth to death, I will give to each of them, one by one,
his due." When the lady heard these words from the king
she was glad, and said, "O king, when thou hast slain the
whole of them, appoint nobles vezirs in their stead, and then

lean thy back against the wall of retirement, and give thyself up to mirth and merriment: till thou hast done thus thou shalt not be at ease." And the king consented to this proposal, and they passed that night till the morning conversing.

CONCLUSION

When it was morning the king was wrathful, and he came and sat upon his throne, and he said, " Where is the youth? let him come." They brought him, and the king said, " Ask ye him if he confesses to the charge of his mother." Thereupon the grand vezir said, " Let him come before you and be asked, and it will be well; bring him, let us ask him." The king commanded that they brought him, and he said, " Youth, speak; how hast thou done by thy mother? " The youth was silent. The king turned and said, " Be not silent, there is leave to thee, speak." The youth was silent. Again the grand vezir said, " Perchance his governor might make him tell."

Straightway the king commanded that they should bring his governor; and they sought him but found him not, and came and told the king. The king said, " This day it is needful to make manifest my justice; let the executioner come." He came; and the king commanded, saying, " Take the youth and all those vezirs; and kill them." And they took the whole of them from the presence of the king; and they made clean the judgment-square and sprinkled it with sand. And they made the vezirs sit down by tens, and they brought the youth too. Then the executioner set the prince upon his knees and bound his eyes, and he drew his sword from its scabbard and bared it, and said, " Is there leave, O king? In thy glory is my arm strong and my sword keen. The cut-off head grows not again, and too late repentance profits not." And he went twice round the divan and asked leave of the king; and the king commanded him, saying, " Smite off his head." The executioner went round the divan once more, and as he was again asking leave of the king, the bearer of glad tidings came, crying, " The prince's governor comes! " The king said, " Quick, seize and bring him."

Forthwith the slaves brought the governor, not letting his feet touch the ground. When the king saw the governor he

was wroth, and said, " Kill him! " The governor said, " O
king, wherefore art thou angry? If it be thy desire to make
the youth speak, bring him and let him speak." Quoth the
king, " Is it thou who saidest to the youth, ' Speak not '? "
The governor answered, " Yea." The king said, " Why? "
The governor said, " O king of the world, I saw the prince's
ruling star in the astrolabe that for forty days it was in evil
aspect, such evil aspect that if he uttered the least word he
should perish, but that if he spake not he should escape. I
taught him a Name, and charged him straitly that he should
not speak the least word. Now is the time accomplished, and I
am come; command that they bring him, and I shall give him
leave to speak." The king commanded that they brought the
youth, and the governor said, " My prince, be my life a ransom
for thy father and for thee! Praise be to God! the evil aspect
of thy star is accomplished; loose thy nightingale tongue and
speak; what is this plight? "

Straightway the youth said, " In the name of God! " And
he related what befell him with the lady from its beginning to
its end; and then he fell upon the ground and began to weep.
And the king put his finger to his mouth and wondered. And
the members of the divan marvelled at this deed of the woman,
and they said, " The prince's words are with reason and truth,
and such like trickery comes from womankind."

Then the king asked the slave-girls, and they bare witness
that they had been behind the wall and had heard the thing,
and that the prince spake truly. And the king saw that the
right was the prince's, and he repented him of what he had
done. And he besought pardon, and kissed the prince's two
eyes, and pressed him to his heart and wept full bitterly. And
straightway he commanded that they bring the vezirs; and
the king made many excuses to them, and clad each of them
in sumptuous robes, and bestowed boundless gifts and favors
upon them, and begged forgiveness of all of them. And the
vezirs said, " My king, whatsoever cruelty and injustice thou
hast done us, be it all forgiven thee; our fear was lest thou
should slay the prince, acting on the woman's word; for our
vezirship is by the health and safety of our king and our prince;
and their existence is a mercy to the world; after they were
perished the perishing of the whole of us were a thing assured."

And they all kissed the ground together, and asked for retribution on the woman.

And the king commanded that they bring a wild ass; and they took the lady to the square of judgment and set her upon that ass, and bound her fast to his tail and legs, and took her forth to the desert. And they smote the ass with a whip, and the ass began to gallop and the woman fell from his back to the ground; and the wild ass looked, and when he saw the woman behind him he shied and ran off. And the woman was torn into pieces small even as her ear, and left upon the shrubs and stones. Thus that which she had purposed against the prince befel herself. The sires say, " Wish good that good may come to thee: if thou dig a pit for another, dig it deep; for it is like thou shalt fall therein thyself; then thou needest not trouble trying to get out." And from that time has the saying been among the folk, " May I see thee on the ass! " After that the king summoned all the vezirs and the nobles and the commonalty, and he made a great feast with all manner of minstrels and music, and for forty days and forty nights they feasted and made merry gratefully. And then they lived for many years, and did justice and dealt with equity.